THE RIGHTS OF LABOR

THE
RIGHTS
OF
LABOR

BENGT
ABRAHAMSSON
and
ANDERS
BROSTRÖM

SAGE PUBLICATIONS   Beverly Hills   London

Translated from the Swedish by **David McCune**

English edition, Copyright © 1980 by Sage Publications, Inc.

Original Swedish edition, *Om arbetets rätt. Vägar til ekonomisk demokrati,* Copyright © 1979 by Almqvist & Wiksell Förlag AB, Stockholm.

For information address:

SAGE Publications, Inc.
275 South Beverly Drive
Beverly Hills, California 90212

SAGE Publications Ltd
28 Banner Street
London EC1Y 8QE, England

Printed in the United States of America

Library of Congress Cataloging in Publication Data

Abrahamsson, Bengt, 1937-
 The rights of labor.

  Bibliography: p. 281- 294.
  Includes index.
  1. Employee ownership. 2. Property. 3. Value.
4. Socialism. I. Broström, Anders, 1946-   joint author. II. Title.
  HD5650.A24|3   331'.01'1   80-16233
  ISBN 0-8039-1477-6

FIRST PRINTING

CONTENTS

ACKNOWLEDGMENTS

We are both sociologists. A review of the problems associated with the principle of the rights of labor cannot, however, be limited to the sociological literature. We are necessarily led into other areas of the social sciences and philosophy, e.g. jurisprudence, economic history, economics, political science, and ethics. We owe a large debt of gratitude to many people for the interest they have shown in our work and for bringing to our attention shortcomings and imperfections in earlier versions of the manuscript. The following is a partial list of those to whom we owe thanks:

for assistance with problems of sociology of law and general jurisprudence: Axel Adlercreutz, Boel Flodgren, Håkan Hydén, Per Stjernquist, Antoinette Hetzler, Alexander Peczenik, and Ulla Bondeson, all at the University of Lund.

Bo Gustafsson and Alf Johansson of the University of Uppsala for their help with economic history.

Ragnar Holte, Göran Lantz, Carl-Henric Grenholm, Göran Collste, and Algot Gölstam of the Institute of Theology at the University of Uppsala.

Villy Bergström, Roland Grankvist, Casten von Otter, Roland Svensson, Marianne Pettersson, and Olle Hammarström of Arbetslivscentrum in Stockholm.

Annika Brickman and Per Eklund have offered valuable criticism of the parts of the manuscript dealing with legal issues. Sven-Ove Hansson and Paavo Bergman took upon themselves the considerable task of reading the entire manuscript as it neared completion. We have also benefited greatly from the discussions of the main theses of the book which we have had with, among others, Steven Deutsch, Val R. Lorwin, Don van Houten, and Paul Goldman at the University of Oregon, Eugene.

The book has been written as part of the work on the project "The Institution and Effects of the Law of Co-Determination: Mandator Questions." We have received economic support for the project from the Bank of Sweden Tercentenary Fund. Nils-Eric Svensson and Agneta Örtegren of the fund's secretariat have—in spite of their heavy work load—always found time to help us solve the problems which have been part of the work on the project.

To all these people, and to those we may have fogotten, we give our warm thanks. We have tried as best we could to make use of the criticism and sound advice we have received. Any remaining imperfections are solely our responsibility.

Stockholm   —Bengt Abrahamsson
                                                       —Anders Broström

PREFACE

One can reason that a person who refines and makes usable a raw material by means of his own labor, thereby adding value to it, should also own that which has been produced. Labor gives rise to capital; it may therefore seem appropriate that the right to dispose of the capital should belong to those who labor. Labor is the most important human activity and is the basis for the individual and social development of any human being. The right to work should therefore be both universal and unconditional, and it should be one of the main duties of society to guarantee work for all.

This is, however, not the case. It is the owner of the raw material who becomes the owner of the refined product, in spite of the fact that his own labor may contribute little or nothing. There is no necessary connection between labor and authority over capital. Once one owns capital, then this capital can often be retained and even increased with no more effort than the mere act of waiting. The right to labor is subject to conditions determined by private capital and by the choice of investments made by the capitalholders. In a few societies, among these Sweden, workers have been able to steer the profits and movement of capital to a certain degree by organizing themselves into trade unions and political groups, thus keeping employment at a high level through public intervention. However, the possibilities of this kind of public control are gradually being weakened as capital becomes increasingly concentrated (as it has in Sweden more than in any other country) and as production is automated and computerized at an increasing rate of acceleration.

Economic democracy has become one of the most important issues of the 1970s, brought to the fore by, among other things, the investigation of employee investment funds and collective capital formation by the Swedish Federation of Trade Unions (LO). This investigation resulted in the report *Löntagarfonder* by Rudolf Meidner et al. (1975). The issue is currently the subject of a government inquiry into employee investment funds. It is our opinion that the question of the rights of labor has received too little attention in the course of this discussion; hence this book.

Note to the reader. Due to lack of space, significant portions of the source material for chapters 8 and 9 have been commented upon in the notes at the end of the book. We ask the readers to acquaint themselves also with this part of the text.

Chapter 1

INTRODUCTION

This book deals with the basic elements of economic democracy and discusses three principles for ownership of means of production: private rights of ownership, civic ownership rights, and the rights of labor.

The debate about employee investment funds has placed in question who should own the means of production in the event that this ownership is expanded to include a larger group than the present owners of capital. The labor rights offensive of the early 1970s—including the law on security of employment, the law on the status of shop stewards, the law guaranteeing employee representation on company executive boards, and the law of co-determination—has at least indirectly influenced this issue. The new laws have in part been justified by the statement that wage earners have a right to influence production and the results of production *by virtue of their labor*. Wage earners have maintained that labor is a factor in production which is at least as important as capital; therefore, the owners of capital should not have the sole right to determine how the means of production are used. A further step is taken when the question of economic democracy and employee investment funds is raised: here the demand is made that labor *take precedence over* capital when decisions are made about production and its goals.

Three main principles underly the debate about ownership of the means of production. Within capitalistically organized economies, the system of production is based on *private ownership*; this principle functions both as an economic blueprint and as a legal guide, legitimized and supported by legal rules and institutions. Private ownership means that the person who supplies the raw materials and the instruments of labor (i.e., the capital) for production and who organizes production and pays wages is recognized as owner of that which is produced. According to this principle, labor is a commodity to be bought by the owner of the capital and combined by him with raw materials and instruments of labor in order to carry out production in the most efficient way possible. Labor cannot be the basis for any claims to *ownership*. However, the amount of *remuneration* for labor is negotiable within the framework of the labor contract.

The second principle of ownership of means of production is closely bound to political democracy and *civic rights*. Capital is considered public property, and the individual citizen can influence decisions concerning its utilization through his right to vote. The state and its subordinate bodies function as administrators of the means of production. The election of representatives follows the principle of one man, one vote. This is in contrast to the system of private ownership, under which, for the most part, influence is allocated in proportion to the amount of capital owned.

One of the most important economic and political issues during the eighteenth and nineteenth centuries concerned unpropertied people and what could be done to improve their lot ("the social question" or "the worker question"). A social-liberal line of thought opposed a socialist or Social Democratic line, with views on labor something of a watershed. Within the economic sciences the battle centered on the significance which should be given to labor in the production process. Socialist economists and advocates of the labor movement drew support from the labor theory of value. They argued that since the value of a commodity was directly dependent upon the labor invested in it, it should also be legitimate to ascribe to labor the right of ownership of that which had been produced. Thus were justified the *rights of labor*.

Advocates of the subjective theory of value argued, on the other hand, that the "value" of a commodity was a phenomenon entirely dependent on market exchange. "Value" was the same as "price," and nothing was changed by any labor invested in the origin of the commodity.

1.1 Individual or Collective Ownership?

In this book we will discuss arguments for the three principles of rights of ownership and the case for a transition from private to collective ownership of the means of production. The book concludes with a recognition of the rights of labor as the basic principle for ownership of the means of production. This position is founded on an analysis of subjective and empirical arguments which can be invoked in support of the different principles of rights. An important point of departure here is the thesis that any discussion of the ownership of the means of production must be founded on some theory of *original acquisition,* i.e., on a notion of the origin of material wealth. This is a central issue in an assessment of both the labor theory of value and the subjective theory of value. Further, *all* forms of ownership—private as well as collective, civic as well as labor—must be justified in terms of acquisition. Thus, it is not sufficient to show that a certain pattern of ownership actually exists; one must also show how it originated, judge its potential legitimacy, and investigate its social and economic ramifications. Nozick writes, for example:

> Those who believe in collective ownership, e.g. those who believe that people who live together in a certain area of land should own the land . . . must also provide a theory of how these kinds of ownership rights arise.[1]

1.2 Plan and Contents of the Book

Chapter 2 is the book's prelude and contains a general definition of our area of inquiry. We review and discuss the transition from private to collective ownership seen from political, sociological, economic, and legal perspectives, with a certain emphasis on the last mentioned. We also discuss a few of the concepts which are central to our later presentation, e.g., means of production, ownership, original and derived acquisition, mandator, organization, simple and composite production (i.e., production based on individual labor vs. that based on the combination of capitalownership plus purchased labor).

Chapter 3 deals with a few theoretical perspectives. One aim of this book is to develop a standpoint vis-à-vis the principle of labor rights. In this context it is important to differentiate between categorical and instrumental value judgments. The latter include value statements, the consequences of which are testable; these should be differentiated from simple, categorical statements of value judgments. The discussion is based primarily on Evert Vedung's reasoning in *Det rationella politiska samtalet*[2] It is our further opinion that Gunnar Myrdal's discussion of the need for "an economic technology" in the work *Vetenskap och politik i nationalekonomin*[3] shows that instrumental value judgments are not only acceptable, but even necessary elements of social science.

Chapter 4 is a short description of economic and historical developments in Europe, including the transition from feudalism to capitalism. This description is presented in order to explain the growth of a specific intellectual production which was one of the prerequisites for the development of the principles of rights. As a basis for this discussion of economic theory, we will use C. B. Macpherson's (1977) distinction between the simple market society (based on individual, independent, small-scale producers) and the "possessive" market society (in which labor is viewed as alienable property.[4] The terminology will also be significant later, e.g., during the treatment of John Locke's theory of the value of labor (Chapter 5). Chapter 4 will also summarize certain main elements in the development of the theory of capital profits and the theory of "value" as a result of labor invested in a commodity.

In *Chapter 5* we examine arguments for private ownership espoused by both conservative and liberal theories. These arguments differ somewhat in character, reflecting the broader philosophic contexts represented, on the one hand by the empirical bent of Enlightenment philosophers and, on the other hand by the philosophy of natural law. Conservative thinkers like Burke saw private ownership as a natural foundation of society, while liberals like Locke, Bentham, and Mill wanted to show through empirical argument that private ownership was "beneficial" to society.

In *Chapter 6* we attempt to show historically that civic rights are closely connected to economic power and private property. Unpropertied people have gradually gained for themselves a broadened decision-making right (the right to vote); meanwhile, the power to execute decisions has been withheld from them. We begin with the basic assumption that power is two-dimensional: it has both a political and an economic side. Herbert Tingsten is one of many writers who has described the advance of democracy in western industrial nations as an almost logically given process which follows naturally from premises established by classical, liberal writers such as Locke. We question this description and point out another possible interpretation: The realization of political democracy signified that unpropertied people, in a struggle with propertyowners, gradually *won* for themselves one of the two dimensions constituting the power to govern social development. In addition, this conquest has at the same time led to a recognition of the division of power into political and economic parts; since the emergence of democracy the struggle has mainly centered on the political, rather than on the economic dimension.

In this context we examine the classical, democratic writers John Locke, Jeremy Bentham, John Stuart Mill, and Alexis de Tocqueville. They underscored the need to expand democracy to include new groups, but at the same time they took care to emphasize that democracy must not go too far. To insure this they recommended that voters meet certain demands such as literacy and arithmetical proficiency or that their incomes be of a certain size. The effect of this was the exclusion of large segments of unpropertied people and wage earners from political democracy.

In *Chapter 7* we describe the labor theory of value and its arguments for labor rights as a basis for ownership of the means of production. We also review the subjective theory of value and its arguments against the labor theory of value and we describe the debate among classical economists concerning labor's value-creating significance.

Modern economics (marginalism) is based on the subjective theory of value. From a political and economic perspective we attempt to explain why this theory of value—and not the labor theory of value—became dominant. The decisive difference between the two theories of value is to be found in their respective premises. The labor theory of value is based on *production* and its historical and social prerequisites. The subjective theory of value is based on *consumption* and the psychological preferences of the private individual. This difference has had decisive ideological, political, and economic-theoretical consequences. In this chapter we establish the necessity of choosing between the two theories of value. Our thesis is that there are logical, ethical, and empirical arguments which support a use of the labor theory of value as a base from which to derive principles for the collective ownership of the means of production. The consequences of this standpoint are described in Chapter 10.

Chapter 8 is mainly a review of the public debate within the Swedish labor movement concerning practical and political standpoints on the discussion of the principles of rights.

Taking international revisionism as a starting point, we attempt to explain how it was that the Swedish labor movement gave priority to civic rights and later accepted the views of marginalistic economics and its subjective theory of value.

A large part of the chapter is devoted to an analysis of the debate of the 1920s and to the ideologue and theoretician Nils Karleby. During the 1920s Karleby, together with Östen Undén and others, founded the so-called "functional socialism" movement. Since then this intellectual tradition has to a great degree directed the programs and actions of the labor movement.

Functional socialistic reasoning—and this is the conclusion of our review—has meant that the labor movement gave priority to *political* power and the *distribution* of production results, instead of giving priority to economic power and power over production itself.

Chapter 9 is an illumination of the conflicts between different interest groups (wage earners, citizens, capitalowners) and the principles and rights advocated and represented by each group through its demands. The conflict between wage earners and capitalowners is exemplified by the debate about employee investment funds. We review certain arguments for labor rights which have been put forth by advocates of the labor movement, and we compare these arguments with economic and legal arguments for private ownership. It is our opinion that a transition to a system of collective capitalownership based on the rights of labor is of such scope and magnitude that a constitutional amendment would be necessary.

The conflict between civic rights and private ownership rights is exemplified by functional socialism. Functional socialism is said to be a method of ending the conflict between these two principles of rights. The advocates of functional socialism maintain that private property rights can be equated with an artichoke: It is a matter of picking away leaf after leaf until private property rights become "functionless." It is by means of civic rights and legislative power in the national parliament that private property rights can be stripped of all their power.

Functional socialism should be viewed primarily as a welfare ideology, lacking in both goals and possibilities to influence the basic power structure of society. It carries with it risks of a development in the direction of state socialism, and it is a worse political alternative than the principle of labor rights (given that the rights of labor can be applied to a system in which local wage-earner influence can be combined with a representation of public interest). Private ownership rights contain a core of protective and legitimizing norms which cannot be reduced without being *exchanged* for others. The right to capital is, in the end, indivisible.

In *Chapter 10*, finally, we discuss the consequences of legislation which would establish the rights of labor as the basis for social power. We present a principle for political representation and discuss the demands necessary for a proper balance between, on the one hand, the public interest and central authority, and on the other hand, wage-earner interets and local influence. We also deal with the arguments against economic democracy which claim that it leads to an ineffective and bureaucratic production apparatus with very little or no growth. These arguments are usually based on an insufficient and overly short-sighted analysis of the incentives which motivate human labor. A recognition of the rights of labor can clear the way for an emancipation of these motivating forces and can make possible the creation of a social system with collective participation in, and responsibility for, production.

Chapter 2

THE CONCEPT OF RIGHTS

The preceding chapter roughly defined our area of study. But the concept of "rights of labor" has not yet been clarified, and the two additional notions of "rights" are in need of definition. The purpose of this chapter is to define these concepts more precisely.

Our goal, however, is broader than this. The very concept of "right" or "rights" is strongly disputed by legal theorists, and the concept of rights has been the subject of a long debate especially within the nordic juridical tradition. The so-called Uppsala school of philosophy (Hägerström et al.) has, for example, maintained that the concept "rights" should be purged from the scholarly language, since the existence of the phenomenon of rights cannot be proved. This point of view has been refuted by Ingemar Hedenius, among others. In the following we shall present a brief review of the most important arguments concerning the be or not to be of the concept of rights.

2.1 Ownership

All concepts of "rights" with which we deal in this book refer to rights to ownership of the property called means of production and the grounds for these rights. (It is important to differentiate between "property for power" implied by these kinds of ownership, and "property for use" inherent in the ownership of an automobile, a boat or similar property.[1] Expressed schematically, ownership can accrue to either individuals or collectives of individuals. In the former case, the property and its yield can be freely utilized according to individual discretion. The latter case demands consideration of the broader group of interested parties which make up the ownership collective.

The primary questions we must treat in this book are, first, what are the reasons for the *transition from individual to collective ownership of the means of production,* and second, *what kind of collective should be mandator of decisions concerning the utilization of the means of production and the distribution of their yield.* The answers to these questions are highly dependent upon one's view of the production process, labor, and other so-called production factors. There are two kinds of mandators which have been topical in the current debate and on which the issue of collective ownership focuses to a large extent. These are, first, the *civic-*collective, and second, the *labor-*collective.

When we use the expression "citizen rights" below, we are referring to *the right of ownership of the property called means of production which in different ways can be connected to the role of being a citizen,* a role which in Sweden includes, among other things, the right to vote and the right to be elected to the national parliament, protection against deportation, freedom of speech and press, freedom of assembly, religious freedom, etc. The role also implies certain obligations to the state, e.g., payment of taxes and mandatory military service. The most important criterion of citizenship is the right to vote. This is the means by which the individual citizen is given the possibility to influence the governing of the state, including the governing of the means of production which are owned and controlled by it.

In a similar way, the "rights of labor" is a matter of *the right of ownership of the means of production being connected to the role of performing labor,* i.e., participating in the production of goods and services with *one's own labor.* An obvious question here is what "one's own labor" means. For example, does the concept include lending money? Does it also include the activity in which one with one's own means buys the labor of others, supplies the labor with the instruments of labor (tools, machines, factory buildings, etc.) and objects of labor (raw materials and semimanufactured goods), gives the employees their contractual pay, and keeps for oneself the yield of the production?

This question is of basic importance to our entire study. The difference between *one's own labor* and *labor through others* has extraordinarily far-reaching economic, political, and juridical consequences, *if this difference is recognized.* It is characteristic of our social system, however, that the distinction between these forms of labor is legally not observed (except in the case of a marginal, but as we shall see, important instance). An object of labor can be reworked and refined and thus increase in value. The person doing the labor is of no significance as far as the ownership of the finished product is concerned. The right of ownership is bound up with the capital used for production, not with the labor.

It is a basic characteristic of capitalist societies that the right of ownership of the means of production lies in the hands of individual citizens and that the power to utilize them is directly related to how much capital the individual owns. The power of decision-making within the private business is determined by the principle of proportionality between capital and votes. The more assets an individual owns in a business, the more votes he or she has in the decision-making bodies of the company. Recognition of this *private ownership* of the means of production is usually connected to recognition of the labor contract as a means of compensating the person performing the actual production. The right of contract will be discussed later (see Section 2.10).

In summary: the three categories discussed in this chapter (and later at different places in the book) are private ownership, civic-collective ownership, and labor-collective ownership, all with respect to the property we call means of production.

2.2 What Are "Means of Production"?

In general, the means of production are made up of instruments of labor (tools etc.) and objects of labor (raw materials). By adding labor to the objects, i.e., by working on the materials, one transforms them and invests them with a greater value than they originally had.

> In the labour-process, therefore, man's activity, with the help of the instruments of labour, effects an alteration, designed from the commencement, in the material worked upon. The process disappears in the product; the latter is a use-value, Nature's material adapted by a change of form to the wants of man.[2]

The product thus created can, in turn, serve as means of production in the next stage:

> The same use value is both the product of a previous [labour-] process, and a means of production in a later process. Products are therefore not only results, but also essential conditions of labour.[3]

Marx's characterization of the term "means of production" clearly precludes any final, absolute, and detailed definition. A certain use-value can, while being a material factor in the labor process, have varying functions. Marx exemplifies:

> With the exception of the extractive industries, in which the material for labour is provided immediately by nature, such as mining, hunting, fishing and agriculture (so far as the latter is confined to breaking up virgin soil), all branches of industry manipulate raw material, objects already filtered through labour, already products of labour. Such is seed in agriculture. Animals and plants, which we are accustomed to consider as products of nature, are in their present form, not only products of, say last year's labour, but the result of a gradual transformation, continued through many generations, under man's superintendence, and by means of his labour. But in the great majority of cases, instruments of labour show even to the most superficial observer, traces of the labour of past ages.[4]

At the same time, Marx draws our attention to the fact that we do not normally think of the means of production as products of labor. This tendency not to view the means of production as products of labor is actually a legitimate demand to be placed on the manufacture of means of production—when in use they should perform so flawlessly that one does not notice them. Only in exceptional cases do we have reason to ponder over their origins, and then the cause is usually some imperfection in the object:

> [I]t is generally by their imperfections as products, that the means of production in any process assert themselves in their character of products. A

blunt knife or a weak thread forcibly remind us of Mr. A, the cutler, or Mr. B, the spinner. In the finished product the labour by means of which it has acquired its useful qualities is not palpable, has apparently vanished.[5]

The specialization of the production process, which was especially dramatic in Europe during the eighteenth century, paved the way for a previously unknown increase in the rate of production. In order to make full use of the advantages of specialization and the benefits of large-scale production, increasing amounts of capital were needed to invest in machines and factories, and to import foreign raw materials (see Chapter 4). The commercial capital upon which mercantilism and early capitalism were built was often bound to individual financiers or families, and this capital gradually became insufficient. The private owner of capital was replaced by a new form of capital accumulation: the *stock company*.

The stock company collects under one roof capital furnished by a multitude of private owners of capital. The management of production is centralized to an *organization*, which becomes the instrument for further growth of the smaller, private sums of capital. Marx writes:

> The world would still be without railways if it had had to wait until the accumulation of a few individual capitals had got far enough to be adequate for the construction of a railway. Centralization, on the other hand, accomplished this in the twinkling of an eye, by means of joint stock companies.[6]

Centralized capital can be split up into shares in the form of stocks or other securities which can be treated as separate units on the capital market. When we now and below refer to "capital," we are referring to these shares of accumulated capital in a concrete sense. The connection between the means of production, the capital which is centralized in the organizations, and the divisibility of the capital deserves emphasis for a special reason. On occasion the development we have described here is portrayed as a continuing democratization of the power over production, e.g., in the expression "owner democracy." The usual objection to this thesis is that the dissemination of stocks does not bring about a broader influence on the utilization of capital. Instead, the tendency is for power to be concentrated even more, i.e., in the hands of the largest stockholder.[7] An even more important objection arises, however, because of the fact that the accumulation of shares in the form of a stock company often represents rather short-sighted and interchangeable interests. The individual invests his or her capital with the intention of making a greater profit than could have been made through an alternative investment. The individual rationale thus evidenced can—because the interest is shortsighted and can be satisfied by any other investment with a higher anticipated profit—easily result in actions of the company as a whole which are irrational as seen from the perspective of public and employee interest.

The point we want to make, in summary, is that the ownership of property has an important organizational significance. The organization is the instrument by which the many individual parties increase their own capital. This capital appears diversified and decentralized in a large number of shares, but it is actually coordinated and centralized in the form represented by the stock company. We will have reason to return to the issue of organization in the section on mandator and executive (2.4).

The right to capital. Ownership includes, as pointed out by Honoré among others, many different dimensions: physical control over objects, the right to use the objects according to one's own discretion, the right to transfer ownership, the right to income from the lending of objects, etc.[8] But these different dimensions are not all equally significant. In particular, the *right to capital* governs, and actually encompasses, many of the remaining elements of ownership.

> The right to capital is the only one of these elements which by itself seems to define the various kinds of ownership. It is the most fundamental of the elements exactly because it includes the right to destroy, consume or dispose. ("Dispose" includes exchange, gift-giving, or simply "getting rid of.") . . . [The remaining instances] can be seen as a protection against, broadening of, limiting of, or development of this right. One who has all the rights on the list but lacks the right to capital may possibly own the object in a derived sense, but one who has the right to capital owns it "essentially."[9]

2.3 Juridical Person

A discussion of ownership becomes somewhat problematic when one considers that this right, according to existing law, is bound to an individual subject. Property right is thus always a matter of possession by or freedom of disposition by one *person* (see Section 2.6 concerning these terms).

This seems to present a difficulty, since both citizen rights and labor rights presuppose ownership exercised by a collective. Juridically, however, the situation is not appreciably different than the case of a stock company or foundation. The group owning the property appears (and can theoretically be treated as) a *juridical person*. Civic rights apply thus to the ownership functions exercised by the *state* or any other representative of the civic group. Labor rights (exercised in the form of ownership of the means of production) can likewise be expressed as the rights of an *association or union of wage earners*. Legally, an employee investment fund, for example, entails nothing new. It is an organization founded on the collective interest in effective production, economic security, and collective control over production, in which each member contributes his or her own labor.

The organizational form "fund" should be differentiated from the property law phenomenon "fund." Honoré differentiates between three kinds of objects which can be owned: material objects and interests in material objects, claims, and finally collections of objects or claims. A "fund" is the financial equivalent of objects or claims (or both).[10]

2.4 Mandator

The concept of "mandator" has been mentioned from time to time in the preceding pages. The time has come to define the term and explain how it relates to the rest of our discussion.

This discussion is based on the notion that there exist in society various interests which arise as individuals are influenced in diverse ways by economic, technological, and political (including legal) social forces. Some examples of socioeconomic forces are changes in a society's industrial base, unemployment, and inflation. Technological changes are evidenced in new machines, new systems of production (e.g., computerization) and innovations within the field of communications. Political changes—which to a great extent are reflections of and reactions to economic and technological conditions—can express themselves as changes in the party structure, the emergence of new political interest groups, and alterations in the political resources of citizens.

These three kinds of changes—of which the first two are often, but not always, linked to the clear intent on the part of the owner of the capital to improve profitability—have effects which can best be described with the aid of a two-stage model (see Figure 2.1). In the first stage, these social changes have effects on the *individual* in the form of altered living conditions, unemployment, and changes in personal finances, means of subsistence, educational opportunities, etc. These individual predicaments may lead in a second stage to a *collective consciousness*, i.e., a process in which numbers of persons perceive the conditions, which they until then had seen as limited to themselves individually, as in fact affecting many others in the same situation. There are several prerequisites before such a collective consciousness (or class consciousness) can arise: besides a high degree of dissatisfaction with living conditions, it is also necessary for people to come into contact with each other.

The collective consciousness, and the common desire to control and improve one's own situation, are prerequisites for the formation of *organizations. An organization is a systematically established structure, constructed by some person, group, or class with the distinct, conscious intent to realize certain goals.* These goals are linked to the interests of the organization's mandator (owner). The mandator of the organization is often identical to the person or persons who initiated the organization and/or supplied the capital and the labor needed for its establishment.[11]

Most organizations grow gradually, the number of members increases, and the work load on the original initiators becomes larger. The mandator gradually realizes that the organization has become too large for decisions to be made and executed simply. For example, as the scope of trade union activity grew, the participatory democracy upon which decision-making had been founded in the early years could no longer be reconciled with the demand for effective protection of the economic interests of the members. It is easy to show that decision-making in the plenum form becomes awkward even in rather small organizations. In these cases, the usual and natural step is to appoint an *executive* group. The task of the executive is to carry on the business of the organization as deputy to, and on behalf of, the mandator.

The executive group usually consists of two main categories of personnel, one of which is elected and the other employed. In the nonprofit organization the elected decision-makers are often called "representatives" while the employees are "functionaries." Within a corporation the board of directors is the elected executive while management and salaried employees are the employed executive.[12]

We will now return to our concept of rights. It should be clear that the mandator for the juridical person *private company* consists of private owners of capital who execute their mandate through the shareholders' meeting either by attending personally or by proxy.[13]

The mandator situation is different in the cases of citizen and labor rights. As mentioned earlier (Section 2.1), the vote in the decision-making body of a private company is generally proportional to the amount of capital owned. In the case of the juridical person *state,* the citizens are the mandators and the rule "one man, one vote" is applied as the principle of decision-making.

It is worth emphasizing that the mandate in reality lies not in the quality of "citizen" but rather in the quality of "citizen entitled to vote." The distinction is important, since the debate about employee investment funds (see Section 9.1) occasionally leaves one with the impression that there is a great difference in the numerical strength of "citizens" and "wage earners." What is often overlooked is the fact that only citizens *entitled to vote* can reasonably be expected to influence the collective formation of capital. (This because it is the right to vote which is the constitutional definition of the decision-making capacity.)

There is a significant overlapping of the category citizen/presumptive mandator in the case of citizen funds (see Chapter 9), and the category wage earner/presumptive mandator in the case of employee investment funds. After all, the citizen with the right to vote is most often also a wage earner. There are slightly more than four million wage earners in Sweden and slightly less than six million citizens with voting rights. Thus, wage earners (i.e., those gainfully employed today) constitute more than two-thirds of all citizens with voting rights.

It is reasonable to assume that the associations of wage earners which would be mandators of funds according to the principle of the rights of labor normally would be made up of the labor unions we recognize today.

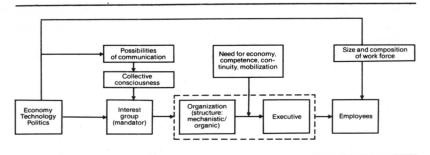

Figure 2.1: A PROCESS MODEL FOR THE STUDY OF ORGANIZATIONS

It should be pointed out, however, that the ownership rights to the means of production can, according to labor rights, be passed on to whichever wage-earner association the legislator chooses to recognize. .

This raises two questions. Can a fund system founded on the principle of the rights of labor be justified, and how then should it be organized? And in what way or ways will the functions of the labor organizations change compared to the present? Both of these questions have been central to the debate about wage-earner funds. The organizational questions present some of the most difficult problems set forth in the spring of 1978 by LO/SAP (the Swedish Federation of Trade Unions and the Swedish Social Democratic Party). Critics from many quarters have pointed out that a system of employee investment funds would mean, among other things, that wage earners would find themselves "on both sides of the negotiating table." We will discuss and attempt to answer these questions in Chapter 10.

Operational definitions. How can one empirically determine who is the mandator? The point of departure for one answer to this question lies in the concept of the executive. The mandator is the person or persons who appoint the executive. In most organizations there are written rules (articles of association, statutes, and similar documents) which dictate who has the right to elect the executive body.

One other answer arises from the concept "right of delegation." The mandator may delegate various questions to the executive for decision (this, as we mentioned earlier, is one of the reasons for appointing an executive leadership). Certain questions, however, *may not* be delegated: stock company legislation, for example, does not allow a stockholders' meeting to delegate to any other body decisions concerning fixed capital, rules for the appointment of executive directors, and responsibility for financial statements. This rule of ultimate responsibility determines, therefore, who is mandator for the organization.

This rule also limits the possibilities of a broadening of the Swedish law of co-determination. According to present legislation, co-determination for wage earners may not go so far as to encroach upon the functions of the

shareholders' meeting. The following was established by a labor department study of the relationship between corporate legislation and co-determination legislation:

> [The shareholders' meeting may not] commit itself to a dispossession or
> limitation of its sovereignty for the advantage of any other corporate body.
> According to corporate legislation, the ultimate decision-making right lies with
> the stockholders by means of the shareholders' meeting. The executive board
> and other representatives of the company are in principle obliged to act upon
> decisions of the shareholders' meeting (prop. 1975:103 pages 234,383). The
> supervisory activity of the shareholders' meeting may not be limited. This
> state of affairs may be considered guaranteed by absolute precepts established
> in corporate legislation.[14]

2.5 Socialization of the Means of Production: Change of Mandator

Political struggle is often expressed as the struggle for the right of
mandate, the most important part of which is the right to control the
means of production, their utilization, and their yield.

One can conceive of the transition from private to collective ownership
of the means of production as a change of mandator. The contemporary
industrial mandate is founded on private ownership, with power being
distributed according to economic investment, while the mandator function of citizen and labor rights is based on collective ownership according
to the principle of one man, one vote. In the case of labor rights, the
investment of each person takes the form of contributed labor. In the case
of citizen rights, there is no actively contributed investment. Rather,
partial control over the means of production is seen as a natural right, a
consequence of the right to vote.

In the case of citizen rights, ownership is considerably more anonymous
than in the case of labor rights. It is impossible to see any *direct* relationship between the role of the citizen entitled to vote and the growth,
administration, and distribution of society's capital. This is simply because
there is no correlation between the role of voter and the role of creator of
surplus value and capital. The role of voter is political, and the role of
creator of capital is economic.

The political role includes more than the capacities for formation and
administration of capital. The voter must take a stand toward political
parties not only in their capacity as administrators of means of production, but also insofar as they are responsible for social, educational,
cultural, defense, financial, and foreign policies.

These issues become important in the discussion of employee investment funds, since any move to transfer ownership of private corporations
to the public will raise the question of how public interests in the
companies will be represented vis-à-vis wage-earner interests. Should only

those gainfully employed have influence over the capital formation of the company? If not, how should other legitimate interests, e.g., those of retired workers, be represented?

> What does one say to retired workers? ... Retired workers, who soon will comprise one of every five adults, do not participate in production. And yet they can claim the right to have a say in determining the principles by which the power of ownership will be exercised. Their labor has created the capital now used for production. How does one argue that only those presently employed should have the right to determine what happens to the capital?[15]

We believe that a way can be found to organize society in accordance with the principle of the rights of labor and which also upholds the rights of those not gainfully employed. In reality there are many similarities between the interests of those employed and those not employed.[16] Pointing this out, however, is not sufficient, since one can nevertheless *imagine* cases in which the will of those employed concerning how the yield on production should be distributed can conflict with the will of other groups, e.g., of retired workers. Legal order demands a system which is able to deal with exceptions to the norm (agreement between wage-earner interests and public interests) such as described by Bodström (see ref. in note 16). In Chapter 10 we will attempt to develop a line of reasoning showing how the assertion of the rights of labor can be reconciled with the principles of solidarity, principles which include those who have left active production and those who have yet to enter another occupation.

2.6 What Is a "Right"? Are "Rights" Fictitious?

In the introduction to this chapter we indicated that the concept of "rights" is a subject of debate among legal theorists, and that the three concepts we discuss in this book are therefore in dispute. We shall now review this debate.

THE UPPSALA SCHOOL

During the early part of the twentieth century and throughout the years between the world wars, scientific debate and the entire cultural climate of Sweden were greatly influenced by the so-called Uppsala school of philosophy, Axel Hägerström being the dominant name. Of basic importance to the Uppsala school was a deep skepticism regarding natural law, metaphysics, speculation, and theorizing based on assumptions which could not be proved by factual observation or empirical investigation. Sweden's social climate at the turn of the century was heavily influenced by continental, and especially German, social philosophy. Great systems, such as those of Hegel and Nietzsche, set the tone. One characteristic of this social philosophy is a blurred boundary between science and politics. The Uppsala school attacked the grandiose ambitions of the continental philosophers who created pretentious systems of thought. Hedenius describes Hägerström's philosophy as follows:

> [This school is characterized] by a striving which is at once both very flexible and very rigid: to forgo every philosophic "system" but attempt to acquire for philosophy some of the exactness of the normal sciences; to methodically examine the reasoning of the constructors of the great systems in order to finally learn something definitive about "the eternal companions"; to neither speculate nor meditate, but rather through logical analysis to attempt to clarify and solve problems; to, if possible, remedy the ancient misery of philosophy, the lack of unity in even the most elementary issues.[17]

The Uppsala school was not alone in its criticism. At the same time, similar thoughts were propagated by the so-called Vienna school (Carnap et al.) in Austria and by Cambridge philosophy (G. E. Moore and others) in England. An important common characteristic of these schools is the demand for logical cogency and conceptual precision combined with the demand that all scientific statements be provable by fact. The goal of scientific work was to arrive at certain kinds of true premises or statements. It was, on the other hand, not the business of science "to pronounce or think theses such as 'this is good,' 'this is right,' 'this should happen,' or 'this should not happen.'" The object was, in the words of Myrdal in *Vetenskap och politik i nationalekonomin* to separate "that which is" from "that which should be." Pronouncements on "that which should be" were the business of politics.[18]

Hägerström, in his inaugural speech *On the Truth of Moral Conceptions*, said:

> Since it is the business of science to present only that which is true, and since it is nonsense to consider a notion of that which should be as true, then it is the business of no science to propose how we should act. . . . [Furthermore], it is not for [science] to set values. Just as it cannot show that given rules should be obeyed, so it cannot show that they should not be followed and that others should replace them. The opinion presented here . . . is that the science of morals cannot *teach morals*, but can merely teach *about* morals.[19]

We shall not enter into a long discussion of the Uppsala school. Our general point is that Hägerström's philosophy makes demands which in reality cannot be fulfilled. Later (in Chapter 3) we shall comment on Gunnar Myrdal's *Vetenskap och politik i nationalekonomin* to show that high ambitions toward a science free from value judgments and an awareness of the problem's breadth are not sufficient to reach the goals of the Uppsala school. But as we shall see in more detail in the next chapter, this does not mean that scientific ambition must be abandoned.

THE UPPSALA SCHOOL AND JURISPRUDENCE

Criticism by the Uppsala school had repercussions in various scientific fields, in the humanities and social sciences as well as in jurisprudence. In the last of these fields, the concept of rights came under fire.

> Juridical concepts . . . were criticized severely. In particular, criticism was directed at expressions like "rights," "duties," etc., expressions for which there seemed to be no observable analogues in the real world. These expressions were thus condemned as "metaphysical." . . . Such concepts were thought to reflect lingering notions from the realm of natural law and similarly untenable scientific beliefs.[20]

The "antimetaphysical" line of thought was especially represented by Vilhelm Lundstedt. Among other things, Lundstedt maintained "that there actually are no rights and that the concept of rights is a logical absurdity, an absurdity which jurisprudence until now has been toying with only because of basic misconceptions."[21] Rules of law must be discounted, according to Lundstedt. It is, he said, "especially important to emphasize the necessity that jurisprudence come to an understanding that what are commonly considered 'rules of law,' be they either written or unwritten, do not exist in reality."[22]

It is probably correct to say that the Uppsala school accomplished "a beneficial house-cleaning and reevaluation in the realm of juridical notions and concepts."[23] But insofar as they concerned the concept of rights, these theses were much too extreme and, as Hedenius shows,[24] bordered on the absurd. Hedenius writes:

> [If] there exists any fixed, desirable quality about that which we call "personal right of ownership," and *if* one can name those kinds of things which criminal law covers with the words "legal obligation," then this means that the words "current rules of law," "right of ownership," and "legal obligation" are not, in the sense of common juridical language, meaningless words. The statement "this is my right of ownership" must be a true statement whenever a fact exists of the type "which we call personal right of ownership" and the person in question is I. . . . In other words, there exist current rules of law, rights, and legal obligations.[25]

It is probably a rarity for contemporary students of law to accept the position of Hägerström and Lundstedt. There is, however, a tendency to avoid taking a stand on the empirical issue whenever possible, and instead to consider the concept of rights as a sort of pedagogical aid to juridical doctrine. The concept has a "function of economizing thought and presentation"; it "draws our attention to the affinity between and the social functions of various legal institutions (i.e., conglomerations of rules concerning a certain subject)."[26] The concept of rights takes on such a presentational role especially in the so-called *notion of the intermediary concept.* Lantz uses the exacting term "theory of the intermediary concept."[27] As will become apparent in the following sections, it would be an exaggeration to call the intermediary concept model a theory. It is hardly a question of a systematic ordering of statements, although it is nevertheless a very significant contribution to juridical systematics.

THE INTERMEDIARY CONCEPT MODEL

Strömholm introduces "rights" as an intermediary concept as follows:

Certain legally significant situations embrace a large number of elements. Suppose that person B purchases real estate from A on July 1, 1960. Within the framework of the current Swedish judicial system, a vast number of legal rules which previously applied to A now apply to B. (This is oversimplified; in reality the transition is successive, occurring in stages marked by sales contract, bill of sale, payment and deed.) The latter, among other things, acquired a number of possibilities for making use of the real estate. One could say that the sale of the real estate is a legal precondition which potentially (in the realm of possibilities) results in innumerable legal consequences. In most cases in which anyone has reason to show interest or discuss B's legal position with respect to the real estate, this precondition—the sale—which created the legal position is, for all practical purposes, of no interest. It does not matter whether B acquired the real estate by means of purchase, gift, inheritance, etc. Of practical interest is that the legal situation has come into being and that it has not been abrogated by some intermediary fact, such as a resale by B to C. It is likewise uninteresting—and for that matter impossible—to enumerate all the potential legal consequences of the acquisition each time one has reason to consider a particular aspect of B's potential legal actions as regards the real estate.[28]

This use of the concept "right of ownership" satisfies a practical need: a summing up of a number of legal preconditions and consequences. The intermediary concept "right of ownership" functions as a "point of rest."

Someone who in 1970 says that "it is B who has the right of ownership to the real estate" has thus stated in condensed form that a legal state was created and has not been abrogated in the intervening years, and that the potential legal claims can be asserted by B.[29]

The economizing intent is evident in the capacity of the intermediary concept to reduce the number of statements needed to express in legal language, say, a property rights situation. The conditional statements "if purchase, then property right" and "if property right, then freedom to use" each expresses a part of the rule of law which in the complete form reads "if purchase, then freedom to use." Similarly, the statement "if inheritance, then authority to sell" can be broken down into a prevenient statement ("if inheritance, then property right") and a subsequent statement ("if property right, then authority to sell").[30] Thus, the prevenient statements express various *legal preconditions,* and the subsequent statements express various *legal consequences*. The notion of property is thus a central point between a large (and in theory unlimited) number of legal preconditions and a (likewise theoretically unlimited) number of legal consequences:[31]

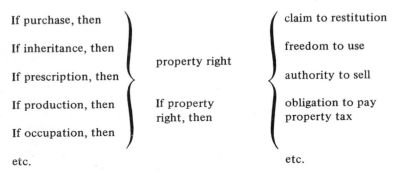

If we do not make use of the intermediary concept, then we are faced with the problem of how to deal with the many combinations of prevenient and subsequent statements. To say that someone has a property right to something is much simpler. Admittedly we sacrifice detail, but on the other hand the details—concerning both legal consequences and legal preconditions—can be rather easily charted by a study of current law.

HEDENIUS: ON THE RIGHT OF POSSESSION AND FREEDOM OF DISPOSITION

The conjoining of the intermediary concept with current law complicates comparisons between various legal systems. The legal preconditions and consequences embraced by, for instance, "right of ownership" vary from country to country.

An issue is how much importance should be attached to these variations. Most legal systems obviously contain a *core* of ideas concerning rights of ownership. Hedenius proceeds from this assumption in his essay "The Analysis of the Ownership Concept."[32]

> My premise implies that when we refer to the right of ownership, as it has been fixed for a long time by many legal systems, then we are speaking of one single relationship, i.e., the ownership relation between the owner and that which is owned. According to this premise then, the right of ownership *as a concept* is the selfsame relationship, even though ownership, both as to origin and legal consequence, has been formulated in various ways at various times by various legal systems.[33]

Manifestations of the phenomenon "right of ownership" may differ widely at different points in time and in different milieus. This may occur "without [the right of ownership] ceasing to be the same phenomenon, as long as we have defined [right of ownership] unequivocally, and as long as the conditions of the definition are fulfilled by all its manifestations."[34]

Hedenius suggests defining "right of ownership" two-dimensionally, i.e., as *protection of possession* and *freedom of disposition*.

Protection of possession refers to the protection granted to an owner by the legal system from being involuntarily dispossessed of a thing to which he has the right of ownership. According to this terminology, possession is not identical to "disposition." Possession means simply having, or having access to, a thing, provided one has not voluntarily relinquished it.[35]

The second dimension, freedom of disposition, comprises according to Hedenius,

a freedom to dispose of that which is owned by means of a sale or any other transference, e.g., by gift, inheritance or contract (concerning, for instance, another person's right to use the property), or without any contract to give away, will away, abandon or destroy the thing which is owned.[36]

These two dimensions are used by Hedenius in a paradigmatic construction. In reality the right of ownership is limited everywhere. But for the sake of logical argument it can be defined as a person's completely unlimited right to a thing.[37] In reference to this extreme point of view, the right of ownership can be determined to be more or less complete. Through the application of Hedenius's dimensions, complete right of ownership can be said to exist when there exist both complete protection of possession and complete freedom of disposition.[38]

We shall not go into Hedenius's concept of ownership in greater detail. The terms protection of possession and freedom of disposition are not very easy to apply in practice. Further, it seems that Hedenius assumes that these dimensions can vary independently of each other. But he does not explain this very well, and this would, in another context, be worth a lengthier discussion.[39]

In spite of the problems, however, Hedenius's discussion is worthwhile since it clearly emphasizes the importance of finding aspects of the right of ownership which are as permanent as possible and which are central to the right of ownership concepts in most legal systems. This is obviously a prerequisite for a comparative analysis by the social sciences.

The "core" of the differing notions of right of ownership for which Hedenius is searching can be specified somewhat further. Earlier in this chapter (Section 2.2) we touched upon Honoré's category "right to capital" and Becker's comment that this is the most "fundamental" element in the right of ownership. There are great similarities between Hedenius's definition of "freedom of disposition" and Honore's "right to capital." The "core" for which Hedenius is searching includes—as in Honoré's concept—the right to destroy, give away, or sell the thing owned.

Another of Honoré's terms should be brought out in this context, i.e., "the right to manage—that is, to decide how and by whom a thing shall be used." As was intimated in the section entitled "Mandator," the relationship mandator/executive is a question of management. The owner of capital—by force of possession of the most fundamental instrument of the right of ownership—may delegate to the executive the right to *manage* the capital; but he keeps—in the terminology of Hedenius—the right of disposition over the capital.

2.7 The Appropriation of Property:
On Original and Derived Acquisition

In the terms of the intermediary concept we have described property right as a summing up of legal preconditions and consequences. We shall now look more closely at the legal preconditions as they pertain to the concept of property.

Property right arises as a consequence of an appropriation (recognized by the legal system) or, in other words, a *legal acquisition*. Undén ties his discussion of acquisition to the three classical factors of production: labor, land, and capital:

> As a private individual, one can acquire property according to current legal order either as compensation for labor and services, or by virtue of possession of and right of disposition over land and capital utilized for production. . . . Wages are acquired through a transfer of the right of ownership, i.e., the transfer of money from the employer to the employee by virtue of a labor contract. . . . But the landowner can also acquire returns on land by cultivating it and profiting from its yield, just as the owner of capital can directly utilize his capital for the production of commodities.[40]

Acquisition usually occurs as rights of ownership are transferred from one person to another (succession). This can happen in various ways, e.g., through inheritance, marriage, will, sale, gift, etc. It is less germane to our study to ascertain how often a certain type of acquisition *occurs* in society. This empirical question is less interesting to us than the question of which means of acquisition *are or are not recognized as legal categories.*

Swedish juridical doctrine differentiates three kinds of grounds for acquisition: original, derivative, and extinctive acquisition. Original acquisition means that a person obtains ownership rights to ownerless property. Derivative acquisition consists of the taking over of property from a previous owner through, for example, inheritance, purchase or gift. We will return to the category of extinctive acquisition in the following section.

There are two main types of original acquisition: "taking" and "making" (in the words of Honoré). Our legal preconditions appear thus:

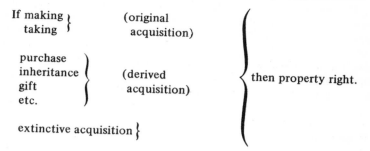

The category of "taking" is legally rather meaningless today.

> In contemporary society it is only in exceptional cases that ownership rights are acquired through appropriation of ownerless property. . . . Under certain preconditions one may, according to current law, appropriate game through hunting or trapping, fish and crustaceans through fishing or other form of capture, and berries, mushrooms, etc. by picking. These objects are not covered by the real estate owner's right of ownership but rather are ownerless.[41]

Most things belong to someone. Only with the consent of the existing owner may they be transferred to a new owner. We will not discuss "taking" further at this point, but instead we refer the reader to the section on Hegel (5.1). Classical philosophy devotes great attention to the "taking" form of original acquisition, as well as to the category of "making." We now turn our attention to the latter.

"Making" is a form of acquisition in which a raw product or another object at a low level of manufacture is transformed to a higher level of manufacture, usually obtaining thereby a greater value.

> A change in the right of ownership can be caused by a change in the object of this right which makes it appear to be a completely different object. Thus all production of commodities includes the creation of new or more or less changed products. The craftsman or industrialist who, either himself or through persons in his service, works his raw material becomes owner of the new creations.[42]

A crucial point here is the phrase "himself or through persons in his service." *What is happening here is that two different kinds of production are being brought together under the same legal category, i.e., the kind of*

production which occurs through one's own labor and that which tran-
spires as the industrialist invests capital and has work performed by hired
labor. The discussion of the rights of labor concerns for the most part
whether or not it is justifiable to combine these concepts. The main theme
of Marx, for instance, is the emphasis on the right of workers to regain
control over the means of production and their yield while ending the
exploitation of the workers through which others acquire the surplus value
of production.

According to other interpretations—including that of current Swedish
law—it is the ownership of capital and of the instruments of labor which
lead to the right of ownership of the product. The person who has
contributed labor to its creation may not lay claim to it. His remuneration
must be arranged through a *contract* by which a certain wage is paid for
certain labor (see Section 2.10 on the right of contract).

The two different kinds of production—and the fact that they are
combined under the same juridical category—reflect an historical process
during which the right of ownership slowly and almost imperceptibly
changed its social function. The process originated in a period in which
social organization was characterized by "simple production of goods."
That is,

> a society in which a majority of all producers of goods are independent
> farmers or craftsmen who own their own means of production, employ few or
> no outside workers, and who in most cases sell their products directly to the
> customer.[43]

This era—which in Europe can be said to have lasted approximately
until the end of the Middle Ages—was gradually replaced by a social
organization based on composite production, that is, production characterized by the means of production being owned and controlled by
individual owners of capital who produce with the help of hired labor.

It is worth noting that the transition from simple to composite production took place slowly and undramatically. The capitalowners themselves
often participated in the production together with one or several employees. The difference between the two types of production were thus not
readily observable.[44]

2.8 Simple vs. Composite Production

Following the delineation between simple and composite commodity
production, we shall use the concepts *simple* and *composite production*
when speaking of the production process. Simple production combined in
one and the same person several different functions which were later
separated. In simple production, the producer buys the raw material,

transforms it with hos own hands into a final product, and sells it to the buyer. The producer is independent and economically free.[45]

What happened during the infancy of capitalism—that which Ambjörnsson[46] calls the commercial revolution—is that the concept of the right of ownership began to assume a changed function. At this time the arguments of the social philosophers concerning labor began to include the labor performed by employees ("servants").[47] Macpherson's documentation of this period is perhaps the most exhaustive, and we shall have reason to return to it later (in Section 5.2).

In the early 1800s the concept of right of ownership was essentially the same as in 1600. "[But] what had happened to its social function? Did it still represent a system of production [similar to that of previous centuries]? No: the producing person now worked in another man's house, with another man's tools. The producer was still the possessor (*detentor*) of the raw materials, the instruments of labor, and the final product, but they were no longer 'his.' "[48]

It is Karl Renner's thesis that the transition from simple to composite production takes place within the framework of the existing concept of property. The owner of capital is considered an independent economic agent. The sociological and economic circumstances of being able to employ one or more coworkers—and the fact that the number of such persons grows—has no effect on the right of ownership seen as a *legal rule*. Employment becomes more common, but it is not regulated by any gradual transformation of the concept of property, such as apportioning to the employees some of the surplus value. Rather, it is regulated by a broadening of the contractual relationship. "[Property] changes its function without a corresponding change in the law."[49] The concept of ownership which we now see applied by Swedish law reflects the permanence—and socioeconomic insensitivity—which is a part of the legal system. In his dissertation on property law, Undén does not consider it a problem that production can happen in two ways. Acquisition by production is not considered a special category, Undén says, "since no change takes place with respect to the owner personally."[50] In other words, the person who owns the finished product is identical to the person who owned the raw material. The *labor* which transformed the raw material to a finished product simply has nothing to do with that. "By keeping the object of labor the basis for the right of ownership, the issue of commodity production—which is economically important—is unproblematic as far as juridical ideology is concerned."[51]

2.9 Specification

The third form of original acquisition is so-called extinctive acquisition. The term signifies the transition of an ownership right from person A to another person B due to disregard or "annihilation" of A's ownership right. A well-known example of extinctive acquisition

> is when a famous artist mistakenly uses someone else's chunk of clay to make a sculpture. If in such a case the value created by the labor is significantly greater than the value of the material and if the person doing the labor was acting in good faith, then this person is of old considered to have acquired ownership rights. This is a case of so-called *specification*. The owner of the raw materials should, of course, be remunerated for its value.[52]

Hydén believes the case of the artist and the chunk of clay is a "pseudoproblem," one which jurists discuss instead of considering "the important question of commodity production."[53] This seems an unduly summary criticism of jurisprudence and, moreover, an interpretation which misses an important point. Hardly ignoring the issue of commodity production the case of the artist and the clay brings the matter of the character of commodity production to a head. The interesting point in this case is that it is *the only case of original acquisition which recognizes labor as a value-creating factor* and where ownership of the raw material does not automatically justify ownership of the finished product. (Hydén states that "juridical ideology" does not recognize any ownership through labor at all).[54] Undén writes on the subject of specification:

> That which characterizes specification is that a new thing is created through the reworking process, e.g., furniture is made from someone else's wood, a suit of someone else's cloth, flour of someone else's grain, boards of someone else's logs. . . . The principle issues raised by specification are whether the specifier's acquisition presupposes any distinct value relationship between the labor done and the raw material, and further whether the specifier's good faith is a necessary condition. According to French, German, and Swiss law the value relationship is a deciding factor even though it is stated in different ways. It is reasonable to give significance to this idea. *In general, the more valuable the invested labor in relation to the value of the material, the more appropriate it would be to recognize the right of ownership of the laborer [our italics]*.[55]

Why then, one must ask, is this rule that an increase in value bestows upon the laborer the right to the product not *generally* applicable? How can it be that if I grind someone else's grain or if I sculpt someone else's chunk of clay, I become owner of the grain or the clay, but if I labor as an employee to cast concrete into a stairway or assemble electronic calculators, then I receive only my wages? There seems to be no difference between the two cases. It is true of most industrial production that labor increases the value of the product just as significantly as in the case of the sculpture and the clay.

There are at least two answers to this question. First, the paradigmatic case of specification is a matter of someone taking possession of someone else's clay *by mistake*. The Swedish legal system does not accept theft or other wilfull action as grounds for specification. "A deliberate use of someone else's material will . . . inevitably be punishable."[56] (Civil law, however, does allow for the possibility that the finished product may be kept even if the raw material is stolen.)

This explanation is based on the acquisition of the clay *in good faith*. But in German and Swiss law, for example, this insistence on good faith is weaker; the emphasis is placed instead on the increase in value. Our question cannot be answered in this case by saying that the raw material came into someone else's possession by mistake. The explanation seems to be another: *Cases of specification are so rare that they possess no real threat to the right of private ownership.* Pressure from the owners of clay to change the law can be expected only if a veritable epidemic of mistakes should arise, resulting in large groups of owners losing their chunks of clay. The probability of that kind of situation is minimal. An increase in value can be recognized as a ground for acquisition since the right of ownership of instruments of labor and means of production is not generally threatened.

If, on the other hand, wage earners—relying on the principle of increase in value—should get the idea to demand the right of disposition over that which is produced (say stairways and electronic calculators), then one could expect a vehement reaction from owners of the raw materials and means of production.

2.10 The Right of Contract

A logical complement to composite production is the right of contract. Composite production is based on the combination of privately owned capital and a "free" labor force. In the beginning, labor contracts were individual agreements between employers and wage earners. But due to the increasing organization of the working class, this is somewhat different today.

> Based earlier on a contract, the labor relationship has now developed into a "position." . . . The "position" includes the demand for reasonable pay (determined by collective bargaining or regulation) . . . the obligation to make certain contributions (to unions and insurance programs) . . . the right to certain benefits (health and accident insurance, pension, funeral costs), and finally certain guarantees against unemployment or in the case that employment is terminated.[57]

Renner directs our attention to the fact that the original private labor contract has become more and more a matter of public concern. To an ever-increasing degree the state has been drawn into the relationship between the two sides of the labor market, both as inspector and regulator.

The private contract has become—through the complementary institutions of collective bargaining, employment exchange, national social security, etc.—an institution of public law. Decisions are still made according to the private will of the concerned individuals, but their influence is constantly decreasing: the state element is almost more important than the private, and the collective element is more important than the individual.[58]

Renner's thesis (reviewed in Section 2.8) is also applicable to the labor contract; the juridical element has remained essentially unchanged while the social functions of the labor contract have shifted. The individual contract has been transformed into collective agreements between the parties of the labor market. But these collective agreements—commitments for *groups* of wage earners and (most often) *groups* of employers—do not change the basic character of the labor agreement: it is a contractual agreement between the individual employer and the individual wage earner. "In the language of the Swedish law of co-determination, worker signifies a person who is *employed,* i.e., a person who by means of a contract has committed himself—in principle *personally*—to do work for another."[59]

Contractual law becomes an important complement to a system in which labor is bought and sold on a market. Contractual law can also be applied to groups other than wage earners: contractors, customers, the state, local authorities—generally anyone or any organization which deals with the corporation in different ways. Advocates of private ownership will often combine a defense of private ownership rights with an assertion of the importance of free bargaining rights. The capitalowner's right of disposition over the means of production often seems more acceptable if wage earners and others have this freedom.

It is symptomatic that the economist Ingemar Ståhl combines a criticism of the Meidner proposal on employee investment funds with a plan for an analysis of corporate ownership and power from the perspective of contractual law.[60] Ståhl's presentation of the interested parties in a corporation is strongly reminiscent of Eric Rhenman's model.[61] The contribution of each interested party to—and its income from—the organization/corporation is defined by contract. The contract element emphasizes the perspective of "balances" which is one of the bases for Rhenman's model.[62]

C. J. Westholm, on somewhat similar grounds, attacks the principle of majority in the proposal on employee investment funds by the Swedish Federation of Trade Unions. According to Westholm, the majority principle seems "strange to those who are used to the corporation making its agreements with the many interested parties by means of contracts."[63] The right of the contract, according to Westholm, better insures that "the individual has more to say as a consumer and at his workplace."[64] The idea of balances is also clear: *"As far as the right of contract is concerned, it makes no difference how many people stand on each side when the contract is signed. Neither side should be able to overpower the other."*[65]

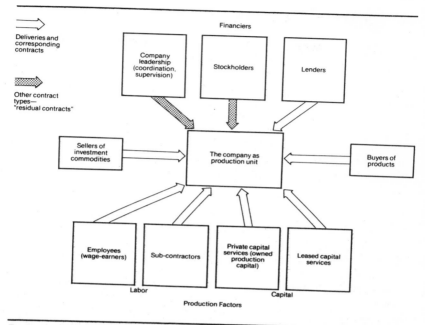

Figure 2.2: THE CONTRACT STRUCTURE OF THE COMPANY

Research on the right of contract has attained a certain popularity recently, especially in the debate on collective capital formation. It does not signify anything really new: it is mainly concerned with the problems of power distribution in the corporation, especially between the two main components labor and capital. The implicit recommendation is that the principle of "one man, one vote" should not be applied to models for power and influence in corporations.[66]

A note on Honoré and liberalism. Honore is of the opinion that the right of ownership is best studied against the background of the basic model of "a single human being owning, in the full liberal sense, a single material thing."[67] As mentioned earlier, the right of contract highlights this liberal model by accentuating the *individual* aspect of the employer-employee relationship. An important qualification of this, however, is that ownership of the material object "means of production" permits control of more than the mere object. As Karl Renner has emphatically stated, ownership of the means of production also implies control over the *people* who use these means of production within the framework of the contractual relationship. A capacity for control over people is inherent in capital, and the contract functions as the agent through which this control is expressed. The right of ownership signifies ownership both *in rem* and *in personam.*[68]

2.11 Collective Production and Collective Ownership

Can the circumstances of simple production be recreated? Is it realistic to believe that the direct relationship individual-labor-capital can be implemented anew? Can production again be decentralized so that the direct connection between the individual producer and his product can be regained?

To a great degree, modern industrial production and services occur in collective and organized forms. Efficiency and competitiveness are largely dependent upon an organization's division of labor and scale of production. A widespread return to labor-intensive forms of production is hardly possible: the decentralization of production has limits set by forces outside our own economic system.

In one way it may appear that the personal, individual labor which characterized simple production belongs to a bygone stage. This is undeniable as far as individual, independent labor is concerned: the production of goods and services today must occur mainly on a large scale and in organized forms. "Individual" and "personal" are, however, not synonymous. Even if the labor is collective, the laborer can obviously consider the production to be "his own." This requires that he sees a direct relationship between the labor in which he participates and its results. In other words, the closer the relationship between the laborer and the capital formation process, the greater the possibility that the principle of the rights of labor will be implemented. Production must be collective, but this does not imply that it must be anonymous. Collective production can indeed allow for active participation in the formation of capital.

But the situation is different in the case of citizen rights. Anonymity and complexity are, so to speak, built into the system. Since citizen rights have nothing to do with the production process, the incentives for monitoring labor and capital are limited. The formation of collective capital, and its administration by the state and secondary bodies, will not differ principally from, say, the national pension system, the value added tax system, or direct taxation. We shall return to these concepts of rights in Chapter 10, as part of our discussion of how the principle of economic democracy should best be implemented. What things speak for citizen rights on the one hand and labor rights on the other as a basis for economic democracy? This is the most important question we must answer.

2.12 Summary

In this chapter we have developed a conceptual apparatus for our discussion in Chapters 3 through 10. Our main concern has been the application of the three concepts of right which have arisen from our discussion of the right of capital, i.e., the private, civic-collective, and labor-collective right of ownership. Economic democracy implies a transfer of means of production from private to collective ownership, but to *which* collective? In a system of collectively owned capital, which collective should make the decisions concerning its use and yield?

Arguments can be made both for the rights of labor and for civic rights. The question is whether these positions can be united, or if we must choose between them. In the latter case, on what basis should we choose, and what difficulties or advantages would this choice entail? This is the subject of our book.

Economic democracy concerns, among other things, the organization of production. We have treated this question briefly within the framework of a model in which the concepts of mandator and executive are central elements. Collective ownership of means of production is first of all a question of the mandator function, the composition of the mandator group, and the legal, economic, and political means by which the state and society will substantiate and legitimate the power of various interest groups. Economic democracy is a matter of decision-making power over the *preconditions* of production, such as capital formation, investment, structure, and long-term planning. Collective influence over the daily decisions in the workplace (e.g., by means of autonomous work groups) may be one part of a system of economic democracy, but it is not one of its distinguishing qualities. Socio-technical reforms (such as job rotation, job enlargement, group organization, etc.) are accepted and encouraged even under a system of private capital ownership. But the issue of broad control over the corporation necessarily brings up the question of mandator and thus becomes a much more controversial problem.

Positivist schools of philosophy (e.g., the Uppsala school) and certain behaviorist writers in the social sciences have questioned the concept of "rights," claiming that it is a mere fiction. Hägerström states, for example, that rights cannot be observed and hence do not exist. Opposed to this view, we have stated—in support of Hedenius—that rights are social and legal facts and can be subjected to scientific analysis. One instrument for this analysis is Eckhoff's "intermediary concept model," according to which the concept of ownership serves as a "resting point," coordinating a number of "legal preconditions" (purchase, inheritance, production, occupation, etc.) and "legal consequences" (e.g., claims to restitution of property, freedom to use, competence to sell).

Among the legal preconditions, we have concerned ourselves with original ("making" and "taking") and derivative (purchase, inheritance, gift, etc.) acquisition. A further important distinction is the one between simple and composite production, simple production being carried out by individual laborers using their own raw material and means of production. Composite production is a combination of privately owned capital plus hired labor. This distinction is relevant to C. B. Macpherson's discussion of the "simple market society" vs. the "possessive market society" to follow in Chapter 4.

Chapter 3

THEORETICAL POINTS OF DEPARTURE

One important aim of this book is to take a stand regarding the principle of the rights of labor. This means making a *value judgment* about the rights of labor, seen in relation to private ownership and civic rights. Is it legitimate for researchers in the social sciences to concern themselves at all with taking a stand on questions of value judgment? (The fact that it is legitimate to *describe* social values—by means of opinion polls and similar empirical surveys—is something with which most everyone will agree.)

3.1 On "What Is" and "What Should Be"

We have seen how Hägerström strongly emphasizes the duty of the scientist to differentiate between "that which is" and "that which should be" (see section 2.6). Gunnar Myrdal takes the same position in his book *Vetenskap och politik i nationalekonomin,* a book to which we shall shortly have reason to return. As we shall try to show, Myrdal's work is a good example of the difficulties involved in Hägerström's recommendations.

If Hägerström's position were to be accepted, then the aim of our own book would have to be abandoned. There is, however, good reason to question the reasonableness of Hägerström's unconditional invocation of "that which is" as the social scientist's given field of inquiry. In the following we shall review Evert Vedung's treatment of this question in the book *Det rationella politiska samtalet.*[1]

Vedung takes as his starting point Hägerström's statement (reviewed in 2.6), and parallel statements of other social scientists, maintaining that disciplines such as economics and sociology should only determine "what is and how it is" (von Mises). "My statement," says Vedung, "is that this position still contains a small but principally important kernel of truth."

> This does not mean, however, that science should stand practically paralyzed before the problem of the validity of value judgements. On the contrary, today there is cause to clearly dissociate oneself from the doctrine that political science is merely a science *about* politics.[2]

It is evident from the context that Vedung means that political science is also a science *of* politics. It is our opinion that his views can, in essence, also be applied to sociology, as well as to economics (concerning this, see Section 3.2 on Myrdal).

Hägerström's viewpoint is often called "value nihilistic." Value judgments are not thought to express statements about reality; they express "an emotion, a command, advice or a recommendation." According to the value nihilistic interpretation, criteria of truth or falsehood are not applicable to these statements of value.[3]

The mistake of the value nihilists, according to Vedung, is that they confuse the *function* of a sentence with its *content*. When the value nihilists say that a value statement expresses an emotion, then they are commenting on how the statement *functions* for the person speaking and/or hearing it. "The import of value statements is said to be their tendency to be caused by, or to cause, the occurence of certain psychological processes in the sender or receiver."[4]

The import of a statement is, however, not just a matter of its function, but also of its content. Language is also a medium for reckoning, and "the import of an act of speech can be the same regardless of which psychological processes have preceded it or which psychological effects follow it."[5]

> We can take as an example the pronouncement, "Abolish agricultural regulation!" As is clear to everyone, the pronouncement of this statement may be caused by many different psychological processes or states, e.g., anger, hate, fear, sorrow, distress, loss, resignation, job, or indifference. The statement can also have several different effects, e.g., surprise, delight, and disgust. But regardless of the causes or effects of the statement, its import in the specific linguistic context is the same. *The import remains constant regardless of causes or effects.* It follows from this that the meaning of a statement cannot be equated with the psychological processes causing it or which it causes. But this is exactly what the value nihilists do when they claim that value statements have expressive or evocative functions. While they believe they have answered the question of the meaning (in the sense of logical content) of value statements, in reality they have answered a completely different question, i.e., the question of the origin and consequences of value statements. It is undeniably odd that this simple rule of thumb—that one must keep separate the questions of origins and effect on the one hand and validity on the other—has not been obeyed in practice even by several of our century's foremost philosophic thinkers.[6]

After some additional consideration, Vedung arrives at his main thesis. Science may not only make assertions *about* value statements (that is, what they are, what their functions are, etc.). Science may also *make* value judgments. "All value judgments are not equally good or bad from a scientific point of view. The slogan [of Hägerström et al.] that scientific (political) moral philosophy may only be a theory *about* morals and not a theory *of* morals is . . . ripe for revision."[7]

Vedung's reasoning in support of this position is based on the distinction between *categorical* and *instrumental* value judgments. An example of a categorical value judgment is, "The power of the people should be increased." This statement can obviously not be tested against reality; the statement is neither true nor false, but is simply a "norm according to which one should act."

Instrumental judgments *can,* however, be tested against reality:

> Assume person A claims that a limitation of the freedom of the press is desirable since this would reduce the risk of domestic espionage activity against foreign powers being revealed. Further, assume person B dislikes such a measure precisely because it is assumed to have this effect. Here we are faced with a conflict concerning how we should judge a possible action. But at the same time there is agreement concerning the consequences this action will have. Statements of the second kind are expressions of instrumental value judgments.[8]

An instrumental value judgment states that action A is a certain or almost certain means of reaching a certain goal:

> An instrumental value judgment can thus be reshaped into a *statement,* expressing a means-end relationship of universal or probablistic nature. And this statement contains no value judgements at all. Even the most inveterate value nihilists should be able to agree that an instrumental value judgment can be given such an objectivist interpretation.[9]

Instrumental value judgments are, in other words, entirely descriptive and can therefore be subjected to the usual analysis of validity. "Given the end, science can thus point out suitable means to that end without suffering pangs of conscience."[10]

But one does not need stop even here. Categorical value judgments are also valid scientific objects of inquiry. They are formulations of ends. Science can assist us in choosing between various ends and supply us with facts which help us in choosing the most suitable alternative.

> [In this respect] it is legitimate for science to discover (a) if the object of a categorical value judgment can in any way be realized physically; (b) if so, which alternative means exist and how great the probability is that they will lead to the end; (c) which side effects and ultimate consequences result from the choice of means besides their probable result in the end; (d) if a point of view includes several categorical value judgments, which of them concern things which are physically possible and which concern things which cannot be realized.[11]

Vedung summarizes:

> At this point it should be clear that the political analysis of theoretical content can in no way be reduced to a theory about political ethics. It can also be a science of political morals. Instrumental value judgments can be rewritten as statements to be tested empirically in the usual way. The significance of this

should not be underestimated, since most value judgments in political language are of this character. But categorical value judgments occur also, and not even in the face of these is the theoretical analyst forced to stop. He can present a number of scientifically supported viewpoints on them.[12]

Value judgments which express pure precepts (of the type, "The power of the people should be increased") must, however, be kept separate from what has been said: these cannot be confirmed or rejected in the same way as judgments of reality may be. Thus far Vedung.

What we are trying to do with our book is to formulate instrumental, not categorical, value judgments. When we write—for example in chapter 7—about the labor theory of value and the subjective theory of value, our statements are concerned with the *effects* of choosing one of the two theories of value. It is our opinion that these effects can be demonstrated both logically and empirically. Our reasoning concerns theories of value as *means* to reach certain *ends*; and it is the relationship between means and ends which we wish to discuss. Examples and details in our continued reasoning will hopefully concretize this statement better than we have been able to do here.

3.2 On the Necessity of Instrumental Value Judgments: Gunnar Myrdal on Science and Politics

The above discussion can be spelled out even more precisely. Instrumental value judgments are not only *acceptable* features in the activity of social science. They are also *necessary*. Social scientific theories have, to the extent that they are applied (and the aim is usually that they should be applicable), consequences of one kind or another for individuals, groups, and classes. The choice of a theory X instead of another theory Y as a rule also means (to the extent that the theories are not too empty or imprecise) that a certain point of view or a certain kind of political praxis is recommended. The consequences of X and Y with respect to, say, politics, economics, or social relations vary. The instrumental content of this is clear: *if* theory X is chosen, *then* this will probably result in other world views, paradigms, economic-political measures, social-political programs, etc. than if theory Y had been chosen. (This does not mean that the choice of a theory means that one gives up all freedom of action. Within the framework of one theory there are usually a great number of conceivable possibilities which can be practically applied.)

An extremely important point is that the choice of a theoretical point of departure cannot be avoided. Social scientific works contain—clearly understood or implied—choices between theories which in different ways affect results. In our opinion, it is important that judgmental points of departure are clearly presented, precisely so that their *consequences* in the form of various practical measures may be investigated.

Certain of Gunnar Myrdal's works provide excellent illustrations of this. In the first edition of *Vetenskap och politik i nationalekonomin*, [13] Myrdal argues intensively and enthusiastically for a judgment-free social science and—in clear reference to Hägerström—for the importance of differentiating between "that which is" and "that which should be." He wishes to build an *economic technology* based on analysis (free of values) of the dominating interests in society. [14] In an edition forty-three years later he has given up the idea of the possibility of a judgment-free social science: he feels now that judgments always steer the scientist, and his thesis is that the researcher therefore must state his value judgments. The same reasoning also occurs in *Objektivitetsproblemet i samhällsforskningen*. [15]

Myrdal's reversal is understandable and reasonable; at the same time it can be claimed that he did not go far enough. *Vetenskap och politik* is a brilliant work, marked by a grand ambition to fulfill the positivist demands for a strictly empirical science. This ambition breaks down completely, however, in the final chapter of the book. Myrdal is there forced to accept the notion of *objective interests* as the basis for his economic technology. He establishes that the charting of the field of social interests stumbles upon a considerable number of problems, partly due to the circumstance that people's subjectively expressed interests are not always their real interests. The interests of the people must therefore become the object of assumptions (which means that the interests are *ascribed* to the people). The conceptual framework of economists can be of assistance here:

> In order that economic technology may be of practical use, then it is necessary that it be built upon the views these people with their general outlook on social problems would have *if* they viewed reality more correctly, let us say if they knew at the start everything we economists know already about the involved chain of events in the mechanism of price formation. . . . In the establishment of the area of opinion relevant to our investigations, we must therefore in some way pull from the views actually established those views which the various social groups *would have* under the entirely hypothetical precondition that their economic insights were more complete and correct. [16]

It is completely clear here that Myrdal is thinking of instrumental judgments: given a certain "outlook on social problems", certain developmental possibilities will follow in the "economic technology."

Vetenskap och politik is a good demonstration of the necessity of social science working with instrumental value judgments, statements of the "if—then" type. Myrdal does not, however, quite reach this conclusion in his treatment of the value issue. He does emphasize that value judgments should be presented, but *why* this should happen is not sufficently explained. Myrdal establishes that value judgments have consequences for scientific work, but he does not offer any appreciable elucidation of what these consequences are and *that* they, in fact, also may be *utilized* in the analysis.

3.3 Social Development and Intellectual Production

Values can provide grounds for rational choices. Thus we may some-what self-indulgently summarize Vedung's position. It is, however, clear that the basis for this position is completely removed if rational choices cannot be made at all. If social development and change take place entirely without the influence of human will and reason, then it is clear that any discussion of choices of alternatives becomes senseless.

Rational analysis is a matter of presenting ends and choosing among alternative means. But obviously, in a purely determinist situation, a specific development will occur, regardless of whether I choose political act A or its opposite non-A. The choice of A or non-A is simply inconsequential.

This will become significant in the next chapter when we discuss developments in economic history and their relation to social philosophy and economic theory. There are various arguments concerning how closely these two phenomena—social development and intellectual production—are related and in which direction any potential influence moves.

The English economic historian Donald Winch has summarized these lines of thought. We shall review them below; this will be one step in our endeavor to formulate a tenable position concerning the problem implied in the chapter heading, i.e., the relationship between social development and attempts to understand and interpret this social development.

DONALD WINCH ON ECONOMIC
DEVELOPMENT AND THE WRITING OF HISTORY

Around the middle of the eighteenth Century a new way of writing about economy and society became common in Europe. In England and France, economic issues had until then been treated in rather ephemeral books, articles, and pamphlets about, say, monetary policy, commerce, population statistics, interest, taxation, etc. Contributions to the discussion were often of current political interest but hardly dealt with comprehensive issues.

What happens around 1750 is that attempts to understand and explain economic events become more cohesive, systematic, and analytic. Political economy is established as an independent science. The growth of political economy is the subject of Winch's dissertation. What we shall treat here is, however, not his description of this process. This is not our problem. We are interested in which *explanatory models* can be used when one deals with the relationship between economic development and its relation to economic theory. Various perspectives are conceivable, according to Winch.[17]

First (1), a distinction can be made between (a) those models which treat the origin of political economy as a product of an independent and autonomous intratheoretical development ("an autonomous shift of perception and outlooks") and (b) those which view political economy as the result of changes in the economy. According to the latter, political economy can be viewed as "a response to new economic problems and interests which excited criticism, explanation, and justification." Thus, the economic changes occur first, and the scientific reactions to them come second.

Position (1a) is called by Winch idealism, and (1b) he calls materialism. Expressed simply, ideas direct reality in (1a), while the opposite is the case in (1b).

The idealist and materialist views of the *origin* of political economy usually coincide with similar notions concerning the further *development* of economic theories. Winch differentiates here between (2a) absolutism and (2b) relativism.

> The absolutist interprets the history of economics as a story involving the progressive development of an intellectually coherent and autonomous body of theory, where progress is judged in terms of conceptual refinement and explanatory power. The relativist is not concerned with this type of progress and may even deny that standards exist by which such progress can be determined; he treats the history of economics more as a reflection of, or reaction against, features of the changing contemporary environment.[18]

Where does Winch stand himself with respect to these explanatory models as he deals with political economy and its development? It seems fairest to describe him as a kind of skeptical materialist and relativist, with the emphasis on the "skeptical." While he demonstrates clearly enough that political economy has, to a great extent, developed as a series of attempts at interpreting and explaining economic development, he takes care to emphasize that this dependency is far from clear-cut and one-sided. There is always a risk, he says, that later readers will overemphasize those elements of political economy which appear connected to material development,[19] while forgetting or ignoring the fact that a good deal of the materialistic development went unobserved or—if it was observed—was never understood by economists.

It is our interpretation of Which that while the economic historian should search for the bonds between economic development and their contemporary interpretations, one should also take care to notice cases of *misinterpretations*; explanations which have been left out; and the political economists' criticisms of developments. One should not only pay attention to "points of correspondence" between theory and reality, but also to "points of dissonance."[20]

3.4 Summary

In this chapter we have asked the question whether it is legitimate for the social scientist to make value judgments. The answer is important, since one can take no position on the three principles of rights without formulating value statements.

We have questioned the thesis of logical empiricism that (social) science should only deal with "that which is and how it is." It may be asserted that social science is not only a science *about* values but also a science *of* values. It can, among other things, lay a foundation for choices between various value systems.

Such an endeavor demands, as pointed out by Vedung, the differentiation between categorical and instrumental value judgments. A categorical value judgments is not testable: it constitutes only a statement *that* a certain position or measure is right, and it cannot be examined with respect to its truth or falsehood. An instrumental value judgment is of an "if . . . then" character. It states that a certain action is a means for attaining a certain end. The consequences of the instrumental value judgment may be examined, i.e., it can be subjected to logical and empirical testing.

What we have to say on the concepts of rights is of the type "instrumental value judgment." When we later (Chapter 7) discuss the labor theory of value and the subjective theory of value, we will do this partly be attempting to show what economic, political, and ethical consequences follow from the choice of one or another theory of value.

Further, with reference to Gunnar Myrdal's work *Vetenskap och politik i nationalekonomin,* we have tried to show that instrumental value judgments are not only reasonable but also necessary features of social scientific activity. Myrdal's own recommendation that the social scientist should present his own value judgments may be defined more exactly to include instrumental value judgments.

As a starting point for Chapter 4, we have, in connection with Donald Winch, pointed out two dimensions significant for the treatment of the relationship between social development and intellectual production, i.e., idealism vs. materialism and absolutism vs. relativism. A materialistic and relativistic explanatory model may seem most reasonable, but at the same time one must take note of, say, cases of autonomous intellectual developments. In other words, one must be wary of the risk of becoming the prisoner of a model.

Chapter 4

SOCIAL DEVELOPMENT AND
INTELLECTUAL PRODUCTION

Economic and Historical Perspectives

4.1 Introduction

In Chapter 3 we touched upon certain theoretical problems, relating to the question of the connection between economic development and the way it may affect scientific activity. We have noted our skepticism toward two extreme formulations of this connection: first, the notion that theoretical developments simply steer social developments and, second, the opposite notion of ideas as mere reflections of economic changes. In general, we have aligned ourselves with Winch's line of thought. Economic historical data are best served by being arranged in such a way that the organization of labor and the utilization of the results of production are the main themes. The distribution of surplus (or, in Marxian terms, who appropriates the surplus value of production) is the underlying issue here.

Within this general framework, history, social science, philosophy, etc. are dependent upon material development in at least two rather obvious ways. First, no science can arise unless human beings spend time and energy producing and transmitting knowledge. This is made possible by using part of the surplus to keep the scientists alive and to supply them with instruments of labor.

Second, it is clear that contemporary economic circumstances define to a great extent *what* social scientists write about and *when* they do it. Few should disagree with the statement that economic science, like social science, can be described for the most part as a running commentary on historical development. It is, as Winch says, significantly more difficult to explain *why* and *how* they wrote as they did.[1] We have, then, returned to the question of social development and the autonomy or dependence of ideas. For the moment we have nothing more to add to the discussion of this problem. The problem will come up again in the section on social democracy and the subjective theory of value (Chapter 8). An autonomous development of theory—in which theory was formed in logical steps as the result of debate and criticism entirely *within* the labor movement—would most likely have resulted in the movement's ideology being given a more direct connection to labor and the production process. But because of external circumstances—economic transformation, the social misery of the working class, the massive academic criticism of the labor theory of value, etc—took another course. The labor movement came in many respects to align itself with the consumption notions of the subjective theory of value, and to profess intentions which signified a just distribution of the results of production rather than controls over the conditions under which they arose.

We shall devote this chapter to an illustration of two issues just mentioned: the general economic conditions for intellectual production and the material circumstances which have been the objects of inquiry for political economists and philosophers during the last centuries. Our goal is limited, both with respect to economic history and to comments on the economic and social debate. We intend primarily to try to place a number of leading classical European authors in their economic and social contexts. The more detailed and comprehensive discussion of the content and consequences of their various messages must wait until Chapters 5 through 8.

4.2 The Transition from Feudalism to Capitalism

This chapter deals with a number of main elements in the development of capitalism and their reflection in economic theory. The period and the area dealt with include Europe from the Middle Ages onward, with emphasis on the period after 1600.

Around 1600, a number of signs that the economic system in Europe was approaching a change were discernible. Locally manufactured goods found a broader market; wage labor increased in scope; the possibilities for creating a surplus grew; the control over the distribution of this surplus shifted to new groups. During the seventeenth and eighteenth centuries, the feudal method of production, which had been on the decline since the fourteenth century, was definitely replaced by a new organization of production—an organization in which owners of capital used it to hire "free" labor for large-scale manufacture and industrial production.

"Feudalism" denotes a social order in which an aristocracy of land-owners/militarists dominates the rest of society, comprised mainly of peasants. The surplus from production—i.e. that which is left after pro-visions for the existence and survival of the direct producers/peasants—is appropriated by the landowners. Compulsory forms for this appropriation were common: slavery and serfdom comprised one form, but there were also systems of day-labor and payment by the peasants of part of their produce to the landowners. The transfer of surplus to the feudal lords was dependent on just such *compulsion*: peasants who can dispose over land need not, in contrast to wage earners, sell their labor in order to survive. The degree and kind of compulsion varied, but it appeared throughout the feudal system of production.[2]

The transition from feudalism to capitalism took several centuries and was a process in which the feudal elements gradually gave way to the new method of production. The change was far from uniform: periods of expansion were succeeded by crises, and only from the larger historical perspective can the existence of the new, capitalistic method of production be established with certainty.

Eric Hobsbawm has—in agreement with Maurice Dobb[3]—summarized the transition to capitalism in the following points:

(a) A period of relapse, following the break-up of the West-Roman empire followed by the gradual evolution of a feudal economy and perhaps a recession in the tenth century A.D. ("the dark Ages").

(b) A period of extremely widespread and rapid economic development from about 1000 A.D. to the early fourteenth century (the "High Middle Ages"), which forms the peak of feudalism. This period saw a marked growth of population, agricultural and manufacturing production, and trade, and virtual revival of cities, a great outburst of culture, and a striking expansion of the western feudal economy in the form of "crusades" against the Moslems, emigration, colonisation, and the setting up of trading-posts abroad.

(c) A major "feudal crisis" in the fourteenth and fifteenth centuries, marked by a collapse of large-scale feudal agriculture, of manufactures and international trade, by population decline, attempted social revolution, and ideological crisis.

(d) A renewal period of expansion from the mid-fifteenth to the mid-seventeenth century marked for the first time by signs of a major break in the basis and superstructure of feudal society (the Reformation, the elements of bourgeois revolution in the Netherlands) and the first clear breakout of the European traders and conquerors into American and the Indian Ocean. This is the period which Marx regarded as marking the beginning of the capitalist era.

(e) Another period of crisis, adjustment, or setback—the "seventeenth century crisis"—coincides with the first clear breakthrough of bourgeois society, the English Revolution. It is followed by a renewed and increasingly general period of economic expansion which culminates in

(f) The definite triumph of capitalist society in the virtually simultaneous Industrial Revolution in Britain, the American Revolution, and the French Revolution—all occurring in the last quarter of the eighteenth century.[4]

The transition from feudalism to capitalism is not a simple process in which the capitalist elements in feudalism are strengthened and gradually break through the feudal "shell." A crisis for feudalism often meant a setback for bourgeois elements as well. During the crisis of the thirteenth century (point c above), not only did large feudal farms experience a setback, but the Italian and Flemish textile industries which had been built by capitalist entrepeneurs who hired wage earners and who approached full industrialization in their organization also had trouble.[5] The crisis of the seventeenth century meant a reversal for international commerce and was a sharp blow to the city-based economies which had begun to blossom in, among other places, Spain and Italy.[6]

4.3 Medieval Methods of Production:
The Beginnings of the "Industrial Revolution"

During the Middle Ages, European society was almost completely dependent upon agricultural production for its existence and growth, which was very slow until approximately the end of the seventeenth century. The economy of the European countries was based on production within the primary sector, above all agriculture, but there was also some extraction of raw materials, used mostly for the production of tools for agriculture and the construction of houses. The great majority of the population was rural; as late as in 1500, there were only six European cities with populations of 100,000 or more, comprising only 1.4% of Europe's population.[7]

Compared to later ages, medieval society was a primarily poor and economically static society. Still, there were trends in its development pointing toward the significantly greater economic, political, and social mobility of the seventeenth and eighteenth centuries.

Economic historians point out that, in important respects, the so-called Industrial Revolution has its origins in the Middle Ages. According to Lilley, humanity has gone through two technological revolutions.[8] The first was during the period from 8,000 to 2,500 B.C. and included the gradual establishment of agricultural techniques, irrigation, the production of textiles, pottery and objects of metal, the utilization of yeast processes for bread and ale, the expansion of sea travel through sailing ships, the development of the harness for beasts of labor, and in some cases (for example, the Egyptian pyramids) the solution to very complicated problems of labor organization.

The second dominant period in the process of technological development occurred in Europe after the year 1000. This period was characterized to a great extent by the growing use of new sources of energy, especially water and wind power. During the period from 800 to 1100, horse harnesses were changed in such a way as to increase the efficiency of draft animals by up to 200%. The introduction of iron horse shoes and double harnesses led to additional significant improvements in agricultural efficiency. As for transport, the spread of the compass during the twelfth century was a significant advance, as was the gradual development of canal navigation, made possible through the use of locks during the fourteenth century.[9]

The introduction of the spinning wheel during the 1200s led to a dramatic improvement in the production of thread for textile manufacture. The extraction of metal was also made more effective: the production of cast iron began during the thirteenth century and came into more general use in the fourteenth century.

A gradual development of the market became noticeable. This affected life in the cities through an increased ordering and planning of economic activity. Le Goff points out that the increased rationalization was noticeable in at least two ways. Working time became more regulated, and the use of standardized weights and measures became more common.

> The need to schedule working time led the towns first of all to demand special bells for the lay townsfolk, and then led to the construction of machines and instruments which divided time into fixed and equal portions—clocks and watches based upon the hours.[10]

Lilley summarizes, saying that the technological advances of the eighteenth and nineteenth centuries can be explained for the most part as an increased use of already existing technological aids, the roots of which are found in the Middle Ages. The first phase of the industrial revolution used mostly medieval sources of energy.[11]

It may also seem natural to consider the medieval methods of production as simple and gradual extensions of the means of production of earlier ages. According to Lilley, however, this is wrong. Medieval methods of production represent a new and independent development, which was to continue at an accelerated rate into the eighteenth and nineteenth centuries.[12]

4.4 Wage Labor and the Need for Labor

Craft production during the Middle Ages is often portrayed as a system of master-apprentice relationships, with masters organized in guilds and apprentices bound to the masters and their households in a paternalistic relationship. But a significant portion of craft and incipient industrial production was the result of pure wage labor. Wages were often paid in accordance with the workers' productivity.

The difference between the labor market of the Middle Ages and that of today is thus not as great as our textbooks would often have us assume.

> Wage-earning at piece rates and at daily, weekly or annual rates was more typical of medieval industry as a whole than the quasi-familial relation between the master and apprentice. In mining and metallurgy and in many branches of metal fabrication, in all construction work except among groups of masons settling in late medieval towns, in the technical operation of mills and saltworks, in the rural textile and leather industries and also in new or unusual lines of specialization in town industries and in rapidly expanding ones, skill was developed and rewarded simply by differential rates of pay.[13]

Spontaneous opposition movements occurred at times among the workers against the employers: well known are, for example, the strikes in the Flemish textile mills during the middle of the thirteenth century. The extent of wage labor in the textile sector is clearly illustrated by the fact that in the area around Douai at this time, there were approximately 150 textile producers, each with approximately 100 employees.[14] At the middle of the seventeenth century in England, approximately 40% of the adult male labor force were wage earners.[15]

Technological shortcomings in the means of production are thus only a partial explanation of slow industrial progress before 1600. Industrial goods could not be sold on a larger scale because the population was forced to work mainly at farming in order to maintain a subsistence level existence. The slow rate of industrial development is largely explained by the scarcity of labor. Production of food established definite limits:

> So long as productivity in agriculture was not significantly raised . . . a substantial transfer of manpower from agriculture to industry was bound . . . to undercut the output of primary goods, and notably of foodstuffs, and thus to impair, beyond a certain point, further industrial progress.[16]

Work intensity was further limited because of religious holidays, which in many European countries reduced the available labor time by as much as 25%.[17] Some labor-saving devices were employed, but in general there was a direct relationship between manual labor and productivity.[18]

The difficulty of obtaining labor for the expanding craft and industrial sectors of the seventeenth and eighteenth centuries was at the time a much noted problem. For example, contemporary economic and political writers argued for expanded immigration:

> [In] the two centuries we are surveying [from 1500 to 1700] manufacturing continued to depend, much as it had in the past, primarily on man's efforts and skills. Contemporaries were aware of such dependence: their emphasis on a plentiful labor supply as a prerequisite for industrial expansion and the policies aimed at attracting workers from other countries must be viewed in the light of an economy in which human energy still played a predominant role and human dexterity could seldom be replaced by the machine.[19]

The lack of free labor functioned as a limitation on industrial production. This was reflected in the economic theory by the attention of the theoreticians to a great extent being directed toward production costs. Certain economists noted that the "true" or "real" value of a commodity—measured in invested labor—tended to be lower than the price which was paid for the commodity. It became increasingly common to study and compare the relation between market prices and production costs and to seek explanations for differences between them, i.e., to try to explain the surplus or surplus value.[20]

> The most important precondition of any such advance is, of course, the "freeing" of an abundant supply of wage-labor. Large numbers of direct producers have to be dispossessed of their means of production before their labor can be organized on a capitalist basis. It is fairly clear from the content of the economic literature of the last quarter of the seventeenth century, if not that this process was already appreciably under way, at least that its

significance and necessity had been widely appreciated. The literature abounds with suggestions for attracting foreigners to the country by encouraging immigration and permitting naturalisation, for "setting the poor to work", abolishing the death penalty for all but the most serious offences, and so on.[21]

4.5 The Transition to Capitalism: What Was the Main Impetus?

Western European feudalism entered a crisis during the fourteenth century and gradually disintegrated thereafter, more or less quickly depending on the region. The beginning of the capitalist period may be dated at the earliest in the latter half of the sixteenth century. The approximately 200 years which passed between the decline of feudalism and the first signs of capitalism may, in accordance with Sweezy, be called a period of "pre-capitalistic commodity production": production increased and wage labor grew, but neither the capitalist nor the feudal organization of production was sufficiently strong to leave its mark on the social order.[22] Changes in the method of production gradually occurred, however, and capitalism was established. How can the transition from feudalism to capitalism be explained? Is there any main impetus in this process, and if so, what is it?

This question has been an object of debate between, among others, Maurice Dobb and Paul Sweezy. According to Dobb, the primary reason for the demise of feudalism is to be found in the demands for increased income on the part of the ruling class and the workers' inability to accomplish additional intensification of production, as well as their revolt against such pressure. Feudalism signified an overexploitation of labor: serfs left the estates in great numbers, and those remaining were too few and too overworked for the system to continue to function.[23]

Dobb's explanation begins with factors within the feudal system itself. Sweezy, on the other hand, thinks that the reason lay in circumstances outside the system. Sweezy presents as the main impetus increasing international commerce and the commercial capital which entered Europe from, say, the Mediterranean countries. The increasing commerce brought with it pressures toward an *exchange economy*, i.e., an economic system directly opposed to feudalism's natural economy.[24] We find further support for this line of reasoning, says Sweezy, when we ask where the serfs who fled from the feudal estates went. According to Sweezy, Dobb has not taken sufficient note of the fact that this flight occurred concurrently with the growth of medieval cities.

There is no doubt that the rapidly developing towns—offering, as they did, liberty, employment, and improved social status—acted as a powerful magnet to the oppressed rural population. And the burghers themselves, in need of additional labor power and of more soldiers to enhance their military strength, made every effort to facilitate the escape of the serfs from the jurisdiction of their masters.[25]

These explanations do not, of course, exclude each other: the demise of the feudal system may indeed have been the effect of the old rulers' overexploitation of the workers and of the lure of the cities and wage labor. As Sweezy himself points out, it may indeed be reasoned that the demands of the feudal lords for increased income were expressions of growing trade and the spread of urban life.[26]

4.6 The Spread of the Market: International Commerce

In the feudal social form, peasants and the rural population had been dependent on local landlords. During the period from 1500 to 1600, there was a very slow, but nevertheless distinct, restructuring of power relationships in favor of the urban population and the middle class. "The peasants went from servitude to lords to servitude to townsmen."[27] This transference of power from lords to townsmen also took on partly new *economic forms* due to the increasing significance of the market. The urban population was dependent for its food supply upon agricultural products from surrounding rural areas. Some city dwellers were able to get agricultural products directly from their own land holdings near the cities. But the greatest number of city dwellers had to buy foodstuffs at the city's market.[28] Along with the increasing size of the cities came an increase in market exchange.

While the internal markets of the European cities were regulated by all manner of central intervention, there were few corresponding limits on international commerce. The risks faced by commercial expeditions were certainly significant (ships sank or were pirated), and the church, by means of religious norms, tried to stop loans of capital for interest. In general, however, profits from international trade were sufficient to offset the risks, and the interest demanded for lent capital was obviously calculated largely in consideration of these risks. Neither were the church's norms insurmountable obstacles preventing the use of capital or international trade. Both covert market transactions and theological excuses were common.[29]

The international commodity exchange and the flow of capital were directed to a great extent by the large commercial houses in Europe, especially in Italy and Germany. To an increasing degree, commercial enterprises were financed by means of various collective commitments with the aid of share or stock systems. The latter form of finance was especially common when it came to undertakings requiring a large sum of capital, such as mining, metalworking, or the building of merchant ships.[30] Increasing competition between various sources of capital and financiers led to decreasing interest rates. By around 1700, interest rates were probably only around half of what they had been 300 years earlier.[31]

The discovery of America led to the opening of new export markets for European products. The dissemination of the news from North and South

America was impressively swift. "Within a century after Columbus' voyages to the Americas, a whole series of native American crops were being cultivated regularly in Europe. Maize, green beans, peanuts, potatoes, cocoa, tomatoes, and sweet potatoes had become the dominant sources of calories in some parts of Europe."[32] As for exports, Spanish industry, for example, benefited greatly: Spain exported large amounts of wool, cotton, and silk cloth, and the demand increased greatly for metal goods and ocean-going ships.[33]

In summary, the period from 1500 to 1700 is characterized partly by the growing ease with which investment capital could be obtained at moderate interest costs, and partly by an increase in potentially favorable investments due to an expansion of the market. In a more long-term way, the European market was also favorably influenced by the new foodstuffs, and the dietary improvement was one of the factors behind Europe's increase in population. According to available calculations, Europe's population increased from a bit more than 80 million in 1500 to approximately 115 million in 1700.[34] This had direct consequences on the supply of labor. The demand for both industrial products and foodstuffs also increased, largely because of the increasing militarization and the growing armies of the European states.[35]

4.7 Economic Theory

Until approximately 1600, production and trade were for the most part local (in spite of what has been said above about the international features), meaning that those who cultivated the land and sold its products had as a rule a good idea both of the origin of these products (that is, the labor and raw materials contained in them) and of the price they commanded. The formation of economic theory—in general theological, like most intellectual production of the time—was clearly marked by these relationships, i.e., the direct market sale of personally produced commodities. The Canadian political scientist C. B. Macpherson's term for this type of system is the "simple market society."

"SIMPLE MARKET SOCIETY" VS. "POSSESSIVE INDIVIDUALISM"

Since Macpherson's conceptual apparatus and his discussion are important to our continued presentation, we shall now describe his terminology and his treatment of the transition from a "simple" to a "possessive" market society.

It should be emphasized that Macpherson's concepts are to be viewed as ideal types. Thus, a pure society of the type "simple market society" has probably never existed,[36] if by "pure" one means a society answering to *all* of the criteria presented by Macpherson.[37]

Expressed most simply, the simple market society is characterized by (1) full freedom to buy and sell and (2) a greater (subjectively assessed) profit from retention of control over one's own labor than from the sale of one's labor. Being a free, independent producer means, from an economic perspective, more for the individual than the income that results from rendering of services in the employ of another person.[38]

In the simple market society, individuals have complete control over their own energy and their own knowledge, and they are free to use them. The only things bought and sold on the market are goods produced through one's own labor. "All individuals have land or other resources through which they can earn a livelihood by means of their labor."[39] There is no *labor market* since—according to the assumptions above— employment results in less subjective gain than the purchase/sale of personally produced goods. Contracts exist, but only as a means of establishing rights and obligations between producers of goods.

Macpherson contrasts this model of society with another in which the purchase and sale of labor are also included ("possessive market society"). Labor is the property of the individual and can be disposed of (just like land and other resources). Macpherson assumes further that some people have more energy, ability, and property than others. It will often be true of this latter group that the sale of their own labor to those with greater resources will be the most efficient way of earning a livelihood. (The designation "*possessive* market society" is used to emphasize that labor is treated as the individual's property which can be disposed of.)[40] According to this line of reasoning, working for others is more profitable for some than using their own labor to produce their own goods for market. Further, the greater degree of efficiency which can be achieved by the organization and division of labor—due to the organization of the labor of those with fewer resources by those with more resources—reduces the prices of products, making individual production of these same commodities through individual labor unprofitable.[41]

Contracts exist as a means of establishing rights and obligations relating to the exchange of both goods and labor. Thus, the possessive market society has both a commodity market and a labor market. Or rather, both labor and physical products become commodities.

> In the fundamental matter of getting a living, all individuals are essentially related to each other as possessors of marketable commodities, including their own powers. All must continually offer commodities (in the broadest sense) in the market, in competition with others.[42]

Macpherson contrasts the two models of society in the following way:

> Competition in this market [i.e., for both commodities and labor], unlike that in the simple market in products, is a means by which men who want more may convert more of the powers of others to their use than others convert of theirs. For the effect of competition in this market is to compel entrepeneurs (who must have had some capital initially, with which to hire labor) to use

increasing amounts of capital as a means to more efficient production. The greater the capital required in order to stay in the market, the less possible it is for men of little property to enter into, or stay in, independent production. As the greater efficiency of more highly capitalized production permits the population to increase, such production becomes indispensible for the larger society. And as the land runs out (which it does the more quickly because land has become a kind of capital), an increasing proportion of the population becomes dependent on selling its labor. Thus a class division between those with land and capital, and those without, sets in (if it was not in existence already.[43]

THE COST OF PRODUCTION VS. "UTILITY"

One of the earliest expressions of economic theory derives from the medieval scholastics, most importantly Thomas Aquinas.[44] The scholastics' contribution has a mostly ethical-moral motivation, and dealt with the church's viewpoints on various elements of economic life. A main problem for the scholastics was the definition of the actual value of commodities, so that one could determine against this background whether a certain price—demanded by the seller or paid by the buyer—was "just" or not. The *existence* of such a value was beyond discussion.

The idea that payment should be in proportion to the producer's expenses or investment of labor was immediately present. The actual economic situation which Thomas Aquinas could observe was one in which production was executed by individual, independent small-scale producers who sold their products in the market and bought their own necessities with the earnings from this sale. The *just price* (*iustum pretium*) consisted mostly of the producer's own expenses. This meant mainly his labor, but the expenses also included compensation for potential economic risk, expenses for raw materials, and transportation costs. Compensation was needed for these investments. They made up the actual value (*real value*) of the commodity, a value which, in turn, could—and often did— differ from the price commanded/payed at the sale of the commodity.

Who should decide if the price was just or not, i.e., if the payment for the commodity was too far above or below the real value? The answer to this question can be summarized by the terms "public opinion" or "sense of justice." Community formations were as yet small and easily surveyed: "In a small, static and relatively self-supporting community, the labor and expenses of various producers could for the most part be directly compared to each other."[45]

But a new kind of economy, in which commodity exchange became increasingly significant, began to evolve, and with it came a new class (businessmen and merchants). Those who lived off the surplus attained through the procurement and sale of commodities grew in number. Improved communications, both within and between countries, as well as the growth of the cities, encouraged the emergence of a category of people who sought their occupational livelihood not only in the production and sale of commodities, but *solely* in sales.

The authors of the canonical writings treat the latter type of economic character with a certain condescension. Thomas Aquinas, for example, differentiates between the "natural" exchange through which "one thing is exchanged for another or for money to meet the needs of life," on the one hand, and the situation in which things are exchanged for money "not to meet the needs of life, but to yield profit," on the other. The latter kind of exchange—professional commerce—is viewed by Thomas Aquinas as "to a certain extent dishonest."[46]

Commerce for profit could, however, be made more defensible if (a) the merchant had in some way improved the commodity, or (b) the price increase could be justified by a "change in location or time" (i.e., transportation or storage), or (c) transportation of the commodity meant a special risk for loss or destruction of the commodity. In other words, "the merchant may escape moral condemnation if he as far as possible behaves like an independent small-scale producer."[47]

The medieval ideal for economic behavior—as the following quotation implies—was breaking down and changing, and the dominant force behind this process was increased commerce. The basic idea of a "just price" was thus also attacked: "The medieval concept of the just price gradually lost its power over men's minds as the impersonal and unconscious market took over the task of regulating prices."[48]

The belief in *costs of production* as the main basis for the value of a commodity remained, however, a dominant part of economic teaching. It was an inheritance from the scholastics which would later be developed by the so-called classical economists (Petty, Smith, and Ricardo in England and Sismondi in France). But before we move on to the classical economists, a few words should be said concerning economic theory under mercantilism.

Toward the end of the Middle Ages, with increasing intercommunication and the gradual emergence of the European nation states, cases of economic problems such as those we dealt with above must have become all the more common, i.e., cases of commodity prices in which production costs were hidden and/or impossible to calculate (imported products, products based, especially after the discovery of America, on previously unknown raw materials, etc.). It was then expedient—especially for the seller—to argue that the price which was *usually* payed and received should be considered just. An ethical-moral incentive could be retained, even though the notion of production cost had been abandoned. One could claim that a commodity still had a value made up of its *utility* to the buyer. "If the buyers of a certain commodity were willing to procure it at a price which was higher than the producer's costs, then this price could be considered as corresponding to the commodity's . . . 'real value' *for them*."[49] With the expanding market, the production cost model became awkward. The concept of utility made the trouble of calculating production costs superfluous.

Meek's treatment of mercantilism is too comprehensive to be dealt with in its entirety here. But attention should be called to a few important points.[50] First of all, as we have already mentioned, it was during this period—the sixteenth and early seventeenth centuries—that an economic theory based on markets began to be seriously formed. The value of commodities was tied more and more often to their actual market price. Supply and demand began to be seen as regulators of value/price; the notion of a relation between utility and price began to be common. Thus a foundation was provided for the economic theory of utilitarianism and for the equilibrium and balance lines of reasoning used by Bentham, among others (reasoning which then appears in the theories of marginal use from Jevons on). This also established perhaps the most dominant theme in the formation of economic doctrine (seen from scientific, technological, as well as political perspectives)—the struggle between a theory based on objective (but difficultly assessed) production costs and a theory based on subjective consumer judgments (cf., Chapters 7 and 8).

Second, it is important to note the relatively limited position of power resulting from the use of commercial capital. The means of production were at this time still mainly in the hands of the immediate producers—peasants and craftsmen. The former were, of course, often forced to relinquish a good part of their production to local landowners, but beyond that, the exploitation which could be practiced affected mainly the people as *consumers*. Commodities could be sold by merchants for a profit; but commodities could still not be produced on a large scale for profit with the aid of other people's labor. Production was local, individual, and—compared to later times—at a low level of organization. The conditions corresponded to—in Macpherson's terms—a simple, rather than a possessive market society. Industrial capital was still without appreciable importance in economic life, and the only kind of profit-making activity which attracted any greater attention was the so-called "profit on alienation," i.e., profit on *things* which were sold.[51] Alienation of labor was, as described by Macpherson, the object of economic theory and doctrine first at the hands of Hobbes and Locke (most importantly the latter, who lays the foundation for, among others, Smith's and Ricardo's presentations of the labor theory of value).

4.8 The Spread of the Capitalist Method of Production

As was intimated above, European commercial capital was of strategic importance for the building up of industry in the individual countries. It began with crafts. Merchants provided capital for investments in buildings and instruments of labor, and thus they came to make the decisions concerning other important economic circumstances. The relationship between capital owner/merchant and craftsman as described by Sylvia L. Thrupp recurs in a greatly magnified and deepened form in the relationship between capitalowner and worker during the heyday of industrial capitalism.

> By themselves, craftsmen could not possibly have built up export industries. They had to rely on the services of merchants, who were gradually drawn into supplying them with work and capital through credit on supplies and advance payment on sales. Ultimately, as is well documented for the textile industries, the merchants organized the whole process of production. The craftsmen lost their independence. The merchants were able to assume this position of dominance . . . because their profits on general wholesale trade, including the growing trade in foodstuffs, made them the wealthiest group in the towns.[52]

The accumulation of capital had begun. As mentioned earlier, the hindrances preventing its use were many—the risks of enterprise, very limited domestic demand, ecclesiastic dogma against capital income (which was, however, rather easily circumvented), a limited labor supply. The period from 1500 to 1700 cleared away many of the obstacles connected with the old social and political order. Central states emerged and grew;[53] rationalism and the spirit and optimism of the Enlightenment grew partly as a result of the new geographic perspectives, and partly because the biting edge of abject poverty had been dulled in many areas.

During the following two centuries (the eighteenth and the nineteenth), the demographic and technological prerequisites for an intensified production were also achieved. The population increase created a massive increase in demand while at the same time creating an increased supply of labor. Technological inventions—which were often better versions of already existing means of production—could be put to increasingly intensive use as economic needs and demand grew.

THE INDUSTRIAL REVOLUTION AND THE MIDDLE CLASS

The truly explosive developments in production were most noticeable in the English cotton industry during and after the eighteenth century. The production of cotton cloth increased tenfold between the years 1760 and 1785, and then grew again tenfold between 1785 and 1827.[54] Technological improvements in the spinning machine contributed somewhat, but this growth was due mostly to a great increase in marketing possibilities.[55]   Lilley's general thesis—and it seems especially reasonable—is that technological inventions and their utilization are effects of the needs created by population increase and the development of new marketing possibilities, and that the technological potential for increased production had actually been latently present for a much longer time.[56] This thesis is applied, for example, in the treatment of iron production and the development of steam power and railroads, as well as in the development of sea travel.[57]

Socially and politically, this epoch brought with it changes which left significant marks on contemporary social thinking and philosophy. New power groups emerged: by the end of the seventeenth century in England, the Industrial Revolution's place of origin, political power had "been redistributed in a way that favored the merchant, banker and capitalist farmer—and to the expense of the nobility, big landlords and small craftsmen."[58]

Commercial and industrial capital were now united. This capital was invested at an accelerated rate in new enterprises for the manufacture of textiles and steel and for the building of railroads and ships. Capital was also used more and more in order to transfer land into the hands of the urban bourgeoisie. In some places, these land transfers were very large.

The concept "bourgeois"—originally the designation for a city dweller active in commerce, administration, crafts, or independent occupations—attained a new dimension once ownership of land was added to the bourgeois' ownership of commercial and industrial capital.[59]

> [The] bourgeois did not confine themselves to the cramped precincts of their towns. . . . They had an ardent desire to acquire land and have it worked by tenants. This brought two advantages: the prestige and authority conferred by ownership of land; and ground rent, which generally yielded lower profits than business or industry, but which had the merit of being more stable. Hence, by the fifteenth or sixteenth centuries, the original meaning of the word bourgeoise began to be lost, and by the 18th century it was no more than a remembrance of things past. On the eve of the Revolution, the French bourgeoisie, which was certainly not the wealthiest, held more than 30% of the cultivated land. In Switzerland or certain regions of western Germany, almost all the land was in bourgeois hands. By contrast, in those countries where great domains were formed at a very early date and the towns' hold on the country was correspondingly weaker (northern Germany, central and eastern Europe, the Iberian Peninsula), the vast majority of land was held by the nobility or the church. England, where the bourgeoisie and the gentry were much more closely interdependent—to say the least—than elsewhere, stood halfway between the two extremes.[60]

During the initial period of capitalism, economic power was transferred from land to city; from feudal lords and landed nobility to the merchants and industrialists of the cities; from local power centers to central state powers, supporte;by a growing military and administrative apparatus. It is, therefore, a logical consequence that the economic power which had been transferred from the landowners to the bourgeoisie gradually expressed itself in the act of the capital-holding city dwellers gaining power by simply buying out the old, established elite classes.

CLASSICAL THEORY OF VALUE

The increasing competition, especially *within* countries, gradually made it more and more difficult for merchants to make their profits by way of the traditional method, i.e., by taking advantage of the difference between the price received for a commodity and the price at which it was bought. Control over the actual production of the commodity dominated under these circumstances as an increasingly common way of guaranteeing continued income. Certain sections of the merchant class began to use their collected resources to steer the manufacture of products, for example, by introducing a division of labor into production and—although still on a small scale—by introducing new technological inventions.[61]

These changes were reflected in economic theory as attention once again was focused on production costs. Certain economists—John Cary, for example[62]—noted that the "true" or "real" value of a commodity—measured in the labor invested in it—generally tended to be lower than the price paid for it. It became increasingly common to study and compare the relationship between market prices and production costs, and to attempt to explain the difference between them, that is, the surplus, or surplus value.[63]

The growing production potential was dependent on one thing more than any other—"liberation" of great amounts of labor.

Classical political economy derives from "this epoch-making discovery of the great forces of production inherent in 'free' labor organized in a capitalistic way."[64] A valuable new commodity, labor, is made available to the market and becomes an important object of economic theory and social scientific analysis.

> General, abstract, human labor slowly begins to be recognized as the primary and universal cost-element in production, the basic cause of that value-difference between output and input upon which national prosperity (and individual profits) ultimately depend. Economists begin to visualize the productive activity of the nation as a whole in terms of the disposition of its labor force.[65]

However, the step from this to a complete labor theory of value is rather large. Locke's thesis on use-value as primarily created through investments of labor can be considered among the first contributions (see Macpherson; and section 5.2). Also, other writers pointed out that wage costs were the most important element of production costs. The primary intention was generally not to present a wage-cost theory in order to explain the meaning of "value." The aim was most often less scientific and more political:

> The primary concern of most contemporary writers was not to formulate a theory of value, but to emphasize the importance of securing an abundant supply of cheap labor. Their efforts were largely directed towards the reduction of wage-costs. The advocates of an increased population, of poverty as a spur to industry, and of increased disciplinary measures against the laborers, obviously had this consideration at the back of their minds, and were often honest enough to admit it.[66]

The idea was clear: labor was more and more often seen as a necessary condition of prosperity and the creation of value. A more complete labor theory of value depended, however, on additional building blocks. The most important of these was an investigation of the function of capital in the economy.

It is remarkable that the question of capital profits—their origins, causes, and their relationship to investments—was not seriously considered until the latter half of the 1750s. Remarkable because the *phenomenon* of capital profits—the increase of resources through "productive" investments—must reasonably have been part of the most intimate reality of the economists. Besides, as we mentioned earlier, another form of profit— profits through the disposal of commodities (which had been bought earlier)—had in earlier times been an important source of income and the object of economic theorizing.

How shall we explain the slowness with which reasoning about capital profits was developed? Not even Adam Smith's Glasgow lectures (1763) contained a systematic treatment of the profit concept; such a notion was first presented by Adam Smith in *Wealth of Nations* in 1776. Meek's discussion is very interesting, partly because of its insight into the actual issue—the emergence of the concept of capital profit—and partly because of its illumination of the relativity of the social sciences and the reflexive nature of economic theories inspired by changes in the state of production.

First, says Meek, it was not easy to keep capital profits separate from two other kinds of income—interest on money and land. The important difference between *money passively collected* and *money actively used* had begun to be noted toward the end of the seventeenth century in connection with the increasing role of commercial capital. Things were similar concerning the use of land. Only as land holdings were more widely *used for market production*—as opposed to production solely for the landowner and any of his subjects—did the phenonmenon "profit" become clear as compared with the "passive" income of land rent.[67]

Second, there were difficulties involved in differentiation between *profits* and *wages for labor*. During the earliest years of capitalism it was still common that the man who purchased labor—that is, who employed others to work for him—was himself an individual producer running his own business. It was not uncommon for him to participate in production himself. The income thus received could therefore easily be seen as "a kind of superior 'wage' for [the capital owner's] personal effort rather than a 'profit' on the capital—which was often very limited—[he] provided."[68]

Third, it was only rather late that the conditions presented themselves for establishing what was an *average profit* on capital. Capital was certainly invested in various industries, trades and regions, but it would take time before these investments, and the profits which followed them, were sufficiently extensive, systematic, and varied to allow the formulation of general laws on the movement of capital:

> Before the profits of stock could come to be regarded as bearing a regular proportion to the amount of capital, in whatever sphere it happened to be employed, it was clearly necessary that the field covered by capitalist methods of organisation should be considerably enlarged, that competition in both internal and external trade should be reasonably free, and that capital should be relatively mobile between different places and occupations.[69]

Most of all, it can be said that classical economy is characterized by the discovery of the function of capital profit and its character as something which regularly arises from the *production* of goods, and not mainly from their *exchange*:

> It became more and more clear that under competitive conditions profit at a reasonably regular rate would be earned on capital in whatever sphere it happened to be employed, and that this profit must be regarded as originating in production rather than in exchange.[70]

Prior to Adam Smith, calculations or predictions of the price of a certain commodity had been difficult. In their most common form, these predictions were based on production costs plus a certain increment ("profit" or "earnings") which was assumed in each individual case to be dependent on supply and demand. Because of this, the potential for general assumptions concerning price formation was, of course, small.

As soon as the idea of a normal or "natural" profit level was accepted, significantly more general predictions of commodity prices could be made, and an economic *situation of equilibrium* could be identified:

> Commodities, it could now be said, tended under competitive conditions to sell at prices equal to "prime costs" plus profit at the "natural" rate. A situation in which the "natural" rate of profit was being earned, so that there was no tendency for firms to enter or leave the industry, could be defined as a situation of equilibrium, in which supply "balanced" or "equalled" demand, and the price at which commodities sold in this situation could be conceived as their "natural" price.[71]

The actual market price was assumed to constantly approach this "natural price"—a combination of production costs plus "normal" capital profit.

THE LABOR THEORY OF VALUE

The theory of production cost—the most important element of which was the thesis of the necessity of labor in the creation of value—now established itself for a long time to come as the supreme principle of supply and demand (which we saw to be common during mercantilism). By about 1800, the labor theory of value seemed to many economists to be an established truth, and the thesis that increased productivity derives from the division of labor also seemed clear. (And not only to economists: the labor theory of value was generally accepted among writers in social and political science. It is interesting, for example, that a conservative such as Edmund Burke is among these.[72] Only thirty years later, conservative writers were to attack the labor value theory with great energy.) Adam Smith's work *The Wealth of Nations* (1776) expressed both the general labor theory of value and particular ideas concerning the division of labor. Labor is, said Smith, the fixed, lasting, and constantly valid measure of the value of different commodities:

> Equal quantities of labor, at all times and places, may be said to be of equal value to the laborer. In his ordinary state of health, strength and spirits; in the ordinary degree of his skill and dexterity, he must always lay down the same portion of his ease, his liberty, and his happiness. The price which he pays must also be the same, whatever be the quantity of goods which he receives in return for it.... Labor alone ... never varying in its own value, is alone the ultimate and real standard by which the value of all commodities can at all times and places be estimated and compared. It is their real price; money is their nominal price only.[73]

A given temporal unit of labor could, however, be used in widely differing ways by *the person who organized production*. Smith establishes one of his primary theses in his first chapter—the greatest improvement in labor's productive power up until that time was the division of labor. His example—which would for all time be a standard feature of economics books—concerned the manufacture of pins. One inexperienced worker would just barely have time to produce one pin per day, says Smith, if he executed all the different phases of the process himself. However, by dividing up the manufacturing process into approximately eighteen different operations, the production of pins could be made so much more effective that even a small workshop with about ten employees could produce up to 48,000 pins per day.[74]

> This great increase of the quantity of work which, in consequence of the division of labor, the same number of people are capable of performing is owing to three different circumstances: first, to the increase of dexterity in every particular workman; secondly, to the saving of time which is commonly lost in passing from one species of work to another; and lastly, to the invention of a great number of machines which facilitate and abridge labor, and enable one man to do the work of many.[75]

The use of capital in order to accomplish—with the aid of employed labor and the division of labor—a more intensive production is what separated wealthy from poor nations and modern from earlier generations.

We are more industrious than our ancestors, says Adam Smith, because more people are occupied with productive labor instead of using up resources in unproductive occupations—as in the case of, say, servants.[76] The accumulation of capital—the expression of the wealth of nations— depends, according to Smith, on the productive use of capital resources:

> There is one sort of labor which adds to the value of the subject upon which it is bestowed: there is another which has no such effect. The former, as it produces a value, may be called productive; the latter unproductive labor. Thus, the labor of a manufacturer adds, generally, to the value of the materials which he works upon, that of his own maintenance, and of his master's profit. The labor of a menial servant, on the contrary, adds to the value of nothing. . . . A man grows rich by employing a multitude of manufacturers: he grows poor by maintaining a multitude of menial servants.[77]

Labor as the most significant value-creating factor, division of labor, the role of capital, the difference between productive and unproductive labor—all of these central concepts were to be taken up again and dealt with more systematically by, among others, Ricardo and, later, Marx. But while *The Wealth of Nations* was met by active contemporary interest and contributed to Smith becoming dean of Glasgow University, the labor theory of value in both Ricardo's and Marx's versions was to be met in part by scornful rejection. The labor theory of value began; already during Ricardo's time, to attain a political significance as an argument for a reforming of society in line with the demands of the working class.

> The labor theory—or, rather, the notion which came to be associated with it that "labor produces all"—had begun to be used by a number or radical writers, and by the working-class organizations with which they were often associated, to support their claims for various measures of economic and social reform. If labor in fact "produced all", these writers were asking, why should it not also receive all—or at least considerably more than it did at present?[78]

Many of the more conservative economists came to view Ricardo's theory of value as not only incorrect but also as socially dangerous.

> In 1829 the English economist Samuel Read wrote disparagingly that the workers "had been flattered and persuaded to believe that they produced everything", but that they must "be informed and understand that they do *not* produce everything." His colleague, John Cazenove, warned at the same time of what he felt was the doctrine—as dangerous as it was false—that "labor constituted the only source of wealth." For this theory offered "an unfortunate excuse for those who profess that all property belongs to the working class and that the shares of others constitute theft or fraud of the workers." Several other academic economists at approximately the same time attacked the theory of surplus value which "was being spread among industrial workers and craftsmen" and "stimulated the persons of the poor and ignorant."[79]

A number of things thus point to the fact that it was not the actual content in the works of Ricardo and Marx which was perceived as subversive, but that rather it was the *use* to which they could be put in the new political situation which began to arise in the industrial countries of Europe during the nineteenth century—a situation in which "the social question," i.e., the impoverishment of the working class, had become a burning issue, and strikes, revolts, and attempted organizations of workers became more common. Both Ricardo's and Marx's works—which, like Smith's, stressed the central role of labor—attained an economic and political explosive power which *The Wealth of Nations* could not attain a few decades earlier, even though it provided the most important analytic tools for a theory of the contradiction between capital and labor.

4.9 The Working Class and "The Worker Question"

The history of the rise of the working class follows in general the same pattern—although not the same timetable—regardless of which country we choose to study. Here we shall only suggest the outline of this development; neither the aim of this book nor available space allow a more extensive review. We would like to refer the reader to Bergier, 1973: 397-451 and the literature mentioned there. For details concerning working hours, labor intensity, and working conditions in factories, we suggest Marx, 1957: Chapter 15. Concerning the rise of the working class in Sweden, we refer the reader to the articles by Hellner and Andrén in Lindblom, and to Heckscher.[80]

Bergier discerns three rough steps in the rise and development of the working class in the European countries. First, there is the growth of the class of industrial workers as a *mass*, i.e., as accumulated groups of wage earners with similar living and working conditions but without a developed consciousness of that which was common to all their experiences. Second, there is the maturing of this mass to a conscious social class with its own identity. Third, there is the organization of the working class into political and trade associations with concrete economic and political aims.[81] The first two elements of this scheme conform—without it being specifically mentioned by Bergier—to Marx's dichotomy "class of itself" and "class for itself." As the reader could observe in Chapter 2, the model presented there of the rise and development of organizations had a similar basic principle. The economic, technical, and political changes which promoted industrial capitalism and the factory system were accompanied by an extreme polarization of the conditions of capitalowners and wage earners. A few examples may suffice to show the breadth of the misery which was the lot of the industrial proletariat in Europe of the nineteenth century—a misery which amounted to both to an almost incomprehensible wear on the workers and to widespread social and political apathy.[82] (The first trade unions were not formed by those wage earners who were worst off, but rather by relatively well-paid, well-informed, and independent occupational groups, for example printers.)

The working day in England in 1832 was twelve hours and was shortened to ten hours in 1847.[83] The intensity of labor increased. Marx quotes a report from the inspector of factories:

> In most of the cotton, worsted and silk mills, an exhausting state of excitement necessary to enable the workers satisfactorily to mind the machinery, the motion of which been greatly accelerated within the last few years, seems to me not unlikely to be one of the causes of that excess of mortality from lung disease, which Dr. Greenhow has pointed out in his recent report on this subject.[84]

Accidents were common:

> Consequently, although it is strictly forbidden in many, nay in most factories, that machinery should be cleaned while in motion, it is nevertheless the constant practice in most if not in all, that the workpeople do, unreproved, pick out waste, wipe rollers and wheels, etc., while their frames are in motion. Thus, from this cause only, 906 accidents have occurred. . . . Although a great deal of cleaning is constantly going on day by day, yet Saturday is generally the day set apart for the thorough cleaning of the machinery, and a great deal of this is done while the machinery is in motion." Since cleaning is not paid for, the workpeople seek to get it done with as speedily as possible. Hence "the number of accidents which occur on Fridays, and especially on Saturdays, is much larger than on any other day. On the former day the excess is 25% over the average of the preceding five days; or, if the number of working-hours on Saturday being taken into account—7½ hours on Saturday as compared with 10½ hours on other days—there is an excess of 65% on Saturdays over the average of the other five days".[85]

Employment of women and children was very widespread; at times, three-year-old children worked ten to twelve hours per day, and among five and six-year-olds this was common.[86] Marx quotes reports of health inspections from 1864 showing a death-rate among children during the first year of life which reaches 26% (varying from district to district, but with 20% being a common figure). An investigation in France showed similar or higher figures:

> As was shown by an official medical inquiry in the year 1861, the high death-rates are, apart from local causes, principally due to the employment of the mothers away from their homes, and to the neglect and maltreatment consequent on her absence, such as, amongst others, insufficient nourishment, unsuitable food, and dosing with opiates; besides this, there arises an unnatural estrangement between mother and child, and as a consequence intentional starving and poisoning of the children. In those agricultural districts, "where a minimum in the employment of women exists, the death-rate is on the other hand very low."[87]

An item from an investigation of workers' living conditions in Sweden during the 1860s may serve as a conclusion. The conditions described below seem to have been hardly better for workers in England or on the Continent.

In the year 1865 Gothenburg's city council appointed a committee to investigate "pauperism and its causes." The following may be quoted from the frighteningly gloomy description of workers' living conditions which was presented that same year: "The living quarters generally occupied by the working class are often apartments in old, dilapidated, decayed wooden buildings, either standing alone or in the courtyard of some newer, better building. The wind blows in here through draughty windows, doors which cannot be closed, and rotted walls. The floors of the upper story are over a wash house, wood shed, or the like and are draughty and cold; on lower stories they are always decayed, often wet with moisture, which during rain or thaw is abosrbed into the joints between the old boards in the walls or ceiling, and which runs down under the building from the surrounding ground and remains there. The hearths most commonly smoke into the buildings. During cold weather, fuel cannot create enough warmth, and this must be carefully conserved by stuffing holes and cracks with rags, which, in turn, contributes to worsening the already unhealthy air. Chill, smoke, moisture, and unhealthful air are thus the most common troubles." Even the newly built houses "for lease to working people" are sharply criticized. They are built from too shoddy materials, they are insulated poorly, and are rented before being finished.[88]

The "social question" or "worker question" became a more volatile issue as increasing concentrations of workers moved to the cities and industrial regions. Attempts at organization within the working class became more common; an international workers' movement began to take form (the First International trade union, for example, had 250,000 French workers as members in 1870).[89] The revolts in Europe (1848 in London, Birmingham, Paris, Brussels, Rome, and Berlin) made the cities into political focal points.[90] Industrial revolts in many countries and a conscious mobilization of worker groups (e.g., in the form of Luddism and Chartism in England), demands for voting rights, etc., necessitated, to a growing degree, concessions from the ruling classes.

These concessions consisted partly of economic reforms (Bismarck's social insurance program being the most spectacular example), and partly of offers to representatives of the working class concerning a division of political power. This paternalism—to use Bergier's term—was caused by, among other things, the revolution of 1848 and its aftershocks:

[Paternalism] aimed to divert the workers from the political temptations held out to them henceforth by the various forms of labor movement, trade-unionism or socialism. The attitude of the German industrial bourgeoisie after 1870 is extremely characteristic in this respect: its gestures to the workers (insurance cover, mutual aid, social clubs) were inspired by a fear of socialism. Addressing his employees in 1877, Krupp voiced a feeling prevalent in his class: "Enjoy what is given you to enjoy. Relax, when your work is over, in the company of those close to you, your parents, your wife, your children; concern yourselves with your house and home. Let that be your policy: it will bring you happiness. As for politics (die grosse Landespolitik), spare yourselves that worry. Engaging in politics requires more time and experience than it is possible for the worker to have."[91]

A gradual redistribution of some of the economic surplus was accepted—even though often reluctantly—by capitalowners, and thus rendered possible compromises between enlightened capitalism and the increasingly strong organization of social democracy. Liberals in Germany and Sweden, among other countries, also agreed to a broadening of voting rights to include larger groups and—gradually—to the abolition of property ownership as a condition for civic rights. As we shall discuss in greater detail below (Chapters 6 and 8), civic rights meant only participation in the power to make decisions. The power to *execute* them lay—and still lies—with the minority who has the right to capital (see Section 2.2).

4.10 Summary

The rise of wage labor, the commercial revolution, the spread of the market, the development of international commerce, and other elements of the emerging capitalist method of production have had clear effects on—and have been reflected in—social scientific thinking and the formation of economic theory since the Middle Ages.

This chapter has had a dual purpose. We have tried to describe the main features in the development of material production, labor, and consumption in Europe from the Middle Ages to around 1900. Also, we have examined how these processes are reflected in the social scientific literature, and how they have been interpreted by authors active in political economy. Among other things, we have been able to establish that the labor theory of value was a common point of departure for the classical economists until around the first quarter of the nineteenth century.

C. B. Macpherson's double concept "simple market society" and "possessive market society" is of importance for an understanding of the formation of economic doctrine. The philosophers of the possessive market society—the most important being John Locke—provide the theoretical and ideological basis for private capitalownership and for the establishment of a connection between private property and the role of citizen. This latter theme recurs in other classical democratic authors such as Bentham, John Stuart Mill, and Alexis de Tocqueville (see Chapter 6). As Macpherson points out in a later work, the identification of property as *private* property is a product of the seventeenth century.[92] Wage labor was also seriously established as an institution during the seventeenth century.

We have examined in broad terms the changes from a system based on compulsory labor controlled by feudal lords to a system of "free" labor controlled and organized by owners of private commercial and industrial capital. As we shall find in Chapter 6, the development of civic rights is connected to the latter phase of this process, i.e., the phase in which workers also began to organize and demand a share in the power over society and its formation.

Chapter 5

OWNERSHIP AND POLITICAL IDEOLOGIES

In Chapter 4 we dealt in broad terms with a few basic features of European economic history and their effect on the contemporary formation of economic theory. But intellectual production dealt not only with *economic* but also with *political* thought.

In reality, of course, these areas were not seen as isolated from each other. On the contrary, the concept "political economy" refers to a formation of doctrine in which economy is considered to be indivisibly tied to the exploitation of the three production factors land, capital, and labor, and where class relations and class interests are marked by the power relationships between the production factors. In the following we shall take a closer look at this political dimension in the formation of economic theory. In particular, we shall investigate how the right to ownership of the means of production was treated by various leading writers of the conservative, liberal, and socialist intellectual traditions.

Our reasoning can be briefly summarized as follows: both conservatism and liberalism strive to legitimize private ownership. The arguments they put forth vary, however. Within the conservative intellectual tradition, private ownership is seen as the actual foundation of the social order, a postulate demanding neither explanation nor justification. (This is not changed by the fact that much energy has nevertheless been spent in this way. The conservative writers present their texts precisely in order to show that no special justification of private ownership is needed.)

Liberalism, however, cannot accept ownership rights as self-evident. For Bentham and others, the existence of ownership rights—like that of other social institutions—is something which must be *explained*. This explanation is founded in empirical observations and in the notion of the utility of the social institutions. Liberalism—a product of the European Enlightenment, philosophic radicalism, and empiricism[1]—is critical of natural law and the conviction of conservative authors that various social phenomena can be justified by pointing out that the phenomena exist by virtue of *custom* or because they are *morally* right.

As for their views on original acquisition—occupation and production—perhaps one can summarize the conservative and liberal positions in the following way: it is relatively unimportant for conservatism *how* property was originally acquired. The important thing is *that* the property is privately owned, through original or derived acquisition, through occupation or production (see Section 2.7). If this is the state of affairs, then it should be preserved.

The liberals express doubt about this; for example, the right of inheritance is not just simply accepted ("just simply" should be emphasized; as we shall see, liberalism developed, through the so-called principle of security, arguments for a preserved distribution of personal fortune). *Production*—the individual's labor to increase his own, and thus the entire society's, well-being through his own efforts—is stressed as the most important form of acquisition.

The theory of liberalism was to a great degree formulated in opposition to the established power-holding groups of l'ancien regime (the church, the royal house, and the nobility) which founded their positions first and foremost on the ownership of land. It became the theory of capitalism and formed an ideological base for the bourgeois revolt, most clearly expressed in the American and French revolutions (1776 and 1789). It legitimized the freedom of trade and the right of the individual to act independently, both in an economic and in a political sense.

The demand for freedom did not, however, carry the same revolutionary meaning for everyone. Wage earners—who already in the seventeenth century made up almost half of the working population of England—had little choice but to accept that the freedom to increase one's own well-being through one's own labor was often limited since employment opportunities and working conditions were fixed by others, that is, by those who provided buildings, instruments, and materials for labor (and who could therefore to a great extent determine conditions of the labor contract).

There were numerous opportunities for wage earners to notice that owning a factory building, a steam engine, and a number of looms was for the most part significantly more pleasant and profitable than—as they did—laboring in front of the steam engine or loom.

In the socialist economic and political literature—which was created with the growth of the working class and spread through eighteenth-century Europe—the conflict between labor and capital is a central theme. Connected with this is socialism's view on the right to acquisition of property. Acquisition through one's own labor—what we above (2.8) called simple production—is contrasted with acquisition through the use of capital and purchased labor (composite production). Labor, one could claim, was the prerequisite for capital being created at all and for its accumulation. Thus it was reasonable that those who labored—and not those who provided the capital—should have a first right to that which was produced.

This genetic argument—labor is the original of capital; without labor, no capital—forms perhaps the most important base for the labor theory of value. At the same time it sheds light on a central point separating socialism from liberalism—the point at which the methods of original acquisition—"production through one's own labor" and "production through the labor of others"—stand in opposition. Liberalism energetically demanded freedom for acquisition through production. But as we shall see, it spoke in a hushed voice about the differences between varying *kinds* of production.

In this chapter we shall look more closely at the conservative and liberal traditions, while excluding, for the time being, socialism and the labor theory of value. The latter will be discussed in more detail in Chapter 7.

5.1 The Organism Theory

The thinking of political scientists during the Middle Ages and the seventeenth century was dominated by the notions of natural law and of the social contract. According to the first tradition, the legal system was conceived of as a law fixed by God in human nature. This law has at times been viewed as the precondition for the laws existing in society (positive law), and at other times has been seen as a challenge to positive law.

According to the latter tradition, the people entered into a voluntary agreement—a social contract—according to which natural rights were given over to a superior political power which was to guarantee order and—in Rousseau's version—execute "the public will."

Both the theory of natural law and the theory of the social contract were often given an interpretation which challenged the established society. The writings of the English and French Enlightenment philosophers contain, as pointed out by Gunnar Myrdal, various elements of the theory of natural law.[2] It was partly in opposition to this radical variant of legal theory that the organic social theory was developed in Europe toward the end of the eighteenth century.

The organic social theories were largely called upon in defense of the existing social order, and were used as weapons against the ever more common challenges to the state-supporting classes. The advocates of the organism theory are to be found almost without exception among the traditional power groups and/or among social philosophers opposed to the American and French revolutions. The organism theories also coincided both temporally and thematically with Romanticism.

In France they were brought forth by de Maistre and de Bonald, in England by Edmund Burke, and in Germany by, among others, Fichte, Hegel, Schelling and Adam Müller.[3] We shall deal briefly with Burke and Hegel and their views on ownership in the following.

Basic to the organism viewpoint is the notion that any described object—be it an individual, a group, an organization, or a society—consists of a number of cooperating, necessary elements. The word "necessary" is worth special attention. By postulating that the existing elements are necessary for the existence of the system, a normative goal is attained. "Organism" then becomes a useful substitute for "natural" or "necessary." If the state or the people is described as an organism, then the impression of an inflexible unit is conveyed. The effects of this are varied.

> The individuals become mere limbs or parts of this unit and can naturally not invoke any rights against it. If the state is viewed as an organism, then one may presuppose a separate state will, which admittedly must be expressed through people, but is not necessarily connected to the presently living will of the people. If the people is said to be an organism and the state is described as an expression of the people's individuality, then the result is the same. In that case people means the people which lives continually through time. This conception of people—which arises through an hypostatization of simple and reasonable ideas concerning the power of tradition, duties to descendants, etc.—makes it possible to place the "real" people's will anywhere, e.g., with the monarch or with certain socially high-ranking groups.[4]

With the support of the organism theory, various antidemocratic theses may be maintained. A common variant is to describe the traditionally ruling persons or groups as parts of the state organism having functions determined by nature. The monarch, for example, becomes the "head" of the social body, and social differences can be explained in accordance with the theory. "Classes are described as limbs in the social organism with definite functions and conditions for survival. All are part of a living, higher unity and thus it is proved that 'in the deepest sense' an harmonic order prevails."[5]

In the organism theories, ideas on harmony, the necessity of the existing division of labor, and the naturalness of the existing division of power are unified. Society is seen as a living unit striving for balance and harmony. Order arises as the product of an inner need for steadiness and stability in the social system, supervised by the "head" of the social body.

The organism theory has a clearly antirational content. That which is "natural," slowly developed, and traditional is extolled above that which is consciously constructed and planned by people. "The human being is assumed to have an instinct which corresponds to the will of the nation, nature and God, an instinct which is contrasted to man's uncertain and dangerous reason."[6]

5.2 Burke and Hegel on Private Property

Burke's main thesis—which includes much of the content of the above— is that society, the state, or the people have developed through a gradual, continuing process, a process which "has only to a slight degree been influenced by conscious attempts to lead and plan."[7] Society as it exists today is the product of a natural and organic process; it must therefore be seen "as a given point of departure for all action, not something undefined and unfinished, clay which may be formed according to the reason and will of man."[8]

The antirationalist element is clear. Burke is suspicious of that which is rational and planned, while at the same time underscoring the value of man's "sure and powerful instincts."[9] In its concrete application, Burke's organism perspective means that *custom* and tradition are given as the most important legal grounds for, among other things, state rule and private property. The French Revolution, which, according to Burke, breaks the link between modern and previous generations and thus rejects that which is customary, is a breach of the social order. The inheritance principle is put forth as a pillar of the well-functioning social system. Through the inheritance principle—upon which English society is said to be built—"we receive, preserve and convey our rule and our rights in the same way in which we enjoy and convey our property and our lives."[10]

The established social hierarchy which has arisen over the ages should be preserved. In Burke we find combined "the impassioned defense of tradition and the inheritance principle" and "a defense of private ownership and private inheritance."[11] The labor-free income of the capitalowner is defended: his income is used to give others work and is therefore valuable.[12]

Just like Burke, Hegel makes an axiom of private property—a premise which needs no detailed explanation. The right to property is the actual foundation of the legal system: "The right to property is the centerpoint in the spider web of the legal system. Everything radiates outward from here. According to Hegel, the entire legal system follows logically from private property."[13]

"First through property," says Hegel, "does a person exist as reason." Hegel's argument for the value of private property should not be understood as an advocacy of property as a *means* of attaining freedom. Property is an *end in itself,* indivisibly tied to the will and self-realization of the individual. Man possesses a thing more totally, the more the various potentials of the thing are realized (i.e., the more the individual works to liberate the forces inherent in the thing).[14]

Production has a particularly important place in Hegel's discussion of acquisition. It is compared to, say, occupation the kind of acquisition which is most nearly in accordance with the *concept* of acquisition. This line of reasoning may also be applied to the shaping of the individual man. Man takes possession of himself by developing his physical and spiritual abilities. Through labor, production, man becomes owner of himself.[15]

5.3 Liberalism: Locke, Bentham, and Mill

The English Enlightenment signaled to social scientific philosophers a break with the speculation of previous ages on natural law and religion. Not that concepts of things presumed natural in a certain social or legal system were abandoned at once. Nor were notions of God's role and God's possible purpose with society quickly abandoned in favor of scientific explanations and a rational world view. The transition occurred slowly. For example, natural law gradually lost many of its theological features, but it was preserved for a long time by means of other justifications. The idea that rights existed "by nature" could, for instance, be defended with a reference to the general reasonableness of these rules.

LOCKE

A basic problem for many classical philosophers has been to explain man's transition from a more or less primitive "natural state" to a society of order and authoritative rule. Locke's ideas concerning ownership and its development make up an important part of his theory on the transition from the natural state. One of Locke's points of departure—one containing strong elements of natural law—is that human beings are born equal, equal as to "life, health, liberty or possessions." God has delivered the earth to men in order that they may make their livelihoods from it. This gift of the earth has been to all human beings collectively. Now if, according to Locke's assumption, men are by nature equal, how then can one explain and defend the origin of private property and therefore material inequality? How can individual human beings be given the moral right to privately own large amounts of property when God gave the right of possession to *all*?

Locke's important contribution to the discussion of ownership—which has made him one of the leading figures in this discussion—begins with labor as the basis for acquisition and as the moral justification of ownership. The common right of human beings to an object is nullified as soon as an individual person acquires the thing. This acquisition can occur through occupation (taking something which is common and removing it from the state in which nature left it; Locke exemplifies this with acorns and apples), but it occurs especially by means of production: Locke's expression for this is "mix one's labor into something."[16]

Both Locke's occupation thesis as well as his thoughts on production fall back on the conviction that the individual has a right to his own life and his own body. In brief, the argument is as follows: since man owns his own body, he should also have the right to own that which he acquires through his body, either by means of occupation or production. The logic in this is not convincing, to express it cautiously.[17]

From a moral point of view, problems arise in connection with the question of how many resources a person may acquire for himself. Locke discusses this question in detail. His method in brief is:

(a) to establish that the right of acquisition in principle should be unlimited,
(b) to enumerate important arguments against this idea, and
(c) to refute these arguments.

Taken together, these steps make up a plea for commercial freedom and an advocacy of "a moral justification of bourgeois acquisition."[18]

Locke deals with three arguments for a limitation of private ownership.[19] First, the claim can be made that it is reasonable for a man to collect only so much property that there is still enough left for others; private ownership should not be carried so far that my own right to acquisition of property prevents others from practicing the same right.

Second, one has the right to collect only so much property that it does not spoil. No one should be allowed to hoard commodities or natural products in such an amount that he cannot use all of them.

> As much as any one can make use of to any advantage of life before it spoils; so much he may by his labour fix a Property in. Whatever is beyond this, is more than his share, and belongs to others. Nothing was made by God for Man to spoil or destroy.[20]

Third, the right to acquisition should be limited to the amount a person can acquire by means of his own efforts; this because it is "the *Labour* of his Body and the *Work* of his *Hands*" which makes the person owner of the thing when his labor is "mixed into" the natural object.

These three limitations may seem to constitute a decisive argument against an economic system based on individual, private capitalownership. All three must be considered reasonable and morally inviting: it would seem an unrewarding task to argue against them. Who would wish to claim that my ownership should stand in the way of that of others, or that I should have the right to accumulate so much as to risk that it spoil? The third limit seems, by the way, definitely to restrict accumulation: even an extremely industrious person can hardly—with the mere use of his own labor—seriously obstruct the livelihoods of others through his private acquisition.

Locke solves the problem, however; he does this with a reference to the economy of money. That which more than any other thing separates the ordered, civilized society from humanity's natural state is the existence of a monetary system—an agreement between people to use money as a means of exchange.

The monetary system removes the first limit. *Land* can admittedly not be equally distributed. However, through the monetary system and the market, the *products* of the land can come to the benefit of all, even if they do not own the land themselves. The act of an individual acquiring and cultivating land becomes an act benefiting everyone:

> [He] who appropriates land to himself by his labour, does not lessen but increase the common stock of mankind. For the provisions serving to the support of humane life, produced by one acre of inclosed and cultivated land, are (to speak much within compasse) ten times more, than those, which are yielded by an acre of Land, of an equal richnesse, lyeing wast in common. And therefore he, that incloses Land and has a greater plenty of the conveniencys of life from ten acres, than he could have from an hundred left to Nature, may truly be said, to give ninety acres to Mankind. For this labour now supplys

him with provisions out of ten acres, which were but the product of an hundred lying in common.[21]

Locke's reasoning presupposes of course that the question of distribution is unproblematical, i.e., that the products of the land can be distributed in such a way that everyone benefits (or, in any case, so that no one is treated unfairly). Locke makes this assumption: the standard of living in a country where all land is cultivated is better than in countries where this is not the case. Even if there is not enough land for all, everyone still has a livelihood.[22]

The monetary system removes the second limitation. Gold and silver do not spoil. Money may be accumulated in any quantity. Not only this: even agricultural products may be accumulated in unlimited quantity since they can be exchanged for money: "a man may fairly possess more land than he himself can use the product of, by receiving in exchange for the overplus, to any one, these metalls not spoileing or decaying in the hands of the possessor.[23]

Finally, the monetary system removes the third limit. The dimensions of an individual's labor can hardly be so great so as to make for a massive accumulation by means of one's *own* labor. But, as Macpherson points out, Locke had a definition of "own" labor which included not only the labor executed by an individual with his body. Also the labor *purchased* by an individual was his, i.e., the labor executed by persons in his service. When in the following sentences Locke speaks of "my" labor, it is completely clear that this also includes his *servant's* labor:

> Thus the Grass my Horse has bit; the Turfs my Servant has cut; and the Ore I have digg'd in any place where I have a right to them in common with others, become my *Property*, without the assignation or consent of any body. The *labour* that was mine, removing them out of that common state they were in, hath *fixed* my *Property* in them.[24]

Labor is individual property, according to Locke. It may not only be owned, but also disposed of. Monetary economy makes it possible to sell and buy labor.

> [The] more emphatically labour is asserted to be a property, the more it is understood to be alienable. For property in the bourgeois sense is not only a right to enjoy or use; it is a right to dispose of, to exchange, to alienate. To Locke a man's labour is so unquestionably his own property that he may freely sell it for wages. . . . The labour thus sold becomes the property of the buyer, who is then entitled to appropriate the produce of that labour.[25]

With this Locke has formulated, as Macpherson writes, a "political theory of acquisition."[26] The solution to the moral problems arising out of the unlimited accumulation of property lay in the monetary system. Through it an inequality in the ownership of natural resources could be defended: the yield from natural resources could, with the aid of the market, come to the benefit of all. Through it the accumulation of capital—which did not risk being destroyed—could also be justified. Finally, the actual foundation for capital accumulation could also be given a moral justification. *Labor* was the foremost motive for ownership rights; here was included not only the labor I do myself, but also the labor which others do for me.[27] It can be said that Locke created a doctrine of private ownership and private enterprise—a theory for the bourgeois revolution.[28] It is logically consistent that Locke's demands for freedom—economic freedom—were invoked in both the American and French declarations of rights at the end of the eighteenth century.

BENTHAM

Locke provided a series of separate arguments for private ownership. But what has not been made sufficiently clear in the above is that he also—as Hegel did later—considered ownership a natural feature of society; property was a natural right.[29] But with Jeremy Bentham—whose productive life fell at the end of the eighteenth century, or approximately one century after Locke's—we do not find private property as a premise, and even less as a premise of natural law. This would have been incompatible with Bentham's pragmatic and empirical philosophy. To the extent that private property needed justification, this had to come through reference to its utility for the individual and society. This utility, said Bentham, could be calculated mathematically; there was no need for moral or legal justification. Bentham was strongly critical of theories containing these features.

Property and the maximization of net pleasure. Bentham bases an individualistic theory on the psychological assumption that human beings seek that which is pleasant and try to avoid that which is painful. Bentham's famous introductory chapter to *An Introduction to the Principles of Morals and Legislation* says:

> Nature has placed mankind under the governance of two sovereign masters, *pain* and *pleasure* It is for them alone to point out what we ought to do, as well as to determine what we shall do. On the one hand the standard of right and wrong, on the other the chain of causes and effects, are fastened to their throne. They govern us in all we do, in all we say, in all we think: every effort we can make to throw off our subjection, will serve but to demonstrate and confirm it. In words a man may pretend to abjure their empire: but in reality he will remain subject to it all the while. The *principle of utility* recognizes this subjection, and assumes it for the foundation of that system, the object of which is to rear the fabric of felicity by the hands of reason and of law. Systems which attempt to question it, deal in sounds instead of sense, in caprice instead of reason, in darkness instead of light.[30]

Man seeks out pleasure and attempts to avoid pain. This thesis becomes the basis not only for *interpretations* of human actions, but also for *recommendations* for a suitable and desirable social order.

How can 'this descriptive statement of how people are in practice constituted be made a basis for pronouncements on how an entire society *should* be constituted? The answer to this question can be given in greater or lesser detail, depending upon how deep we wish to dig into the layers of problems contained in Bentham's superficially simple thesis. Since our aim in this chapter is mainly to illustrate how various theories treat private property, we wish to refer the reader to other sources for an elucidation of utilitarianism and its predecessor, hedonism.

In brief, however, the answer goes like this. The foundation for utilitarian reasoning comes from Locke. All people at all times strive through their own actions to create the greatest possible well-being for themselves. An act is justified when its aim is to create in the long run the greatest possible well-being for the actor. This acting for one's personal well-being does not conflict with the common good. Locke had said: "[He] who appropriates land to himself by his labour does not lessen but increase the common stock of Mankind."[31] Similarly, Bentham claimed that the interest of society was bound to the interest of private individuals, i.e., "the sum of the interests of the several members who compose it."[32]

The principle of personal utility is clearly and unequivocally formulated. It is not only *that* people strive for the greatest possible well-being. Man *should* also strive for a maximization of pleasure. If everyone acts in this manner, then the result will be an "increase in the common stock of mankind." It should be pointed out that for Bentham the "common good" was no abstraction. This quantity could be estimated through an arithmetic totaling of each individual's net pleasure ("the felicific calculus"). Bentham also provided a comprehensive manual for how sensations of pain and pleasure could be totaled by referring to prefixes (positive and negative) and various dimensions (intensity, duration, probability, proximity in time, etc.).[33]

To a great degree, the explanation is to be found in the emerging natural sciences of the seventeenth and eighteenth centuries. Bentham obviously believed that pain and pleasure were objectively measureable phenomena and that observations could be made with the aim of determining their relative strengths with respect to a given number of variables. We will return later to this recurrent feature of utilitarianism (Chapter 8).

It is also worth underscoring the empirical and positivistic character of utilitarianism for intralogical reasons. Bentham may not—if he wants to remain consistent with his own theory—claim as an *axiom* that property rights are the foundation of the legal system. According to utilitarianism, different social phenomena must be justified by their *utility* to people (and thus to society). And neither can Burke's device be used, according to which the wisdom of humanity collected through the ages—administered by the ruling classes—was the precondition for the continued existence of society. Within the intellectual framework of utilitarianism, every phenomenon must be judged according to its utility *here and now*, and not according to the functional effect the phenomenon might have on the future state of society. Metaphysical arguments, like those based on the value of custom or tradition, are foreign to utilitarianism. Nevertheless, in his discussion of private property Bentham comes very close to Burke's argument on the same subject.

For Bentham it is conceivable *in principle* that the pleasure arising from the ownership of private property could be counterbalanced and superseded by other pleasurable sensations; the reverse is also true that the pain arising from the loss of property may be counterbalanced or superseded by other losses. It could thus happen that an individual who is robbed of everything he owns could be compensated for this through the enjoyment of "pleasures of the senses," "pleasures of skill," "pleasures of a good name," or any of the other nice things which Bentham enumerates.

It is, however, clear that Bentham puts private property in such a special position among his pleasure-creating factors that its loss can only with great difficulty be compensated for by the high values of other components. Bentham says, in his list of various types of pleasures:

> By the pleasures of wealth may be meant those pleasures which a man is apt to derive from the consciousness of possessing any article which stands in the list of instruments of enjoyment and security, and more particularly at the time of his first acquiring them; at which time the pleasure may be styled a pleasure of gain or a pleasure of acquisition: at other times a pleasure of possession.[34]

Here Bentham establishes a close connection between "wealth" and "security." It is through the emphasis Bentham places upon the security motive that private ownership attains such a central position in the utilitarian system.[35]

According to Bentham, people—as opposed to animals—live not only for the present; man also has long-term goals. The sense of security is something that contributes to man's ability to plan and look to the future. Social conditions should be such that human expectations are not disturbed or overthrown. Besides the utility principle, it is the security principle which requires that individual expectations not be frustrated. This principle is, in turn, the basis of property.[36] Property is, as one commentator puts it, *an established expectation* that one will be allowed to act in a certain way (e.g., by having control over property), while at the same time others will be prevented from having control over the same property without permission.[37] This expectation is created by law. The law should be such that no sudden or unexpected shifts are allowed in the distribution of society's resources. The legislator "should preserve the distribution which in actuality has been established."[38]

How does this fit in with advocacy of the principle of equality, which seems to imply that some forms of redistribution—even relatively rapid ones—must take place? The answer is quite simply that a conflict between the two principles must be solved through a yielding of the demand for equality.

> When security and equality are in opposition, there should be no hesitation; equality should give way. . . . The establishment of equality is a chimera; the only thing which can be done is to lessen inequality.[39]

The state could, according to Bentham, remove obstacles preventing the free circulation of wealth and thus facilitate equalization. The state could also reform the right of inheritance, for example by ascribing equal inheritance rights to all the children of a propertyowner. But the security motive clearly excluded the complete abandonment of inheritance rights. Only if there were no heirs, should the individual's property be administered by the state for further distribution.[40]

In the preceding paragraph Bentham appears to advocate an emancipation of the forces of capital. He emphasizes the importance of free circulation of capital resources and underscores the principle that owners of capital should, with a satisfactory degree of security, be able to expect returns on the capital. He emphasizes that the state, by means of legislation, should remove obstacles to each individual's striving for "subsistence and abundance" while also guaranteeing *possibilities* of growth for others. Further, a more equal distribution of capital is desired (in the interest of the market economy), but should not be carried so far so as to frustrate the expectations of the economic participants.

The same motivation is clear in Bentham's critique of the declaration of rights of the French Revolution. Bentham's attack on the revolution was not less vehement than Burke's.[41] He attacked the thesis of the declaration of rights: "Every man is sole proprietor of his own person, and this property is inalienable."[42] This statement is false, said Bentham. It is worthwhile reviewing his argument:

> In what manner is the legal relation of the husband to the wife constituted, but by giving him a right for a certain time, to the use of certain faculties of hers, by giving him, in so far a property in her person? And so on with respect to the legal relations of the father to the child under age, and of the master to the apprentice or other servant, whatever be the nature of the service.[43]

Bentham criticizes by means of *empirical arguments*—concerning how things are in practice—the *normative* statement in the declaration of rights. The passage is therefore not particularly logical. The interesting thing, however, is that Bentham implicitly points out *that* it happens in society that labor is sold and bought and that therefore "the proposition that no man shall be suffered to have any property in the person of another would be a mischievous one, and mischievous to a degree of madness." It is clear that ownership, according to Bentham, must include access to the efforts of others, whether they be one's children, servants, or wife. In this way Bentham's philosophy may be seen as an additional reinforcement of—and individual-psychological justification for—the "possessive individualism" which Locke, among others, claimed to interpret.

JOHN STUART MILL

The significance of John Stuart Mill lies mainly in the interpretation of the utilitarian theory and the adaptation of the theory to a new social situation. What happened between Bentham's contribution to the social debate (around 1800) and the corresponding period in Mill's life (middle and late nineteenth century) was that industrial capitalism had more securely consolidated its position in English society, and the working class had begun to organize itself politically and in trade unions. Productivity increased to a previously unknown extent, while at the same time the misery and inhumane working conditions of the wage earners became more and more obvious. "The worker question" or "the social question" had become an acute problem which, if not solved, threatened to lead to widespread social conflict.

Besides the developments in the economy and in labor, the political and social scientific debate changed. Many writers before Marx had presented the thesis that labor was the main source of wealth, and that the yield of labor should fall to those who had invested their labor (Smith, Ricardo, and others). But not until the organization of the working class on the continent did this thesis become *politically* meaningful (see Section 8.1).

The debate had been going on for a few decades when John Stuart Mill entered it. It is symptomatic that Mill, in his chapter on property in *Principles of Political Economy* (1848) finds it necessary to begin his discussion with an analysis of communism. The increasingly common demands for an equalization of property could not be belittled or dismissed with impunity. They demanded counterarguments.

After a thorough review of the reasons which seemed to speak *for* communism, Mill dealt with the reasons for what seemed to him a superior solution to the social question—an improvement and perfection of the system of private ownership.

Mill on communism. Those who attack the principle of private property may be divided into two classes, says Mill—those who demand absolute equality in the distribution of "physical means of life and enjoyment"[44] and those who accept a certain amount of inequality with the understanding that this is motivated by some principle of justice or expediency (Mill obviously includes himself in the latter category).

To the first group belong, among others, "Mister Owen and his followers." The term for their program is communism. The concept "socialism" has a similar meaning, says Mill. It is not entirely identical to communism, but its aim is still a system "which requires that the land and the instruments of production should be the property, not of individuals, but of the communities and associations, or of the Government."[45]

A first question is whether communism and socialism can be put into practice. Yes, says Mill. No reasonable person would doubt that, say, an agricultural collective consisting of a few thousand people with collectively owned land and collective labor could produce enough for the subsistence of its members. The objection, often heard, that some people would try to avoid the collective labor, is of little value, according to Mill. Is it not so, asks Mill, that wage earners in the *present* system of production most often have a minimal interest in actively contributing to it? He answers:

> I am not undervaluing the strength of the incitement given to labour when the whole or a large share of the benefit of extra exertion belongs to the labourer. But under the present system of industry this incitement, in the great majority of cases, does not exist.[46]

A communistic system is likely to be less productive than one in which the farmers own their own land or in which the workers keep for themselves the products of labor, but it will probably be more effective than a system—like the one in effect in England during Mill's time—in which a great deal of the labor is done for a monthly salary by employees from "the middle or higher classes."[47] Much energy could thus be liberated if the system were changed. "Mankind are capable of a far greater amount of public spirit than the present age is accustomed to suppose."[48] People can be made to feel a collective spirit; the statement that productivity would decrease under communism is thus questionable.

> To what extent, therefore, the energy of labour would be diminished by Communism, or whether in the long run it would be diminished at all, must be considered for the present an undecided question.[49]

As to the second question: one of the objections to communism is one which also is often raised against poverty laws, i.e., if society supports the poor and their children, then the population will increase catastrophically. But a communistic system, says Mill, can be expected to take measures to limit the population if the system is threatened.

> The Communistic scheme instead of being peculiarly open to the objection drawn from danger of overpopulation, has the recommendation of tending in an especial degree to the prevention of that evil.[50]

A third objection is that the division of labor will become problematical in the communistic society. All people are not suited to all kinds of work. Rotation of jobs—which communist writers readily advocate—could therefore hardly be entirely realized. But Mill thinks that the system could nevertheless accomplish a somewhat more equal division of labor than that which existed in contemporary England.[51]

Mill summarizes with an assessment of communism:

> If, therefore, the choice were to be made between Communism with all its chances, and the present state of society with all its sufferings and injustices; if

the institution of private property necessarily carried with it as a consequence, that the produce of labour should be apportioned as we now see it, almost in an inverse ratio to the labour—the largest portions to those who have never worked at all, the next largest to those whose work is almost nominal, and so in a descending scale, the remuneration dwindling as the work grows harder and more disagreeable, until the most fatiguing and exhausting bodily labour cannot count with certainty on being able to earn even the necessaries of life: if this, or Communism, were the alternative, all the difficulties, great or small, of Communism would be but as dust in the balance.[52]

But, says Mill—and this is his main point—communism must not be compared to the system of private ownership as it now appears in contemporary England. The comparison must instead be made with private capitalism as it *could* appear. And here Mill formulates a surprising thesis: "The principle of private property has never yet had a fair trial in any country; and the less so, perhaps, in this country than in some others."[53]

The social arrangements of Europe derive not from a simple distribution of land or from advances through labor, but rather from "conquest and violence." "[A]nd notwithstanding what industry has been doing for many centuries to modify the work of force, the system still retains many and large traces of its origin."[54]

The property laws, says Mill, have never yet been in accordance with the principles which justify private property.

It is toward this goal—the realization of what Mill believes are the sound principles of the system of private property—that Mill is striving in his continued discussion. These sound principles demand that everyone be allowed an equal chance to begin "fair in the race" and that ownership of property be diversified instead of concentrated. If this is achieved, says Mill, then one would find that "the principle of individual property would have been found to have no necessary connexion with physical and social evils which almost all Socialist writers assume to be inseparable from it."[55]

Mill founds his positive picture of private property rights on the notion that this is the true expression of the individual's *sacrifices*. Like Bentham (and, as we saw, basically also Locke), he includes not only one's *own* *labor* among the grounds for private acquisition. The sacrifices which motivate acquisition also include expenses for the purchase of labor and the cost of refraining from immediate capital returns in favor of later profits ("abstinence").

Mill's reasoning on the significance of the property concept is worth a detailed review. This is because it assumes a clear position of *equating labor and capital* as production factors: an equating which is theoretically founded on utilitarianism (both labor and the lending of capital are seen as subjective sacrifices) and which during the eighteenth and nineteenth centuries was to be endorsed further by, among others, Condillac, Cournot, Say, Senior, Menger, Jevons, and Walras, and in Sweden by Gustav Cassel (see Chapter 7).

What makes up the concept private property? Mill allows the following definition:

> The institution of property, when limited to its essential elements, consists in the recognition in each person of a right to the exclusive disposal of what he or she has produced by their own exertions, or received either by gift or by fair agreement, without force or fraud, from those who produce it. The foundation of the whole is, the right of producers to what they themselves have produced.[56]

The objection may be raised, says Mill, that private ownership rights as they have been formed in practice, recognize property rights for individuals with respect to certain objects in spite of the fact that these individuals have not produced the objects *themselves*. For example, workers in an industry are allowed by law only rights to wages. The actual product is transferred to the ownership of someone who has only provided capital, perhaps without even having carried out supervisory duties. Is this just? Mill writes:

> The answer to this is, that the labour of manufacture is only one of the conditions which must combine for the production of the commodity. The labour cannot be carried out without materials and machinery, nor without a stock of necessities provided in advance, to maintain the labourers during the production. All these things are the fruits of previous labour.[57]

And further:

> The capitalists can do nothing without labourers, nor the labourers without capital. If the labourers compete for employment, the capitalists on their part compete for labour, to the full extent of the circulating capital of the country.[58]

The paragraphs cited here are noteworthy in their lack of agreement with Mill's earlier reasoning. We have seen how Mill, in connection with his analysis of communism, maintains that it should be compared to "the regime of private property, not as it is, but *as it might be made*" (our italics). [59] The defense of private property lies not in existing social conditions, but in the *ideal* of private ownership. Mill emphasizes this additionally by sharply criticizing the existing state of property ownership in England.

In the paragraphs cited just above, however, Mill *uses precisely the existing conditions* to justify private ownership. This is not particularly logical in relation to his own recommendation of method: a statement of the ideal outlined by him should have been sufficient. The conclusion is that Mill, in spite of his earlier criticism of the circumstances of production in England, *nevertheless* feels that these circumstances basically meet the most important demands to be placed on a good system of private capitalism. In the end it is Mill's *theoretical* theses of the blessedness of the private system of ownership which dominate over his empirically gained insights into the disadvantages of the system.

5.4 Summary

Two basic positions on the question of a justification of ownership (especially of the means of production) have been discussed in this chapter. According to one of these, the right of ownership is a necessary element of all societies; private property is the foundation upon which society rests. We find the clearest expression of this in the conservative theoreticians (for example, Burke and Hegel), but we also find private ownership rights as an axiom (of natural law) in John Locke's writings.

According to the other position—exemplified by Bentham—one may not presuppose a priori that private ownership is a natural and necessary social institution.

To utilitarianism private ownership, like other social phenomena, is a *problem*; in accordance with the theory of utility, such elements of society demand an *empirical* justification. Custom and tradition are not sufficient as reasons, and neither may axiomatic lines of reasoning (like Hegel's) be presented. Bentham defends private ownership by bringing up the security motive. Particularly in the work of John Stuart Mill, apparent sympathy with the pure specification argument (property *only* through one's own labor) is united with a defense of "possessive individualism." The argument for this is the claim that production factors carry equal value: the abstinence motive is equated with the labor motive.

This latter distinction will be important for our continued presentation. Is it reasonable to consider the provision of capital an effort of the same kind and degree as labor? May one—as in the utilitarian subjective theory of value—consider these to be equal "subjective sacrifices"? The question is related to another terminological distinction which has been used several times above, namely the distinction between production through labor (simple production) and production through capital investment plus the investment of purchased labor (composite production). It is impossible to speak—as Locke, Bentham, and Mill do—of the phenomenon "labor" without further definition. Direct labor—the carrying out of production—must be analytically separated from indirect labor—control over the circumstances of production. In spite of the mystification and confusion surrounding them in the subjective theory of value (see Chapter 7), both of these functions are economically, politically, and legally of a fundamentally different kind. Any line of reasoning about private ownership and economic democracy must consider the distinction between simple and composite production.

The social and economic development we discussed in Chapter 4 was expressed not only in economic theory but also in contemporary political literature. This chapter dealt with how the question of ownership has been treated by writers of the conservative and liberal theoretical traditions.

Both conservatism and liberalism contain argumentative schemes in support of private property. Conservatism views private property as the actual basis of the social order, i.e., as a postulate or axiom needing no further justification. Liberalism cannot approach the question in this absolute and uncompromising way. To liberal writers such as Bentham, private property, like other social institutions, must be provided with a theoretical justification.

Why is private ownership necessary? The explanation is given in terms of utility. A social institution must, in order to be accepted, be shown to contribute to human happiness and thus have utility for the entire society. "Society" should be understood here as the sum of the individuals in it: they constitute the units upon which are based the computations of individual net pleasures which make up the sum total of utility.

The individual "felicific calculus" consists of the difference between "pleasures" and "pains," calculated for a number of separate dimensions. The theory of utility, developed in detail by Bentham but based on classical hedonism, forms the foundation for the subjective theory of value, the content of which—in different variations—will be discussed in Chapter 7. In the area of economics, the subjective theory of value is a point of departure for the theory of marginal utility and later for "marginalistic" theory. Politically, it would come to form an offensive front against the labor theory of value, which was based on premises of production and class analysis.

Utilitarianism presents no real theory with which to carry out the computation of individual pleasures into the sum pleasure—a computation presupposed by utilitarianism itself. Lacking this, utilitarianism seeks to solve the problem by assuming that the laissez-faire principle by itself will contribute to social harmony and balance. This is facilitated by the organic view of society. According to this, society is comprised of a number of interdependent and necessary elements. Various social institutions, such as private ownership of the means of production, can thus not be eliminated or brought to an end without having damaging consequences for the whole organism. Stability and security are, for Bentham among others, of greater value than equality.

Chapter 6

CIVIC RIGHTS

This Far, but no Further?

The concept of civic rights—in the application of interest here, i.e., the collective ownership of the means of production—includes the ownership functions practiced by the juridical person "state" or any other legally recognized representative of the group "citizens entitled to vote" (cf., 2.3 and 2.4). According to this model, citizens are seen as the mandator for the elected executive state (parliament and government).

The right of decision-making is practiced indirectly: those citizens entitled to vote elect representatives who appoint a government which appoints administrators of the collectively owned capital. Having civic rights implies "constitutive authority" (see below 6.4), i.e., influence over the formation of the society's constitution with respect to capitalownership and disposition.

The connection between civic rights and capitalownership is primarily a twentieth-century phenomenon. The question of collective ownership by a state under the people's control arose first with the growth of the labor movement and its demands (sometimes expressed in revolutions) for a just share of society's resources. Ironically enough, many of the societies where this has become a reality are now characterized by features which most people consider opposed to democracy. Thus, capitalownership by means of civic rights is formally practiced today in countries such as the Soviet Union, East Germany, Poland, and Romania. In these countries state ownership and administration of the means of production are combined with only slight or even nonexistent possibilities for citizens to influence the direction of the state apparatus through the free formation of public opinion. Civic rights usually prevail *formally*; in *reality* they are often very limited.

This is, of course, not to say that there exists any necessary connection between a state-socialist and an undemocratic system. Highly oversimplified assumptions of this kind have been made by writers such as von Hayek and Herbert Tingsten.[1] We will return to the question of civic rights and other forms of democracy in Chapter 10.

The issue of civic rights has, as we shall attempt to show below, almost always been closely bound to economic power and the right of ownership.

When new socioeconomic groups demanded economic rights, these demands concerned not only the right to *make decisions,* they also—and especially—concerned the power to *execute* the decisions. This power depends ultimately on ownership of the means of production. And quite in keeping with this, many of the classical contributors to the theory of democracy have been cautious in two ways. They have expressly demanded that decision-making rights be extended to new population groups; but they have also been careful to point out that decision-making rights must be limited. Those groups whose influence should be restricted are the unpropertied, the uneducated, those who lack employment and income, those who are poor and rely on social support.

There exist extensive writings in political science and history concerning the so-called emergence of democracy, writings which often maintain as a thesis that the expansion of universal suffrage has its origin in the demands for freedom, equality, and brotherhood presented by the French Revolution and its theoretical and practical instigators. In this chapter we shall take a closer look at some examples which indicate that universal suffrage is far from an obvious outgrowth of the liberal bourgeois revolution and its ideological contributors. If one examines the consequences of the definitions of "citizen" which have been applied through the ages, then one may easily conclude that universal suffrage did not come into being because of but rather *in spite of* the contributions of the classical democratic authors. The expansion of the democratic form of government occurred as new, previously unrepresented social groups were recognized as mandators for the state.

The passive form ("were recognized") in this statement is vague and obscure. It conceals the circumstance that certain groups and classes judged the knowledge, maturity, and rationality of other groups and classes against the background of their own political aims. For example, throughout the history of the democratic process men long considered women to be insufficiently competent to make decisions; older members of society see to it with a certain zeal that voting rights are not given to people who are too young; and—most important for our discussion— propertyowning groups have in various ways sought justification for the exclusion of unpropertied people from power over the governing of the state. A main theme in the following discussion concerns the ways various authors have sought to limit civic rights to certain social groups.

6.1 The Enlightened Development Model

Descriptions of the expansion of civic rights often follow what could be called the *enlightened, natural development model.* It is implied that by virtue of their superior arguments for the expansion of democracy, the established power groups have perceived the importance and value of more and more groups of citizens being able to enjoy the advantages of democracy. Liberalism is said to have played an important role in this process, and the liberal notions of freedom urged it on. The conservative forces in their alliances with the absolutist state, the monarchy, the nobility, and the church were forced to give way to the demands for spiritual and material freedom put forth by liberalism and the bourgeois social strata which supported it. The most prominent expressions of these tendencies were the American and French revolutions. Especially the motto of the latter, "freedom, equality, brotherhood" laid the foundation for the nineteenth- and twentieth-century development of democracy in Western Europe and North America.

It is implied that the persuasive force of the liberal demands, combined with a good measure of foresight and attention to the neglected social groups, in particular the working class, has led the established economic and political power-holders to gradually relinquish control of the state to the popular majority.

A wonderful example of this method of presentation is found in Tunberg and Söderlund's *Svensk historia för gymnasiet.* The political development during the nineteenth century was marked by liberalism, according to the authors. The liberals opposed the personal power of the king as practiced by Karl XIV Johan. The liberals demanded therefore

> that the government should show greater consideration for the will of the people as manifested in the parliament, and that the power of the people's representatives should be increased. The parliament should be constituted in such a way as to be able to express public opinion in a better way than the parliament based on estates. The abolition of the division by estates was especially in agreement with liberalism's notions of equality. The reform of representation was therefore a main point in the liberal platform.[2]

One gets the impression that the demands applied equally to all social groups, including the working class. But it is mentioned in passing that "many liberals" also "advocated . . . the necessity of altering economic policy to bring it into agreement with the theories of the advantages of free trade presented by, among others, Adam Smith." However, compared to the ideals of enlightenment and equality this is a subordinate motive.

This theme is even clearer somewhat later in the authors' argument. Under the heading "Social Reforms" they write:

> Early Swedish liberalism had a marked humanitarian outlook. The liberals eagerly supported better care for the poor, sick and imprisoned, more humane criminal punishment, more effective education for the people, and generally better living conditions for the most neglected social groups. Bentham's famous thesis that the duty of the state was to insure the greatest possible happiness for the greatest number of its members won great approval also in Sweden. Public opinion was also influenced by the notions of equality which liberalism had inherited from the Enlightenment, according to which it was not justifiable that certain social classes should hold privileged positions.[3]

The model occurs, however, in a subtler form in other areas where its effect on the scientific discussion can be expected to be greater than in the case of Tunberg and Söderlund. Below we shall deal rather extensively with Herbert Tingsten's book *Demokratiens problem,* a standard work in Swedish political science, a work which to a significant extent has influenced the Swedish debate on popular rule.

6.2 Civic Rights and the Theory of the Enlightened Development

"Political thought of our time," says Herbert Tingsten by way of introduction to his book, "is in crucial respects founded on the ideas developed during the centuries after the Reformation which appeared in a mature form during the latter decades of the eighteenth century in connection with the establishment of the American Republic and the great French Revolution."[4] These ideas are codified in the American Declaration of Independence of 1776 and the French Declaration of Rights of 1789.

> The significance of these ideas in their most general form can be elucidated most simply by a few key words, a few words of honor. which during the past 150 years have enjoyed an authority disputed only by certain largely reactionary movements: reason, progress, happiness, equality, and freedom.[5]

The state based on privilege is successively replaced in many countries by constitutional democracy. Political privileges had appeared in various forms over time—an inherited autonomous monarchy, representation by estate, political influence by virtue of descent or official position, voting rights or elegibility for election based on income or fortune. (Freedom of the press, freedom to organize, and similar rights were, however, at the same time entirely or partially recognized in many places.)

It is from the state of privilege, says Tingsten, that modern democracy gradually developed.

> The legal influence on state government has been equalized and generalized. Governmental power has, even where monarchy has been preserved, passed in reality to a government dependent upon representation, or else it has been given over to a person or assembly chosen by direct or indirect popular election. Either those groups which in the state of privilege had a right of precedence in the formation of representation have been stripped of these rights, or else that part of the representation which had been appointed in this way has lost most of its perogatives. Limited or graded suffrage has thus been replaced by universal and equal suffrage. Those rights connected to political activity are maintained and preserved. The combination of legal equality and civic freedom thus becomes—expressed schematically—the hallmark of democracy.[6]

In the continuation of his presentation, Tingsten stresses the advocacy of *individual* rights contained in the idea of democracy. In various formulations he establishes a connection between that which is democratic and that which is individual. "Democracy appeared as a means to emancipation from state force, an instrument for liberal individualism."[7] The American and French declarations of rights are parallel in significant respects. In the American polity democratic and liberal principles were brought together. "Ownership rights, inheritance rights, and freedom of contract were considered just as inviolable as political freedom. The activity of the state was to be limited to protection and preservation of the legal rules which were necessary for the co-existence and peaceful competition of individuals."[8]

The liberal-individualistic arguments erected upon the foundation of equality have been used for criticism of existing constitutional disparities.

> The advocates of democracy have been able to show that the regulations or the praxis through which certain persons or groups attained a special position of power were irrational and untenable.... Why, it was asked during the debate on the Swedish representation reform, should a nobleman because—at most—one of his ancestors had made a patriotic contribution, have greater political opportunities than a bourgeois or a peasant with the same or greater level of wealth or education? Why, it was said 40 years later, should a craftsman or worker be excluded from voting rights if his income was not 800 crowns but attain political majority if he reached this limit; how could it be defended that a person with an income of 15,000 crowns be allowed many times more votes in local elections than a person with an income of 1,500 crowns? Why should a woman lack the right to vote when she did the same work as a man with voting rights? And why should the woman working in the home—who by the way was constantly extolled by the conservatives—be placed in a lower class than those working in a factory or in an office? In this way all exclusions, limitations and gradations could be marked as arbitrary means for preserving the power of those who already held it or as inconsistencies in the application of a certain principle.[9]

A common problem with Tingsten's method of presentation is his delight in using passive clauses (e.g., "could be marked as arbitrary means") and paraphrases starting with "it was". It is thus not sufficiently clear where various demands originated and which economic and political power resources were used to implement them. This facilitates a historiography which views the democratic development as a natural political-ideological process in which the superior standpoints almost by themselves break through the existence of the old regime. The following quotation is an example. It gives the impression that Bismarck, because of the internal logic of neo-liberalism, perceived the importance of expanding democracy:

> [One] noteworthy fact is that Disraeli in England and Bismarck in Germany stood behind the new regulations on suffrage. The old liberal ideology gradually yielded to a neo-liberalism which in part accepts the democratic principles

and in part, and connected to this, works for socio-political reforms and more modest state intervention in accordance with a preservation of the principle of private ownership and enterprise.[10]

A relaxation of political tension during the latter decades of the nineteenth century plus "the rise of mass education, increasing prosperity, industrialization, etc." helped engender this willingness on the part of the rulers.[11] It is true that the political behavior of these groups often showed traces of a sustained defense of the old order, but on the whole the development is seen moving toward an increasingly broad citizen influence.[12]

The picture which Tingsten paints contains strong features of a constant development of democracy toward broader political power. The development is not without moments of stagnation or even reversal (the dictatorships of Italy and Germany between the wars), but it is generally true that democracy has advanced by virtue of the power contained in its ideological premises and through the political victories it has reaped. We see, says Tingsten, popular government as "an ideal which can be realized for all everywhere."

> This form of government means that it becomes possible for all people to attain a certain degree of political insight, that it becomes possible for all to assert their own views, and that this influence on the affairs of society is united with the possibility for people to live a rich personal life in freedom.[13]

Civic rights as a goal of the labor movement's struggle is a motive which for all intents and purposes is completely lacking in Tingsten. He speaks, for example, of "those excluded from voting rights" who were "allowed to gain power" by the privileged, about the fact that the privileged "agreed to the popular demands,"[14] or that one motive for democracy is that by it "the condition of the poor, neglected social groups is improved."[15] The *labor movement* as a political participant is conspicuous almost only by its absence (also the chapter "Democracy and Socialism," pp. 110-136 is couched almost entirely in terms of the history of ideas).[16]

The drama in the occurrences which preceded the workers "being allowed" to gain power was often such that it corresponded poorly with the enlightened development model. We shall, in order to exemplify this point, recount a couple of descriptions from the days around the constitutional reform in Sweden in November 1918.

Widespread upheavals took place at this time in Europe, aftershocks of World War I. In Germany a general strike had been proclaimed beginning on November 9; the soldiers were in widespread revolt; the German Kaiser abdicated and fled to Holland. On November 9 Karl Liebknecht raised "the red flag personally over the palace in Berlin"; the republic was proclaimed.[17] Unrest was also widespread in Sweden, partly due to a scarcity of foodstuffs and a high cost of living, and partly due to remaining limitations on suffrage.

The jolting force of the German landslide spread through Sweden and many other countries. There was an intense flaring up of the demand for a democratization of the constitution; the masses moved immediately for this and for other reforms, of which, in the sociopolitical arena, the old demand for the eight-hour working day stood in the foreground. But many believed that now the final bell had tolled for the existence of bourgeois power and that the decisive blow should be directed not only against limited suffrage but also against the House of Lords as an institution and against the monarchy, and with this, capitalist expropriation should be placed on the agenda.[18]

The Swedish Minister of Education and Ecclesiastic Affairs, the Social Democrat Värner Rydén, noted in his diary, among other things, that the military units in Stockholm could no longer be trusted. The Ministers of War and Naval Affairs testified to Rydén that "the atmosphere was very much one of revolution."

Cautionary measures had been taken in several respects. Especially untrustworthy troop units had been demobilized, and in the navy they had been dispatched to Karlskrona. The bolts had been taken from all arms in the supply depots and left with trustworthy officers. In Norrbotten the arms in the depots of the veteran reserve had been moved to Boden. On the recommendation of the chief of police [in Stockholm] the machine guns had been stripped of their bolts.[19]

The Edén government had presented bills on the introduction of women's suffrage in political elections, and on a reform of local voting rights. These proposals had been defeated through the numerical superiority of the Right in the House of Lords. The impression remained, therefore, within the Left that the issue had reached a dead end.[20] The Liberal party did not want to take the full step and abolish the taxation limit in local elections in spite of the fact that, among others, the large liberal newspaper *Dagens Nyheter* had recommended that "the table be cleared of the so-called limitations."[21]

It seems that [for prime minister Edén] deference to the mood of the Liberal Party . . . was decisive. He would have firmly persevered in his position and even declared his intention to resign if the Social Democrats had persisted in their view on this point. The situation was justifiably characterized as "a crisis."[22]

Public meetings on the constitutional issue were scheduled for the People's Hall on November 15, 1919. The Left-Socialist party had demanded in a manifesto on November 11 that

a republican polity with a unicameral system, initially in the form of a "constitutional national assembly," should be inaugurated; a general strike was recommended as a means of applying pressure if this should prove necessary.

This extreme movement threatened to spread further; the government was conscious of this, not least through the Social Democratic cabinet ministers' contact with their party.[23]

Värner Rydén wrote in his diary:

Thursday, November 14, 1918. During the past night I didn't sleep until 1:25 in the morning. Thoughts have chased through my brain, and I have tried to think through all eventualities. A revolution (which can be averted through wise and resolute action) must not be aroused. The risks for the workers and the country are tremendously large. It is my conviction that full democracy can now be instituted in a legal way. We all have an irrevocable duty to do our best. This is a frightful day with respect to responsibility to the present and the future.[24]

Pressured by the excited mood, the government accepted the demand for local suffrage with no limitation. Gerdner summarizes:

By giving its approval to a form which under normal circumstances would be radical and by binding itself to quickly carrying it through, the government took the mood and movements on the leftist, radical side heavily into consideration.[25]

After the government's decision, the previously scheduled worker meetings in the People's Hall were canceled. "The tension was simply appalling," noted Rydén. After presentations by Branting, they concurred with the government communiqué. Rydén concludes his diary notes from the November days in the following way:

The government's communiqué had been presented with great acclamation, and Branting had had an overwhelming majority. It is true that the resolution of the Stockholm workers demanded quite a bit more than the government program, but all the meetings had been marked by an intense aversion to the bolshevic minority dictatorship in favor of democracy in principle. These paths should lead us to the goal without a violent upheaval.[26]

Descriptions of the type which have been related suggest that an explanation of the existence of civic rights in terms of gradual development is often faulty. It seems that a *revolutionary* rather than an *evolutionary* development model is justified in the case discussed above. The question is what expansion of civic rights would have occurred if the labor movement had not been mobilized and if—as in the example above—a revolt had not been the obvious alternative to a constitutional reform. Against the assumptions of the evolutionary model concerning civic rights as a natural extension of liberalism should be placed the hypothesis of the revolutionary model that civic rights are rather the result of demands and mobilization carried through against the will and active resistance of the existing power groups.

6.3 On Political and Economic Power

Tingsten's book gives a description of the development of democracy according to which civic rights are expanded as a successive abdication—heavily motivated by the persuasive power of liberal and social-liberal arguments—of the established classes from their previous positions of power. In the section above we have stated certain doubts concerning the explanatory power of such an abdication model. In any case, hypotheses of this kind must be complemented by the counterassumption that democracy was instituted primarily due to organized demands from an increasingly large and politically conscious working class.

Tingsten's treatment of the question contains one additional problem, however, a problem of perhaps greater interest than the one just mentioned. As we have seen, civic rights meant for Tingsten that "those excluded from voting rights" were "allowed to gain power" by the privileged. This equation of "voting rights" and "power" is symptomatic of his presentation. Throughout he treats social power as a quantity which becomes the object of various decisions; the implicit main issue which one glimpses through all of *Demokratiens problem* concerns who should be allowed to participate in decision-making. The fewer people allowed, the less democracy; the more people, the greater the democracy.

This is a one-dimensional and much too limited conception of the character of power. Power is exercised not only through the making of decisions: often it is exercised by *preventing* decisions from being made and—still more importantly—by preventing decisions which have been made from being *executed* (or by executing *other* measures than those which were decided upon).[27] The possibility of counteracting decisions, of blocking the execution of decisions, is related to basic structural factors, particularly economic ones, and especially such economic factors as have to do with the ownership of the means of production. The mere knowledge among political decision-makers that private capitalowners have the legal right to dispose of their capital however they see fit is especially important. This right of disposition determines to a large extent society's regional and employment policies and the economic planning of local communities. The right to capital—as we stated in Section 2.2—is the most fundamental part of the right of ownership: and it is ownership which to a large extent determines the conditions for the system within which political decisions are made.

Power is two-dimensional: it is political, but above all it is economic. As we shall find, Tingsten's reasoning is dependent upon *not* observing this. The theory of democracy may be presented in such a way that the goal is an extension of power in general to increasingly large groups of citizens. There is, however, no such general power. It is common to all the classical democratic writers that they were quite conscious of the fact that "power" was primarily an economic issue.

"The Enlightened Man," writes Tingsten, directed himself in the principle of equality "against the system of privileges and the stable hierarchy
which supported the old society." He continues:

> The concept equality was thus first and foremost polemical and negative,
> signifying an attack on certain forms of inequality instituted or at least
> sanctioned by the state. For the men of the Enlightenment, legal, formal
> equality was the common goal.[28]

In his elucidation of motives and background for this line of thought,
Tingsten points particularly to the English debate at the middle of the
seventeenth century. Tingsten mentions the role played in this debate by
the so-called Levellers (radical Puritans). The Levellers tried, according to
Tingsten, to "assert the rights of the poor in both social as well as political
respects."[29] The radical opinions came most clearly to the fore in the
break with the ruling, more conservative view within the revolutionary
army's Council of Officers in Putney during the autumn of 1647. The
representatives of the radicals, says Tingsten,

> demanded general suffrage with the justification that a person could not be
> bound by laws which had originated without his participation, or even with
> the assertion that only by free choice could a person become a member of a
> political society; thus, they viewed society in the same way as their own
> religious association.[30]

Tingsten feels that the equality incentive is obvious:

> It is characteristic that in the debates of 1647 which we just mentioned, the
> leading spokesman of the conservative line argued that the aim of government
> was to protect the right of ownership and that therefore only those owning
> property should be allowed the right to vote.[31]

The cited passages are central since Tingsten allows the Levellers to be
representative manifestations of thoughts which he generally says are
represented by "democracy and liberalism" (notice the combination).[32] It
is therefore of interest to investigate to what extent the Levellers really
attempted to assert the rights of the poor and unpropertied.

The Canadian political scientist C. B. Macpherson devotes one chapter
of his book *The Political Theory of Possessive Individualism* to just the
political theses advocated by the radical Puritans. The conclusion of this
very careful review is a direct refutation of Tingsten's position. It is quite
true that the Levellers proposed expanded voting rights, but they in no
way claimed that these voting right should be *universal*. In a letter sent to
various army regiments containing information on the debate in Putney, it
is said that a vote determined

that all soldiers and others, if they be not servants or beggars, ought to have voices in electing those which shall represent them in Parliament, although they have not forty shillings per annum in freehold land.[33]

Servants and those relying on public support are thus excluded from the Levellers' demands for civic rights. This was a significant limitation of civic rights. There is reason to find out *how* significant, since this is of consequence for Tingsten's thesis.

In the seventeenth century "servants" had a much broader meaning than the word has today. It was used generally to mean *all who worked for wages*.[34] The category of wage earner was broad already by this time, including employees doing domestic work as well as workers in agriculture and industry. According to Macpherson's calculations, 754,000 is a likely figure for the number of "servants and beggars" at the time of the Putney debate in 1647. Since the total number of adult men may be calculated at not quite 1.2 million, then those excluded from voting rights are *approximately 65% or nearly two-thirds of the adult male population*. The majority were thus not covered by civic rights; this becomes even clearer when one also considers that women were excluded.

How can it be explained that the Levellers could make themselves advocates of expanded suffrage while at the same time excluding all wage earners, beggars, and poor people? This is related to their view on *birthright*. This could be lost by, among other things, criminal activity or if the individual was or became a "servant or beggar." The loss of birthright also meant a loss of voting rights.[35]

The concept of birthright was in turn related to the medieval religious doctrine of ownership rights as derived from possession of and disposition over one's own person. Against this background, it was not unreasonable for the Levellers to exclude the categories mentioned above. Wage earners and recipients of public support—as well as women—could not entirely dispose over their own persons. They were dependent upon the will of others and were included within the area of command of their superiors.[36]

The notions discussed here have broad consequences. They embrace a social order based on (a) free ownership, (b) suffrage practiced on the basis of this ownership, and (c) "ownership" which also includes ownership of the labor of others.

The Levellers perceived that freedom in the society they sought to build was a function of owership. Ownership was defined as the right of ownership, which excluded the will of others, is what made a human being a human being, a belief which broke abruptly with the traditional theory according to which social life defined human life. In the Puritanical analysis, society became a series of relations between individual owners. No person could alienate his entire person for the sake of another. He could, however, sell his labor. Ultimately, society could be said to be a series of market relations. The unions which human beings create are temporary, contractual: they are brought together and they are dissolved; they are, as it is said, free.[37]

The Levellers recruited for the most part from the petty bourgeoisie, from among free craftsmen and retail merchants. They found the rationality which they judged necessary to steer society mainly within their own social strata. Social power would be practiced by virtue of their ownership. Thus it was clear that civic rights not only needed to be expanded; they also needed also to be *limited*. Macpherson summarizes:

> The Levellers have generally been regarded as radical democrats, the first democrats in English political theory. We may now suggest that they ought rather to be considered radical liberals than radical democrats. For they put freedom first, and made freedom a function of proprietorship.[38]

6.4 How Democratic Were the Classical Democrats?

The limits on civic rights which were conceived by the classical contributors to the theory of democracy have usually been treated briefly in the literature in comparison to their contributions to the expansion of democracy.

We shall therefore devote some additional space to a discussion of this question. We shall remain in England a bit longer. We have previously dealt with Locke, Bentham, and John Stuart Mill in those sections which were relevant to their views on ownership of the means of production (Chapter 5). What we wish to emphasize in the following is that their views on these matters cannot be detached from their view on civic rights. *Because* they viewed ownership relations as fundamental, *they were also eager to limit civic rights to those who could represent owner interests.* What they have to say about civic rights does not stand separate from their opinions on ownership rights. A few excerpts from their works may illustrate this.

LOCKE ON THE WORKING CLASS

John Locke states very clearly—unlike the Levellers among whom the subject was mainly implicit—the thought that unpropertied people lacked the ability and sufficient maturity for political activity. The working class could temporarily become a political force, but then in a destructive sense and in revolt against the ruling classes:

> [T]he labourer's share [of the national income], being seldom more than a bare subsistence, never allows that body of men, time, or opportunity to raise their thoughts above that, or struggle for the richer for theirs, (as one common interest) unless when some common and great distress, uniting them in one universal ferment, makes them forget respect, and emboldens them to carve to their wants with armed force: and then sometimes they break in upon the rich, and sweep all like a deluge. But this very rarely happens but in the male-administration of neglected, or mismanaged government.[39]

In Locke's opinion it is a poorly run state in which the workers have reason—and are allowed—to revolt. For Locke, says Macpherson, the working class was "an object of state policy, an object of administration, rather than fully a part of the citizen body"; it was "incapable of rational political action."[40] "Where the hand is used to the plough and the spade the head is seldom elevated to sublime notions, or exercised in mysterious reasoning."[41]

It is clear that Locke, when he observed his own society, saw two classes with differing rights and differing degrees of rationality—those who owned and those who lacked property. That person who is without property loses the right to ownership of his own person, which is the basis of the individual's original, natural rights. Locke underscores further that the division of property is natural, and that society is set up to protect this inequality of ownership.[42] The actual significance of rational behavior is the private acquisition of land and its yield, as well as the striving to improve it for the purpose of securing a comfortable life for oneself.[43]

Locke recommended the majority principle for the governing of society. This explains his reputation as a pioneer of democracy while also providing a key to the connection between Locke's doctrine and the American Declaration of Independence, which in large part drew inspiration from Locke. Locke was, however, conscious of the fact that the majority in England of his time consisted of unpropertied people. It may seem, therefore, that Locke's theory contains an inner contradiction, but this is only illusory. It disappears with the explanation that "Locke assumed that only property owners were full citizens in the society, and thus were in the majority."[44]

An interpretation which claims that Locke was a democrat, says Macpherson, ignores

> all the evidence that Locke was not a democrat at all. It reads into Locke a concern with the democratic principle of majority rule which was to be the focus of much American political thinking in the late eighteenth and early nineteenth centuries, and again now, but which was not Locke's concern.[45]

Full rationality, says Macpherson, lay for Locke "in the acquisition [of property] rather than in labor."[46] The bourgeois Whig revolution in England during the seventeenth century established not only the superiority of the Parliament over the monarchy:

> [I]t also consolidated the position of the men of property—and specifically of the men who were using their property in the new way, as capital employed to yield profit—over the labouring class.[47]

BENTHAM ON "CONSTITUTIVE AUTHORITY"

Bentham represented, according to Tingsten, "a variant of the equality principle" in his assertion (like other English utilitarians) of the principle that "the happiness of each person is of equal value."[48] And Tingsten quotes Bentham: "The only form of government which entails or can entail the greatest possible happiness for the greatest number both as regards intent and result . . . is a democracy."[49]

It is interesting to study Bentham's definition of the concept of citizen against this background. It may seem illogical if Bentham excludes unpropertied people. This would seriously call into question Bentham's demand for a good constitution, that is, one which can achieve "the greatest happiness of the greatest number."[50] If unpropertied people are excluded, then the majority are excluded, and statements concerning "the greatest number" would lose credibility.

How does Bentham define the mandators for the state he wants to see realized? In Bentham's own terms, with whom lies the "constitutive authority"? Bentham is brief and direct, especially in his comments on who should be excluded from civic rights.

> The constitutive authority is in the whole body of electors belonging to this state: that is to say, in the whole body of the inhabitants, who, on the several days respectively appointed for the several elections, and the operations thereunto preparatory, are resident on the territory of the state, deduction made of certain classes.
>
> Classes thus deducted, are—1. Females. 2. Males, non-adult: that is to say, who have not attained the age of (21) years. 3. Non-readers: that is to say, those who have not, by reading, given proof of appropriate aptitude. 4. Passengers.[51]

It is almost obvious that women are excluded. Bentham sees them as subservient to the man/guardian (the man has "a property in her person").[52] The same is true of persons under twenty-one years of age. The category of passengers (transients) is excluded due to the territorial criterion.

The discussion of suffrage usually concerned only adult men (thus excluding a priori categories 1 and 2 from the discussion of civic rights), and it is through the third criterion that Bentham's notions of democracy are most clearly elucidated. Bentham does not explain himself in greater detail, but the motivation for this limit is—as with Locke—a belief in differences in rationality between various social classes. Only those who are mature enough for political power can be allowed to have it. Because of theoretical considerations Bentham cannot claim that rationality is bound to private property. But in practice there was need for a rule which protected democracy against abuse from the lower classes. The literacy demand established a limit here which, in any case in Bentham's time, rather effectively excluded unpropertied people, wage earners, and poor persons.

Bentham was motivated by the same rational, enlightened principles as Locke and the radical Puritans. Like them, he was critical of the absolute dominion of the royal sovereign. "Owing to intellectual blindness and weakness, absolute monarchy is still established by law in so many more countries than any better form of government is." [53] And like them, he was, however, also interested in seeing that the expansion of civic rights remained within limits which did not disturb the power which the new bourgeois groups had acquired.

MILL ON THE WORKING CLASS

The leading advocate of utilitarianism during the nineteenth century was John Stuart Mill. He has been applauded for his endeavor to extend popular government and for seeing democracy not only as a means for the practice of representative social power but also as an end in itself. For example, for Sten Johansson and Carole Pateman he symbolizes the value of political participation—a value which is presented as a competitor to the so-called theory of democratic elitism (government through representatives who gain their posts in competition for the votes of the people). [54]

The common reviews of John Stuart Mill's writing—as is the case with Locke and Bentham—have emphasized his formulations of the advantages of democracy, his advocacy of general suffrage and its function as an educator of the people. This interpretation is represented by the following passage from Tingsten:

> Democracy or representative government is, writes J. S. Mill, obviously the "ideally best form of government," that is to say, the form of government which is best if the necessary conditions for its institution and maintenance are present. With regard to the immediate results for human welfare, its superiority is based on two axiomatic statements. "The first is that the rights and interests of each human being are insured against encroachment only when the person concerned is able and habitually prepared to defend them." "The second is that the level and dispersion of the general prosperity stand in proportion to the extent and variation of the human forces which are aimed at furthering this prosperity." Both of these viewpoints are fulfilled by democracy, in which each citizen has an equal opportunity to influence the government and in which all cooperate in matters of common concern. [55]

But Mill gives clear indications of the ways civic rights must be limited. C. J. Westholm, among others, has argued that Mill considered certain portions of the working class to be insufficiently mature for an assumption of political responsibility. [56] Suffrage should therefore be limited.

> The problem for Mill is that democracy, general suffrage, and free discussion can lead to an abuse of absolute power. And the absolute power is in the majority. The problem is not diminished for Mill by this majority consisting of a class which is "to say no more, not the most highly cultivated." During Mill's time it was the conditions under which the working class lived which were the basis for the anxiety Mill felt concerning its political role; it had reason to demand improvements, to acquire increased power, but at the same time

precisely these reasons were—for the moment—a reason for not giving free rein. Mill felt, quite simply, that portions of the working class were not sufficiently mature for political responsibility.[57]

The means which were to be used to avoid giving free rein will be recognized from Bentham. In order to acquire the right to vote, an individual must, according to Mill, be able to read, write, and apply simple arithmetic.[58] Bentham's educational criterion is thus expanded significantly here. Further, a limit based on the amount of taxes paid should be applied. Those who do not pay taxes would otherwise be allowed "to put their hands into other people's pockets for any purpose which they think fit to call a public one."[59] Neither should recipients of public assistance be given voting rights: "He who cannot by his own labour suffice for his own support has no claim to the privilege of helping himself to the money of others."[60] We recognize here a principle of incapacity from Locke and the Levellers.

One may, like Westholm and Tingsten, refer to Mill's expectation that the need for limitations on suffrage would gradually decrease—concurrently with the increased knowledge and political maturity of the population—and that suffrage would thus for all intents and purposes become general.[61] The question is, however, how this expectation for the future should be weighed against Mill's striving to protect the groups representing industrialism and capitalism *in the present*. Tingsten deals with this when he writes "[Mill fears] that the 'evil' interest will assert itself in political struggles between the rich and the poor and especially between employers and workers; primarily he seems to fear that the workers may be able to force into being a law which conflicts with his own beliefs concerning the demands of the public interest for an economically liberal policy.[62]

Mill's skepticism of the working class is underscored by, among other things, pronouncements (in connection with the discussion of the demand for education) of the following sort: "An employer of labour is on the average more intelligent than a labourer, for he must labour with his head, and not solely with his hands."[63] Or there is the following thought inspired by the question of what will happen when the votes of the working class are made available to the politicians:

> The English working classes have had no encouragement to think themselves better than, or as good as, those who are more educated than themselves. But once let them become the ascendant power, and a class of base adventurers in the character of professional politicians will be constantly addressing them with all possible instigations to think their own crude notions better than the theories and refinements of thinking people, and I do not deem so highly of any numerous portion of the human race as to believe that it is not corruptible by the flattery which is always addressed to power.[64]

DE TOCQUEVILLE ON THE UNPROPERTIED AND DEMOCRACY

Few have more clearly expressed the double desire that democracy *both* should be expanded to new bourgeois elements *and* should stop there than the Frenchman Alexis de Tocqueville, the author of *Democracy in America* (1835-1840). A short review of a central passage from de Tocqueville will conclude this chapter.

Every people, says de Tocqueville, consists of three classes.

> The first class consists of the rich. The second includes those who, without being rich, live in prosperity. In the third class come those who have only small or no wealth and who mainly live on the work offered to them by the first two classes.[65]

How will these various classes administer the state finances if they gain power? What policies will they advocate with regard to the taxation of wealth?

The rich can be expected to be moderately thrifty, according to de Tocqueville. They will propose taxes with the knowledge that they will be affected only very modestly: "A tax which falls upon a great fortune . . . [only] skims off the surplus and is not very noticeable."[66] It is clear that de Tocqueville here is thinking of proportional and not progressive taxes. The reasoning would not fit very well into a situation in which the rich make laws which tax their wealth more heavily than that of the less wealthy.

The most moderate solution is having the middle class make the laws, according to de Tocqueville.

> One may confidently assume that the taxes levied by them would not be too heavy, since nothing is more calamitous than large taxes on small fortunes.

> Of all democratic regimes, therefore, rule by the middle class seems to me to be—if not the most enlightened and in all certainty not the most generous— then at least the most economical.[67]

What happens if the lowest class gains power over legislation? De Tocqueville warns that then the "public burdens" would be increased instead of diminished. Taxes would then be unequally distributed, to the disadvantage of the more well-to-do:

> Since the greatest part of those who vote do not have any taxable fortune, it seems that all money spent for public purposes could only benefit and never hurt them; and those who have some small fortune would easily find such methods for the distribution of the tax burden so that taxes fall only upon the rich and benefit only the poor, something which the rich would not be able to do if they had the power.[68]

Taxes do not hurt those who make the decisions concerning them. And de Tocqueville states his judgment on "the democratic wastefulness": *"In other words—democracy is the only regime in which those who decide upon a tax can exempt themselves from paying it"* (italics in original).[69]

General suffrage gives the ruling power to the poor. Democracy thus becomes a very expensive form of government. It functions better, the more citizens there are who own something:

> From this point of view, general suffrage would be less dangerous in France than in England, where almost all wealth is collected in a few hands. American, where the great majority of citizens own something, is in an even more favourable position.[70]

A DIGRESSION CONCERNING POLITICAL DEMOCRACY IN THE UNITED STATES

Walter Korpi deals in an article with changes in voter participation in elections in the United States during the industrial breakthrough around the end of the nineteenth century.[71] His analysis shows that the political development parallels in important respects the arguments put forth by the classical liberals. Around 1830 almost all white males in the United States had voting rights. Participation in elections was high: for example, in the South in the 1870s and 1880s, it was around 85%.

The industrialization process changed this. In various ways, universal suffrage was in practice made less universal. Various measures aimed at restraining immigrating laborers were implemented. Korpi writes:

> The still large rural population, the native middle class, and the growing bourgeoisie saw their interests threatened by the teeming masses of workers—in great part new immigrants—in the industrialized countries.
>
> How could the privileged groups in American society protect their interests and at the same time preserve the democratic state? The solutions which gradually emerged did not, of course, follow any master plan aimed at diminishing democracy. But combined, the various measures led to a sharp decrease in voter participation after the turn of the century and the partial exclusion of large groups from democracy.
>
> One type of protective measure made it much more difficult for the lower classes to vote. In cities over a certain size the demand for personal registration long before election day was instituted. Citizens who had retained their foreign citizenship were no longer allowed to vote. Literacy exams in English were instituted in many states.[72]

The parallel to the suffrage limitations discussed by Bentham and John Stuart Mill (see 6.3), among others, is clear.

Civic rights carries a heavy ballast when introduced as a basic principle for economic democracy. Historically it is tied to the liberal argument for private property and economic freedom. The labor movement has restricted itself to dealing with general suffrage as the primary means of struggle; politically, this has meant the acceptance of a sharp distinction between political and economic power, and it has meant that the labor movement has been satisfied with being a participant in the former. Such a thought was rather foreign to the classical liberals; for them political power was indivisibly bound to economic power. Alf Ross, in his classic *Varför demokrati?* says that democracy should be seen as "political method, a pan-ideology, not a norm for the ordering of the content of social relations."[73] As we have seen, the classical theoreticians of democracy were most often quite conscious of the fact that "the ordering of the content of social relations" (i.e., property relations) was of extraordinary importance for the form of democracy *they* wished to see realized.

6.5 Summary

Tingsten concludes the section in which he comments on Mill in the following way:

> It is superfluous to give any further examples of the line of reasoning in the democratic discussion with which we have dealt here. The thought that democracy takes care of the interests of all or of the great majority still belongs to the most commonly and energetically asserted arguments in the debate. . . . [One] says that popular government, because all may assert their influence, must favor the common well-being, promote the good of the great majority, etc.[74]

The examples of arguments from certain of the democratic authors which we have presented suggest—to express it cautiously—that the efforts to "promote the good of the great majority" contain significant reservations. If one reads critically, one cannot preclude the interpretation that these limitations have been made precisely in order to *prevent* the "interest of the great majority" from being executed, or in any case that the classical writers readily reserved for the propertyowners the right to determine what the interests of the unpropertied people were.

Much of what, for example, Locke, Bentham, and Mill write may be interpreted to show that these writers were in favor of a complete expansion of civic rights. The weakness in this method of interpretation becomes apparent, however, when their conceptions of who should be viewed as a citizen are studied. Here a clear distinction is often made between various categories of the population and various classes in terms of differing degrees of rationality. Those who have the capacity to rule society are the men; they are the educated, but above all, they are the property owners. The real effect of the argumentation of the classical authors on this issue is that power—both political and economic—for the most part remains in the hands of the social strata which already hold it. For example, during the French Revolution a distinction was made between "active" and "passive" citizens; an income limitation excluded the latter from the right to vote.[75] The National Assembly "made suffrage dependent upon a certain wealth and made the right to be elected dependent upon the possession of a certain amount of real property."[76]

The traditional link between economic and political power was first broken as the unpropertied social groups, through increased class consciousness and political organization, began to demand power during the nineteenth century. The power they won for themselves was *political* power, not economic—the latter remained for the most part where it had previously been. The breakthrough of political democracy, i.e., civic rights, signifies the attainment of power by previously unrepresented elements of the population. But this authority could only be exercised over a sharply reduced portion of the social field of power.

Chapter 7

THE LABOR THEORY OF VALUE AND THE SUBJECTIVE THEORY OF VALUE

In earlier chapters we have reviewed a number of legal principles related to the question of original acquisition (Chapter 2); we have studied certain features of European economic and historical development and the relationship between this development and economic doctrine (Chapter 4); we have studied the connection between notions of ownership and political ideology (Chapter 5); and we have looked closely at the foundations of the democratic theory implemented in Western Europe and the United States since the nineteenth century (Chapter 6). A pervasive theme throughout this study is the concept of *composite production* as the most important principle for economic organization, legal systems, and the formation of economic and political doctrine. This concept draws strength from the subjective theory of value, which began to successfully compete with the previously widely accepted labor theory of value during the nineteenth century. The subjective theory of value is, in economic, historical, theoretical, and political respects, an expression of the expanding market and the increasingly widespread capitalist method of production.

What demands may be made on a theory which is economically and politically oriented toward wage earners, i.e., toward the direct producers? It is our opinion—presented below—that the subjective theory of value is severely handicapped in this regard and is in important respects antagonistic to the workers' interests and endeavors, and that the merits and strengths of the labor theory of value to a great extent have been neglected in the debate, even within the labor movement. (Evidence for this assertion follows in Chapter 8.) In this chapter we shall compare the two theories against the background of the broader goal of creating a basis of organization and principle for a social order which recognizes labor as the original source of acquisition.

The foundation of the labor theory of value is the thesis that an object acquires value by virtue of the amount of human labor invested in it. "Objects" include tools, machines, buildings, etc., that is to say, means of production (see Section 2.2) or—more generally—capital. The explanation of the origin of capital is unequivocal and definite: labor gives rise to capital, and labor is, together with the raw materials which become the objects of production, a necessary precondition for the creation of capital.

In the next stage, the growing capital is in turn a condition for expanded production.

.But as regards the simple, genetic question—which comes first, labor or capital?—the labor theory of value gives an unequivocal answer: labor constitutes the starting point for further economic development. "Every child knows that a country which ceased to work . . . would die."[1]

7.1 Objections to the Labor Theory of Value

For most economists today, the labor-value thesis seems unreasonable for several reasons. First of all, they say, the determination of the value of a commodity is made up not only of remuneration to those who contributed their labor, but also to those who provided machines, buildings, land, and working capital. It is, according to this point of view, in other words, not justifiable to ascribe specifically to *labor* the dominant role as a production factor.

Second, the notion that commodities have any real, inherent, objective value of their own is usually denied. The exchange-value of a certain commodity is determined entirely by the potential buyer's *subjective estimation* of the value of the commodity in relation to other commodities. Value is the same as price or exchange-value.

Third, the labor theory of value is attacked on purely technical grounds. In the complicated process involved in the modern production of commodities, the part which arises through human labor becomes less and less visible and thus less and less possible to measure. Extraction of raw materials, prefab production, production and assembly of the finished product, packaging, and distribution—all of this is done to an increasing degree by machine. According to the labor theory of value, the labor which is invested in the production of, say, machines should also be included in the value of the commodity. This, according to modern economists, makes empirical investigation almost insurmountably difficult. The theory of marginal utility—which places the primary importance upon what occurs in the *exchange process* and not in the production of the commodity—offers much better assistance by assigning to supply and demand the main roles in the determination of value. "Value" is assessed as a property of the commodity at the moment of exchange (for, say, money) and not as a permanent property deriving from the amount of labor invested in it.

These three arguments—the notion of production factors equal in principle, the denial of the notion of real value, and the calculation argument—will be dealt with in this chapter, although the latter only very briefly. Let us begin with that.

To an extraordinary extent the criticism of the labor theory of value is based on empirical arguments derived from an interest in technical (in contrast to legal-political) knowledge. There is an intensive discussion between Marxist (Dobb, Robinson, Morishima, and others) and non-Marxist (Samuelson, and others) economists concerning the advantages and disadvantages of the value theories with respect to the possibility of predicting price variations and changes in the supply and demand of commodities on the market. This discussion will be passed over here, partly for lack of space, but partly—and most importantly—because it deals with very limited aspects of the labor theory of value. A treatment of the two theories of value on technical grounds would presuppose the assumption that the labor theory of value—in any case, in Marx' interpretation—was created for the purpose of aiding in the analysis of relatively short-term price variations. But this is not the purpose of the labor theory of value: it was created as a means of dealing with historical changes in production relations and relations between classes in a society based upon private ownership of the means of production. A primary element in the discussion of this was the treatment of the concept surplus-value:

> [T]he value theory was never intended as a theory of price, which, as a superficial manifestation of the bourgeois economy, Marx considered worth very little attention, but was instead designed to explain something to him far more fundamental: the process of production, i.e., the extraction of surplus values in the various sectors of the economy.[2]

Marx did, of course, devote a significant amount of attention to the so-called transformation problem, i.e., how value is transformed to price. The reason, however, according to Baumol, was not because he considered the question important to his own purpose. For Marx it was a matter of dealing instead with the more important problem of the relation between profit and surplus-value. Here the discussion of relative prices constituted a pedagogical obstacle: "To Marx, indeed, it was worth discussing only to reveal its irrelevance . . . so that the basic truth about the production of surplus value could be revealed."[3]

Two additional circumstances should be noted. The labor theory of value has met with resistance on political grounds ever since Ricardo. Academic economists began to attack it seriously during the first decades of the nineteenth century when it was adopted as a theory by representatives of the emerging working class. It cannot be precluded that this constituted an obstacle to its development as a technical economic tool.

Second, it may be claimed that the subjective theory of value is correct because it has been *used* for economic prediction and analysis for a long time. But the fact that a theory has been in use is not an argument for its correctness. The geocentric theory—the thought that the earth is the center of the universe—was used for centuries in astronomy. The phlogiston theory—the idea that all combustible material contained a special element, phlogiston—for a long time enjoyed considerable popularity among chemists of the eighteenth century. Many observations could be shown to agree with the theories; nevertheless, there are few today who would claim that they are correct.

In a similar way, observations of variations in supply and demand which seem to accord with the predictions of marginalistic economics cannot be used as proof of the correctness of the theory (especially if it is claimed that marginalism is the *only* correct theory). Modern marginalism—derived from the subjective theory of value—is a theory which is applicable to the study of price formation and market relations. If higher goals are set, so that they also include demands for an explanation of socioeconomic historical changes, then it has little to offer.

7.2 The Labor Theory of Value: Ricardo and Marx

During the course of the eighteenth century the idea was gradually developed that commodities consisted of amounts of accumulated or "crystallized" labor, with each different part of the division of labor contributing its share. It was not enough that *labor* had been invested in the commodities; in addition, it was a question of *social labor,* i.e., the collected efforts of people who stood in definite social relationships to each other—relationships governed by productive forces and the prevailing method of production. The amount of labor-time which had to be invested in the production of a commodity in a particular society at a particular level of economic development could thus be seen as a constant measure of the value of a commodity ("socially necessary labor").

This thesis—formulated first by Ricardo and later developed by Marx—signified an important modification and purging of Smith's theory. Smith had differentiated between two kinds of measures of labor-value: a measure of the labor embodied in a commodity and a measure concerning how much labor could be *bought* or commanded:

> The value of any commodity, therefore, to the person who possesses it, and who means not to use or consume it himself, but to exchange it for other commodities, is equal to the quantity of labour which it enables him to purchase or command. Labour, therefore, is the real measure of the exchangeable value of all commodities.[4]

The most obvious interpretation of this statement is that the value is dependent upon *wage costs.* Money or commodities "contain the value of a certain quantity of labour which we exchange for what is supposed at the time to contain the value of an equal quantity."[5]

Smith's concept "commandable labor" was sharply attacked by Ricardo. Smith had intended to create a constant and nonvariable measure of value. He presented, however, *two* measures with differing properties, of which only one—the labor invested in the commodity—could be accepted, according to Ricardo. Commandable labor made the value dependent upon the *price* which was paid for the labor, and Smith's assumption seems to be that the price always stands in relation to the worker's productivity. Smith reasons, says Ricardo, "as if because a man's labour had become doubly efficient, and he could therefore produce twice the quantity of a commodity, he would necessarily receive twice the former quantity in exchange for [his labour]."[6] Ricardo thought that this was wrong: paid wages in no way paralleled the increase of productivity. "It is very seldom that the whole additional produce obtained with the same quantity of labour falls to the lot of the labourers who produce it."[7]

Ricardo's contribution meant, among other things, a reduction in the ambiguity contained in Smith's concept of commandable labor and a distillation of the notion of the socially necessary labor invested in the commodities (including the labor time spent for the production of the means of production).[8] Thus were laid the most important parts of the foundation upon which Marx was to build the labor theory of value. Marx's recognition of Ricardo's contribution is also clear and distinct, especially with respect to the definition of value:

> At last, however, Ricardo comes on the stage, and calls to science: Halt!—The foundation, the starting point for the physiology of the bourgeois system—for the understanding of its internal organic coherence and life process—is the determination of *value by labor time.*[9]

The conceptual skeleton outlined by Smith and Ricardo would later be filled out and given form by Marx in his thinking on capital accumulation, surplus-value, and class contradictions. Before we enter into this section, a few words should be said about the reception of Ricardo's work and the criticism it received, especially after his death in 1823.

The retreat of the labor theory of value—and, as we shall discuss below, its replacement by utilitarian lines of thought—was related partly to certain ambiguities in Ricardo's own formulations and partly to the fact that the defense of Ricardo's theory after his death was managed by disciples who were often more devoted than talented.[10]

MARX AND SURPLUS-VALUE

The axis around which this political criticism moves is surplus-value. Since we are beginning here a discussion of the specific Marxian variant of the labor theory of value, a section briefly summarizing Marx's theory is in order. There are considerable difficulties in making a *short* summary. We choose, therefore, to quote from a work by a group of writers who have wrestled with the task and who, in our opinion, have done well:[11]

> Marx begins his analysis of the capitalist social system with an analysis of the *commodity,* since this constitutes "the cell of the bourgeois society, containing in itself all the contradictions of the system."

Like Ricardo, Marx differentiates between the *use-value* and the *exchange-value* of the commodity. Use-value is a qualitative property of the commodity, while exchange-value is a quantitative property.

> Every useful thing, as iron, paper, etc., may be looked at from the two points of view of quality and quantity.

That commodities have exchange-value means that there exists a common property or substance in them which makes it possible to quantitatively compare them to each other. This property is that all commodities are products of human labor. It is thus the *quantity of invested human labor* in the commodity which determines its exchange value.

The quantity of invested human labor is measured in *labor-time*. But the exchange value for each individual commodity is measured not by the labor-time invested in the individual commodity, but rather by the *socially necessary labor-time:*

> The labor-time socially necessary is that required to produce an article under the normal conditions of production, and with the average degree of skill and intensity prevalent at the time.

Socially necessary labor includes both the labor invested *directly* by the laborer and the labor which has previously been *indirectly* invested in the other commodities and tools which have been used in production.

Does profit arise through all sellers selling their commodities *above* their value and all buyers buying them under their values? No, says Marx, for then the seller would lose what he has won as a seller as soon as he appeared as a buyer.

The exchange of equally large values thus constitutes a starting point in the explanation of the origin of profit. And still the capitalist must get out of production a larger value than he puts in. . . . The capitalist must therefore find in the market a commodity whose actual use-value is being a *source* of value. This commodity is *labor* or the ability to labor.

In order for this transaction to take place, certain historical conditions must be fulfilled. There must exist a class of unpropertied people who own nothing more than their labor and who must sell it in order to live.

As with all other commodity values, the value of labor is determined by the labor-time which is necessary for its production and reproduction. It is equal to *the labor-time which is spent to produce the necessities for the subsistence of the worker and his family.* This value is determined not only by minimum physical needs, but also by historical and cultural factors, which vary from country to country and from time to time.

Assume that the commodities needed for the reproduction of labor each day are produced in four hours. The worker receives a wage each day which corresponds to four hours of labor. The labor is thus sold (exchanged) for its value. But the worker does not work four hours, but rather eight hours per day, and during this time he produces a value corresponding to eight work hours. The time the worker labors to compensate for the value of the labor Marx calls *necessary labor-time,* and the rest of the day consists of *surplus labor.* The value of this surplus labor is *surplus-value* (s), which the capitalist appropriates. This is how profit originates.

The value of the raw materials, tools, machines, etc., expended in the production of the commodity is called by Marx *constant capital* (c), since its value is not changed in the production process but is only transferred to the new product.

On the other hand, that part of capital, represented by labour-power, does, in the process of production, undergo an alteration of value. It both reproduces the equivalent of its own value, and also produces an excess, a surplus-value, which may itself vary, may be more or less according to circumstances. This part of capital is continually being transformed from a constant into a variable magnitude. I therefore call it the variable part of capital, or, shortly, *variable capital.*

If the variable capital is labeled v, then the value of the commodity may be written:

$$C' = c + v + s$$

The *rate of surplus value* (s/v) indicates the degree of exploitation, i.e., how great the capitalist's exploitation of the worker is. The *rate of profit* (s/c + v) indicates the size of the profit which the capitalist receives on all of the invested capital (c + v).

The constant capital is expended for the replacement of exhausted means of production, the variable capital goes to the worker, and the surplus-value goes to the capitalist. In Marx's theory of value we can thus see *a direct connection between the relations among people in production and the income distribution in society.*

Once Marx—by assuming that commodities are sold at their values—had shown how profit arose, he wanted to show how surplus-value was distributed within the capitalist class. Or, and this is the same thing, that what on the surface of society appeared as profit, interest, etc. had arisen through exploitation of the worker.

He shows how the total surplus-value in society is distributed through competition among the various capitalists in the form of profit and interest in proportion to their invested capital. By showing how values are *transformed* to production prices it is also shown how surplus-value is transformed to profit, interest, and land rent.

MEEK ON THE NOTION OF SURPLUS-VALUE

According to certain opponents of the labor theory of value, the concept of surplus-value is derived from the labor theory of value and thus is an abstract, theoretical construction. If this thesis is correct, says Meek, then the most frequent accusations against the labor theory of value as an instrument for political motives would make sense. This is, however, not the case, he claims; on the contrary, the labor theory of value was formed in order to explain the *manifest existence* of surplus-value.

The difference in value between input and output in production was viewed by the classical economists as an empirical fact, the existence of which could not be denied, but the origin and extent of which were in need of *study*. Not surprisingly, the economists' value judgments on surplus-value vary. Smith considered it for the most part a good and obvious fact that landowners and capitalists appropriated surplus-value, while William Thompson, for example, largely condemned such a system.[12] It was, in Meek's opinion, the emergence of a strong and articulate labor movement which caused the concept of surplus-value to be accused of being ethically and politically loaded.[13] These accusations— which arose long after the labor theory of value had begun to be formulated—hardly give reason to deny the labor theory of value its scientific worth.

7.3 The Labor Theory of Value: Some Problems

Marx does not—in keeping with what was said above—go to the trouble of addressing the accusations against the notion of surplus-value which contend that it was primarily politically motivated.[14] Rather, preparatory works for *Capital* show many traces of efforts to solve problems which had been insufficiently treated by the classical economists and to supplement the labor theory of value (primarily Ricardo's version) in the areas where it met criticism.

Marx summarizes the criticism and suggests answers in the following way:

Since Ricardo gave to classical political economy its final shape, having formulated and elaborated with the greatest clearness the law of the determination of exchange value by labor-time, it is natural that all the polemics among economists should center about him. Stripped of its puerile form this controversy comes down to the following points:

First: Labor itself has exchange value, and different kinds of labor have different exchange values. We get into a vicious circle by making exchange value the measure of exchange value, because the measuring exchange value needs a measure itself. This objection may be reduced to the following problem: Given labor-time as the intrinsic measure of exchange value, develop from that the determination of wages. The theory of wages gives the answer to that.[15]

[Concerning this, Marx has previously said the following:] In order to measure commodities by the labor-time contained in them, the different kinds of labor must be reduced to uniform, homogeneous, simple labor, in short, to labor which is qualitatively the same, and, therefore, differs only in quantity. . . . [I]n so far as labor is represented by exchange values, it may be defined as human labor in general. This abstraction of human labor in general virtually exists in the average labor which the average individual of a given society can perform—a certain productive expenditure of human muscles, nerves, brain, etc. It is unskilled labor to which the average individual can be put and which he has to perform in one way or another. The character of this average labor varies in different countries and at different stages of civilization, but appears fixed in a particular society.[16]

Second: If the exchange value of a product is equal to the labor-time contained in it, then the exchange value of one day of labor is equal to the product of that labor. In other words, wages must be equal to the product of labor. But the very opposite is actually the case. Ergo this objection comes down to the following problem: How does production, based on the determination of exchange value by labor-time only, lead to the result that the exchange value of labor is less than the exchange value of its product? This problem is solved by us in the discussion of capital. [And by developing the concept of surplus-value—our note.]

Third: The market price of commodities either falls below or rises above its exchange value with the changing relations of supply and demand. *Therefore,* the exchange value of commodities is determined by the relation of supply and demand and not by the labor-time contained in them. As a matter of fact, this queer conclusion merely amounts to the question, how a market price based on exchange value can deviate from that exchange value; or, better still, how does the law of exchange value assert itself only in its antithesis? This problem is solved in the theory of competition.[17]

Fourth: The last and apparently the most striking objection, if not raised in the usual form of queer examples: If exchange value is nothing but mere labor-time contained in commodities, how can commodities which contain no labor possess exchange-value, or in other words, whence the exchange value of mere forces of nature? This problem is solved in the theory of rent.[18]

COMMENTS

The first problem addressed by Marx above concerns the issue of labor-time as a measure of exchange-value. The value of each commodity is best expressed in the time it takes to produce it. At once the problem arises that commodities produced by slow and unskillful workers seem to be of greater value (since more time has been expended). Marx answers that such an argument is a misunderstanding of the idea of the value of labor. Basic to it is the concept abstract ("average") labor, i.e., as we mentioned earlier, the socially necessary labor-time which is used for the production of a commodity, given the skill and intensity of production existing in society at a given time. Marx exemplifies:

> The introduction of power looms into England probably reduced by one half the labour required to weave a given quantity of yarn into cloth. The hand-loom weavers, as a matter of fact, continued to require the same time as before; but for all that, the product of one hour of their labour represented after the change only half an hour's social labour, and consequently fell to one-half its former value.[19]

The second problem, along with Marx's contributions to its solution, is so well known that it may largely be passed over, after what has been said in the review above. The exchange-value of one day of labor was, as Marx pointed out, in no way equal to its product. On the contrary, the worker produced far more than he received in wages. Exploitation is a given *consequence* of the natural laws of commodity production under capitalism. "However much ... the capitalist mode of appropriation may appear to flout the primary laws of commodity production, it nevertheless arises, not from any violation of these laws, but, on the contrary, from their operation."[20]

Third, how should one interpret Marx's formulation that "the law of exchange-value is merely realized in its opposite"? Pointing out a temporary "balance" between supply and demand was, for Marx, more than anything a *beginning* of the problem, not its solution. The fact that there was a "balance"

> was taken by Marx as an indication that the level of the equilibrium price could not be adequately explained merely in terms of the interaction of these forces. The relation of supply and demand could certainly explain *deviations* from the equilibrium price, but it could not explain the level of the equilibrium price itself. It was in fact precisely *through* fluctuations in "supply and demand" that the law of value operated to determine the equilibrium price.[21]

Both Marx's own presentation and Meek's interpretation of his reasoning on supply and demand are complicated and difficult to follow. As we implied above with our reference to Baumol, this seems to be due in large part to the fact that the problem Marx dealt with was confined to the process which *led to* the product attaining a certain value around which the price could fluctuate. The fluctuation itself was of lesser interest, even if the market price—to be discussed in the next section—had some mysterious properties.

To deal with Marx's last problem, how was it possible that commodities which clearly contained no labor could attain an exchange-value? Did this not conflict with the theory, which had tied exchange-value to labor-time?

Ricardo had wrestled with this difficulty—without arriving at any solution—in connection with attempts to explain how wine, stored in a cellar, could increase its value from year to year, in spite of the fact that it had not been the object of any additional labor. Ricardo's colleagues and disciples—among them James Mill and J. R. McCulloch—had drawn a certain amount of ridicule by stating that "hoarded labor" (i.e., capital) created the growing value of the wine or that the "labor of nature" caused it.[22] The dogmatic confinement to the labor theory of value was so strong that explanations other than those couched in terms of labor were unthinkable.

Marx comes to the aid of Ricardo with the concept of rent. More specifically, this concerned the extra advantages which accompanied the possibilities—for those capitalowners who possessed, say, a waterfall or especially productive land—for monopolizing the forces of nature. "The surplus profit for the factory using the waterfall" could be explained neither with capital as the only factor nor through reference solely to labor:

> The increased productiveness of the labour used by him comes neither from the capital and labour itself, nor from the mere application of some natural force different from capital and labour but incorporated in the capital. . . . The possession of this natural force constitutes a monopoly in the hands of its owner; it is a condition for an increase in the productiveness of the invested capital that cannot be established by the production process of the capital itself; this natural force, which can be monopolized in this manner, is always bound to the land.[23]

However, the problem concerning "the exchange-value of mere forces of nature" did not take up much space in Marx's theory. In practice, it was often disregarded by assuming the value of landed property to be zero.[24]

TO START WITH PRODUCTION

The notion of value as an expression of "embodied labor" fulfills, among other things, the important function of pointing out "that the economic process should be analyzed in terms of people's relations with each other and in terms of people [engaged] in the production of commodities." This thesis summarizes what may be Marx's most important contribution to the labor theory of value—the thesis that relations between people in the commodity-producing society are often disguised as relations between things. The thesis of commodity fetishism is expressed as follows:

> Since the producers do not come into social contact with each other until they exchange their products, the specific social character of each producer's labour does not show itself except in the act of exchange. In other words, the labour of the individual asserts itself as a part of the labour of society, only by means of the relations which the act of exchange establishes directly between the products, and indirectly, through them, between the producers. To the latter, therefore, the relations connecting the labour of one individual with that of the rest appear, not as direct social relations between individuals at work, but as what they really are, material relations between persons and social relations between things.[25]

Because this apparent "relation between things" must be penetrated, it is necessary to investigate the production process, and to begin the social analysis at that point. Marx thought a study of consumption to be an incorrect method for political economy:

> If you proceed from production, you necessarily concern yourself with the real conditions of production and with the productive activity of man. But if you proceed from consumption, you merely declare that consumption is not

at present "human," that it is necessary to cultivate true consumption, and so on. Content with this, you can afford to ignore the real living conditions and the activity of men.[26]

As we now go on to describe and comment upon utilitarianism and the theory of marginal use, it is worth noting that they do just what Marx argues against in the passage cited above: they start with consumption.

7.4 The Subjective Theory of Value

The emerging labor movement and revolutionary movements in Europe attained through Marx and the labor theory of value a theoretical and political justification, an explanation in terms of historical development and economic contradictions.

The labor theory of value was, however, gradually pushed aside. The time after Ricardo's death up to the end of the nineteenth century is characterized by a paradigmatic shift in economic thinking. During this time, the labor theory of value and political economy were replaced by the subjective theory of value, in the form of various theories of marginal utility derived from utilitarianism.

The theories of marginal utility, which we will have reason to discuss in more detail below, were, in turn, the foundation for modern economics or "marginalism." The explicit reference to the utility concept has disappeared or been toned down in these later theories. In the theory of marginal utility it was, as T. W. Hutchison has said, "the adjective rather than the noun which was preserved."[27] However, the bonds between early marginal utility theorists like Jevons, Menger, and Walras, and modern economics are strong.[28]

Who were the main contributors to the new economic thinking, and what were the economic and political reasons behind it? The first question has been treated in detail by Eric Roll; and we shall later refer to his reasoning in *A History of Economic Thought*. But when it comes to the possible *reasons* for the historical shift of doctrine, Roll has little to say. Naturally, a discussion of this point must be more speculative. Considerable evidence shows, however, that the emergence of the subjective theory of value was not primarily the product of an internal scientific process, but is better explained with reference to the economic and political development in Europe during the nineteenth century. A few hypotheses on this will be presented later in the chapter.

THE PARADIGMATIC SHIFT: SCIENTIFIC PRODUCTION

Smith's version of the labor theory of value was built upon the trisection capital/labor/land, and it brought attention to the distribution of the surplus between the classes capitalowner/wage earner/landowner. Both Smith and Ricardo clearly hint that capitalowners should be allowed greater returns through emancipation of market forces and that the privileges of the landowners should be subjected to debate.

During the period we are discussing here it gradually became clear that the conflicts between industrialists and landowners were being resolved to the advantage of the former. Another conflict emerged—that between capitalowners and wage earners. The surplus from production tended to grow; at the same time the consequences of its distribution became increasingly clear. The thought that each class of economic participants was allotted its own portion of the surplus accorded less and less with a situation in which *one* of these groups—capitalowners—became increasingly dominant. Thus, the trisection of the classical theory was no longer especially correct.

The theory's problems were exacerbated by the use of labor as a general measure of value. One did not need to have notable economic powers of observation to see that the labor investment received unproportionate reward. The labor theory of value fit like a poorly tailored suit: it needed either to be resewn—i.e., complemented and provided with new elements—or replaced. As Roll points out, a complement would probably have meant the addition of a line of reasoning on exploitation.[29] The contradictions in the distribution issues would then have been brought more to the fore, without other questions (e.g., the explanation of price formation) being brought any closer to their solutions.

Instead, the theoretical development took another path:

> Instead of continuing the attempts made by Ricardo (and later by Marx) to preserve the labour theory through the complications of a developed capitalist system, a number of economists in France, Germany, and England chose a different path. They did not try to show that, in spite of certain modifications, the labour theory of value held good . . . nor did they continue to use the concept of the surplus in the explanation of the capitalist's profit. *They gradually abandoned the labour theory of value in favour of a different principle of explanation which eliminated the ides of the surplus*—in so far, at any rate, as it implied a theory of exploitation.
>
> *In technical terms this involved the development of a utility theory of value and, as a corollary to it, the admission of the productivity of capital* [our italics].[30]

Perhaps the most important consequence of the utility line of thought was—as the quotation suggests—that capital and labor were equated as production factors in the theoretical treatment.

Important contributors to the emerging theory of marginal utility were Abbé Condillac, J. B. Say, and Augustin Cournot. In England, the paradigmatic shift from the labor theory of value to the subjective theory of value was represented primarily by Senior and Bailey. There were also a number of German economists working in the same vein.

Condillac launched the thought that "utility" as an economic concept is not an inherent property in the *commodity*, but rather something which the individual/consumer *ascribes* to the commodity according to his needs. Thus, utility is not an absolute concept, but rather a *relation*; utility increases or decreases according to the wants of the individual.[31]

This idea has several consequences. First, attention is drawn to the *exchange process* rather than to the production process. The main question becomes how the commodity is received and subjectively judged. Against this background, it is expedient to see the exchange process as a direct determinant of the commodity's value. One part to an exchange offers something which to him is less useful than that which the other party offers in return. Third, the *supply* or *scarcity* of a commodity becomes an important factor in determining its exchange-value. The production costs become merely an indirect determinant. "Value in exchange was an expression of subjective estimates of utilities in terms of quantities. Cost of production influenced price only through changes of supply."[32] Fourth, Condillac and Say, among others, took a decisive step away from the distinction in the labor theory of value between productive and unproductive labor, i.e., between labor which does and labor which does not create surplus-value. According to Say, all participants in the production of utilities which give rise to a market price should be viewed as productive.[33]

A fifth consequence of the adaptation of utilitarianism and the subjective theory of value to economics was a new and radically different way of dealing with the distribution issue. Once the labor theory of value was abandoned, the concept of "surplus" had to be abandoned also. Surplus had been defined by Adam Smith in terms of the labor which had been invested in the commodity and which gave it an *added value*.[34] This definition caused significant theoretical problems for Smith, problems which Marx later tried to attack through the use of the theory of surplus-value.

Once the question of surplus-value and its distribution was eliminated, the door was open to the formal equation of labor with other production factors. Condillac and Say saw production as a cooperative process in which all factors held the same position. "All factors possessed both qualities necessary for the creation of value: scarcity and an indirect utility."[35] Say anticipated a great number of later economists with his idea that the market and consumer demand determine the economic yield for each production factor.

> [Say] regarded the prices of all factors as dependent upon the prices of their products, thus ultimately on consumers' demands. Although he did not, perhaps, express it very clearly, Say seems to have had in mind the sort of functional connection between cost, price, wages, rent, interest and profit which was to be developed later by the equilibrium school.[36]

Labor was thus no longer seen as the principal value-creating factor. According to this point of view, *all* production factors offered their services to the market and were rewarded according to relative demand. With the subjective theory of value as a foundation, it now became possible analytically to treat labor and capital as equals. It was the British economist Nassau Senior who most clearly developed this line of reasoning.

Senior used a production cost concept which included both labor and capital. Production cost was defined as "the sum of the labour and abstinence necessary to production."[37] Abstinence is Senior's term for the capitalowner's sacrifice when he abstains from immediate use of his money. According to Senior, abstinence stands in "the same relation to profit as labor does to wages."[38]

For Senior, both labor and capital constituted subjective *sacrifices*. Also the lending of money was seen as a psychological cost, a "sacrifice of saving."[39] It is a very small step from this assumption to another, i.e., that capital is also productive.[40]

It is easy to understand the attempts to simplify the theory and the motivation behind an equation of labor and abstinence from capital as "sacrifices." Theories are not, however, mere technical aids; they also have political and ideological functions. In an ideological sense, there are significant differences between the subjective theory of value and the labor theory of value. The former entails as a logical necessity the evaluation of labor as a cost to the individual, i.e., as a negative factor. In the labor theory of value there is no built-in theoretical demand of this type. On the contrary, labor is often seen as a positive, creative activity having important consequences for the individual's development.

> Labour is, in the first place, a process in which both man and Nature participate, and in which man of his own accord starts, regulates, and controls the material re-actions between himself and Nature. He opposes himself to Nature as one of her own forces, setting in motion arms and legs, head and hands, the natural forces of his body, in order to appropriate Nature's productions in a form adapted to his own wants. By thus acting on the external world and changing it, he at the same time changes his own nature.[41]

Further, it should be pointed out that the economists of the subjective theory of value signaled a new methodological direction which was to have far-reaching consequences for the social sciences. The break with political economy signified a departure from the concentration on macroeconomics and the analysis of broad economic developments which had characterized the works of Smith and Ricardo, among others, and which recurred in a somewhat new form in Marx. The object of investigation of the subjective theory of value was the *individual*, not society.

7.5 The Explanatory Ambitions of the Labor Theory of Value and the Subjective Theory of Value

The classical labor theory of value had claimed that society could always be analyzed through a study of labor, landownership and capital (a division which was revised by Marx through a combination of the last two categories). The theory was considered universally valid, and the economic functions which were tied to the three classes comprised parts of a permanent structural pattern.

The advocates of the theory saw before them

a stratified society in which particular social groups were made to correspond to functions in the economic process. This identification (labour—wages, rent—landowners, profits—capitalists) was taken as an implied, but never-changing pattern.[42]

The labor theory of value attempts to explain the function of the economy through a study of *production* and the *social relations* arising from it. The subjective theory of value seeks explanations in how the *individual* functions *psychologically* and investigates which behaviors this evokes in the market.

The labor theory of value concentrates on social structure; production and the economic base are its constant objects of study. The subjective theory of value also claims to be generally valid, but for a different reason. The schools of thought based on utility theory "claim that they develop a theory of value which is independent of any specific social order."[43]

Rather than stressing the permanence of classes, the emphasis is placed on the universality of individual *psychological properties*, what is assumed to be the pervasive human tendency to strive for the satisfaction of needs through a surplus (as Bentham says) of "pleasures" over "pains."

One effect of this was that historical analysis of society was removed from the domain of social science. The subjective theory of value provided a theoretically well-founded reason for economists to abandon the study of specific social forms and the factors related to their development (e.g., class structure). The subjective theory of value could thus also be used as a means of dismissing troublesome questions concerning the distribution of the surplus between social classes as well as demands from the growing working class for more just economic policies. The economic participant now studied was the individual person and not his class. As Roll maintains, the theory of marginal utility became usable as an apology by means of, for example, the thesis that capital was also productive.

The retreat of the labor theory of value

was effected by the introduction of a subjectivism which absolved economists from concerning themselves with a particular social order. Theorems which had been developed on a basis of equal individuals undertaking abstinence and toil and trouble could have nothing to say about the real social differentiation of these individuals.[44]

In spite of partial changes in the original theory, the core of marginalist economics is still a view of the economy as a system composed of individual participants seeking on the market the most advantageous exchange possible for the purpose of attaining the maximum satisfaction of their needs. The mathematical and purely formal features have been refined, however, and few modern economists would claim that their work is directly dependent on an understanding of the utility concept. Augustin Cournot (1801-1877) signaled the separation of the theory of marginal utility and marginalism. The visible ties between the subjective theory of value and modern economics were thus weakened, but as we have already mentioned, this did not change the subjectivist foundations of current economic analysis. We shall discuss in greater detail below the relationship between modern economics and the utility concept.

MARGINALISTIC ECONOMICS AND "UTILITY" PLUS SOME COMMENTS ON COURNOT

A description of the content of modern, marginalistic economics is best served by beginning with the problem which it claims must be solved. Roll explains this problem in the following way:

> The first thing which confronts the economic theorist is an economic reality which, in spite of all its complexity, is at once reducible to a network of exchange transactions in the market. The surface phenomena are those of supply, demand and price. Comparatively little reflection is needed to recognize these factors in all the markets which are the theatre of modern economic activity. In regard to the goods and services which individuals require directly for the satisfaction of their wants, the general purchase-and-sale character of individual behaviour is easy to recognize. But even the transactions of the productive process are seen to resolve themselves into the purchase and sale of raw materials, capital goods, money capital, and labour power. If, then, we regard the economic system as an enormous conglomeration of interdependent markets, the central problem of economic inquiry becomes the explanation of the exchange process, or, more particularly, the explanation of the formation of price.[45]

Regardless of whether the object of explanation is consumption or production, the same model, based on the factors supply and demand, is used. In the utilitarian theory of marginal utility—for example in Jevons's version—there was the additional striving to give utility a fundamental, theoretical explanation which penetrated beyond the "superficial phenomena" supply and demand. Such an explanation was attained through the assumption of a permanent psychological characteristic in the individual. The basic assumption of the "profit of pleasure" was taken from utilitarianism and Bentham, but it has a much older origin in classical hedonism and Epicurus.[46]

As Myrdal says, exchange-value (price) is the only concept of value recognized by marginalism, while both the "fundamental" explanations of "utility" as well as the classical notion of real value (based on incorporated labor) have been abandoned.[47] As for the utility concept, it is certainly true that modern economics does not to any great extent devote itself to deep psychological and metaphysical inquiries into the subjective theory of value. The connection to utilitarianism and hedonism is, however, clearly visible in the marginal utility and equilibrium reasoning which is of central importance for marginalism. Marginal utility is the utility one would have from an additional small unit of the commodity, or the sacrifice which would be part of doing without a small unit, any unit of the entire supply. Myrdal explains the connection between marginal utility and equilibrium in the following way:

> [It is natural that the marginal utility] must be just as large as the price of a commodity (or more correctly: just as large as the marginal utility of money or of whatever else is given in order to acquire the commodity). If the marginal utility were greater, then one obviously would continue to exchange things for it until the marginal utility had sunk to this level (which actually would have risen somewhat). The underlying thought is that marginal utility usually decreases with an increasing total amount of utility, with "the degree of saturation," as it is expressed. In this way one arrives at the state of equilibrium. If, however, the marginal utility should be lower, then one exchanges as much of one's supply as needed to thereby bring the marginal utility up to parity with the marginal utility of that which one receives in exchange.
>
> At equilibrium, i.e., when one has acquired as much as one wants of everything, then the marginal utilities of all commodities are directly proportional to the exchange-values of these same commodities. This means, if we view the problem from the point of view of monetary income, that the marginal utility of what we acquire for one dollar is the same for all commodities. Otherwise it would be profitable to do other things with the monetary income.
>
> One would thereby raise the sum-total utility of monetary income if one acquired more utility than one abstained from in exchange. The reasoning may at once be transferred to the sacrifice side of the felicific calculus. A worker works and a capitalist saves up to the point that an additional effort on his part would cause him more pain than is counterbalanced by the pleasure of payment.[48]

Regularities in the economic behavior of individuals can be shown to exist *without* being given any more profound explanation. Cournot constructed his theory of exchange in this way in the 1830s. The theory was purely formal:

> [Cournot] saw that relations in the market could be regarded as purely formal relations; that certain categories, demand, price, supply, could be regarded as functions of one another; that it was possible, therefore, to express the relations of the market in a series of functional equations; and that economic laws could be formulated in mathematical language.[49]

It is on these grounds—a "value-free" and "nonmetaphysical" formalized rendering of the connection between supply, demand, and price, with no philosophizing on the concept "utility"—that mathematical, marginalistic economics builds its models. The contributions of the Austrian School and Jevons will be briefly mentioned below. We refer the reader to Roll for additional information concerning the development of modern economics.[50]

7.6 Jevons, Menger, Walras, Böhm-Bawerk, and Others

Toward the end of the nineteenth century, an increasing number of economists appeared as interpreters of the subjective theory of value. These later contributions are of a lesser significance in this context since they are primarily further codifications and more systematic presentations of the lines of reasoning demonstrated by, among others, Condillac, Say, and Senior. A few words should, however, be said about them since they, rather than Say, Senior, etc., are often said to represent the paradigmatic shift with which we are dealing here.

The "Austrian School" (Menger and others) occupies a particularly prominent position when the precursors to modern economics are presented in the literature. As we saw above, the decisive steps in the theory of marginal utility were taken much earlier.

The English statistician W. S. Jevons in his book of 1871 *The Theory of Political Economy* (a remarkable title considering that it hardly dealt with *political* economy) presented a coherent and formally consistent theory of value, exchange, and distribution.

Jevons's concentration on the individual as the active subject recurs in Carl Menger (1840-1921). In a polemic with Gustav Schmoller, who was oriented toward macroeconomics and a historical perspective, Jevons maintained the thesis that economy must be studied as the product of a great number of individual behaviors. Menger's "methodological individualism" has modern descendants in, for example, the economists Ludvig von Mises and Friedrich von Hayek, the philosophers Karl Popper, J.W.N. Watkins, and Joseph Agassi, and the sociologists Max Weber and George Homans.[51]

The influence of Cournot converges in Léon Walras's (1834-1910) work *Eléments d'économie politique pure* with the attempt to create a "value-free" economic theory. The conceptual apparatus is essentially the same as that of Jevons, and the definition of exchange-value is based on a combination of utility and scarcity.

We find the basic features of the subjective theory of value once again in Menger's student Eugen von Böhm-Bawerk. The individual and his wants make up the alpha and omega of Böhm-Bawerk's analysis. "Utility" is seen as a factor determining the behavior of the individual. Unlike the case of, say, Cournot, the utility concept has its own theoretical function here.

The independent contribution of Böhm-Bawerk is mainly to be found in a refined theory of capital and rent. Böhm-Bawerk is, however, also known for his criticism of Marx's *Capital*—a critique which we shall discuss below.

Perhaps the most interesting thing in Böhm-Bawerk's contribution is not its detailed content but rather its intent. As is evident below, Böhm-Bawerk's arguments to a great extent miss Marx, since he argues with the subjective theory of value as a practically self-evident premise and reasons as if "value" (subjectively understood) were an unequivocal concept, common to both his own and Marx's theories. Take, for example, the following quotation from Böhm-Bawerk's book *Karl Marx and the Close of His System* of 1869:

> We will begin with a question which will carry us straight to the main point: in what way did Marx arrive at the fundamental proposition of his teaching—the proposition that all value depends solely upon incorporated quantities of labor?
>
> That this proposition is not a self-evident axiom, needing no proof, is beyond doubt. Value and effort, as I have stated at length in another place, are not ideas so intimately connected that one is forced immediately to adopt the view that effort is the basis of value. "That I have toiled over a thing is one fact, and that the thing is worth the toil is another and a different fact, and that the two facts do not always go hand in hand is far too firmly established by experience to admit of any doubt. It is proved by all the labor which is daily wasted on valueless results, owing either to want of technical skill, or to bad speculation, or to simple misfortune; and not less by each of the numerous causes in which a very little toil has a result of very great value."[52]

By postulating a subjective definition of "value," Böhm-Bawerk automatically invalidates Marx's definition of the same term. According to the labor theory of value, a clause such as "all the labor which is daily wasted on valueless results" would be unreasonable, since labor is precisely the factor which endows a product with value. Böhm-Bawerk avoids a discussion of this assumption in the passage cited above. Instead he reasons as if it were self-evident that "effort" and "value" do not belong together. Thus, "labor" (the objective measure of the labor theory of value) could be contrasted with "valueless results" (which is a subjective judgment), and further, "very little toil" (objective) could be contrasted with "very great value" (subjective). By mixing together value concepts of opposite types, and by implicitly assuming that only one (the subjective one) is correct, Böhm-Bawerk then automatically determines the result: Marx's labor theory of value must be dismissed as unreasonable. (It should be interjected that Böhm-Bawerk is wrong when he says that it was Marx's contention that value is determined only by labor. Böhm-Bawerk says that even natural resources must be counted among the factors which give value to a commodity. [53] Marx himself, however, stated this in *Capital,* Vol. I.) [54]

Sweezy maintains that Böhm-Bawerk was not alone in this method of writing. [55] It was commonly assumed among established economists that the subjective theory of value was *the* science of the economic system; thus it was felt that Marx's contributions could be criticized with the aid of the concepts of the subjective theory of value.

The Swedish economist Gustav Cassel in his book *The Nature and Necessity of Interest* made a contribution to the debate on capital and labor which in large part concurs with the above-mentioned authors in the tradition of the subjective theory of value. Cassel's main thesis is that capital as a production factor must be equated with labor, and that the person who provides the capital should be remunerated for the waiting for want-satisfaction which is part of the lending of capital.

"Waiting" as a general production factor is explained to be a universal phenomenon, something which may be applied to *all* economic participants. Whether the person in question is a worker or a capitalowner is of no consequence here. The following quotation is a good example:

> Supposing a set of workmen have built a house, they may themselves wait for the money the use of the house will bring in year after year for a long time to come. But they may not be willing to do so; they may prefer to get the reward of their labour at once; in this case they may find another person willing to take over the function of waiting in their place. This man will then buy the house; the workmen will immediately get their wages; and the buyer will settle down to wait. This shows that waiting is a quite separate function of economic life. It may be taken over by any one who chooses to do it; but there can be no doubt about the fact that somebody must do it. [56]

Commentary. Notice the hypothetical situation which Cassel constructs. He imagines that the laborers are in a situation where they themselves can mobilize the capital necessary for building the house. Then he assumes that they may choose between being immediately remunerated for the construction of the house or waiting to be rewarded for their labor. If they don't *want* to wait, then they may look for a person who is willing to bear the cost of abstinence in their place, i.e., who is willing to wait for the yield.

Admittedly, we are dealing here with a hypothetical example, and it should not be supposed that Cassel had any but purely pedagogical intentions with this line of reasoning (with the emphasis on *this*—in other contexts he could be strongly polemic). Nevertheless, the example is interesting as a reflection of the severe simplifications—not to say distortions—of reality which are necessary in order to make the theory function. In reality it is extremely rare that workers build houses with the hope of obtaining long-term income. The situation for them is usually completely different than for the capitalowner. They can usually not *choose* to leave their remuneration on deposit; quite to the contrary, for the most part

they must withdraw their payment at once in order to cover the immediate costs of their own subsistence and that of their families. In reality it
is usually not the workers who find a person well equipped with capital
who is willing to assume the abstinence function. Rather, in the great
majority of cases it is the capitalowner who "finds" workers for building a
house.

7.7 The Paradigmatic Shift: Hypotheses
on Political and Economic Causes

An explanation of the breakthrough of the subjective theory of value
solely in terms of its own properties is insufficient. The emergence of the
subjective theory of value seems to a great degree related to its ability to
summarize, formulate, and interpret phenomena connected to mass production and mass consumption which became increasingly visible in European industrial societies during the rise of capitalism.

The continuing industrial capital concentration and the increased efficiency of industrial production had created a market of a previously
unknown kind. The violently expanding production (for example in the
textile sector) and the less expensive products which followed soon made
parts of Europe's population potential consumers of the new industrial
products. The new theory seemed to provide explanations of consumer
behavior and a rational explanation of the phenomenon supply and
demand. Price formation, which until then had been explained with
reference to the production process, could now be given a significantly
simpler interpretation, based on the individual psychology of the consumer. As a by-product of this, questions of long-term changes in society
lost their interest. "One searches in vain for a theory of development
among the marginalists. . . . In spite of the fact that they lived in a time
marked by revolutionary change, their theories were essentially static,
short-term theories, in contrast to the essentially dynamic conceptions of,
say, Adam Smith and David Ricardo."[57]

Further, the complexity of the production process increased immensely
with industrialism's expansion. The more a production process is marked
by the craft element, the more reasonable it is to try to estimate a
product's value with the aid of the labor-time which has been invested in
the product. It is not unreasonable to imagine that a person who bought a
product via the medieval market was well acquainted with its labor
content—perhaps because the buyer had seen the craftsman do the labor or
because he had himself participated in similar production within his own
household. Thus, the justness of the price asked by the seller could most
likely be rather easily judged against the background of what the buyer
knew about the production process.

Because of the increasing expansion of production by machine, because
the number of steps on the path between raw material and finished
product increased, and because the opportunity for direct, personal obser-

vation of production decreased, the purely technical difficulty of calculating the amount of labor contained in a product increased. This seems to
have contributed to the decreasing interest in the labor theory of value,
and to the fact that the subjective theory of value became correspondingly
more attractive.

In addition, the subjective theory of value could—as Roll points out—be
used to legitimize the existing capitalist system of production. The subjective theory of value introduced the thought that even capital was productive, and thus labor and capital were equated as production factors. Labor
was regarded as a subjective sacrifice. The same was true of forgoing
capital, or "abstinence." One by-product of regarding labor as a sacrifice
was the indirect underscoring of the role of the consumer. Jevons, for
example, speaks of "the irksomeness of work" and "the painfulness of
labor," which the laborer puts up with only because of compensatory
rewards.[58]

Related to this—and a direct consequence of the theory—was the
abandonment of the thought that society could be analyzed as composed
of various classes (capitalowners, workers, and landowners). Attention was
instead shifted by the subjective theory of value to the individual as an
"atomistic" unit and an autonomously active participant in the market (a
participant who in the typical case stands for the supply of labor and the
demand for industrial products).

It is not difficult to imagine that those who were economically and
politically powerful in the industrial countries regarded the theories of
marginal utility as both correct and welcome interpretations. One could
say, after all, that the economy ultimately depends upon the individual's
decision to buy or not to buy a certain commodity. And individuals, like
their market behavior, could be observed; "class," on the other hand, was
an abstract phenomenon which no one could claim to have seen (even if
the theoreticians of the labor movement stubbornly maintained that
classes existed). In addition, a number of prominent economists had
clothed the subjective theories of value in authoritative formulations and
invested them with sophisticated formal and mathematical presentations.
Scientifically the issue seemed clear (the subjective theory of value also
made strong impressions on the labor movement as we shall see in Chapter
8); the fact that the theory also seemed to demolish a good part of the
foundation for socialist agitators didn't make it worse.

One additional element in this enumeration of possible explanations
should be mentioned. The ideas of marginal utility meant that attention
was directed to the mechanisms of balance and equilibrium and to the
permanent tendency of the supply and demand factors to counterbalance
each other in the market. Questions of growth could thus easily fall into
the background. Perhaps it is natural, as Bo Gustafsson has pointed out, to
see the development of the subjective theory of value as a theoretical
complement to the long economic stagnation which marked the European
countries during the period 1873-1896.[59]

If this line of thought is correct, then the notion of balance in economic *theory* is a kind of academic reflection of a "balance" which chracterized the economic *reality* of the age.

7.8 The Choice Between the Labor Theory of Value and the Subjective Theory of Value

Both the labor theory of value and the subjective theory of value claim to be general theories for the explanation of economic processes. We have attempted to show this above. Because an understanding of economic processes is of basic importance for the understanding of society, further, because the two theories are not compatible, and because there exists no third theory with the same scope, we must choose between the labor theory of value and the subjective theory of value. We arrive at the starting point of our discussion by returning to Locke.

LOCKE'S THREE OBJECTIONS: ARGUMENTS FOR COLLECTIVE OWNERSHIP

As we saw in Chapter 5, Locke presented a general justification for ownership through production. He who "mixes his labor" into an object should be considered its owner. Locke also assumed that the value of the mixed labor was several times greater than the value of the original object (i.e., the raw material).

We saw also that the definition of the expression "his labor" was so broad that the labor executed by employed persons was also considered as belonging to the individual (that is, the labor of his "servant"). Locke was actually trying—as Macpherson shows with persuasive evidence—to justify the capitalowners' opportunities to freely carry on production (with their own *and* with the labor of others) and to freely sell the products on the market. A very large portion of English workers during the middle of the seventeenth century were wage earners. The resource contained in their labor was to be used. The theory of "possessive individualism" justified them freely selling their labor and the capitalowner freely buying it. It was *composite production* as a principle for original acquisition (see Section 2.8) for which Locke mainly argued.

In order to do this, Locke was first forced to clear away a few objections against private acquisition—the objections (1) that acquisition not be allowed to be so extensive that there was a risk of spoilage of what was owned, and (2) that there must always be enough left over for others ("enough and as good left in common for others"). Locke added the statement (3) that the amount of the property was limited in fact since the individual's acquisition had physical limits which were determined by the extent of the individual's labor. One simply *could not* acquire an unlimited amount of property through labor.

As we have seen, Locke's answer to these objections was that they are dismissed by the monetary economy. His assumption about the function of the monetary system and the market is central. It is our position, however, that it is untenable; and *that it is untenable is shown by exactly those three objections which Locke himself makes.* In actuality, Locke with his three objections has provided good arguments for *collective* ownership of the means of production.

Let us begin with Locke's empirical notation (3)—that the monetary economy makes accumulation possible. This statement is correct, today to a much greater degree than during Locke's time. In fact, a very large private accumulation *can* occur thanks to the monetary economy and the market system.

That (3) is correct means in turn that (2)—that there *will* be enough left over for others—is untenable. In most countries there exists not only inequality, but *extreme* inequality, often to the ultimate limits of starvation and misery. Today—as in Locke's time—people die because there is not "enough and as good left in common for others." They lack not only a share in land and property, but, quite in contrast to what Locke presupposed, they lack also any possibility of acquiring a share in the yield of land and capital. The control of this—the distribution of the production results and employment opportunities—lies in large part in the hands of those who dispose over the rights to the means of production.

Finally, Locke's comment (1)—money does not spoil. It is admittedly correct that money does not spoil; but money represents large amounts of value, the accumulation of which today often means precisely the despoliation and waste of resources: weapons and weapon systems; the pollution of air and water; the devastation of areas of land which are vital to the human being (e.g., the Amazon). One may reverse Locke's reasoning. Precisely because money *can* be accumulated in great amounts, there is waste of the resources which should benefit everyone.[60]

Locke's answers to his own objections are untenable as a defense of the system of composite production, at least as it appears today in the capitalist industrial countries. The objections are in actuality valid arguments *against* unlimited private acquisition, especially of means of production. If one is serious in demanding that there be enough left over for others, then it seems to us that the system of composite production cannot be defended. Locke's principle of labor-value ("mixing in of labor" leads to ownership) is not invalid because of this. The demand that there be enough left over for others is quite compatible with a system based on *simple* production.

LOCKE'S THEORY AND SIMPLE PRODUCTION

Locke intended not only to create a theoretical justification for composite production, but also to achieve a justification of production in general. His is a theory of value-creation through labor. The theory includes the labor carried out by the individual himself with his own bodily forces and intellectual ability. Let us examine Locke's objections against the background of the idea of *simple* production.

Just as important as Locke's *answer* to objection (3) with regard to composite production is the *objection* with regard to simple production. The scope of each individual's labor is limited, and it is only through the use of the labor of others (organized by means of machines, offices, factories, centralization of energy sources) that any massive private accumulation can occur and that criterion (2)—that there be "enough and as good left in common for others"—is seriously endangered. The same is true of objection (1). While it is true that waste can result even from the personal labor of the individual, the risk that this could cause injury to other citizens of the society is significantly less if there is no massive individual accumulation.

The objections raised by Locke are arguments for simple production, for the individual's *own* labor being the legal ground for original acquisition. The importance of the argument increases with the scarcity of common natural resources.

This is all fine, but it can be extremely uneconomical. Shall we go back to the simple market society of individual, autonomous production with privately owned spinning wheels, hand saws, and cobbler's tools? Is this the way for the workers to regain control over the means of production and what is produced? Doesn't this put us in an extremely disadvantageous position in international competition?

As we said in Section 2.11, the production of goods and services today must to a great extent take place on a large scale. It is neither possible nor desirable to recreate the social and productive organization which characterized the society of simple commodity production. Production by means of well-organized *collectives* of workers is the only possible way to preserve the energy and administrative advantages of large-scale production. But even if production is collective it can take on the character of "one's own" labor. The prerequisite is that the person who carries out production has a *share in the decisions* concerning how this production shall be carried out, and that he have a share equal to that of every other member of the wage-earner collective. When the individual has an opportunity to participate in the decisions concerning production and in the distribution of the company's income, then he also has the opportunity to comprehend what his own labor means for the final product. Collective influence over production means that there can be no massive *individual* accumulation (Locke's second criterion), and that a common insight into the building up of resources is created. Experiences from wage-earner-controlled companies and similar associations (for example, Israeli kibbutzim) suggest that a significant pressure exists in the direction of an equalization of incomes within organizations.[61] The possibilities of meeting the demand in Locke's objection (2) within each production organization seem to be rather good.

Collectively organized production does not, however, exclude "company egoism." Even if each company is democratically directed with full equality in the exercise of influence over decisions, it cannot be excluded (1) that the companies may act in such a way that society's common resources are wasted, or (2) that a company seeks to attain profits which damage other companies. It is also possible (3) that one or a few companies can accumulate much more property than other companies. This occurs under the assumption of a free market, that is to say, that each company is free to use the economic advantages it may have or which it may acquire.

This raises the problem of the relations between the companies and society and whether restrictions should be placed upon the actions of the companies/wage-earner collectives. We will return to this question in Chapter 10.

OWNERSHIP WON OR LABOR LOST?

The above-said concerns primarily the question of the distribution of the products of labor. In that discussion we have accepted the premise of the labor theory of value that personal labor (simple production) justifies ownership of what is produced. The argument for this has been mainly that composite production is seen to lead to such great inequality that Locke's criterion (2) ("enough and as good left in common for others") can hardly be maintained.

There are, however, besides this almost empirical argument, at least two additional *theoretical* objections to the idea of labor-value. One—which we will treat at the end of this chapter—is that the notion of labor-value is based on a real value argument and that real value arguments are unreasonable. The other objection is that labor which, according to Locke, is "mixed into" an object may be regarded as having disappeared (and is thus no grounds for acquisition of the object). This line of thought also occurs in Jevons.[62]

Nozick presents the notion of lost labor in the following way:

> Why does mixing one's labor with something make one the owner of it? Perhaps because one owns one's labor, and so one comes to own a previously unowned thing that becomes permeated with what one owns. Ownership seeps over into the rest. But why isn't mixing what I own with what I don't own a way of losing what I own rather than a way of gaining what I don't?[63]

There are several answers to this. First, it does not sound reasonable. Why should my labor on an object mean that I lose that which I previously owned? To whom in that case? According to Nozick, the argument concerns a previously unowned object. Can it really be maintained that I as a living subject lose that which I own to a passive and possibly dead object?

Second, labor often means an increase in value of the object (a statement which Nozick accepts). It may be claimed in part that I should at least be allowed the *increase in value* (again an idea which Nozick does not dismiss). It may also be claimed—as in the case of specification (see Section 2.9)—that I should be awarded the *object*, and that the person who provided the raw material should be compensated for it. According to this principle, the capitalowner negotiates with the workers for compensation—the reverse of the relationship which we find today.

Third, Locke's argument of labor-value concerns both composite and simple production. Nozick finds himself in difficulty when he objects to the labor-value argument. He accepts a system of production based on privately owned means of production in which the owners compete for the available labor force.[64] Nozick recognizes composite production which, like simple production, is built upon Locke's notion of labor-value. Composite production means that the person whose employees' labor gives rise to commodities is recognized as owner of the commodities. How can this be justified if one claims, like Nozick, that *labor disappears*? In that case this must also be true of the *employees'* labor. Why should the labor which an employee performs on the object, and which according to the notion of lost labor "disappears," suddenly materialize as a profit for an *entirely different* person who may not even have touched the object?

If the argument of labor-value is to be refuted, it must be refuted for both composite and simple production, and *especially* for composite production. In addition, if it is refuted, then there is the unreasonable consequence that only occupation remains as a form of original acquisition (see 2.7). The reasonable alternative is an acceptance of the labor-value argument.

7.9 Summary

The starting point of the labor theory of value is the thought that the labor invested in the refinement of a natural product adds a real value to the product. The notion of real value is denied by the subjective theory of value, which is based instead on the premise that the value of a commodity arises in the exchange process, that is to say, in the relation between individuals exchanging commodities ("commodities" includes even money) and thereby trying to attain for themselves a "pleasure profit," a surplus of "pleasures" over "pains."

None of these premises may be verified by observation. Both the notion of real value and the hedonistic pleasure principle are mere theoretical starting points and foundations for continued discussion. It is thus not possible to *prove* that a commodity attains a value through the incorporation of labor into it; it is only possible to show *de facto* that the commodity has been worked on. Nor is it possible to *prove* that a commodity attains a value by being exchanged for, say, money. We may observe the exchange, but it is not possible to prove that the commodity which the individual receives gives him greater satisfaction than the money he gave for it. We *assume* that this is the case (for why else would the exchange take place?); but in the same way we would have assumed that the *money* was of greater value for the individual if the exchange had not taken place (for why else would he have chosen to retain the money?). The hedonistic principle has the serious theoretical disadvantage that it can be used to explain both a certain action and its opposite.

It may be objected that we can always ask the consumer whether his purchase meant a "pleasure profit" and thus gave the commodity an (exchange-) value. But in the same way we can ask the producer of a commodity if his work on it has meant that its value has increased. The questions and the possible answers do not help us in the choice between the two theories of value—neither the consumers' not the producers' subjective opinions are satisfactory criteria.

Rather, the choice must be made after a comparison of the economic, political, and ethical consequences of the two theories of value. The following points are relevant here:

(1) The starting point of the labor theory of value is that labor precedes the creation of capital. From the genetic perspective labor and capital may not be regarded as equal. Instruments of labor, technological aides, and machines arise originally from labor (the refinement of natural resources). In reverse: it is theoretically conceivable (even if in practice it would be extraordinarily uncomfortable and unpleasant) to remove all capital existing today from society and still retain society. A primitive social organization could probably be maintained and production could begin anew as long as human beings could work. Only if human labor ceases does the society cease to exist.

The labor theory of value provides a reasonable explanation for the *original* creation of capital. Capital derives from labor, without labor there is no capital-creation. This question is on the whole of no interest to the subjective theory of value; it satisfies itself with an analysis of conditions which exist *after* capital has been created (and there are thus things which can be exchanged).

(2) The labor theory of value emphasizes the *production side* of human economic action; the subjective theory of value emphasizes the *consumption side*. Related to this are various aspect of the distribution of society's collected wealth: while the subjective theory of value directs attention to what *comes out of* production, the labor theory of value emphasizes the distribution of the *conditions* for the production results. The subjective theory of value says nothing about how commodities are produced. As far as the subjective theory of value is concerned, the primary issue is a matter of the processes which are related to the *exchange* of commodities. As Roll points out, the subjective theory of value is "independent of any specific social order." If we are interested in how society is changed, how a certain "social order" is succeeded by another, how production is ordered, etc., then the subjective theory of value is severely handicapped.

(3) The labor theory of value sees labor as the primary source of prosperity, while the subjective theory of value does not make any real distinction between the production factors labor and capital. (From the historical perspective this thesis is, of course, much too weak: if one looks to the effect of the subjective theory of value on economic theory, then it leads to capital—abstinence—being *especially* emphasized as a production factor as compared to labor). This leads to two things which are of importance for the *ethical* interpretations of the theories of value. Regarding (a) the incitement (impetus) for human behavior, the subjective theory of value stresses the *material motive* (capital accumulation, economic compensation for performed labor): economic compensation is seen as the primary answer to the "subjective sacrifices" made by the capitalowner (through abstinence) and the worker (through labor). The labor theory of value to a great degree sees the motive for behavior in the *labor itself,* that is to say in the rewards which are part of the actual labor process (so-called inherent incitement; more on this in Chapter 10). As for (b), the assessment of labor—which is, of course, basic to what has just been said under (a)—the labor theory of value sees labor as a positive and necessary factor for human development as an individual, as a social being, and as a species. The subjective theory of value tends to regard labor mainly as something negative, as a sacrifice ("toil and trouble") tied to the individual.

(4) The emphasis on original acquisition, the concentration on production aspects, and the positive assessment of labor as the source of prosperity are connected in the labor theory of value with the notion of a reunification of the laborer with the means of production and with that which is produced. In the labor theory of value, labor is seen as a creative activity—an activity through which human beings take possession of nature and at the same time develop their own abilities.

This line of thought—elucidated by the young Marx in his reasoning on alienation and reification and thereafter presented and discussed by a great number of social scientists—has been treated by us under the heading *simple production* above. Even if modern industrial production must occur for the most part in collective forms, simple production can be realized by all workers having an equal share in decisions about the aim and direction of production. The subjective theory of value does not recognize any difference between simple and *composite production,* i.e., the combination of capitalownership and purchased labor. The reason for this would seem to lie mainly in the fact that capital and labor are regarded—and formally treated—as equal production factors. The employment contract—with an employer who buys labor and a worker who sells it—is the concrete expression of this assessment, and the labor market parallels the commodity market with its "free" participants. The labor theory of value does not recognize any equivalent "freedom" here; this is consistent with its emphasis on capitalownership as the dominant means of power in a society built upon private ownership of the means of production.

(5) As for the explanation of relative *prices* and the use of the two kinds of theories for an analysis of market mechanisms, this is a principal goal of the theories of marginal utility and marginalism which are derived from the subjective theory of value, but it is a subordinate goal of the labor theory of value. The latter sees price fluctuations almost as a superficial phenomenon and as a much less important issue than the circumstances which determine what is produced and under what conditions this happens. The level of commodity prices, and, given this level, the distribution of the surplus-value from production, are more essential areas of inquiry for the labor theory of value.

The following table summarizes points 1-5 above:

	The labor theory of value	The subjective theory of value
1. Premise	the notion of real value (value through labor incorporated in the commodity)	Hedonistic calculation, "pleasure profit" (surplus of "pleasures" over "pains"); Value = exchange-value = price
2. The relationship capital-labor	Labor superior to capital; without labor, then no capital	Labor and capital are equal production factors; no position on the origin of capital
3. Historical data	Relevant (important for, among other things, for analysis of class relationships)	Irrelevant (the exchange process is a psychological ever-existing phenomenon)
4. Analytic unit	Classes, class relationships	The individual
5. Production and consumption	Emphasis on the production process	Emphasis on the consumption process
6. Evaluatoin of labor and the incitements for labor	Necessary grounds for human development (as an individual and as a species); inherent incitements	Labor is a "subjective sacrifice"; material incitements
7. Method of production	Simple production	Composite production
8. Explanation of relative prices	Subordinate issue	Principal issue

Thus: *if* it is a reasonable premise that an object attains value through labor being incorporated into it; *if* we recognize that labor is a necessary precondition for the creation of capital; *if* the examination of the production process is judged to be more important than the examination of consumption, and *if* the role of the human being as producer is seen as more important than the role as consumer; *if* labor is seen as a necessary and positive factor in human development rather than as a "subjective sacrifice" (or if it at least is judged necessary for labor to become a necessary and positive factor in human development); *if* the recovery of the workers' direct control over the means of production (simple production) is seen as an important political measure; and *if* the technical analysis of price variations is an issue subordinate to the aforementioned theoretical goals—then the labor theory of value seems to offer such starting points that it, rather than the subjective theory of value, should be accepted as an instrument of analysis.

Chapter 8

POLITICAL POWER, THE LABOR THEORY OF VALUE, AND SOCIAL DEMOCRACY

8.1 Before Revisionism

Background: The dependence of Swedish Social Democracy on German Social Democracy. The theoretical development of Swedish Social Democracy is characterized by a strong dependence on continental, that is to say, mainly German but also English intellectual currents during the latter half of the nineteenth century. German socialist ideas influenced Sweden in the person of August Palm, who conveyed the thoughts first of Ferdinand Lassalle and later of Karl Marx.[1] English social-liberal ideas of the 1880s were spread to Sweden via the revisionism of the 1890s. Demonstrating this dependence is of some interest since it points to the lack of autonomy in the Swedish debate. The fact that the debate was almost entirely taken from foreign sources was often the cause of theoretical ambiguity and conflict. The Swedish Social Democratic writers and debaters were not even particularly well-acquainted with the original texts. To the extent that they read, they read reviews, interpretations, articles, and translations of Liebknecht, Kautsky, and others, sometimes even of Marx and Engels.[2]

It is clear that the pioneers of Swedish Social Democracy in its first hundred years based their theory only slightly on the study of the primary sources of scientific socialism, that is to say, Marx's own works, especially *Capital*. Hjalmar Branting's view of Marx shows clear traces of the prevalent misunderstanding which followed Kautsky's popularization of the theory in *Karl Marx' Ökonomische Lehren*. Branting also read Bernstein's "revisionist" book, though he and the other social democratic leaders were led to reformistic practical policies by our own actual domestic situation and our own historical conditions.[3]

We shall restrict ourselves to the following issues in this chapter: how did the German and Swedish Social Democratic parties view the question of political power and the creation of value? There are two possible positions to take in answering both of these questions: political power may be won either through reform or through revolution; the value of commodities is derived either from production or from consumption.

8.2 The German Labor Movement and Lassalle

The February Revolution of 1848 in Paris, the revolutions in Berlin, Vienna, and Rome, and the June Revolution in Paris in 1848 may be regarded as important points for the emergence of the labor movement. With the exception of the June Revolution in Paris, these revolutions were the revolt of the bourgeois Left against the remnants of feudal society.

During the period from 1850 to 1860, Germany experienced an economic upswing which favored the bourgeoisie and worsened the conditions for the organization and mobilization of the working class. It was in this climate in 1862 that the diplomat Otto von Bismarck started out on the path which led to his appointment as Premier of Prussia and his immediate evocation of the idea of national unity. Two trends arose in German socialism during this period. There was a reorganization of the Communist League, an association which had participated in the revolts of 1848, but which was dissolved in 1852. This movement, based entirely on Marx, later (1869) led to the Social Democratic Workers' Party. The other trend was dominated by Lassalle, who in 1863 founded the first large workers' party, the Allgemeiner Deutscher Arbeiterverein (ADAV). Both of these parties existed side by side until 1875, when they were united into one party, the German Workers' Party (SPD, Sozialdemokratische Partei Deutschlands), at a congress in Gotha. The program adopted there shows clear traces of Lassalle's writings. Thus, Lassalle remained the dominant intellectual inspiration of German Social Democracy long after his death in 1864.[4]

Lassalle was very close to Marx during the 1850s. They exchanged letters frequently, and Lassalle was well acquainted with Marx's writings. When Lassalle decided to form the ADAV, however, their friendship ended. A contributing reason for the break was that Lassalle—*realpolitiker* that he was—initiated a close collaboration with Bismarck.[5,6] (See below, Section 8.3.)

LASSALLE AND POLITICAL POWER

In the socialist debate, the question of how political power should be won by the labor movement—through universal suffrage or through revolution—depends upon one's view of the state. It was primarily in their positions on the state and rights that Marx and Lassalle differed. Lassalle saw in the idea of the state the basis for right, reason, and morals. From this basic position on the state, Lassalle argued that the working class should form autonomous labor organizations and work to attain universal suffrage. Through universal suffrage the working class could, by virtue of its majority position, control the parliament; thus, the socialist society could be created through acts of state. Lassalle regarded universal suffrage as the *first step* to political change; and he did not see parliamentarianism as an end in itself but rather as a means.[7] The first step to social change—a solution to the "social question"—was that the bourgeois state should grant credit to labor-controlled production unions. Brandes writes:

> The overestimation of the state as the highest moral unit into which the individual may ascend is one of the many things in Lassalle's basic view which derives from Hegel and attains supremacy with Bismarck. To Lassalle with his hunger for power it made no difference if society's forceful transformation was imposed from above or if it was slowly developed to the greatest possible extent through political freedom.[8]

Lassalle advocated production unions primarily against the background of the unequal distribution of the results of production. It was, thus, neither an efficiency argument (increasing production) nor a legal argument (giving the workers the right of determination over production) but rather an argument of a sociopolitical character.[9]

LASSALLE AND THE RIGHT OF LABOR

Lassalle's economic outlook was above all inspired by the state-socialist economist Karl Rodbertus, who was twenty years older than Lassalle. In 1838 Rodbertus presented his theory of the falling wage rate in *Die Forderungen der arbeitenden Klassen*; Lassalle dubbed the theory "the iron law of wages." Rodbertus's ideas were a further development of the Malthusian notion of population increase and subsistence minimum. Rodbertus claimed, like Smith and Ricardo, that labor is the primary value-creating factor. Rent is the difference between the production value and the wage, and the cause of "slavery to rent" is private ownership, which should therefore be abolished. According to Rodbertus, however, this will take several centuries; in the meantime the state must create greater equality through social reforms and through the regulation of wages and prices.

Marx was of little importance for Lassalle's economic views. Lassalle died in 1864, the first part of *Capital* was published in 1867 and Volume III appeared in 1894.

Lassalle maintained, as Marx did later, that labor creates value. But his view on the ownership of the means of production differed greatly from Marx's view due to their widely divergent positions on the role of the state. Lassalle emphasized the right of possession and the right to a share of the yield after investment. The state—an amalgamation of the population and an expression of the public interest—should have the right to ownership of the means of production. Marx in turn stressed the direct right of ownership by the producers. In complete contrast to Lassalle, Marx saw the state as an instrument of the ruling bourgeois class directed against the workers. In the future society based on worker power, the state would die out.

8.3 German Social Democracy Under Bismarck

Marx's practical political contributions came mainly during the 1840s when he founded the League of Communists and wrote the *Communist Manifesto*. In 1849 Marx moved to London, where he lived and was scientifically and politically active until his death in 1883.

Capital, Vol. I was published in 1867 and was probably read by only a very few active Social Democrats of the time. Marx's significance for contemporary Social Democracy was thus mainly indirect and theoretical. Droz claims that Marxism during the 1870s mainly took the form of "phraseology" and that the dominant party after 1875 was a democratic and social party and not a Marxist party.[10] Bo Gustafsson maintains the same thing: "[One] cannot on the whole speak of an initiation of Marxism into German Social Democracy before 1878."

In 1875 the SPD was formed through the merger of Lassalle's party, the ADAV of 1862, and the SAP from 1869. The "Marxists" forming the leadership of the SPD were under the influence of intellectual currents such as Malthus's population theory, Darwin's theory of evolution, Lassalle's theory of state, and the utilitarian theory.

This union, or rather this juxtaposition, of various ideas had as a consequence "that the dialectic to a great extent was replaced by, or mixed with, a shallow evolutionary outlook"[12] and further "this evolutionary tinge to Marxism led to socialism being presented as an almost predetermined product of social development."[13] The paradoxical situation arises that, on one hand, "Marxist theory before 1890 [could] not have had time to penetrate very deeply,"[14] and, on the other, *when* it became politically significant in the Erfurt Program, its practical policies were formed in close collaboration with liberals and liberal ideas. Marxism in Germany during the 1890s may be described as theoretical; it was parliamentary Social Democracy under the leadership of Vollmar and Bernstein which attained practical significance.

In the election of 1878 the Social Democrats won considerable victories, which led Bismarck to institute the so-called Socialist Law the same year. Social Democratic organizations were forbidden, their newspapers lost their publication permits, and the opportunities to spread propaganda in an organized manner were curtailed. The only possible socialist activity was limited to participation in the election for the national parliament. The Socialist Law contributed to severe inner conflicts between the left and the right factions of the party. In the beginning of the 1880s the right wing of the party was dominant.[15] By the middle of the 1880s the conflicts had become so intense that Engels feared a split in the party. This never occurred, however, and when the Socialist Law was repealed in 1890, the left wing had grown stronger and dominated the party. At the same time the election of 1890 showed that the Social Democratic party had become the country's largest during the time of the Socialist Law. The dominance of the rightist faction during the first half of the 1880s had lasting effects on the activity of the party during the 1890s. Eduard

Bernstein (see 8.4) was among those on the Right who advocated cooperation with the liberals and a deemphasis of the class struggle.[16]

MARX AND ENGELS ON PARLIAMENTARIANISM AND REVOLUTION

When one examines Marx's and Engels's positions on the issues of
parliamentarianism and revolution, one should keep in mind their constant
reservations. Universal suffrage can only be regarded as a short-term tool,
and the labor movement must constantly preserve its "real, historic
right" to make a revolution.[17] What Marx and Engels seem to mean is that
certain limited reforms are possible and even desirable in the capitalist
society. These limited reforms can strengthen the fighting spirit and
consciousness of the labor movement so that the movement can *contribute*
to the fall of the class society *from within*. This was a viewpoint on
reforms which Branting would later (1906) develop.[18]

When Marx uses the expression "democracy," he is referring to a social
form in which the state does not exist. Democracy is synonymous with
social justice. We find the following elements among Marx's conditions for
a democracy: an ordering of production determined by the producers, the
absence of the state, and a formal constitution founded on the ordering of
production.[19] It is against this background that Marx addresses the value of
general elections, representation, and other formal rules of a democracy.

Marx also dealt with the issue of the "dictatorship of the proletariat."
Can this concept be made compatible with "democracy" in the Marxian
sense just mentioned?

Hansson has commented on the use of the expression "dictatorship of
the proletariat" in Marx and Engels.[20] The word "dictatorship" in the
sense of absolute power first came into use through Lenin in the 1920s.
Both Marx and Engels used the concept "dictatorship" to "describe the
power of a popularly elected assembly in a newly established democracy."
In the idiom of the late nineteenth century, dictatorship was not the
opposite of democracy. Hansson continues:

> They [Marx and Engels] never maintained that the dictatorship of the prole-
> tariat should be exercised in any other form than that the working class should
> utilize its majority position in a popularly elected assembly and subjugate all
> centers of power which did not derive from the people. For them it was never
> a question of the leadership of any special revolutionary group. This interpre-
> tation of the notion belongs to a later era of the history of political ideas.[21]

The issue of parliamentarianism and revolution was also dependent upon
the question of the development of the capitalist order of production.

The capitalist order becomes superfluous when production is centralized, production forces become socialized, and the private capitalists
no longer can finance production through credits.[22] Meanwhile the conditions for a socialist society grow; this occurs partly through the political
organization of the workers into a party. But the working class should be

prepared to exercise its "real, historic right," that is, the right to make revolution if the bourgeoisie does not accept the fact that development has led to the need for a new economic order.

8.4 Revisionism

THE PREREQUISITES FOR NEW POLICIES

Politically, the transition from the 1880s to the 1890s brought a definitive change. In Germany the Emergency Powers Act ended in 1890 and parliamentarianism experienced its breakthrough.

The SPD became politically legal when the Socialist Law was repealed. At the same time, under pressure from the successes of the Social Democrats, that part of the bourgeoisie which was favorable to reform began to suggest sociopolitical reforms in a number of areas. Within the SPD there were several prominent people who saw a path open to the labor movement once the SPD had been accepted and the bourgeoisie was inclined toward reform. The activity of the SPD was therefore directed in part at an inner consolidation of party activity and party organization and in part at reforms which were supported by the bourgeoisie and which could facilitate the activity of the SPD.

During the greater part of the 1870s and the entire 1880s there was a severe depression in Europe. This was succeeded in the beginning of the 1890s by improved economic conditions; investments increased, increases in real wages could be obtained, unemployment decreased, and trade unions increased their membership. On the whole, the political and economic climate improved after the 1880s and the beginning of the 1890s. It was in this climate that revisionism, not only in Germany, expanded. This line of thought received its label because it reinterpreted and refuted—i.e., revised—the basic ideas in the theories of Marx and Engels. Revisionism attained a great significance because it so clearly and unequivocally pointed out a program of action for the labor movement in both the short term and the long term.

REVISIONISM AND BERNSTEIN

Revisionism has been associated primarily with Eduard Bernstein. Bernstein was active as a journalist and author. Because of Bismarck's Emergency Powers Act Bernstein was forced to spend time abroad, and from 1888 on he lived in London, where he came into contact with the Fabian Society, which had been formed in 1883. These contacts were to greatly influence Bernstein's intellectual development.

Bernstein can hardly be called the originator of revisionism, though he was its modern chronicler and its most consistent interpreter.[23] He says himself that his criticism of Marxism has been presented by others and that the justification of his critique is that he "recognizes that which has already been discovered."[24] In 1896 Bernstein began a series of articles in

Die Neue Zeit entitled "Probleme des Sozialismus," and in 1899 he published this series under the title *Evolutionary Socialism: A Criticism and Affirmation.* This book summarizes contemporary criticism of Marxism on a series of central points.

BERNSTEIN'S POLITICAL PROGRAM

Recounted briefly and summarily, Bernstein's theory is the following. Capitalism is not approaching its imminent breakdown, but instead people and organizations have been able to adapt themselves to the economic development, which in turn has shown that it can be directed. In the very long term—so long that it is actually uninteresting—socialism is a natural necessity, and in the meantime the labor movement should concentrate on the daily struggle. The SPD should put aside its Marxian phraseology and appear as "what it is in reality, a democratic, socialist reform party." The party should concentrate on the present; the movement is everything, and the goal is nothing. A few of the most essential parts of Bernstein's theory are summarized in this thesis. First there is the assumption on human nature. It doesn't really matter which developmental tendencies we are concerned with, since it has been shown that the human being is "adaptable" and "elastic."[25] Bernstein says also that "the economic foundations" are not decisive for development. The human being has shown "an increased ability to direct economic evolution" and, Bernstein continues, there is

a growing understanding of the laws of evolution, especially of economic evolution. Hand in hand with this insight goes, partly as its cause, and partly as its effect, an increased ability to direct the economic evolution. To the extent that man recognizes its nature, the economic natural force, as well as the physical force, is changed from the ruler to the servant of mankind.[26]

Individuals, organizations and nations "succeed in freeing an increasingly greater part of their lives from a necessity which acts against or without their will."[27]

Second, socialism is a natural necessity. Socialism, the moral demand for social justice, is gradually and spontaneously realized within the capitalist system because human beings want it. The immediate consequence for the socialists' political activity "signifies not a decrease but rather an *increase* and a *heightening* of the sociopolitical tasks."[28]

Third, there is Bernstein's view of the state. Bernstein does not question the construction and function of the bourgeois state. He merely establishes that since Lassalle German Social Democracy has been positively inclined toward the state and some form of state socialism.[29]

Against this background it is understandable that Bernstein often appeared as a pronounced antirevolutionary. His arguments often center on the maturity of the working class. His opinion is that the working class is politically, economically, and socially immature. He writes that the working class is "not yet sufficiently evolved to assume political command."[30] He denies the existence of a unified working class and because of this, he says, solidarity is also not possible. Rather, the working class is heterogeneous because of a hierarchical division according to occupation.[31] In addition, the industrial worker is both "indifferent and unsympathetic and even hostile towards social democracy."[32] One may, if one wishes, see Bernstein's entire political program (trade unions, cooperative stores, political party, communalization) as one great educational program for the working class.[33] In keeping with this, he believes, exactly as Lassalle did, in the elite of the labor movement.[34] His goal for the individual members of the working class is to make them "petty bourgeois, professionals and advocates of temperance."[35] "Social Democracy does not wish," says Bernstein,

> to dissolve this society and make all its members proletarians; rather it works incessantly to raise the worker from the social position of the proletarian to that of the citizen and thus to make citizenship universal.[36]

Bernstein adds in a note: "I do not hesitate to explain that I consider the bourgeois class—including the German—to be on the whole not only economically but even morally rather sound."[37]

Bernstein's view of democracy may be said to be decisive for his position on Marxism. He bases his view on the utilitarian principles of the personal freedom of the private individual.[38] Democracy is a form (a contract) for power which these equal individuals (none has power over the others) erect between themselves. This form guarantees to all the highest possible degree of freedom[39] and "the democratic right to vote makes those who possess it legal and formal partners in the society, and this legal partnership must in the end lead to real partnership."[40]

Because reality has so clearly demonstrated that democracy is "a powerful lever in the issue of social progress," it is quite consistent, according to Bernstein, that the political liberalism which he defends will become "the means to the attainment of socialism and the form for its realization."[41]

Bernstein concludes the formulation of his political program with the following position:

> With respect to liberalism as a world historical movement, socialism is not only its chronological descendant, but also as regards the content of ideas, socialism is its legitimate heir, as is shown moreover in every question of principle on which social democracy must take a stand. As soon as any of the economic demands of the socialist program have had to be executed in such a manner or under such circumstances that the development of freedom could thereby be endangered, Social Democracy has never hesitated in taking a position against this. The protection of civil freedom has always stood higher in its view than

the fulfillment of one or another economic demand. The development and protection of the free personality is the goal of all socialist measures, even of those which on the surface appear coercive. A careful examination of these will always show that it is a question of coercion which will *increase* the general freedom of society, that is to say, which will deliver *more* freedom to *broader* circles than it takes away. The legal normal working day, for example, is actually a fixing of minimum freedom, a prohibition against daily selling one's labor for a longer time than a fixed number of hours, and thus this stands in principle on the same ground as the other prohibition favored by the liberals against selling oneself for life to personal slavery. It is thus no accident that the first country in which the maximum number of working hours in a day was fixed was Europe's most democratically progressive state, Switzerland. Democracy is merely the political form of liberalism. Being a counter-movement to the oppression of nations imposed by institutions from without or by those resting merely on tradition, liberalism at first sought its realization as a principle of the sovereignty of the ages and of the nations, both of which principles formed the eternal subjects of discussion for the philosophers of the rights of the state of the seventeenth and eighteenth centuries, until Rousseau in his social contract set them up as fundamental conditions for the legal validity of every constitution and the French Revolution—in the democratic constitution of 1793 which was filled with Rousseau's spirit—proclaimed them as inalienable human rights.

The constitution of 1793 was the logical expression of the liberal ideas of the times, and a cursory glance at its contents shows how little it stood in the way of socialism. Babeuf and "the egalitarians" also saw in it an excellent starting point for the realization of their communist strivings, and accordingly they placed the restoration of the constitution of 1793 at the head of their demands. What later presented itself as political liberalism was only a weakened form of it, adjusted so that it corresponded to and satisfied the capitalist bourgeoisie's need for the overthrow of the old regime, exactly as the so-called Manchester School was only a weakened and one-sided presentation of the basic principles which had been set up by the classics of economic liberalism. *Actually, there is not one single liberal thought which with respect to intellectual content does not also belong to socialism.* Even the principle of economic personal responsibility, which appears to so completely belong to the Manchester School, can in my opinion be neither theoretically denied by socialism or under any conceivable circumstances be made inoperative. Without responsibility, no freedom; we may think theoretically as we wish about man's freedom of action, but in practice we must start from responsibility as the foundation for moral law, for only under this condition is social morality possible. Similarly in the age of communication, in the states which encompass our millions of members, a sound social life is impossible if economic personal responsibility is not assumed in all who are capable of labor. The recognition of economic personal responsibility is the individual's compensation to the state for the services it shows or offers him [our italics].[42]

It is evident in this quotation that Bernstein practically equates socialism with liberalism. Not only does the former follow liberalism chronologically, but their contents are also alike with respect to every principal issue.

In the quotation above Bernstein also reveals his basic view of economics. It is a good beginning for a description of his view on the labor theory of value.

BERNSTEIN'S ECONOMIC PROGRAM

Bernstein's revision of Marxism also contained a denial of historical materialism. It is not a society's mode of production which is the only or most important factor in social changes. It is a matter of the mode of production in relation to other forces.[43] These other forces are, according to Bernstein,

> notions of law and morals, the historical and religious traditions of every age, the geographical influence plus other influences of nature, among which are included man's own nature and his spiritual disposition.[44]

Together these forces are more significant than economic relations, which are merely one part of the economic environment which influences the human character.[45] At the time of his critique of Marx (1896-1898), Bernstein was well acquainted with the theoreticians of marginal utility through the Fabians (Wicksteed, Shaw, and Wallas), the Austrian School, and also through Jevons and Böhm-Bawerk (see Chapter 7). The marginal utility theoreticians were important for Bernstein in two respects. First, they emphasized the empirical; they made experience the basis of scientific theory. Further, they stressed that the value of a commodity depends on its utility.[46] One of Bernstein's objections to Marx was that he had created a theory of value which was not rooted in "real society." This theory of value was an abstraction which, according to Bernstein, could not explain the value of any one *particular* commodity.

Bernstein's own theory is concerned with the empirical study of the *distribution* of production results, not with their *origin*.

He studied exchange—not production—and attempted to find in it the origin of value. It is for moral reasons that the working class—and soon even the healthy bourgeoisie—rises against inequitable distribution. Bernstein was consistent in theory and opinion, and he carried out empirical studies of the reality he perceived in order to refute what he considered to be the errors of Marx's theory.

Bernstein claimed that stock companies (which were becoming increasingly common under capitalism) contributed to the spread of ownership and that this was reflected in an equalization of income.[47] Therefore, said Bernstein, it was

> entirely wrong to assume that the present development shows a relative or even an absolute decrease in the number of the wealthy. the wealthy class is not growing "more or less," but quite simply *more*, that is to say, both *absolutely* and *relatively*. If the activity and prospects of Social Democracy were dependent upon a decrease in the number of wealthy persons, then it

could lay down to rest at once. But the opposite is the case. *The prospects for socialism do not depend on the decrease, but rather on the increase of social wealth.*[48]

Bernstein's most important evidence, which was to be of decisive political significance, was that the middle class was growing in both number and importance.[49] His other theses are in brief:

- the size of companies shows no definite tendency toward large units;[50]
- the same is also true of agriculture;[51]
- capitalism does not lead to economic crises.[52]

Thus, according to Bernstein, the conditions which Marx had given for socialism did not exist. The tendency toward large-scale production had only been partially manifested.[53] There was no united proletariat which could make a revolution,[54] and production was not becoming more socialized.[55] By "socialized" Bernstein referred only to the organizational forms. He could not imagine that the lessening of the importance of credits and investments for capital could be sufficient reason for the socialization of production.

The political consequence of Bernstein's economic-theoretical position was that ownership was not a fruitful scientific problem; nor was it, at least in the short term, a fruitful political problem. Bernstein drew the conclusion that a mixed economic system was sufficient to give the working class a more just share of the results of production. Social Democracy should act in a parliamentary fashion and gradually extend its influence, at the same time as the working class matured through democratic work in the parliament, the state, the community, the trade union, and the cooperative.

The same year that Bernstein published his book (1899), he was sharply criticized by Kautsky in *Vorwärts* and *Die Neue Zeit*. Kautsky wrote a series of articles which he later published in the book *Social Democracy and Socialism* (1908). Kautsky's criticism was just as comprehensive as Bernstein's program. He worked systematically and tested each statement by Bernstein. With respect to the empirical evidence, Kautsky clearly demonstrated Bernstein's mistakes, showing that he had used unreliable sources and that he had exploited data for his own purposes.[56]

Kautsky's criticism of Bernstein is shared by Gustafsson, to name just one example. It is, in our opinion, undeniable that Bernstein was wrong on central points (of which a few have been discussed above). This does not, of course, necessarily mean that *revisionism* as a whole must be dismissed. But beyond the comments above, we do not have the opportunity to go into Bernstein's work. The reader is referred to the sources which have been cited here.

SUMMARY

Bernstein did not accept Marx's labor theory of value which had been formulated on the basis of the mode of production. Once the labor theory of value had fallen in Bernstein's view, the theories of class struggle and the breakdown of capitalism also fell. What was left, according to Bernstein, was the fact that the capitalist economy showed certain "tendencies." Marx's mistake was that he described these tendencies "incompletely."[57] This led Marx away from "real society." Since social development was evolutionary, the labor movement should not worry about the goal. Bernstein thought it was a natural necessity that the capitalist order of production would play out its role and be replaced by something else. It was, however, not a natural necessity that socialism should replace capitalism (even if it was probable). Socialism was instead a moral tool.

Revisionism gave to the labor movement a pedagogical instrument and concrete directions. This stood in contrast to Marxism, which was more exploratory and theoretical. Revisionism also contained views, for example on liberalism, which were already existing elements in society. It was probably simpler to understand this and to build further on these ideas than on Marx's more complicated and demanding theory. Revisionism's proximity to liberalism also increased the possibilities of prompt solutions to the social question.

It should be pointed out that revisionism was not a peculiarly German phenomenon. Revisionist lines of thought emerged everywhere and almost simultaneously throughout Europe during the 1890s. Much significance must, of course, be ascribed to the Second International which was formed in 1889 and to the conventions at which contemporary Social Democratic leaders met. The conditions for a revisionist development were approximately the same in Germany as in a number of other countries. Social Democratic mass parties were formed in the 1880s in Italy, Russia, England, Belgium, Norway, Austria, Switzerland, and Sweden. This had happened earlier in Germany, France, and Denmark, and in all of these countries both a revisionist and a Marxist line emerged within Social Democracy. Revisionism was decidedly an international phenomenon.[58]

8.5 Swedish Social Democracy's Struggle for Independence

Swedish Social Democracy developed considerably later than German Social Democracy, and in many ways it was influenced by its German counterpart. In Sweden there was already a spiraling interest in socialism during the 1840s (Pär Götrek, and others), but this left no direct traces in the form of organizations or programs. It would take about thirty years, until the end of the 1870s, before there were serious attempts to organize the working class and systematically disseminate propaganda.

THE RELATIONSHIP TO THE LIBERALS

Two circumstances dominated the labor movement during the 1870s; first, it was the liberals who with notions of self-help and with worker associations attempted to organize the working class, and, second, it was Lassalle's ideas and not Marx's which first reached Sweden.[59]

The bourgeois social reformism which emerged during the latter half of the nineteenth century on the whole did not discuss reforms aimed at a spread of power—be it economic or political—to the labor movement. Rather, social reformism was motivated by strivings to put a damper on social unrest so that the issue of power would not come to a head. Two reasons for social reforms can be delineated: "one, a humanistic [reason], to do something about the social misery, and two, a politically conservative [reason], to secure social peace."[60]

The labor associations which emerged were used at an early date as educational organizations and laid the foundation for our present education associations. The lecture meetings which were held were led by educated liberals like Anton Nyström. What kinds of ideas and lines of thought were presented and discussed at these meetings? Gunnarsson states:

In the minutes of the Social Democratic Union we read about discussions on utilitarianism and positivism and, naturally, Marxist lines of thought. The minutes from associations and youth clubs testify to a considerable interest in religious issues. Marx's and Engels's "Communist Manifesto" had been translated by Për Götrek, and the highly talented Atterdag Wermelin, who passed on much too soon, popularized Marxist ideas in two brilliant little writings. Utilitarianism has certainly meant a great deal for the development of many workers.[61]

In 1879 the first Swedish workers' meeting was held under the leadership of the liberals. The question of political suffrage was on the agenda, and the debate evidently became very heated.[62] Universal suffrage was never a demand on the program of the liberal Swedish Workers' Union. Tingsten claims that the following decade, the 1880s, saw the drawing of battle lines between liberalism and Social Democracy, and he continues:

The following centuries may, from an important perspective, be seen as a gradual settlement of the large conflicts of principle. In the struggle for popular rule, liberals and Social Democrats were united in collaboration, which sharpened the willingness to reform of the former and softened the social revolutionary demands of the latter. When democracy had been instituted, it gradually became a foundation for the politics of compromise and mutual understanding from which none of the large parties was excluded.[63]

THE STRUGGLE FOR UNIVERSAL SUFFRAGE

When August Palm came to Sweden from Germany in 1881, he presented to the Swedish workers his own translation of the Gotha Program and its Danish counterpart, the Gimle Program. There are only small discrepancies between the Gotha Program and the program which the Swedish Social Democratic Workers' Association adopted in 1882. Lassalle's state socialism remains and universal suffrage is a demand.[64]

> From the left-liberals was drawn the idea of economic organization, in particular the consumer cooperative; and from the early English labor movement were taken ideas [developed theoretically by the Fabians[65]] on trade union and economic organization.

In his examination of the intellectual development of Social Democracy, Tingsten argues for the thesis that Social Democracy was a Marxist organization which perceived the illogical and unreasonable elements in the Marxist theory. Social Democracy therefore became a parliamentary democratic reform party. In order to maintain this thesis, Tingsten must in part distort the actual theoretical development. He does this by strongly emphasizing Marx's importance for Social Democracy. Tingsten writes: "Marxism and the entire complex of notions which belonged to it gave Social Democracy its distinctive characteristic,"[66] and further he writes that "it is on Marx's ideas that one primarily builds."[67] We have already established that this is false.

There are at least two reasons for Tingsten's analytical mistakes. First there is a question of method. Tingsten's empirical data consisted primarily of Social Democratic publications—programs, brochures, motions, newspaper articles, and books. Tingsten subjected these data to a relatively strict theoretical analysis; but it was more seldom that he compared practical policies with ideas. Second, during the period when Tingsten wrote his theoretical history, the 1930s, Marxist analysis was poorly developed and contained few nuances. Tingsten's application of Marxist ideas of class struggle, exploitation, surplus-value, etc., shows clear traces of an unwillingness to adapt the concepts to the actual development. The question is whether Tingsten, like Böhm-Bawerk before him, rejected Marx for the simple reason that the subjective theory of value was assumed *a priori* to be correct. Concerning the Marxian theses, he wrote in his memoirs:

> I condemned the theses as an expression of an outlook which was not only obsolete but which had always been untenable; I stressed that the exploitation concept was a link in Marx's theory of value, a theory which had been abandoned by all.[68]

Common to the theoretical development of Social Democracy during the period from 1881 to 1890 were, on the one hand, the front which was established *against* the liberals and, on the other, the internal debate which to a great extent concerned the possibilities of cooperating *with* them. The pressure from liberal circles was great; liberal parliamentarianism was tempting also because it was a faster and, in all likelihood, a surer path to political influence. The internal debate took place, therefore, against this background of pressure from the liberals and the heritage of Lassalle. It was Lassalle's ideas which were used in the struggle against the liberals, and it was primarily with a foundation in these ideas that the organizations of the labor movement became independent. During the aforementioned period the liberals lost their direct, concrete power over the labor organizations but at the same time won significant ideological influence over the labor movement. The struggle for universal suffrage and parliamentarianism became the main path for the labor movement. The link between *production* and politics remained weak while the role of the citizens as *consumers* was emphasized.

AGAINST PARLIAMENTARIANISM

The growth and consolidation of Social Democracy in Sweden is strongly tied to Hjalmar Branting. Branting became a member of the Social Democratic Union in 1886. Before that he had been one of the leaders of the liberal labor movement, and intellectually Branting was under the influence of liberals like Ibsen, Anton Nyström, and, above all, Georg Brandes.

During his time as a student in Uppsala, Branting, together with August Strindberg, Karl Staaff, Pehr Staaff, and Knut Wicksell, was one of the most prominent members of the Republican Club.[69] Branting was also in personal contact with internationally known revolutionaries and contemporary Western European Social Democrats.[70]

Branting's speech before the Gävle Workers' Club in 1886, more than any other, stands out as a manifesto for the future. According to Zeth Höglund, the speech can "be said to constitute the declaration of independence of the Swedish labor movement and the first program of Swedish socialism."[71] Branting's speech is entitled "Why the Labor Movement Must Become Socialist."[72] The speech begins with a critique of Manchester liberalism. It is a consequence of free competition that wages are forced down below the subsistence minimum (the iron law of wages).[73] Large-scale production entails a sharpening of class conflicts, but at the same time the workers' class consciousness is aroused. The worker sees that the fault "is much more profound, contained in the circumstance itself that he must sell his labor to others who own the means to make it fruitful."[74] At the same time—"and this is the most important thing"[75]—large-scale production and private ownership of the means of production lead to the "extreme increase in the *inequality of the distribution of wealth.*"[76]

The reason behind the social question (or the "worker question" as Branting also calls it) is the right to private ownership of the means of production, and in the long term the goal is "ordered, collective. socialized production"[77] and "to expropriate the millionaires' capital, to make the capital also in the sense of civic law what it already has become economically—society's collective property."[78] In the short term, however, it is most important to distribute the results of production more equitably and justly.

The historical review which Branting makes in the Gävle speech leads "to an outlook on the on-going social development, according to which socialism becomes the natural result of this development."[79] A bit further on in the text it is said that "socialism thus appears as a necessary, logical consequence of this actual development."[80] Karl Kautsky's views,[81] among those of others, are brought out in these statements, views with which Branting was well acquainted, concerning the "natural necessity" of socialism. Kautsky's position is *deterministic*. Branting maintains in another essay that the theory of evolution as formulated by Darwin and Spencer has replaced the "dialectical thought forms."[82] Capitalism does not lead to poverty or breakdown because it bears socialism within itself; it is "corroded from within by socialism's ideas and socialist realities."[83] The movement must therefore concentrate its activity on the present: "[T]he main emphasis must to an increased degree be placed on practical activity aimed at immediate goals."[84]

The determinism developed during the 1880s makes socialism into something mechanical. Revisionism, which emerged during the 1890s unites the mechanical aspect with a socialism which is primarily founded in ethics and morals.[85]

Revolution or parliamentarianism? Well, ultimately this depends on the action of the upper class, says Branting:

> If, however, the upper class respects the popular will, *even when this demands the abolition of its own rights of precedence*, then it will not be the socialists who will appeal unnecessarily to violence. But the first condition for a peaceful labor movement is that it shall have means to make itself heard. *Universal* suffrage is thus the price for which the bourgeoisie can buy settlement by means of administration instead of through bankruptcy brought before the court of the revolution.[86]

In a newspaper article twenty-three days before the Gävle speech Branting wrote: "If we wish to make the approaching period as gentle as possible, well, then we should do as our brother party in Denmark—cooperate with the bourgeois radicals." The reason is that class conflicts have as yet not developed because "the middle class still plays a very important role."[87] The working and middle classes need each other, and the Danish example shows that cooperation is possible "without the slightest concession of one hair's breadth of our principles for a definite, immediate political purpose: to defeat the Junker reaction, to reconquer political freedom, and to gain respect for the popular will."[88] In order to win

universal suffrage, the Social Democrats should "take the hand extended
to us in cooperation from the opponents of Social Democracy. . . . Such a
policy would show, it seems to me, that Swedish Social Democracy has
correctly judged *the most immediate prospects for the future.*"[89]

In 1869 Sweden's Social Democratic Workers' Party was formed.
Instead of a program, a series of separate resolutions were adopted.
Concerning the question of cooperation with other parties, the convention
adopted a resolution which stated:

> With such groups as show themselves seriously willing to defend and expand
> the people's rights, may cooperation therefore take place for the time being
> and for definite, immediate goals at elections, in agitation for voting rights,
> and similar things, but always with the expressed reservation that this occurs
> with the recognition of the equal rights of Social Democracy as a political
> party and that the representatives of the party, whose opinions should always
> be heard for the prevention of unworthy compromise, find the conditions
> otherwise acceptable.[90]

8.6 Revisionism in Sweden

Branting's life-work in practical politics and in writing testifies to the
fact that his primary goal was universal suffrage. To this end he developed
means which were usable and "allied with the bourgeois Left in order to
bring victory to the workers."[91] He mistrusted the revolutionaries, and
against their Marxist ideas he contrasted his own and those of Bernstein
and other leaders of the Second International.[92]

The years between 1890 and the beginning of World War I in 1914 were
of great political, economic, and social significance for practically all
industrial nations. These were years following a very long recession;
decisive structural, economic, and technical changes were made in production. Hentilä has summarized the following changes in Swedish trade and
industry:

(1) Production was expanded and became more diversified; export industry grew
especially.

(2) When the balance of payments became positive in 1910, Sweden became a
capital-exporting country, which at the same time increased the country's
economic independence.

(3) The transition to large-scale enterprises in the central areas of production.
This development was reinforced by the transformation of stock companies,
which began in the 1890s and which brought down the old milling and mining
towns, which had been based on ownership by one family.

(4) The emergence of financial institutions and the transfer of the business of
finance to commercial banks.

(5) The ability of Swedish industry to apply the most modern technical advances
in production; for example, the development of methods of metal refining
and the so-called "genius industry" which refers to the rise of modern

Swedish capital industry at the turn of the century (modern methods for the manufacturing of milk separators, ball bearings, refrigerators, telephones, etc. through companies such as ASEA, AGA, Electrolux, L. M. Ericsson, SKF, etc.).[93]

Social and economic development probably had consequences for Social Democracy's view on the issue of consumption and production, and for the view on the labor theory of value and private ownership.

The discussion of the labor theory of value in the Swedish labor movement was at first linked to the variation on Smith and Ricardo which was later developed by Rodbertus and Lassalle. Thus, it became more a question of the distribution of the results of production than a question of the origin of value.

The practical political significance of the labor theory of value involved mainly the redistribution of the results of production. In relation to what the labor theory of value is actually about—the *origin* of value in production and ownership of the *means of production*—the emphasis on the distribution aspects entails a diversion of the discussion from the actual subject. Due to this shift in the discussion to the distribution issue—justice and equality in the distribution and consumption of useful products—there was a common platform for the materialism of the socialists and the idealism of the radical bourgeoisie.

BRANTING ON THE RIGHTS OF LABOR

Branting's views on private ownership are clear—it is the root of society's evil. He formulates the idea of socialism from the perspective of ownership rights and writes:

[Three] primary points in all of socialism:

- that it takes its starting point in the misery of the masses;
- that it finds the reason for this misery in the unequal distribution of the fruits of labor, which is connected to private ownership; and
- that it sets as its goal social equality, won through a greater or lesser curtailment of private ownership rights.[94]

The central problem for Branting—"the social question of our time"—is the decision-making right over surplus-value and its distribution. This issue sharpens class conflict, writes Branting, but *simultaneously* it contributes indirectly to raising the class consciousness of the workers. And he continues:

I am referring now to the further increased *inequality in the distribution of wealth* which is a consequence of large-scale production ... as long as the unnatural state of affairs remains that the means of labor do not belong to the whole society but rather to private, privileged individuals.[95]

It was clear to Branting that, in the absolute sense, things could not get worse for the labor movement. What he reacted against was the fact that the fruits of labor went not to those who labored but rather to those who owned. Branting saw that the differences in wealth increased in the relative sense: the distribution of the total wealth became more inequitable.[96] This created class conflicts which would remain "as long as private ownership of the means of production remains untouched."[97]

In a central essay, "Socialism in the Labor Movement," Branting formulated the goals of the labor movement in the following way:

> The remolding of [society] in such a way that every privilege of wealth might disappear, and that labor adapted to the prospective profits of a ruling class might be replaced by planned, collective labor for the common good.[98]

Against this background, the equation of labor and capital may have been a strategic means determined by the current political situation, but it was not a goal. For Branting the equation of labor and capital was "an adjustment and an improvement within the framework of existing conditions."[99] Co-determination in companies without decision-making rights over decisive capital issues seemed to Branting to be a half-measure. He thought that the right of co-determination of one's own working conditions with "the reservation that all aspects of management should rest in the employer's hand with despotic power" was merely half of the demand of the labor movement.

> It is, however, remarkable that some people do not want to see that this thought stops at the half-way point and even in the best case leads merely to an extremely uncertain, unstable equilibrium.[100]

Branting continued: "the advocates of the theory of equilibrium" claim that

> the majority and the minority, with preserved conflicting interests and with preserved privileges for the latter group, would simply continue to produce in the same forms as at the time when the ruling position of the wealthy had not yet been shaken by any impertinence. By what right?[101]

In his criticism of the equilibrium theory, Branting borrowed images from physics in which a state of equilibrium between two forces pulling in opposite directions is always unstable, that is to say, "only the slightest disturbance is needed on either side for it to be ended."[102] The demands were obvious, wrote Branting, "that *labor*, not capital, should be the deciding factor in social relations."[103] The struggle for democracy included political, economic, and social justice founded on labor.[104] The struggle for political democracy was the first step. Once this had been won—which happened with the decision on universal suffrage in the national parliament in November of 1918—then the struggle for social and economic justice could begin. We shall return to this in Section 8.8.

Branting's thoughts on the rights of labor did not seem to have been of any direct consequence for his view of the two competing theories of value. He referred to "Marx's theory of value which was criticized from many quarters" and felt that "fortunately, socialism does not stand and fall" with it.[105] He obviously accepted the subjective theory of value and did not seem to see any conflict between it and the thesis that "labor, not capital, should be the deciding factor in social relations."

Branting considered the question decided in 1906. The theory of value which most researchers and socialist theoreticians accepted was "the one which often has been named after the Englishman Jevons, but which has also been independently developed by 'the Austrian School'."[106]

8.7 Summary: Social Democracy at the End of the Nineteenth Century

In the first place, Lassalle's ideas led to a positive view of the state in the program of Social Democracy. Lassalle defined the state as an association of the population and saw in this association the bearer of rights, reason, and morals. This confidence in the state has survived Lassalle in various ways and remains a lasting heritage. He saw universal suffrage as a first step in political struggle.

Lassalle's economic theory was primarily concerned with the iron law of wages. He made the issue of the value of labor into the issue of the distribution of the surplus of production. Though Lassalle died in 1864, his ideas were very important until the end of the 1870s. In many ways the SPD, formed in 1875, built its program upon Lassalle.

During the period from 1850 to 1880 Marx and Engels developed their views of the assumption of power and the value of labor. Marx and Engels answered with a "yes and no" to the question of parliamentarianism or revolution. The working class can improve its situation through universal suffrage. This does not, however, entail a complete acceptance of parliamentarianism. The working class must retain its "real, historic right" to make a revolution.

The labor theory of value's theoretical development was a threat to the capitalist theory of exchange, and the theoreticians of marginal utility tried very hard to refute it. In general, one may maintain that the discussion of the theories of value became very significant not because it led to theoretical development and programmatic changes, but because Social Democracy—in Sweden represented by Branting—definitively accepted the utilitarian theory of marginal utility. The political effects of this would make themselves felt much later.

When German Social Democracy entered the 1890s, it did so under partially new conditions. When the Socialist Law had been repealed, the party and the trade unions had grown, industrialism had expanded enormously, real wages and company profits had increased, and the bourgeois Left had shown a willingness toward reform. It was in this climate that the Marxist Erfurt Program was adopted. It was of very little practical importance. In the same year, 1891, the leader of the SPD, Georg von Vollmar, signaled that it was time to reevaluate the party's tactics. He said it was a matter of making use of the present state and social order. Lassalle's state socialism received renewed confidence, and practical policies were also developed along these lines. Collaboration with the part of the bourgeoisie which showed a willingness toward reform became more intense.

It was also in this climate that Bernstein began to revise Marxist doctrine around 1895-1896. Bernstein replaced Marxism with a kind of ethical theory of social development. According to the theory, socialism was in large part a question of morals and ideas. In the future capitalism would become unnecessary as an economic system. But the road was long, and developmental tendencies thus far had shown that man had succeeded in adapting himself to capitalism and that he was able to direct and lead development. The labor movement should therefore concentrate on the *present* and try to achieve improvements in the existing society.

It is clear that such a theory entails taking a positive position on the issue of parliamentarianism. Bernstein entirely accepted both the political and economic content of liberalism.

In the 1890s the criticism of Marx's labor theory of value by established liberal economists was widespread. Bernstein, who was not an economist, took note of it and in large part joined in the intensive criticism.

During the period 1860-1885 the Swedish labor movement was characterized by emerging social liberalism. The issue of parliamentarianism or revolution was not the essential one; it was, rather, the social issue (i.e., poverty), and the bourgeois Left wished to solve it through self-help, for example, through consumer cooperatives.

In the beginning of the 1880s when the labor movement made its first attempt to form its own organizations, it did so entirely on the basis of Lassalle's ideas. The first decade was characterized by struggle with the liberals for leadership of the labor organizations and by the development of a political program.

Branting's speech in Gävle in 1886 is an important document for an understanding of the 1880s. Branting maintained that social democracy was revolutionary in principle since it wanted social transformation. The means for bringing about change was universal suffrage, he continued, but the working class could not relinquish its right to make a revolution if the bourgeois class opposed the demand for universal suffrage.

Branting's views of the labor theory of value were in many ways influenced by Lassalle. The most important thing, at least in the short term, was the distribution of the results of the value-creating process. Nobody could help feeling indignant in the face of the inequitable distribution of the results of production and the misery of the working class.

From the middle of the 1890s, Branting developed, under the influence of German Social Democracy and especially of Bernstein, a Swedish revisionism. At the turn of the century he initiated direct consultations with the liberals concerning universal suffrage.

In 1917 Branting participated in a liberal cabinet, and one year later the national parliament adopted a law of universal suffrage. It was not to be seen mainly as a victory for the working class, said Branting, but was rather of common concern for the country. The political consequences of the labor theory of value were revealed to Branting mostly in the *inequitable distribution* of the results of production. For moral reasons endeavors should be directed at achieving a more just distribution and consumption in the present. Instead of the labor theory of value, said Branting, Jevon's theory of utility was now valid.

8.8 After the Institution of Universal Suffrage

INTRODUCTION

We established in the introduction to this chapter and in Chapter 6 that the emerging labor movement, through its organizational and intellectual proximity to liberalism, came to accept the latter's "division" of power into a political and an economic sphere. Not only was this differentiation *accepted*—the labor movement *concentrated on* the demand for political rights in accordance with Branting's recommendation. Thus, it reinforced and crystallized this division of power.

The struggle for political power became so central that it might easily appear as if with its help one could attain all other social and economic goals. There was no sophisticated discussion either of how capitalism had developed or of how it would develop if the working class attained political power. We would therefore like to maintain that up to the formation of the first Social Democratic government in 1920 the party leaders were overly optimistic concerning the possibilities for continued democratization. In the parliamentary debate on December 17, 1918, Branting said:

> It was time to make a reality of democracy. And so, it was time to go out and work for our program. We were driven by our party's demand, the demand that the right of labor stand up to the accumulation of capital.

> We wanted to realize the potential of the working class. We wanted the working class and all working people to assume a position worthy of human beings, and to enjoy the fruits of their own labor. This we would accomplish by grasping the political power which the working class possessed in a democratic society. This path is open to us now, and it is ours to tread.[107]

The quotation is testimony to the great importance which Branting ascribed to the suffrage reform and to the way in which the term "the rights of labor" was almost equated with political democracy. It opened the way for all necessary social and economic reforms. The road to emancipation was thus the conquest of political power, social reforms, and the democratization of the economy. Two main lines of thought developed with respect to this latter point, i.e., socialization in the sense of nationalization, and in the sense of industrial democracy.

In 1920 Branting appointed the Committee on Socialization and ordered the Inquiry into Industrial Democracy.

FROM THE STRUGGLE FOR UNIVERSAL SUFFRAGE TO THE STRUGGLE FOR SOCIALIZATION AND INDUSTRIAL DEMOCRACY

On March 10, 1920 the first purely Social Democratic cabinet was formed. The parliamentary base was so weak that the SAP (Social Democratic Workers' Party) could not maintain independent policies. This, however, did not prevent the initiation of inquiries "concerning the issues of the profound social and economic transformations which time itself has brought to the fore," as the cabinet wrote in its declaration of government.[108] These issues were industrial democracy and socialization. According to the cabinet minutes, Branting said:

> It is my conviction that an objective investigation of these lines of social development which takes no account of preconceived opinions will indicate feasible ways to abolish existing acute conflicts in the society while strengthening the productive forces of our people and thus laying the foundation for a brighter future for our entire nation.[109]

The socialization issue had previously been raised in parliament. It is worth noting the motives presented by the Social Democrats for socialization. One case concerned the sugar industry. Representatives of SAP felt that private production of foodstuffs, which had attained a monopoly position, should be socialized "so that the powers of state may have unlimited opportunity to regulate production in consideration of the just demands of *all* of society's members and with no regard for private interests tied to such industry."

Another case concerned natural resources such as ore. It was felt that these were national resources, comprising for all eternity "capital invested by nature in a given nation." The administration of such capital should not be conducted on a private basis "but rather above all with responsibility for both living and unborn generations". Similar arguments were put forth in dealing with a new water law in 1918.[110]

The dominant arguments concern the politics of distribution—everyone has just demands for a share in important foodstuffs and resources which are created by nature.

In no case can one assert that the arguments were founded on the rights of the workers to control and own the means of production. On the contrary, this was the consummation of a line of thought which had appeared earlier—being able to control the networks of distribution and consumption. This idea was reinforced from 1914 to 1918 as Sweden pursued emergency policies in a war-time economy. Tingsten maintains that "what was typical for 'war socialism' was . . . that regulation was not followed by expropriation or intervention in private ownership of a character permanent in principle."[111]

In the debate after the World War the thought was rejected that the war-time economy entailed any form of socialism. This debate was very significant since it was the prelude to the decision by the Social Democratic government in June of 1920 to appoint a Commission on Socialization.[112] The general preconditions for this debate were evident, says Tingsten, who continues:

> The institution in principle of democratization in the autumn of 1918 meant that the questions which had stood in the center of Social Democratic activity for 25 years had found a solution. With democracy came increased power for the party . . . it was under these conditions unavoidable that the question of the economic remolding of society was taken up, the question which was ideologically central to the party and which, it was said, had been deferred because of the necessity of first winning democracy.[113]

There were an additional number of factors which encouraged Social Democratic optimism for the future. The conclusion of peace injected thoughts of peace and continued democratization, and last but not least, the revolution in Russia *at this point* was a positive inducement to debating socialization. However, during the next decade the bourgeois parties turned the example of Russia against Swedish Social Democracy. The struggle between the bourgeoisie and the SAP culminated in the so-called Cossack Election of 1928. We shall return to the "Bolshevik Struggle" later on in this chapter.

In the first stage of the debate, socialization was a question of nationalization. But during 1919, largely due to Ernst Wigforss's commitment to the idea, guild-socialistic ideas found a larger audience.[114] However, "any generally accepted notion of how socialization without state management would appear was never developed." Tingsten says that the socialization debate showed "great confusion" and that the only thing to come of it was that "the concept economic or industrial democracy was . . . generally accepted and asserted."[115]

Certain lines of thought and ideas appeared in the socialization debate of 1918-1920 which have followed SAP up to the 1970s. For one, there is the notion that *private ownership makes up a part of the incitement structure* for the renewal of production; there is the notion that *socialization in the sense of nationalization should refer,* to the extent that it is necessary at all, *to raw material resources* and other *functions essential to the whole nation* (such as the communications system); there is the idea that an expansion of influence should take place so that the working class and society mature; finally there is the idea that *different forms of ownership* (state, municipal, private, and cooperative) *can be imagined as existing simultaneously.* The latter idea points toward the very central idea of ownership as an aspect of functional socialism, i.e., the question of the taking over of certain functions which had previously been privately controlled (see Section 9.2). The powers of state decide what is needed to satisfy the public interest and then extend or limit ownership rights according to this need.[116] The functional socialist elements in the theoretical development of Social Democracy appear here for the first time.

The socialization debate had certain concrete effects. For one thing, it seems likely that the program revision before the party convention of 1920 was influenced by the debate.[117] At the convention Rickard Sandler stated on behalf of the program commission: "We stand to such an extent before a new breakthrough that it is the problem of socialization which will dominate hereafter."[118] The debate led to the appointment of two committees (the Commission on Socialization and the Inquiry into Industrial Democracy) which were to solve the problems.

THE COMMISSION ON SOCIALIZATION

On June 22, 1920 the Commission on Socialization was appointed with Rickard Sandler as chairman and Gustav Möller, Nils Karleby, and Gustaf Steffen as members. Branting gave a detailed motivation for the appointment of the commission in the cabinet minutes: There was a problem of efficient and effective production, and a problem of the utilization of profit from the perspective of economic and social justice.

In the election of 1920 SAP lost votes for the first time in its history. It was generally felt that the diffuse socialization debate contributed to the election defeat.[119] The party resigned the government.

The period after 1920 was strongly marked by economic crisis and by a palpable weakening of Social Democratic agitation. In the following election campaign before the 1921 election socialization was no longer a clear element of SAP policy.

The actual activity of the Commission on Socialization was relatively anonymous. The first report was presented in 1924 and contained a proposal that the state railway be made a public enterprise. It was established in the report that state enterprise should fulfill the same criteria as privately owned ones. They should, among other things, cover their own costs. Rickard Sandler defended this position by saying "that one should also trust in the ability of the freely acting forces and in the fact that people in our modernly organized society to a certain extent are capable of taking care of themselves."[120]

In the parliamentary debate of 1925 SAP was accused by the bourgeois parties of not openly accounting for the work of the Commission on Socialization. Sandler, who at the time was temporary prime minister following Branting's death, gave a deferential answer. First he testified that the Social Democrats were not about to socialize by means of legislation since "socialization [is] quite simply a continuing process of development" which for the most part goes on without state intervention.[121]

During the latter half of the 1920s enthusiasm for socialization waned. In its place a group of young Social Democrats from the party's youth organization SSU appeared with the demand that both ideas and current policy be adapted to reality as it was perceived to be. In 1926 Nils Karleby published his book *Socialismen inför verkligheten* (*Socialism Meets Reality*), and in 1928 Richard Lindström published *Socialistisk vardag* (*Everyday Socialism*). In addition there were Karl Fredriksson's writings on the editorial page of the newspaper *Socialdemokraten* and the influence Gunnar Myrdal gradually began to exercise with his theories, primarily those on price formation but also on financial and credit policies. [122]

Common to these writers was that they questioned the value and the possibility of a socialist economy founded on the collective ownership of the means of production. Karleby, Lindström, and Fredriksson worked to make SAP a social liberal party.

In the parliaments of 1927 and 1928 the socialization issue was a main topic, and the bourgeois parties took the offensive in their criticism. Against this background, the election of 1928 promised to become a new confrontation. This was also the case. The election has been called the Cossack Election because of the descriptions by the bourgeois parties of the SAP as a Bolshevik party. The election was a catastrophe for the SAP, which lost fourteen seats. It would be twenty years before the SAP once again lost political ground. In 1948 the party was once again were pressured by a socialization debate, this time launched by the bourgeois parties under the motto "PHM" (planhushållningsmotstånd, Resistance Against Planned Economy).

The Commission on Socialization continued its work in spite of the criticism and released two additional reports. Between 1932 and 1935, however, the commission was gradually dissolved. It could not agree on a final report of principle after fifteen years of work. Rickard Sandler therefore published his own "Draft of a Report on Principle." [123] One year later, in 1937, Sandler published two additional reports. Tingsten's summary comment on the three reports is that "the interesting thing in it, as in the second part of the draft, is the fact that the program of Swedish Social Democracy is hardly heeded, and pronouncements are constantly made which indicate that the author considers the statements made in this program about society's development and structure to be either incorrect or misleading." [124]

In another place Tingsten has summarized the significance of the Commission on Socialization:

> The Commission, which functioned for almost 15 years, was of extraordinary importance for the ideological discussion. Not that it presented any comprehensive and guiding proposals concerning the institution of socialism; its work never got that far in practice. But it did serve as a symbol of the large and principal goals of the party, as proof that these goals were still living realities but also as a reason to put their realization off into the future. . . . The idealistic existence of the socialist principle was secured while at the same time its realization was postponed. [125]

The work and value of the Commission on Socialization were constant topics of debate in the labor movement. Much consideration was given to the tactical appropriateness of pressing the demand for socialization. The result was, as Tingsten writes, that socialization was chosen as a symbol to rally around, but the demand was dismissed from practical politics in reality.[126]

At the party convention of 1932 a decisive struggle was fought between those who wished to place the socialization demand at the center of attention and those who wished to dismiss it entirely from the program. The latter line was asserted by the party executive board, which prevailed. For our purposes, an interesting contribution to the debate was made by Ernst Wigforss. It concerned "concrete guidelines for the policy of social-ization." Wigforss said that there were in principle two possibilities: one was that a catastrophe would occur, in which case the party would act, and the other was that development would go on by itself, in which case the party would not act due to inner disunity. Wigforss said that this was the party's weakness. The reason for this state of affairs, he said, was that the party had two roots, Marxism and economic liberalism. Marxism entailed passivity in relation to economic development until the time was ripe for the party to intervene. At the same time the party had maintained a liberal economic policy: "it has in every case stood in the way when it has been a matter of giving the party a positive direction in its economic policy . . . one hears and reads statements within the Social Democratic party which show such solicitude toward what is called the free economy that nowadays one can hardly find anything like it in the whole world except among the most ossified economic liberals."[127]

THE INQUIRY INTO INDUSTRIAL DEMOCRACY

Parallel to the socialization debate there was another debate after World War I on industrial democracy, that is to say, it was actually a debate on how greater influence in companies could be ensured for the employees.

A special debate on industrial democracy was arranged at the party convention of 1920. Wigforss opened the debate and presented industrial democracy as a preparation for the remolding of society. The party convention decided upon an inquiry into the question. In June of the same year the first Social Democratic government appointed the Inquiry into Industrial Democracy.

The issue of economic democracy was given much play in the election campaigns of 1920, 1921, and 1922. In March of 1923 the inquiry committee presented a report which proposed management committees. These committees would have only an advisory function, and the goal would be to give the workers "broader insight into production," "the power of active involvement," and "improve cooperation" between labor and capital. The proposal was said to be founded on a "mutual will to cooperation."

In spite of the fact that the proposal thus had very limited ambitions, it was voted down by the members of the inquiry committee from bourgeois parties. One of the Social Democratic members (Johan-Olof Johansson) registered his dissent against the proposal, stating as his reasons that there was a basic difference between labor and capital and that the first condition for an equalization of the two was that "the workers obtain the right of co-determination on the issue of the hiring and firing of workers and the management of work plus an equal right to a seat and votes on the various boards of the company."[128] The leaders of the trade union movement were also critical of the proposal for essentially the same reasons.

In spite of the very cool interest in the proposal, the Social Democrats presented a motion to the parliament in 1924. This was rejected and with it the question was dismissed from the agenda of the labor movement for almost fifty years.

THE BOLSHEVIK STRUGGLE

A contributing reason for the SAP not enjoying more success in its ambitions was probably that the bourgeois parties launched an unexpected counteroffensive. The bourgeois forces also drew unexpected support from the developments evident in the Russian Revolution. This led to an inner dissolution of ideas, which in the longer term had devastating consequences. One may speak here of a "two-front war," one front directed against the bourgeoisie and the other against tendencies toward schisms in the party.[129]

When the Russian Revolution took place in 1917, the SAP sent a telegram which said:

> Swedish Social Democracy is eager to be among those sections of the International which first hasten to offer heartfelt congratulations to their Russian comrades on the speedy and complete victory in your political revolution, a victory which the socialist proletariat so forcefully helped to win for the benefit of the Russian people and for all of humanity.[130]

The telegram continued with a comparison of the Russian and the French revolutions, stating that both had the same significance in crushing reaction around the world.

In the first years after October 1917 the Russian Revolution was considered a promising event, which inspired Swedish Social Democracy to an ideological debate, resulting in, among other things, the aforementioned inquiries. In 1920 the political terror began which culminated in Stalin's concentration camps. It resulted in the definitive erosion of the Marxist intellectual tradition in Sweden, and contributed to the development of the "People's Home" ideology of the 1930s. (The Swedish Prime Minister Per Albin Hansson coined the phrase "People's Home" in a speech in 1932. What he meant was that during a period of relative lack of prosperity, the nation needed a "contract" between workers and private owners as a condition for peace on the labor market. Thus economic growth could be attained, and a society for the whole people could be realized.)

At first Swedish Social Democracy reacted with enthusiasm to the Russian Revolution. The enthusiasm was gradually succeeded, however, by an inner schism: communist factions were formed, and conflicts arose around what the Russian Revolution actually stood for. A few people, among them Artur Engberg and Nils Karleby, were capable of a sophisticated and theoretically well-founded critique of the Russian Revolution, but their contributions were too vague and ambiguous for the internal ideological debate. Karleby most of all dissociated himself entirely from the Marxist intellectual tradition and became increasingly social liberal (see Section 8.9).

Lindhagen has characterized Engberg and Karleby in the following way:

> We anticipate the consequences of the Bolshevik Struggle which turn up early on in Engberg's text of 1920. In the agitation for peaceful revolution we already find ambiguous statements in these two educated Marxists, statements which can be used just as well by their modern descendants to justify social reformism. This risk of a diluted Marxism had been noted long before Social Democracy reached Sweden.[131]

The break of 1917 between Social Democracy and communism broke "the synthesis between reform and revolution which is the most profound Marxist heritage in early Social Democracy. Revolution became the expression of the brutal Leninist praxis of the Swedish Communist party, and reform became with time the shallow reformism of our party."[132] The break between revolution and reform also meant the disappearance of the conditions for educating and organizing the working class toward a "double consciousness," i.e., the possibility of *simultaneously* cooperating with other than socialist forces *and* retaining a socialist consciousness. Instead there was a "simple consciousness" of political power and the possibilities of accomplishing reforms through it.

It was the young members of the party and the SSU, Richard Lindström, Karl Fredriksson, and Nils Karleby who during the late 1920s and the early 1930s came to be associated with the "new" Social Democracy. The 1930s was a decade of conflicting tendencies. The debate was marked by the fronts against Stalinism and the bourgeoisie and also by the "new alternative," which, in spite of everything, injected much optimism into Swedish Social Democracy; this was the alternative which later came to be called the "Per Albin line" or the "People's Home ideology."[133]

The 1930s became a decade of praxis and action. It was a matter of protecting society against fascism and the economic depression. The latter led to the party's establishment of a collaborative line, which meant that, at least as a historic compromise, the notion of the rights of labor as a basic principle was abandoned (cf. the statements on the rights of labor by Branting in Section 8.6). *Instead the right of labor was equated with that of capital.* The problems of distribution and consumption once again became a moral issue (cf. Section 8.7). In accordance with the "new" ideas of the 1930s, Fredriksson, for example, saw the problem as one of organizing capitalism, and Lindström was concerned with differentiating between an economic description of reality and the ethical justification for socialism. [134] These lines of thought had a good deal in common with the so-called Austromarxists, who (above all Rudolf Hilferding) launched the idea of "organized capitalism." [135] In the writings of Richard Lindström, Karl Fredriksson, and Nils Karleby there were clear demands that Social Democracy abandon both in word and deed the theories of class struggle, surplus-value, state, and revolution. Lindhagen writes:

> The Bolshevik Struggle led not only to a decreasing interest in classical Social Democratic intellectual work and theoretical debate. What was broken, in a slightly more profound sense, was the connection between practical politics and theoretical analysis. Thus, neither praxis nor theory lived up to what it could have been. Neither of them was finished creations with the generations of Branting or Per Albin. There was an endless amount left to do on both planes. This was what Karleby's appeal to the SSU (Social Democratic Youth Organization) was about [an appeal to theoretical work—our note]. Not only was our heritage forgotten—that would have been unfortunate enough—but what took place was even worse. *Social Democratic policy, in theory and in practice, stopped growing.* The heritage of Branting and his younger and older comrades did not become what it could have become [our italics]. [136]

The program revision of 1944 should have crowned this development. But there were significant conflicts, and the result was that Ernst Wigforss had to formulate a compromise. [137] Practical policies in the postwar period were instead marked by "the optimistic vision of a practicable social reformism of Karl Fredriksson and his comrades." [138]

THE EXAMPLE OF UNEMPLOYMENT POLICY

The first Social Democratic government—even though it did not have a majority in both houses of parliament—"controlled" political power in a certain sense—it had the political initiative. However, it was forced to resign after only seven months. The second Social Democratic government was formed one year later, in October 1921. That year unemployment increased from around 5% at the beginning of the year to around 20% by year's end. In other words, the economy was marked by a severe and deep depression. Against this background it is interesting to ask the question: On what basis did the Social Democratic government act?

Unemployment policies during the prewar period entailed an active redistribution. The notion of redistribution was mainly inspired by Social Democracy. When the Social Democrats formed a government in 1921, they were incapable of pursuing their own ideas, and they adapted their policies to other interests. Öhman summarizes his view of the unemployment policy under Social Democratic leadership:

> It is quite clear that to a great extent it gave consideration to employer interests; the formation and restrictiveness [of the policy] were defended by saying that unemployment could not "unduly" favor the employees. [139]

According to Öhman, the explanation for this is as follows: First of all, there was no parliamentary base for a majority policy, and the Social Democrats were forced to compromise. Second, there was "the intense fear of inflation." It was thought that a decrease in unemployment would contribute to an increased inflation. Third, there was economic determinism in the party. According to Öhman, "the party was not ideologically prepared for the planned economy notion of the type seen in the 1930s."[140] In spite of the fact that he can point out some likely reasons, Öhman finds the Social Democratic adherence to liberal ideas difficult to explain. He continues:

> There is no logical necessity for the tactical retreat being followed by an ideological retreat, but this seems to have been the case to a great extent. . . . The Social Democratic crisis of the 1920s illustrates the dilemma of reformism: pursuing realistic everyday policies while preserving the long-term goal. It is hardly an exaggeration to say that Social Democracy failed at this during the 1920s; its everyday policies were hardly marked by socialist ambitions.[141]

The economic crisis policies of the 1930s led to practical political advances for Social Democracy. There was an applicable Marxist intellectual tradition which was quite compatible with Keynes's political program.[142] Öhman also believes that the similarities between the Social Democratic intellectual tradition and that of Keynes were so great that the party "would have acted in approximately the same way in the economic crisis regardless of Keynes."[143] Wigforss himself maintains that there were considerable similarities between Social Democratic and Keynesian notions.[144] Lewin also supports this.[145] Unga sharpens the thesis: "the representatives of Social Democracy can hardly be considered to have had different theoretical starting points from the bourgeoisie in their evaluation of unemployment during the 1920s."[146]

8.9 Nils Karleby

In the preceding section we maintained that the practical policy of the Swedish Social Democratic government in the 1920s was for the most part a traditional liberal economic policy which did not differ decisively from the policy of the bourgeois governments. The theoretical expression of this policy was formulated by, among others, the economist Knut Wicksell, who was not a member of the SAP but was assumed to be closely aligned with the party. Wicksell thought that an active monetary policy could partially alleviate the economic crises of the capitalist system. Monetary policy (financial, credit, and interest policy) became the central theme in the economic debate.[147]

Tage Erlander, the successor of Per Albin Hansson and Sweden's Prime Minister 1946-1969, writes in his memoirs that "the study of Wicksell was important to the formation of my social values. But Nils Karleby meant even more."[148]

Nils Karleby (1892-1926) was a trained typesetter and attended the Brunnsvik Folk High School. Karleby worked for a short time as a typographer before be began working as an assistant editor. In 1916 he became editor of the newspaper *Skånska Social-Demokraten.* A year later he became editor-in-chief. Along with this job he was active as the editor of the SSU newspaper *Frihet,* and for ten years up to his death he often published long articles in the journal *Tiden.*

Karleby belonged to a group including Branting, Sandler, Möller, Wigforss, and Engberg which was relatively well acquainted with the Marxist debate. The Russian Revolution and the Bolshevik Struggle led to an extensive involvement for Karleby. He sharply attacked both the Russian Bolshevik leaders and the Swedish Communists for their "un-Marxist" line.[149] The Marxism which Karleby advocated before the revolutions in February and October 1917 changed. Lindhagen feels that "his insights were submerged by the Bolshevik Struggle, both on the personal and political level."[150] The result was a poorly thought out and simple Marxism based on the development notion, i.e., that capitalism develops toward socialism more or less for logical reasons. In the book *Socialismen inför verkligheten,* Karleby tried, according to Lindhagen, to formulate

> a progressive synthesis of liberalism and Marxism in the areas of economics and constitutional law. lt was theoretically not very successful. But the texts have attained what I feel is a rather unfortunate significance as an affirmation of the special and cautious reformism which was to become clearer in the party's policies.[151]

The struggle between Social Democrats and Communists during the Bolshevik Struggle "obscured other more profound and more important distinctions and led at times to something which can perhaps be called political pacifism. The peaceful social transformation of the Social Democrats had a touch of the peaceful social reformism of the radical Free Church."[152]

In 1920 Karleby became a member of the Commission on Socialization. He, like many others, attached a very great significance to it and said, for example: "There still exists a sort of vacuum in Social Democratic policy. This will be filled when the large inquiries are finished."[153] Karleby's contribution to the commission was his preparation of the report on the state railway which was published in 1925. This report was based on an economic viewpoint which Karleby was later to develop more fully. It was a liberal economic viewpoint: the business activity of the railway should pay for itself.[154] Between the years 1920 and 1923 Karleby studied history and economic history under Eli Heckscher and the economist Gösta Bagge. This was probably of considerable importance for his intellectual development in a liberal direction.

Erlander and von Sydow summarize their views on Karleby as follows:

Science and values pointed in the same direction. Social life could be improved through workers and other wage earners being rendered a greater share in the economic decision-making process. Companies and individuals would, however, function best in accordance with economic market principles. The state could gradually institute general reforms. Because given of the gold standard, however, consideration had to be given to economic development in other countries. International free trade and stable monetary value were especially in the interests of the working class. Was Karleby liberal in the midst of his socialism?[155]

Erlander thinks that Karleby succeeded in explaining and creating understanding for the differences between the party's program and its day-to-day policies. *Socialismen inför verkligheten* was met therefore "with a feeling of great liberation."[156] "Karleby's outlook has served as a foundation for many of the leaders in the Swedish labor movement, especially in its second and third generations. Thus, his outlook has left its mark on much of Swedish social development in the last decades."[157]

ON SOCIAL DEMOCRACY

Karleby was eager to give the SAP a distinctively Swedish character. This led him to deny the influence of German Social Democracy. Karleby sought to derive the intellectual origins of Swedish Social Democracy from the Reformation, the French Revolution, and Marx.[158] He described German Social Democracy as "awkward," "doctrinaire scholasticism," and inferior to Swedish Social Democracy "with respect to theoretical clarity and independence and with respect to practical competence."[159] Swedish Social Democracy was in Karleby's words "social-relativist," by which he meant that the party, based on the starting point "that the state is an indespensible form of organization," gradually wanted to transform society so that it approached "the vital demands of the working class".[160]

Karleby underscored the close connection between Social Democracy and Liberalism. Depending on the social development, Social Democracy was a natural consequence of older liberalism: "The modern notion of Social Democracy is a natural outgrowth of classical liberalism. Its connection to socialism comes from the observation of the consequences of the development of production as regards the methods for determining production."[161] "Even economically," Karleby stated, "Social Democracy is a consummation of, not a break with, the ideas of the bourgeois class."[162]

There was one more essential similarity: both Social Democracy and liberalism intended to establish "harmony of interests." What separated them in certain respects was the method of doing this.[163] Another of the peculiarities Karleby attributed to Swedish Social Democracy may be worth noting. It lacked theoretical doctrinism and was characterized by "a sense of reality." "That Swedish Social Democracy has become 'Marxist' is not due to any study of Marx. That is surely the least of what it dealt with."[164] The theory had, as Karleby said, "been expressed in practice." Instead of a theoretical and ideological debate, the driving force behind the labor movement had been the following:

> It was an unreflecting sense of justice, along with immediate need which supported their strivings. The innermost chord of the movement sounded in the demand for human value. It was a mighty enthusiasm and an inten- pathos of justification which was the living force of the movement. It was not a question of theory or dogma, but of fellowship with Swedes excluded from their own country, fighting for their own simple rights as citizens.[165]

Karleby's characterization confirms what we were previously able to establish: instead of a deepened theoretical development with scientific ambitions and the simultaneous ideological education of the working class so that theory and praxis could be united, an ethical socialism was developed, the primary goal of which was the politics of distribution.

ON OWNERSHIP RIGHTS

Karleby states that "the views of liberalism and socialism on the significance of ownership are identical in principle."[166] Social ownership is a part of democracy, but "it is, however, not the goal of the movement." And the reason, according to Karleby, is that it is impossible to realize due to various difficulties and obstacles.[167]

Ownership is not an absolute "problem of rights." The decisive thing is "how it affects human development."[168] It is the limits on ownership as they have been established by the state through legislation that are of interest. According to Karleby, it is the *right of disposition* which is to be limited, i.e., private ownership should not cease, but because of constantly growing collective needs, the yield of private ownership must be distributed differently. "The demand for 'social ownership' as the term is commonly used is actually just a euphemism for the demand for a certain kind of *distribution,* such as 'equal,' 'just,' or something similar."[169]

Once he has turned the issue of ownership into an issue of disposition or distribution, Karleby finds many examples:

> Take urban zoning laws, the health statute, all social legislation, taxation laws with a socioeconomic purpose, etc.—what is this but a series of formulations of ownership according to the norms of social utility, or in other words, the formulation of the co-determination right of nonowners over the utilization of objects?[170]

And he continues with a description of the progress which has been achieved:

> The modern worker participates in the formation of working conditions through his trade union; he is co-owner of important economic enterprises through his cooperative association or through his state or municipality. Through state-supported health insurance programs he is insured against illness, and through accident legislation he is insured against accident. Good schools and educational opportunities are open to him and his children, and he has the benefit of publicly provided control of hygienic and technical conditions. He is insured a rather high degree of freedom and security of life and limb through social legislation, won at the cost of the employer's right to use "his" property as he sees fit. In his old age he is ensured of aid in the form of pension—perhaps scanty but still an important beginning—or care which is so good that his grandfather with memories of the poor house would consider it the pinnacle of luxury. Through universal suffrage he may participate in the legislative determination over property, and gradually, according to his own opportunities and needs, increasingly form it in a socially satisfactory way. Does not this comparison with all its actual reforms of the rights of disposition over property show to what a high degree bourgeois property, bourgeois society, and the proletarian lack of property actually belong to a bygone age? The socialized society, social property, and the participation of the working class have emerged.[171]

In the capitalist economy labor is a commodity which the individual must sell to someone who can buy it. The buyer does not buy the commodity unless he can make a profit, i.e., unless he gets something more than the labor itself costs. In this way surplus-value arises. Surplus-value accumulates and grows. The relevant question for Karleby is therefore: Which party, the worker/working class or the capitalist/upper class has over a long period of time (50 to 100 years) received the larger absolute and relative share of the total growth once necessary investments have been subtracted? The answer depends upon how one views labor and its value-creating role in the production process.

KARLEBY'S INTERPRETATION OF THE RIGHTS OF LABOR

Karleby poses the question whether labor could be a basis for rights. His answer is a definite no.

The slogan "the fruits of labor to those who labor" is, according to Karleby, only "acceptable as a general ethical postulate." "Basically, the term is of petty-bougeois origin" and not applicable to a modern capitalist society. It presupposes that "the laborer should be his own, should himself produce his product, and should himself receive its price." But the laborer is not his own, does not produce the whole product, does not create all of its value, but rather is "a mere cog in a large machine of industrial and commercial workers," says Karleby.[172]

Thus there is no inherent value in labor. Its value is determined solely and merely by the market, by *the utility which others feel they gain by a certain labor.* Through the example of Rockefeller, Karleby shows that "the right to the full yield of labor is an empty phrase." Rockefeller has created his fortune through labor, but those who demand "the fruits of labor to those who labor" will not begrudge him his earnings! Karleby expresses this as follows:

> When one looks at Rockefeller's millions, one may become angry and perhaps speak of exploitation. But one cannot deny that Rockefeller began with two empty hands and had earned his fortune by organizing world oil distribution in a way which was better for consumption. In other words, through *labor* [our italics]. If he earns millions through this labor, then it is still certain that consumers have saved many more millions thanks to his more practical organization, and that the subjective value which consumers placed on his oil and in an emergency might well have paid him for it is far greater than his earnings. Thus, Rockefeller has, on one hand, received much more than the fruits of his labor, measured according to what labor usually pays, but on the other, he has doubtlessly not received most of the fruits of his labor![173]

Labor is a production factor whose price is determined by the employer's marginal utility with respect to it. The marginal utility of a company can, "all else being equal, be increased in part through a rise in the general level of productivity, and partly through a decrease in the number of persons."[174]

Capital is accumulated labor, but only in the sociological sense, says Karleby. In the economic sense this is "completely meaningless for *price formation,* which represents an inner social mechanism of balance." From the point of view of price formation, "capital and land represent independent production factors just like labor, and the investment of capital and land is part of the value of the products just like the investment of labor. And they *must* be."[175] Karleby thinks that the labor theory of value and the theory of marginal utility are *valid simultaneously.* The former for society as a whole and the latter in order to explain the value of a commodity.[176] That was the common interpretation which spread within Social Democracy after Bernstein's revisionism.

ON CAPITAL

For Karleby there was no fundamental conflict between labor and capital. In part due to the numerical growth of the working class and its gradual assumption of political power, social development was moving in the direction of pruning the unlimited rights of capital bit by bit. He called this tendency "the organization of the market."[177] Another analogous tendency was for the working class itself—through political power (and the trade union movement and the cooperative) and social reforms—to mature and create the conditions for socialism.[178]

It was therefore natural and logical that the primary task of the working class, given the capitalist society, should be to organize production as *effectively* as possible and to *economize* with scarce resources.[179] The preconditions for this task were in part that the working class had a share in political power and further that the working class was gradually made a participant in the production process.[180]

There was in Bernstein (see Section 8.4) an optimism concerning the possibility of organizing and directing capital which recurs in Karleby. For example, Karleby writes on the subject of risk:

> It can be decreased through prudent foresights based on good statistics and a well-organized intelligence operation, and above all by a discount rate policy of the central bank which keeps the economic cycles within narrow bounds.[181]

Karleby takes into account three production factors: capital, land, and labor. They are all necessary, but capital and land are more important since, in Karleby's words, they "shape human activity more fruitfully."[182] How can he come to this conclusion? The answer is that for Karleby the elements that are of primary importance for society's economic activity and its foundations are *social utility, society, the public need*, etc.[183] Indirect labor (i.e., saving) is also labor, says Karleby, but this is of interest only from a sociological perspective and does not affect economic conditions. Karleby writes: "But this total perspective is completely meaningless for *price formation*, which represents an inner social mechanism of balance."[184] Karleby develops this carefully and in so doing makes it completely clear that there are two things which must be kept separate: (1) The objective and value-free economic science, which is only a question of effective organization.[185] (2) The injustices which are consequences of economic conditions and which have nothing to do with economic science. Injustice is a *political* problem of participation, or as Karleby expresses it:

> From the perspective of the economic machinery it is completely unessential to *whom* the right of ownership and thus the income from the objective production factors belong. That is a problem of participation in society. It is a main social problem, but it is of no direct importance to the actual economic theory.[186]

Karleby feels that price formation is the only theory of value which is possible in a modern society. As he expresses it, it has "had the decidedly greatest importance for the development of theoretical social economics," while Marx's theory of value "has had an equally predominant importance for the practical, sociopolitical refashioning of the science."[187] It is not just that Karleby thinks that the subjective theory of value is necessary and unavoidable in order to explain a capitalist economy; on the contrary, it is "universally valid" and is thus important even for a socialist economy (cf., Böhm-Bawerk and Branting above).

Karleby also maintains that the two theories of value complement each other. He feels that people's *desires* (subjective theory of value) must be kept in *balance with the economic preconditions* (objective theory of value). In this way the theories of value complement each other so that "the sociological starting points of the Marxian economic theory form the foundation and the framework, and the subjectivist analyses of social economics form the content."[188] The subjective theory of value *is* the science while the objective theory of value describes political conditions; thus it is not science, according to Karleby.

Then what constitutes economic science? What are the basic concepts? We have mentioned one above, i.e., social utility. How does "the public need" arise in the social utility? Karleby's answer is as follows:

> Man's will is the original driving force in economic life as in social life. But the generator by means of which this will is transformed to an economic value-determinant force and thereby to an acting factor in the entire economic process lies in the changes in the effectiveness of the productive investments.[189]

Human will is expressed through a "balance between future and present values" and through a "calculus of pain and pleasure." It is thus the separate calculations of pain and pleasure of individuals which, taken together, comprise social utility.

The difference between the labor theory of value and the subjective theory of value is merely a difference in method and intent, says Karleby.[190] One way to elucidate this difference and at the same time to comprehend how social utility is a condition of price formation is to understand competition.

> It is through the fact that competition on the free market treats the concrete labor invested by all producers in the production of a commodity as one unit and pays for it only to the extent that it was socially necessary that it can be determined to what extent this concrete labor actually participated in the formation of value and in establishing the corresponding price.[191]

In other words, it is in the exchange of a commodity that the price is established, and the value of labor is thereby established indirectly through commodity exchange. Or as Karleby phrases it: "Far from labor being that which determines value, on the contrary, it is [commodity exchange] which establishes to what extent labor will be counted as a component of value."[192]

CONCLUSION

Karleby's economic approach is an attempt at an integration of a Marxist and a liberal approach. It seems clear that in his striving for such an integration, he reveals what is primarily a liberal point of view. Central to Karleby's economic view is the process of price formation. The price of a commodity, and thus its value, is determined by the utility people judge the commodity to have. That price is just and gives to each production factor (labor, land, capital) its fair compensation which "corresponds to its importance for its [social utility's—our note] attainment."[193]

How can it be that resource distribution will be just? Karleby answers:

> The same notion that underlies the democratic equality demand in general underlies the notion of the equal rights of those who share the production factors—an interesting fact which in its own way testifies to the uniformity of human thinking and shows why authoritarian rule and authoritarian price determination (as in the Middle Ages) go together, as do democracy and democratic price formation (in the present). Democracy is based on the abstract equal right: decisions are a result of citizens exercising this right. Free price formation also rests on abstract equal right: the development is the result of the production agents exercising their equal rights. The equal right, exercised by the various parts to a production factor, has the effect that, abstractly, equal receives equal. The condition for the result is, however, that each part is free to choose the place he desires; it is through this competition that equalization is brought about.[194]

Erlander on Karleby. According to Erlander, Karleby's book *Socialismen inför verkligheten* gave "answers to our questions."[195] Erlander makes this judgement while at the same time admitting that neither the second (Karleby) nor the third (Erlander) generation of leading social democrats was so well versed in Marxism that it could discuss the significance of the ideological influence of Karleby's book.[196]

Karleby, according to Erlander, succeeded in putting the theoretical discussion of ownership into "the center of politics."

Now, if it was the case that ownership was not whole and indivisible, then "the entire question of society's change in a socialistic direction came into a new and more easily handled position."[197] And Erlander continues:

> The socialization question was not, as it previously was, the dominant question in socialist theory, but rather was a question of appropriateness exactly as in practical politics. This is not a matter of the breakdown of socialism, but rather of its intensification so as to cover all of reality.[198]

Karleby's ideological works had, according to Erlander, an additional merit which is important to point out: "More important was that Karleby's answer was such that the dividing line between Social Democracy and the bourgeoisie became sharper and was not erased."[199] This statement agrees poorly with Erlander's question of whether Karleby "in the midst of his socialism [was] liberal." Karleby's work doubtless had liberal features and contributed to erasing, rather than sharpening, the border between Social Democracy and the bourgeoisie.

In his writing Karleby laid the foundation for a functional socialist development of social democracy which obscured problems of ownership and thus tended to dismiss continued and deepened ideological debate. Erlander concludes his treatment as follows:

> Nils Karleby's contribution was to prove that the step by step reformation of society, far from conflicting with the Marxist critique of capitalist society, actually was the only true Marxism. Reformism worked in the spirit of Marx, that is, with careful observance of the chances for reform which reality gradually created. That was good for us. We no longer needed to make excuses for our daily reform work.[200]

Of course not—but it was also a question of how far-reaching the reform work would be. Karleby's work contributed to removing private ownership from discussion.

8.10 From Transformation to Just Distribution

The 1920s, the 1930s, the Inquiry into Industrial Democracy, or the Commission on Socialization; none of them were any real break with previous ideas and traditions, nor did they entail any renewal. What happened during the 1920s and later can better be described in terms of continuity and analogies.

Above, in Sections 8.1 and 8.6, we have described the intellectual development of socialism. The conclusion of this description is that the party that was founded in 1889 can hardly be described as based on a Marxist perspective. It was a combination of influences from German and English socialism, from radical bourgeois thinkers and liberals. Instead of being directed toward a deepening of the debate on the labor theory of value and surplus-value, the debate was characterized by ethical and moral discussions of the distribution of the results of production. Therefore, it was the concern of theoreticians like Karleby and others to give the actual policies an explanation and a legitimacy, to show that the party's daily policies really were connected to its ideological tradition and long-term goals.

In the place of socialization came planned economy. Karleby laid the foundation for what he thought would be a transformation with a socialistic import by arguing for a market economy in a planned economic system.[201] According to Karleby, there existed in capitalist societies organizational tendencies in the direction of making the economy more efficient. What was left was to let the state, i.e., the political powers, take the initiative and direct these organizational tendencies. It was organized, planned capitalism that he wanted to see realized. It would allow the greatest possible efficiency of production and thus a constantly increasing production result, which from then on would be distributed justly. Karleby concluded his "program" as follows:

> The guide is not a mechanical exploitation theory, which in reality cannot be a guide to practical work, but can only be important as a general ethical starting point. Neither is it an a priori demand for public ownership or a general system for production. Rather it is the working class demand for equality and its view of social utility and the developmental needs of production; in other words, always the practical need.[202]

Planned economy in the sense in which it was used toward the end of the 1920s and during the 1930s became synonymous with capitalism organized for efficient production.

The key words in the development which now lay before the party were efficiency and cooperation. The notion of cooperation meant that the economic views of labor and capital as two equal production factors were adopted in day-to-day policy. In other words, it was a capitalist economy which the social democrats said they were willing to administer and, in addition, to make more efficient than before. It seems logical that they drew their primary support in this from established economics. Lindhagen formulates the change as follows:

> This is no abstract question. Without doubt, the position on socialism slips during the 1930s under the influence of an economic outlook which was bound to the theory of marginal utility. Consumption and not, as in Marx, production is the starting point for Jevons's and others' formulation of the value problem. This corresponds to the newly aroused hopes of the time for a rising standard of living and a more just distribution of prosperity.[203]

Lindhagen also points out the moral element in the policy of cooperation. A popular morality must replace the Marxist theory of value, but it happens on a considerably more primitive level.[204] Lindhagen and Nilsson summarize the 1930s in the following way:

> The Social Democratic policy of the 1930s may have been devastatingly effective. The party had to show that it was capable of governing. That its possession of power was to the benefit of all the people. . . . But the policy led to the party being viewed less as a class party than before. Both within and outside the party the tendency was reinforced to see it as a *popular party*. Its goal was the good of all. The path there did not at all assume the execution of the power of one class.[205]

And they continue:

> The classless society which socialism wanted to establish after the victory of
> the working class began to be seen as something which should be born today.
> The notion of class struggle had long since disappeared from the vocabulary of
> the party. Now it began to be replaced in practice by the people's home
> ideology—a synthesis of socialism's demand for the power of the popular
> majority and liberalism's programmatical classlessness. And thus was justified
> the long on-going transformation of what we call social democracy's revolu-
> tionary action to what we may call a *distributive ethic*. The party and the
> labor movement no longer expressly intended to transform society through
> their actions. The expressed goal was rather to attain a just distribution of the
> increasing value of the present society.[206]

Lindhagen and Nilsson feel that the policies of the 1930's entailed a
definitive affirmation of the separation of politics and economics.[207]
Private capital is for the most part and in spite of some intervention in the
economy free with respect to the right of disposition.

8.11 Summary

In the preceding chapter we discussed the labor theory of value and the
subjective theory of value primarily from the starting points of logic,
testability, and theoretical fruitfulness. In order to be in any way complete, however, the discussion demands a review of the practical use to
which the two theories were put. This has been the subject of Chapter 8.

Briefly, our thesis is that, due to various circumstances, Social Democracy in Europe—exemplified by Germany and Sweden—chose the theory
which had been developed by groups alien to or antagonistic toward the
interests of the working class. The subjective theory of value, which was
based on liberal individualism, was accepted, while the labor theory of
value was rejected as logically faulty and practically useless.

The reasons for this are, in summary, the following. First, the early
social democratic leaders (for example, Lassalle) did not have access to
Marx's formulation of the labor theory of value. Second, Bernstein's
critique of Marx and Social Democracy's acceptance of "revisionism"
came to function as obstacles to the spread of the labor theory of value
when it *became* available through the publication of *Capital*. Third—and
probably decisive—Europe's continuing conversion to a capitalist system of
production meant that purely factual considerations drew attention to the
phenomena of consumption and the market. The subjective theory of
value was an expression of the "methodological individualism" in social
thinking which was stimulated by the spread of the market, the emphasis
on consumption and the role of the consumer, and the academic doctrines
(of Menger, Walras and Jevons, among others) which followed and inter-

preted these changes. Fourth, the labor theory of value, founded in the circumstances of production and with its emphasis on the *origin* of value, could not be easily adapted to questions which involved the solution to the enormous problem of the *distribution* of the products of labor.

Fifth, it was easy for Social Democratic leaders to feel an affinity with liberalism's opposition to the state based on privilege and to hope that changes could be accomplished in cooperation with the liberals. Universal suffrage became the political reform which Social Democrats and liberals could unite around. An unintended, and for Social Democracy fateful, effect of this cooperation, was that political and economic power were treated as separate issues. For a long time to come, the labor movement concentrated on the first part of this complex of problems. Hjalmar Branting's life-work is perhaps the outstanding example of these strivings.

In summary, one may state that the working class found itself in the weaker position with respect to both political and economic power, which meant that a larger share of the results of production could be obtained only if the bourgeoisie's conditions for ownership of the means of production were accepted.

Political suffrage could be presented as the means by which the labor movement could gradually and peacefully attain parliamentary power. The limits to the potential of parliamentary power were seldom mentioned, and the question of how far the wishes of the majority could be *executed* under a system of private capitalownership was, with few exceptions (Wigforss) not subject to a systematic treatment. The functional socialist tradition which includes Nils Karleby, Östen Undén and Gunnar Adler-Karlsson—and which has exerted a strong leadership in the theoretical development of Swedish social democracy—does not regard the question of ownership of capital as a main problem. More on this in the next chapter.

Chapter 9

CONFLICTS BETWEEN PRINCIPLES OF RIGHTS

In this chapter we shall elucidate some concrete manifestations of conflicts among various interest groups and the principles of rights which are thereby brought to light. Three cases are of interest. The first is the *debate on employee investment funds,* which illustrates the conflict between wage earner demands (for control over production and for a greater share in the results of production) and the demands of private capitalowners (for continued private ownership of the means of production). In this case, the *rights of labor* are asserted against the *rights of private ownership.* We will discuss this further in Section 9.1.

The second case is exemplified by functional socialism. According to its advocates, functional socialism is a strategy for the assertion of the *public interest* against the rights of private ownership. In other words, *civic rights* and subsequent parliamentary demands are asserted against the *rights of private ownership.* This conflict has come to be of interest mainly in connection with the distribution of the results of production and to a considerably lesser extent with regard to the control and ownership of the means of production. It is thus a common occurrence in Western industrialized countries that the state, i.e., the parliament, is forced to legislate on taxes, employer taxes, social security taxes, etc. This is usually accompanied by resistance of the capitalowners, and the laws which are passed are often subject to attack and demands for revision. At the same time, a small part of the means of production is owned by the public interest—between 10 and 30% in most industrial countries. The tendency is toward a concentration of private ownership partly among fewer and therefore larger owner groups and partly among internationally based corporate conglomerates.[1]

The potential and the limitations of functional socialism with respect to the conditions for overcoming the claims to power of private ownership will be discussed further in Section 9.2.

A third kind of conflict between principles of rights and interests concerns the demands and claims of employees vis-à-vis the public interest. This conflict arises mainly within the public sector where employees assert the right of labor as grounds for influence in public administration. Political democracy, which claims to assert and represent the public interest, stands opposed to these employee demands. The conflict between employees in public administration and politicians, who represent the public interest and political democracy, is the object of extensive debate, mainly among political scientists.[2]

Certain of these political scientists[3] argue against increased wage-earner influence because in practice it gives labor unions, when compared with other interest groups (nonworkers), too great an influence over areas of decision-making which are the exclusive domain of political democracy. They warn against a corporatist development, in which union and political interests—which should be separate—converge, allowing them to exercise undue power over other groups.

The conflict between the demands of employees and the public interest will be treated further in Chapter 10.

The conflicts mentioned here are of almost daily interest. It also seems that the developments of the 1970s have entailed a sharpening of these conflicts. In our opinion, it is important that they be discussed and that solutions to the problems arising from them be found. In Chapter 10 we shall discuss a solution to the problems which arise when the rights of labor are placed before the rights of private ownership. A further special discussion will be devoted to the relationship between the rights of labor and civic rights.

9.1 Employee Investment Funds: The Conflict Between the Rights of Labor and the Rights of Private Ownership

The purpose of this section is to describe the debate on employee investment funds from the perspective of the conflict between the principles "rights of labor" and "rights of private ownership."

Collective ownership of the means of production may be arranged in a number of ways, from completely state-owned companies to companies entirely owned by the workers.[4] History gives many examples both of theoretical constructions and of practical attempts at collective ownership.[5,6]

A LIBERAL IDEA

The nineteenth century may be described in terms of a violent power struggle between the old feudal society and the rising bourgeois class, on one hand, and between the propertied bourgeois class and the unpropertied workers, on the other. It was a power struggle fought both through outright wars and through a battle for ideological hegemony. The demands of the unpropertied people were for a just share of the results of production and, further, for influence over the utilization of the means of production and for influence in political bodies.

The awful misery under which workers were forced to live during the rise of capitalism was the visible expression of the dominance of capital over labor. This misery—"the social question"—drew attention not only in the labor movement but also in radical bourgeois circles. There was thus a basis for limited cooperation between these circles and worker representatives.

The attention given to the "social question" by bourgeois radicals was ambiguous. Of course, it was partly a matter of actually helping the needy, but to a great extent it was a matter of using this help to prevent the organization of the workers and a development toward socialism.

John Stuart Mill was one of the early bourgeois economists who saw where the development was headed. As early as 1848 in his *Principles of Political Economy* he argued for a system of profit sharing. Through this idea, Mill, who was conscious of the potential conflict between labor and capital, wanted to create the conditions for a harmonious and conflict-free relationship between capitalowners and workers. He formulated this in the following way:

> The aim of improvement should be not solely to place human beings in a condition in which they will be able to do without one another, but to enable them to work with or for one another in relations not involving dependence. Hitherto there has been no alternative for those who lived by their labour, but that of labouring either each for himself alone, or for a master. But the civilizing and improving influences of association, and the efficiency and economy of production on a larger scale may be obtained without dividing the producers into two parties with hostile interest and feelings, the many who do the work being mere servants under the command of the one who supplies the funds, and having no interest of their own in the enterprise except to earn their wages with as little labour as possible.

> The speculations and discussions of the last fifty years, and the events of the last thirty, are abundantly conclusive on this point. If the improvement which even triumphant military despotism has only retarded, not stopped, shall continue its course, there can be little doubt that the *status* of hired labourers will gradually tend to confine itself to the description of workpeople whose low moral qualities render them unfit for anything more independent: and that the relation of masters and workpeople will be gradually superseded by partnership, in one of two forms: in some cases, association of the labourers with the capitalist; in others, and perhaps finally in all, association of labourers among themselves.[7]

The idea of profit sharing became the radical bourgeois groups' own idea and was advocated by the liberal labor associations, among others. Profit sharing has been a liberal demand in Sweden from the middle of the nineteenth century to modern times. In 1892 a motion on the question was presented in parliament by Rudolf Klinckowström in order to solve the "social question" and to prevent the workers from becoming socialists. Parliament rejected the motion with the argument that this was not a question for state intervention but rather a problem which had to be solved on a voluntary basis by the involved parties.

The issue lay dormant until 1949 when the Liberal party presented a motion on profit sharing in order to increase productivity. In 1952, 1956,

1968, and 1974 the Liberal party again presented motions with the same basic demands. The last attempt resulted in a government investigation of the question, but the first four attempts were rejected with the argument that this was a question for the parties involved in the labor market. This argument was reinforced by the Saltsjöbaden agreement, which established freedom in the labor market, i.e., freedom from government direction. (The agreement, signed at Saltsjöbaden in 1938 between the SAF [the national employers' organization] and the LO [the Swedish Federation of labor], established long-term peace on the labor market and laid down the principle of central negotiations on wages and working conditions since then practiced in Sweden.)

There was a certain connection between the liberal notion of profit sharing and the ideas on worker cooperatives of the early labor movement, which were inspired by Lassalle. The difference was that Lassalle proposed that the state transfer the necessary capital to the worker cooperatives, while Mill, for example, was of the opinion that a certain share of company profits should be transferred to the workers. The important thing, however, is that there was a common problem—the "social question"—for liberals and socialists (see Chapter 8). This made possible a dialogue and, later, cooperation on the suffrage issue. The failure of the Social Democrats to discuss profit sharing to any meaningful degree is most probably due to the fact that interest was focused on the political struggle and universal suffrage, and further, when working-class participation in the economy was discussed, it was, at least in the beginning, in terms of nationalization.

THE REACTIONS OF THE FEDERATION OF LABOR

The Swedish Federation of Labor (LO) discussed the notion of profit sharing at its conventions in 1909 and 1917. The idea was dismissed as "extremely problematical" because, among other things, it would mean that the workers would have to take some responsibility for the companies. During the 1920s the LO reacted coolly to proposals for industrial democracy, arguing that they did not resolve the basic conflict between labor and capital.

Questions of profit sharing and industrial democracy were not to be discussed at an LO convention until 1961. But the LO was forced to react in various ways to the offensive of the Liberal party. The LO's press officer, Gunnar Dahlander, wrote in an article in 1952 that the notion of profit sharing counteracted the system of collective bargaining, the wage solidarity policy, and solidarity in the labor movement. Another argument presented was that the trade union movement would be forced into a position of double loyalty, to both members and owners.

Both the LO and the SAP were extremely defensive on the issue of the growth of wealth and the distribution of power. Two politicians, Per Edvin Sköld and Ernst Wigforss, participated in the debate during the 1950s after their respective resignations from cabinet positions. Sköld argued for a system of collective salary-savings, and his primary aim was the achievement of stabilizing political solutions. Wigforss started from guild-socialistic ideas and proposed "social companies without owners." To a great extent Wigforss shared Sköld's ambitions for policies of stabilization, but he added arguments for policies of growth and distribution. Rudolf Meidner, at the time investigative head of the LO, also participated in the debate and emphasized the arguments for growth and efficiency. During the 1960s the LO participated in two investigations concerning funds for the rationalization of branches of industry (1961, 1966). Neither of them led to any practical results, and there was only slight interest within the labor union movement.

The situation was different in 1971. In December 1969 a long and widespread strike broke out among the several thousand miners in the mining company LKAB. The strike was not primarily a matter of wages, but rather a result of dissatisfaction with conditions of labor organization, labor management, personnel policies, etc.[8] The strike took a severe turn and was given much attention by the mass media. It attained opinion-making significance, and collections were made throughout the country for financial support for the strikers. In the following years, 1970 and 1971, a wave of wild-cat strikes swept the country.

The LKAB strike and those which followed it had something in common with the student unrest in Sweden and abroad in 1967-1968: they were partly protests against authoritarian and hierarchical labor and educational organizations. The workers also struck against the effects of the (Swedish Central Organization of Salaried Employees) in cooperation with the Employers' Association (SAF). The complaints concerned deterioration of the working environment, monotonous labor processes, acceleration of the labor process, the elimination of workers from the labor force, etc.

Korpi points to the existence of a consciousness of income differentials among wage earners and the growing knowledge that economic growth does not necessarily lead to increased welfare.[9] Toward the end of the 1960s the West, including Sweden, suffered from stagflation, i.e., a stagnant economy *with* inflation.

Dahlström points also to structural changes in the economy as reasons behind the changes of course in the LO and the SAP around 1970-1971.[10] He points out the concentration of power within private industry, increasing state interventionism in the economy, increasingly rapid technological changes, rationalization, and stagflation tendencies.[11] At the same time as conditions for the workers worsen, there is a rise in their level of expectations. The origins of this rise can be found in long-term changes in education and democratic consciousness in general and, further, in concrete occurrences such as student unrest and wild-cat strikes.

After a while, the political and union leaders of the labor movement understood the on-going debate and the above-mentioned occurrences as expressions of demands for reforms. During the years 1970 and 1971 the legislative offensive of the labor movement began, culminating in the Law of Co-determination in 1977.

At the LO convention of 1971 a resolution was made demanding co-determination in companies and an investigation was commissioned which resulted in the so-called Meidner Report in 1975.

A motion of the Liberal party in 1974, when Sweden was governed by the "deadlocked parliament" (with the bourgeois and socialist blocks having 150 parliamentary seats each), led to an economic agreement with the Social Democrats, which resulted in the appointment of a state inquiry into the growth of wealth and influence. This so-called Mehr Investigation is not expected to present its first report until at least 1981.

The Meidner Report was received favorably by the LO convention of 1976 and was adopted with minor changes. The SAP lost government power the same year for the first time in forty-four years, and in the following debate one of the reasons was assumed to be the predominant role taken by ownership issues in Meidner's report. The LO and the SAP decided therefore to work out a new proposal, and it was presented in the spring of 1978 (see pp. 207 ff). The proposal was entitled "Guidelines for a System of Employee Investment Funds" and in principle it entailed only the addition of one more goal for the fund system beyond the three which had been adopted by the LO convention two years earlier. The authors of the proposal were careful to note that their proposal concerned only guidelines and that it was "one step in the extensive preparations which must precede a decision by the parliament."[12] These preparations consist mainly of the public inquiry which, up to 1979, was led by Hjalmar Mehr.

At the party convention in the autumn of 1978 the proposal was of no great significance either for the pronouncements of the executive board on motions on economic democracy or for the subsequent debate. The executive board sought an approval from the convention of a few main guidelines without committing itself to any concrete solution. The guidelines proposed by the executive board were:

(1) a reinforcement of the Law on Co-determination;
(2) a widening of the law allowing wage-earners representation on corporate boards;
(3) collective savings; and
(4) a planned economy.

The party executive board felt that this was the most feasible avenue *in the short term*. The party leadership proposed continued investigation of the long-term question of shares in profits. With minor changes and additions, the convention decided that the party executive should, starting from the four goals and in cooperation with the LO and the consumer cooperative, investigate the issue of employee investment funds with the intent of bringing the issue up "for new consideration and decision at the party convention in 1981."[13]

The liberals' demand for the introduction of some form of individual profit-sharing system has not met with approval within the labor union and Social Democratic movements. Not until 1974, when the SAP was faced with a weak parliamentary position due to the "deadlocked parliament," did the party agree to investigate the issue as part of a more comprehensive agreement. In the subsequent debate, in the LO/SAP proposal, and in the convention decision of 1978, it has been emphasized that in any future fund system the capital should be collectively owned. However, in the LO/SAP proposal there is the suggestion that a combination is possible:

> If in addition some of the yield from the national development funds went to the wage-earner collective, then this would result in substantially greater amounts, amounts which would make possible the consideration of dividends allotted directly to the wage earners, for example, in the form of education, paid leaves of absence, or similar things.[14]

The proposal concludes as follows:

> Suffice it to say that here exists a possibility for establishing some of what has been called the individual connection to the employee investment fund system.[15]

This suggestion may be significant for the continued development of the employee investment fund issue. In 1978 the TCO assumed a position which is similar in principle. The funds should be collectively owned, but there is room for discussion of the form of the individual connection. The TCO report rejects a fund system of individual *shares*. Such shares would conflict with the capital formation goal, the distribution policy goal, and the goal of strengthening wage-earner influence.[16] On the other hand, says the TCO report, a system is conceivable with an individual *connection* in the form of collective consumption. Examples of such consumption are "the financing of union activity, research and development, efforts at improving the working environment, and union education."[17] Some form of individual withdrawals is advocated, and "Such a system could, for example, mean that the fund system financed some leaves of absence, which could be used for study, recreation, etc., however one chooses."[18]

Within the Swedish consumer cooperative, Allan Larsson, editor-in-chief of the magazine *VI* and previously Undersecretary of State and investigator for the Steel Workers' Union, has proposed a cooperative model for employee investment funds, a model which would entail "one man, one vote" and the individual ownership of shares which could not be cashed but which would allow for some individual share in the yield. (In 1979 Larsson replaced Hjalmar Mehr as the chairman of the employee investment fund inquiry.) Similar proposals have come from the Center party. As this presentation suggests, there are certain similarities between the proposals. In other words, given certain preconditions (the political and economic situation and the positions taken by the labor unions), a broader solution based on mutual understanding may be possible if an acceptable balance between collective and individual ownership is found.

THE RIGHTS OF LABOR IN THE DEBATE ON EMPLOYEE INVESTMENT FUNDS

The first time in modern history that the rights of labor were asserted against the rights of capital was at the LO convention of 1971.[19] It was in the demands for an industrial branch fund system that a change in property ownership and property formation was presented as a goal.[20]

There is, however, no extensive discussion concerning why the rights of labor underlie an industrial branch fund system and the wage-earner influence in it. Rather, it is goals and demands concerning distribution policy which dominate in the motions placed before the LO convention. The effects of distribution policy to be changed concern wealth formation in profitable companies resulting from the wage solidarity policy.[21] Through the "withholding" of wages in profitable companies, greater profits arise than in less wealthy companies. In another motion the problems with the wage solidarity policy went unmentioned.[22] Rather, attention was drawn to the need for capital formation in general and the need for increased wage-earner influence over it in order to decrease the concentration of wealth and power. In other words, the main problem in the motions is the conflicting results of the wage solidarity policy, on one hand, and the LO-supported economic policy, which aims at growth through rationalization, on the other. This inner conflict in the LO's own policy was probably more than anything else behind the decision of the LO convention to delegate to the national secretariat the task of "taking measures so that the issue of industrial branch funds and other fund formation of profits and wage-earner savings for capital investment in companies is investigated."[23] There are three problems at the core of this investigative task: the issue of capital supply, the wage solidarity policy, and increased wage-earner influence. The dominant motive is the effect of the wage solidarity policy.

1973 and 1974 were successful years for Swedish industry. Profits increased very substantially, leading to a discussion of so-called "excess profits." This seems a somewhat inappropriate concept: in a primarily privately owned industry, the primary goal is to organize production in such a way that returns on invested capital are maximized. It seems therefore anomalous to accept privately owned production and at the same time talk of excess profits.

However, the debate on these so-called excess profits became so widespread that the parliament decided to establish a special investment fund into which companies had to pay a certain part of their profits. The debate on excess profits gave an added push to the fund debate. When, in August of 1975, Rudolf Meidner published the first version of his investigative report, the problems concerning the wage solidarity policy had become a secondary issue. Meidner writes that he interpreted his task in such a way

> that the wage solidarity policy certainly must be the starting point for the discussion of capital formation in the hands of the wage earners and/or profit withdrawals under the supervision of society, but that the question of the right to the constant capital growth in our society—a result of the common efforts of all workers—must be taken up for discussion. Thus it also becomes necessary to deal with the question of the power and influence over our economy and to try to point out methods, based on collective capital formation, for strengthening wage-earner influence over the production apparatus.[24]

This entails a significant change in argumentation. Meidner's starting point is that the capitalist economy is characterized by a conflict between propertyowners and unpropertied people.[25] The former appropriate the value of the labor of the latter. (Capital is defined as accumulated labor.) The propertyowners constantly expand their ownership rights to the means of production while the great majority of people are forced to sell their labor to the owners of the means of production. Actually, the industrialized countries have developed into welfare societies, but still there remains

> a basic, and for an industrial society unavoidable, phenomenon: the increase of real capital which is created by constant new investment falls to the owners of capital. This means, in a country with private ownership of the largest part of the means of production, that the economic growth, the increase in wealth, falls to this group of private owners.[26]

Why is this concentration of private ownership unacceptable? There are, according to Meidner, two main arguments:

(1) *General equality perspectives:* It is a question of justice. Meidner exemplifies this with the "German economic miracle," which is founded on wage earners restraining wage demands so that industry will attain sufficient production capacity and competitiveness. This policy "has given the owners of the real capital enormous benefits, at the same time as the financial claims of small-scale savers have been annihilated."[27] The criticism of this injustice has been formulated "not only by the German labor movement but also by the churches, liberal economists, and progressive bourgeois groups."[28] The similarity to the nineteenth century debate on the "social question" is evident. *Moral injustice* is manifested when certain groups benefit from the labor of the majority. That which during the nineteenth century united the socialists

and the bourgeoisie in a moral ethic—an ethic of distribution, according to Lindhagen and Nilsson (see p. 190)—appears 100 years later as an important link between the two groups. Meidner feels that "even if the development in Germany has been extreme in several ways, its main elements can be found in other Western European countries, including Sweden."[29]

(2) *Economic power:* "The owners of the means of production exert a large and often decisive influence over the utilization of these means of production, over the orientation of production, over investments, over industrial location; in short, they—by themselves or via their proxies in the corporate leadership—make all important decisions."[30]

In other words, one group—the owners of the means of production—acquires the results of the labor of others and uses it in order to make all important decisions. This state of affairs must be changed, says Meidner.

It is important to keep these two arguments separate. The first, the justice argument, concerns an equitable distribution of the results of production and equitable *consumption.* Politically, the demand for a more equitable distribution of production is relatively uncontroversial and can unite advocates of varying principles of rights: the Liberal party and the Moderate party (private capital), the Center party (land), and the Social Democrats (the rights of labor).

The second, the power argument, concerns wage-earner power over *production.* This is a considerably more difficult issue because the demands constitute a threat to other interest groups (land- and capital-owners).

It can be added that an argument has been put forth in the debate which states that wage-earner power over production is a precondition for a more just distribution of the results of production (see p. 204).

MEIDNER'S PROPOSAL

The proposal presented by Rudolf Meidner and his colleagues entails the following. First, there is the goal:

> The equalization of differences in the wealth structure and the democratization of the economy through increased wage-earner influence are thus the main goals for employee investment funds. But at the same time the funds should fulfill the demands for sharing profits which arise as a result of the *wage solidarity policy,* i.e., through the restraint of the higher-paid groups. This may be seen as a partial goal, contained within the comprehensive striving toward justice.[31]

The proposal means that the funds would not be allowed to influence employment or price development. Further, the proposal would lead to an equalization of wealth between the capitalowner and the wage earner as well as within the wage-earner collective.

The proposal aims at transferring a certain percentage of the yearly profit to the wage earners through the controlled and obligatory issuance of shares. These shares of stock would go to the fund system but would remain in the company as working capital. In principle the capital would be frozen in the funds with the exception of dividends on shares, which would be used for research, education, investigation, personnel administration, worker environment, and worker protection.

The fund capital would be administered collectively by a central fund. This would be complemented by branch or regional funds. Corporate funds are rejected for the following reason:

> Funds bound to companies is a construction which suggests local, worker-run companies. But a fund which encompasses several companies is based on the thought that the right of determination over the means of production should fall to a larger collective than the few who use these means of production. It is this latter alternative which most nearly agrees with the basic principles and traditions of the labor movement.[32]

The authors of the proposal discussed setting a lower limit for the companies which were to be included at either fifty or one hundred employees but did not commit themselves to either alternative.

The central fund (or possibly several central funds) would function as an "equalization fund." It would be built up by representatives from branch councils which formally own the stocks within their respective industrial branches. Regional bodies are proposed as an alternative or complement. The central fund or the branch councils would, acting on suggestions from the local union organizations, appoint representatives of the fund owners to the company executive boards.[33] The relationship between central and local wage-earner interest would in the long term be developed in such a way that the latter takes on the primary responsibility for the organization and management of work.

The proposal of Meidner et al. was, as we mentioned above, especially far-reaching and surely surprising for many in its emphasis on power issues. The attempt was unusual. Those who have advocated some form of wage-earner influence in the debate have either started from the justice argument, which also contains an ethical assessment of labor's equal value, *or* they have started from the other argument of economic power. Only exceptionally do both arguments appear in the same contribution to the debate.[34] By far the largest number of contributions deal with the first argument.[35] The power argument has been considered in few articles. We shall now review two contributions which have focused on the power issue, i.e., which have argued for wage-earner power and control over the means of production based on the principle of the precedence of the rights of labor over private rights of ownership.

"EMPLOYEE INVESTMENT FUNDS:
A REINFORCEMENT OF DEMOCRACY"

The first article is by Anna Hedborg.[36] The starting point for Hedborg's paper is the following thesis:

> First, and in the practical political sense perhaps most importantly, the lack of democratic control over the economy is a potential threat to every political decision of importance for the economy. That person who has the power to make decisions concerning production and employment possesses the strongest means to power which exist in relation to politics.[37]

Democratic control over the economy is defined as participation for the working people. Democratic control, i.e., the possibility of asserting the interests of the working people in deciding and controlling economic determinants, is a *precondition* for justice.

It is not possible, according to Hedborg, to argue only for an expansion of political democracy or for planned socialism. A certain measure of systematic planning is needed in order to create "work for all, a just distribution, production according to need, direction of the technical development, economization with energy and raw materials, a good external environment, a fight against inflation, and regional balance."[38] But it seems that Hedborg wants to dismiss this as a primary goal. For her, it is a matter of "uniting and balancing" the demands for systematic planning and the rights of labor, of asserting the workers' interest in participation in and control over economic determinants.

There has always existed a tension in the socialist debate between those who argue for a planned or state-socialist economy and those who argue for an economy based on worker rule or on socialist worker councils. This is a tension between centralization of economic decisions and the need for direct influence over one's own working conditions. It is this tension which must be resolved through economic democracy.

Hedborg's primary reason for pressing the issue of wage-earner power over the means of production is the following: The political system, parliamentary efforts, and the work of the various people's organizations has led to a general improvement of the standard of living and a democracy which for the most part is secured. But in one area there have been only small changes—working conditions. "The greatest inequalities existing in Swedish society today are found in working conditions," writes Hedborg.[39] Due to the conflict between labor and capital, the developmental tendency is negative. Hedborg continues:

> Opposing this tendency is another, the only one offering hope. Wage earners demand the improvement of working conditions, and they are prepared to enter the decision-making apparatus of the companies in order to influence decisions in accordance with their own interests.[40]

The conclusion of Hedborg's article is that the present developmental tendency is a threat to our prosperity and democracy in the long run. In the same way that the people's movements (i.e., the labor movement, the temperance movement, the Free Church movement, etc.) took the initiative and responsibility for political democracy, they now assert their readiness for economic democracy, which is the only escape from the threatening scenario that is approaching.

"LABOR IS THE SOURCE OF ALL WEALTH"

The second article is by Sven Ove Hansson.[41] It is introduced as follows:

> Labor is the source of all wealth. It is through labor that together we create our standard of living, both in the form of goods and in the form of services such as health care, education, and social welfare. None of this could come into being without labor, without the utilization of human labor-time. Therefore, labor is the basic production factor in society.[42]

It is the cumulative labor-time used which creates capital. In the course of production, decisions are made concerning how much labor-time will be used for

(1) production of goods for *immediate* sale and consumption; and
(2) production of instruments of labor *for the future,* i.e., various forms of investment for the improvement and increase of production in the future.

Hansson's thesis is that the emphasis is on the first kind of production in a capitalist economic system. Investments for the future occur only to the extent that this is absolutely necessary to maintain an acceptable and expected profitability on capital. Why is this so? Hansson answers that in the capitalist system there is

> a profound contradiction between labor and capital. Since capital is basically an expression of labor, this is no insoluble contradiction. It has arisen out of the special way in which capital is used in a capitalist system in order to rule labor.[43]

The conflict between labor and capital will be resolved through economic democracy; this will occur as wage earners are assured of control over the labor-time (capital) which is used. The power of capital (private ownership) will cease to exist, and corresponding functions "will be divided up between local wage-earner control and coordinating organs (i.e., the society and the wage-earner collective). The demand for an active democracy in which all wage earners may participate and make decisions is the motivation for giving local wage-earner control as much room as possible without encroaching upon other important political goals."[44]

According to Hansson, it is in the workers' interest to gain control over the factors which determine economic decisions through a system of economic democracy. Hansson's main argument is that the capitalist economic system, seen from the social perspective, is *inefficient*. This is true not only of the form of orientation of the investment program, but

> also of the *insufficient extent* to which such efforts are made. The capitalist system in the West has, especially in the postwar years, shown that from the perspective of the national economy it uses an unacceptably small portion of the available labor-time for investments in future production. This insufficient investment in the future has necessitated various forms of state stimulation in order to achieve sufficient investment in industry.[45]

To Hedborg's argument—that employee investment funds reinforce democracy—Sven Ove Hansson adds another: economic democracy increases the potential for efficient production and the economization of resources.

The conditions and forms of production in a capitalist system which Hansson feels are wrong are, first, the systems for increased efficiency in production, which "have been demeaning for wage earners who have suffered from poor working conditions and sometimes been forced from their workplaces," and, further, the orientation of the production capacity, which "in great part has been used in ways other than those we consider most appropriate."[46]

In summary, Hansson directs the following criticisms at the capitalist system:

(1) Insufficient investments for *future* needs, which leads to a waste of resources;
(2) the placing of the profitability demand above all other demands, and the fact that capital is not recognized as accumulated labor;
(3) ways of increased efficiency of production and growth of productivity which are not only demeaning for the wage earners but also contribute to the waste of resources; and
(4) the orientation of production.

A democratization of the economy should encompass an entire strategy with many different reforms. Hansson specifies five areas:

(1) Decisions concerning the internal affairs of the company are transferred to local wage-earner control.
(2) The administration of capital fixed in a company is transferred to the wage-earner collective.
(3) The administration of working capital (credit) is transferred to social institutions, where decisions are made on the basis of consideration of the whole of society.
(4) The present form of private ownership of land is replaced by a right of disposition which does not allow for profit on speculation.

(5) Extended planning through restrictions:
 —control over the establishement of new firms
 —product checks and requirements on product quality
 —environmental requirements and requirements for the economical use of resources.[47]

An economic democracy formed according to such a strategy, which gives the wage earners power and control over the utilization of the means of production, would, according to Hansson, eliminate the shortcomings in the capitalist economic system.

THE PROPOSAL OF THE LO AND THE SAP

In the proposal presented early in 1978 by the LO-SAP committee, the emphasis in the argument shifted compared to Meidner's proposal of 1975. The power issue was no longer dominant.

After the successful years 1973 and 1974, the Swedish and Western economies entered a long and deep recession. The overwhelming problem became inflation and the need for capital for industrial investments. The economic debate of the time seems to have influenced the authors of the LO-SAP proposal so that they speak more about efficiency and capital formation than about power. In the proposal it is said, first, that economic democracy has an inherent value, and, further, economic democracy is presented as a "necessity"[48] for the "creation of a strong industrial economy, capable of development and providing secure employment and increased welfare for the country's citizens."[49] The division between planned and market economies and between economic democracy and wage-earner influence are clearer and less far-reaching in this proposal than in Meidner's. This is presumably a result of the criticism directed against Meidner's proposal. The fact that the LO-SAP group speaks in such strong terms of the "necessity" of employee investment funds should probably be seen against the background of the economic crisis. The group adds a fourth goal to the three proposed by Meidner and adopted by the LO convention in 1976, i.e., "to contribute to collective saving and capital formation for productive investments."[50]

The difference between the present economy and the one proposed by the committee concerns "the method for using the freedom of action allowed by the economic preconditions."[51] The market economy should be preserved primarily because it allows for "the possibility of greatly decentralized decision-making in production and the possibility of providing for the interest individual people have in free choice in consumption."[52] The common social interest should be placed above the wage-earner interest in order to institute an efficient and planned economy and also to ensure solidarity between groups in the society.

Thus, according to the committee, employee investment funds become "an expansion and a deepening of economic democracy in one area, that is, as concerns decisions on the organization of production" (decisions on production methods, organizational plans, and planning systems).

Wage earners must expect capital needs for the future—or at least for the 1980s—to be so great that they must abstain from private consumption in favor of public saving. This saving (for investment in industry) must be initiated in order to have "an efficient and modern production apparatus," which is vital to secure employment. This is, according to the committee, a precondition for continued democratization. In the early stages of a capital formation system it is also assumed that wage earners "should be able to cooperate" if capital "is used for a democratization of economic life and leads to collective ownership under democratic control."[53]

The power argument, as formulated by Rudolf Meidner, is toned down considerably in the LO-SAP proposal. The most important aspects are capital formation and a long-term, future-oriented planning. It is more a question of wage earners "buying" themselves some influence at the price of lower wages than of asserting the rights of labor as the basis for influence. One could claim, in connection with Hedborg's and Hansson's articles, that there has been a shift from arguments for democracy, power, and control over the means of production to arguments concerning the just distribution of the results of production and an efficient production apparatus.

We may summarize the way the rights of labor have been asserted in the employee investment fund debate as follows: The focal point of the argumentation is the demand for just distribution; workers should be guaranteed a larger share in the results of production. This argument is of special interest since it represents a continuity which spans the time from the liberal labor movement's humanitarian goal of solving "the social question" through the late 1800s and the emerging Social Democratic movement's interpretation of the labor theory of value, which stressed the distribution aspect, up to "modern" Social Democracy, represented by Nils Karleby and others, and through the equality debate of the 1960s. It is worth noting that, from the perspective of theoretical history, ethical socialism is very close to liberalism and the bourgeois revolution, or, as Karleby expresses it: "The spiritual origins of modern socialism flow from the same humanistic principle as do the ideas of the Reformation and the French Revolution."[54]

Other people, including Hedborg, argue for economic democracy (economic power to the wage earners) because this is a precondition for a just distribution of the results of production.

Finally, there are arguments based on the rights of labor. According to Hansson, it is labor which creates capital, and from the workers' (wage earners') perspective it is therefore justified that they, as the creators of capital, have control over the economic determinants and over the use of the means of production.

As for this latter line of reasoning, it is remarkable that it has been presented so sparingly. It is all the more remarkable since one should have learned from the socialization debates of 1918-1920 and 1928, the PHM debate in 1948 (see p. 174), and the pension debate in 1958 that it is precisely the power argument which most arouses the defenders of the rights of capital. The need for ideological preparedness on this point is therefore very great—but the debate has been weak.[55]

In the debate which has been carried on in the mass media since August 1975 the advocates of the rights of capital have followed two lines of thought:

(1) It is necessary that total capital formation increase. This can occur without any change of power. The best method is by instituting a fund system of individual shares. If a fund system is to be instituted, then it must be some form of civic fund, *and* there must be many of them in order to preserve competition on the credit market. The decisive thing is that the credit market principle of decentralization and competition be reinforced.

(2) The power argument is rejected a priori because it changes the balance of power and because it is said not to belong in a pure market economy model.[56]

In order to illustrate the critique of the rights of labor and the defense of private rights of ownership, we shall now briefly examine the theses presented by the economist Assar Lindbeck and the legal scholar Stig Strömholm.

"CAN PLURALISM SURVIVE?"

Among Swedish economists, Assar Lindbeck is probably the most energetic defender of the bases of the present economic system. He sees fund proposals based on the rights of labor both as a threat to the objectives of the economic system and as a threat to political democracy (civic rights). [57] The fact that the rights of labor become a threat in Lindbeck's interpretation and not, as in Hedborg's and Hansson's, a promise, is because the primary goal of social organization, according to Lindbeck, should be *pluralism*. Lindbeck feels that "other demands are placed on economic systems" than mere economic demands. One such demand is

that the system create a significant *pluralism*, i.e., that it lead to the existence of many somewhat independent power groups, having differing interests, values, and ambitions, so that no one single organization or type of organization dominates the society.[58]

Lindbeck's counterproposal is therefore the institution of "a system of civic funds" within the framework of a capital-market characterized by "fund pluralism." [59] The basic principle for Lindbeck's proposal is built upon private ownership rights and aims at an improvement and strengthening of the traditional market economy.

The Swedish model (the mixed economy) "has thus far had a marked decentralized and pluralistic character," according to Lindbeck. What "deserves to be especially emphasized is the importance of a pluralistic administration of capital." He continues:

> It is this combination of an unusually free and innovative private enterprise, an *unusually* well-functioning cooperation between the parties to the labor market, and an *unusually* ambitious security and service-oriented public sector which is characteristic of the *Swedish model* for economic and social development and which has made the Swedish "mixed economy" an interesting model for many other countries.[60]

The pluralistic system—which Lindbeck feels really exists (see below)—is threatened by, among other things, the expansion of the public sector. This expansion creates serious conflict between the goals of the market and the goals of society. Politicians strive for solutions to these conflicts, but their solutions merely result in additional conflicts, decreased market pluralism, increased regulation and intervention.[61] Lindbeck feels that as an economist he cannot oppose the politically formulated social goals; he can, however, point out the consequences of *choices of differing methods of intervention* in the economy. The methods which are coming into increasing use entail the following:

> First, there are the very important consequences for the functioning of markets and prices. If the mergers of firms and the accompanying concentration of market power go very far, competition will sooner or later be hurt—with the likelihood of increased difficulty in the entry of new firms, less innovation, and a general deterioration of efficiency in the allocation of resources as a result.[62]

Increased direct political influence in the economy means increased room for incompetence and a contribution to "a major deterioration in the efficiency of economic decision-making."[63]

Why does increased political influence lead to decreased efficiency? Lindbeck feels that political decision-making is often "extremely short-sighted and 'prestige conscious' because of the overwhelming concern of politicians for short-term party tactics."[64] Thus, politicians buy votes with promises of investments and subsidies without reflecting on the consequences. For corporate leaders and stockholders this leads to a decreasing consideration of the market and to a "pursuit of subsidies and protection" from state authorities. These tendencies are also reinforced, according to Lindbeck, by wage-earner organizations, which become increasingly unwilling to accept what was previously regarded as normal profit.

The real threat to a market system, however, comes from the power changes that can be expected. Lindbeck writes:

> However, the most drastic effects of the proliferation of government intervention are no doubt the wider political, social, and cultural consequences. The distribution of power in society will change in a complicated and dramatic way.[65]

Lindbeck paints a picture of the future which consists of the concentration of power and production in small, intimate, cooperating groups who are more interested in compromise and the exercise of power than in creativity, knowledge, and capacity for competition. According to Lindbeck, there is a risk in Sweden that

> some of the organizations which at the beginning of the century contributed to the pluralistic nature of our society, such as labor unions, now tend to be so strong in some European countries that they in fact may dominate these societies and hence be a threat to the pluralism which they themselves helped to create.[66]

This whole process of development is reinforced by the proposals for employee investment funds, which would concentrate power over capital in a few gigantic private funds, the public sector, or—as in Sweden, says Lindbeck—in some "corporatist" organization, "which would mean that the labor union movement would also become the employers' association." If this prophecy comes true, then we will have in Sweden "a corporatist, if still democratically organized, trade union state."[67]

Assar Lindbeck proposes eight countermeasures. Common to all of them is that their aim is the perfect market, and Lindbeck speaks of his recommendations as utopian. Three of his proposals are interesting as counterproposals to employee investment funds and the arguments for these funds outlined above.

First, says Lindbeck, it is essential to counteract all forms of corporatism or the fusion of different interests into large units. The methods for this are a decentralized (individual) ownership of finance capital, and a general and decentralized system for the public financing of culture, education, and research.

Second, decentralization of decision-making is necessary in companies and other organizations—"what is often called 'employee participation,'" says Lindbeck.[68]

Third, a better policy of distribution would "make the market system—in particular profit-making—more socially acceptable." It would also reinforce individual ownership and improve the conditions for decentralized finance capital.

As a final addition, there is the role Lindbeck feels the state should have in a market economy. The state should concentrate on goals which the citizens feel to be of "major importance." "Clear examples" of such goals are to

> remove poverty and to create better employment opportunities among handicapped citizens, to improve the urban and natural environment, to achieve better macroeconomic stability, and to improve the quality of the supply of collective goods.[69]

Direct collaboration between the state and the market may be tolerated only in areas where the parties complement each other, i.e., transportation, energy, and urban development.

LINDBECK'S MISTRUST OF REPRESENTATIVE DEMOCRACY

The article by Lindbeck quoted above was published in 1977.[70] The article may be said to be a summary of Lindbeck's position on and criticism of existing proposals for employee investment funds.

One feature present throughout Lindbeck's writing is his strong polemic tone. Often, as in the article cited here, this leads to sweeping and, above all, unproven characterizations and generalizations. One example is Lindbeck's statement that it is a "fact that political decision-making is often extremely shortsighted and 'prestige conscious' because of . . . short-term party tactics."[71] The statement is presented as a fact without a hint of proof. It is our opinion, on the contrary, that the political decision-making process is to a considerable degree long-term and systematic. Examples of this are labor market policies formed during the 1930s, 1940s, and 1950s, the social policies of the 1940s, the pension system formed during the 1950s, the education reforms of the 1950s and 1960s, plus various programs for health and child care, etc. In our opinion, these examples show how politicians seek long-term solutions of *common* interest, and not narrow solutions bound by party considerations. This has been done in order to create security for the individual and the *conditions* for the existence of industry and the market. If, as Lindbeck thinks, the opposite were true, then we would most probably not have the welfare system we now have nor would we have had the stability which has marked economic and political developments. Swedish society would have been more similar to Finland or France with constant political changes and considerably less potential for creating the conditions necessary for the welfare society.

WHAT IS "PLURALISM"?

Pluralism consists, according to Lindbeck, of "many rather autonomous and at least in part competing power groups," and, further, of "the private citizens . . . having considerable freedom to look after their own affairs without asking the permission of public authorities or other powerful organizations."[72]

Pluralism's features are "built into the organization of our economic system." And, Lindbeck continues;

> more precisely, they are largely based on an extremely sophisticated and very fragile mechanism, that is, the market system or, in other words, the interaction in fairly free markets between demand, supply, and price for various goods, services, capital, labor, and information.[73]

Three questions deserve to be asked in connection with Lindbeck's definition of "pluralism":

(1) Is today's Swedish "mixed economy" an expression of decentralization and pluralism?
(2) To what, if any, extent are labor unions a threat to pluralism?
(3) If pluralism is in need of reinforcement, then are the "civic funds" advocated by Lindbeck the most reasonable solution?

Concerning the first question, it is—as we pointed out earlier—important to make a clear distinction between political and economic power. If one examines political power, i.e., the power to *make* decisions, then one ends up with a different result in the analysis of pluralism than if one examines the power to *execute* decisions and to create the long-term conditions for society's development (economic power).

Social development has entailed increased pluralism. For example, as political power has come to be shared by the labor movement, "different interests, values, and ambitions" have had greater opportunity for expression than before the breakthrough of political democracy. It is thus difficult to see how increased public influence has *decreased* pluralism. Decisions today have a broader base than, say, during the time of the estate parliament.

If attention is directed instead toward economic power, then the result is almost the opposite. Lindbeck's most important criterion for pluralism is that the situation must be avoided in which "one single organization or type of organization dominates the society." If we look at the total value of commodity production in Sweden today, we find to an overwhelming degree that it is the result of decisions and measures within "one single . . . type of organization," the privately owned company. Further, the *degree* of organization is very high. Sweden is ranked first in the West when it comes to the concentration of private capital—2.6% of all households own 86% of all stock. As far as economic power is concerned, this is far from the "pluralism" advocated by Lindbeck.

Next comes the labor union movement. Lindbeck writes: "There is a clear possibility that some of the organizations which at the beginning of the century contributed to the pluralistic nature of our society, such as labor unions, now tend to be so strong . . . that they in fact may dominate these societies and hence be a threat to the pluralism which they themselves helped to create." The collaboration of a strong government and a strong labor union movement seeking together to collaborate with capital (the picture Lindbeck paints of Sweden) will result in negotiations among the leaders for mutual advantages, even when this is not necessary for reasons of allocation and/or coordination. In short, according to Lindbeck, this development leads to corruption. In the first place, it is worth noting that nowhere today is there a labor union movement strong enough to dominate an entire country. In the majority of industrial countries the degree of union organization has nowhere near reached the level where the organizations would be able to "dominate" even the *wage earners,* if this were constitutionally possible. Even less can they dominate political life in these countries. Given a situation where a very small number of companies under private control govern the greatest part of the economic system while—in most countries—less than half of the employees are organized, then, to say the least, Lindbeck's fears seem misdirected.

Further, Lindbeck includes in his concept "pluralism" competition and some form of "balance" between organizations, *regardless of how these organizations are ruled.* An economy where private interests have significant influence and stand opposed to public interests is, thus, more "pluralistic" in Lindbeck's view than a society where public interests dominate. The fact that the executive leadership of the labor union is elected on the principle of "one man—one vote" has, in Lindbeck's view, nothing to do with "pluralism." On the contrary, it would seem that a labor union movement which is well organized and strongly supported by its members would be a greater threat to "pluralism" than would weak labor unions.

The explanation is to be found in Lindbeck's solicitude regarding the *market.* The market economy, he seems to say, can only be guaranteed through the influence of *private* interests. It is desirable that these interests be decentralized, says Lindbeck, and he proposes certain measures in this direction.

Lindbeck's proposals include the following: Wealth, which he defines only in terms of human and housing capital and not as means of production, should be distributed more equally. Further, he proposes a more equal distribution of power and of opportunity for initiative in the economy. The detailed proposals involve increased influence for the *individual* employee, consumer, and entrepreneur. Lindbeck doesn't think it worth discussing whether these people would have common interests which would induce them to unite in organizations. He also proposes various "civic funds," which would be "owned" partly by owners of the means of production, partly by organizations and popular movements, and partly by political associations.[74]

Further, Lindbeck's proposal includes an increased rate of saving with a balance between private and public saving, an increased supply of risk capital, the prevention of "excess profits," the solution to the problems of

the wage solidarity policy by means of special taxes and fund appropria-
tions and a more flexible wage relationship, i.e., the payment, in practice,
of higher wages for heavier work. In other words, Lindbeck is speaking of
a different solidarity than the one upon which the wage solidarity policy is
now based.

Finally, Lindbeck proposes increased acceptance of company profits. It
is clear that for Lindbeck the private element is of strategic importance to
the success of "pluralism." To express it more acutely: a nondemocracy
with market competition is, in Lindbeck's view, more "pluralistic" than a
democracy in which the market system is regulated by public actions.
Lindbeck tacitly implies that a democracy without a market system is
inconceivable; in fact, his reasoning could even be interpreted to mean that
democracy and market system are nearly identical concepts.

It would seem that Lindbeck is guilty of incorrect reasoning here. He
seems to equate private ownership, which is a *principle of property law,*
and the market, which is an *organizational form* and neutral in the sense of
property law.

Lindbeck is conscious of the high degree of organization and concentration which characterizes the private capitalist system today, and he realizes
that these features, more than any others, subject the present economic
system to criticism and debate. He therefore advocates a solution which is
aimed at simultaneously (1) preserving features of private ownership, (2)
decentralizing the economy, and (3) broadening influence over companies.
The solution is called "civic funds."

Lindbeck's proposal on civic funds involves the creation of a number of
funds which administer stock capital. The funds would be financed by
taxes and would function on the open capital market. If the goal is
pluralism, decentralized decision-making, and an efficient economy, then,
according to Lindbeck, it is necessary

(a) that financing occur through the payment of money from the companies (and
not through obligatory stock issue),
(b) that there be many autonomous funds, and
(c) that no fund or conglomerate fund group dominate.

We would thus have a system of "civic funds" within the framework of a
capital market characterized by "fund pluralism." The members of the executive boards in these funds could be appointed in various ways in various "civic
funds." In some cases it might be conceivable that the shareholders in the fund
choose the board members. In others, various organizations and popular
movements may appoint board members. And in still others, board members
may be appointed via political organizations or via special elections in conjunc-
tion with the general election.[75]

To what extent might these funds be a way of attaining Lindbeck's
goals? There are two circumstances here which constitute important
obstacles. As for (1) preserving features of private ownership, Lindbeck feels

that private ownership has already assumed so anonymous and diffuse a character that the power of the capitalowners is neutralized. Thus, he does not feel that private ownership will have a negative effect on the spread of power. Lindbeck's position seems marked by an extensive mistrust of any form of organization into large units. He is equally suspicious of politicians and executives of present corporate and credit organizations.[76] He proposes, therefore, "broader and more democratically based recruitment for the posts of capital administrator in existing credit institutions and capital funds." This proposal derives from Lindbeck's starting point that ownership is in fact relatively decentralized in a number of institutions and not in physical persons.[77] It is the recruitment of executives for these institutions which should be democratized. Lindbeck's argument on this point is poorly supported. He points out that only 9% of stock capital is owned directly by private persons, but he does not discuss the forms of ownership in the various institutions.

If one examines the data underlying Lindbeck's statements, one finds that 16% of all stock is owned by institutions and organizations which are democratically organized and in which a broader recruitment of executive leadership is possible. This includes the Fourth National Pension Fund, charitable institutions, pension institutions, and interest groups.

The remaining 75% are *indirectly* owned by private persons and private interests which are not democratically organized but rather are organized according to the extent of private ownership. These private owners appoint the executive leadership which, in their opinion, can best administer the capital. One of the most important elements in owning productive capital is that one has the right to *appoint the executive leadership.*

As for (2), (decentralizing the economy), one must question whether it is at all possible to decentralize the economy into small, independent, and competing capital markets. The international market situation is an important obstacle here. Modern industrial production is largely oriented toward capital-intensive mass production in large factory units. Perhaps the foremost examples are the automotive industry, the electronics industry, and the chemo-technical industry.

Concerning (3), (broadening influence over companies), it remains to be shown that civic funds entail any real change of mandator. Lindbeck gives the impression in his presentation that civic funds will exist along with private capital. The important question in this context is who will possess the *controlling* holdings of stock. Even if citizens owned the majority of shares in some of the funds, it is by no means certain that the real control would not be exercised by the previous private owners. The civic principle involves individualization, which Lindbeck almost programmatically strives for. His proposals aim at increasing the influence of the individual wage earner, the consumer, and the entrepreneur. But being an individual wage earner or consumer is something quite different from being an individual entrepreneur. The latter possesses power both politically (as a voter) and economically (as a propertyowner). Now if part of the capital is transferred to civic funds—in which all wage earners and consumers have influence as political participants—but part still remains in the hands of the previous owners, then the likelihood is great that the latter will be the ones who control the economy in reality (cf., the proposals for "owner democracy" through the spread of stock capital which are now and then brought up by political groups connected with private interests). This is even more likely since Lindbeck expressly wants to prevent the collective interests from organizing through the state or the labor union movement.

In summary, the proposal on civic funds assumes (1) that it is possible to return to a decentralized capital market, (2) that the character of ownership is essentially different from earlier times, and (3) that an individualization of economic power will also entail a spread of power. But this is not the case. The capital market is becoming increasingly centralized; ownership, in spite of the fact that it is becoming more *institutionalized*, is still private; and the executive leadership is appointed by private interests in proportion to the amount of owned capital; and an individualization of ownership will in all likelihood lead to the concentration of control over ownership in minority groups in a way similar to the case in existing large stock companies. As we shall discuss again in Chapter 10, it is possible to have democratic control of large amounts of capital and a production based on the production role (and not on passive ownership) and *simultaneously to preserve* essential and crucial market elements in the economy.

THE LEGAL DEBATE

The legal theorist and jurist Stig Strömholm has written an article discussing "the proposal on so-called employee investment funds."[78] Strömholm's elucidation is based on positive law, i.e., he starts from what he calls "relevant legal perspectives" and "existing law." "Existing law" includes civil law, constitutional law, and other legislation. [79] It is worth noting that Strömholm's review of public documents and laws "gives few concrete results when it comes to clarifications."[80] This, he says, is because the "Meidner fund construction is entirely new and alien to Swedish legal notions and the earlier Swedish debate."[81]

After his review, Strömholm states that the fund proposal entails "*a compulsorily regulated transfer of property from one legal subject to another,* in other words, an intervention into the ownership rights of the stockholders"[82] and "that the Swedish legal system in its present framework *does not at all allow for a transfer of wealth* as intended by the proposal."[83] As for other legislation, Strömholm points out "that legal rules on expropriation, taxation, and determination over property in current Swedish law are formed in such a way that a compulsory transfer of property in accordance with the fund proposals is not accommodated by the complex of rules."[84]

The only possibility which remains after Strömholm's legal examination is, in his opinion, a constitutional amendment. He admits that legal notions change with time,[85] but he is hesitant when it comes to the question of whether they should be allowed to influence the constitution in this case.

> I do not doubt that those holding political power, if they want to realize the proposals on employee investment funds, must effect such *constitutional amendments*, so as to make such compulsory transfers compatible with positive law. This is an extremely far-reaching intervention.[86]

The premises upon which Strömholm builds his argument are scantily presented. For example, concerning the conflict between labor and capital as related in the economic, historical, and sociological literature, Strömholm has no other view than that capital is "the resources which *have been accumulated* in the form of profit in one or another company"[87] (our italics). Further, he says that it has always "been understood as obvious" that protection of the individual's ownership right "without a reasonable doubt belongs to ... the fundamental principles of the Swedish legal order."[88]

How capital may "have been accumulated," that is to say, what determining factors were and still are conditions for the private ownership of the means of production and for the capitalowner's right to appropriate surplus-value is not discussed by Strömholm. These rights are, he says, "fundamental principles" which are only a starting point for discussion.

Strömholm's argument has been opposed by Nelhans, among others. Nelhans feels that Strömholm's conclusion that employee investment funds cannot be instituted without a constitutional amendment is incorrect. Nelhans' starting point[89] is that in Meidner's version of the employee investment fund proposal it is not a question of maintaining the precedence of the rights of labor over the rights of private ownership of the means of production, i.e., it is not the power and control over the means of production which is to be changed. Rather, according to Nelhans, it is wage-earner demands for a more just distribution of the results of production which underlie the employee investment fund proposal. This somewhat surprising interpretation of Meidner's fund proposal has been criticized in a rebuttal by Strömholm, criticism which we share with Strömholm since, as he says, Nelhans "mixes *demands for economic and other benefits in contract relations* with the *right to a certain specified property*."[90]

Nelhans equates the meaning of Meidner's fund proposal with bargaining and contract rights, social legislation, and labor union strike action. "This is," he says, "the expression of a changed power function in society which in Sweden has been validated by law without necessitating a constitutional amendment."[91] The labor movement offensive of the 1970s has also been carried on without constitutional amendment, and it, like

Meidner's proposal, is an "intervention concerning influence over yield on capital," says Nelhans.

This conclusion is also odd. We have shown above (Chapter 2) how the powers of state placed stock company legislation above co-determination legislation, with the result that the shareholders' meeting determines profit disposition. In other words, it is the *owners* of the means of production who decide how the yield of the capital after taxes is to be used. Nelhans exemplifies his position with the law on security of employment, the law on the status of shop stewards, the work environment law and the law on co-determination, which will

limit to an even higher degree the right of the capitalowner to personally command the yield of his property, the working capital. And the creation of this law did not necessitate a constitutional amendment in order to legalize a change in fundamental position. [92]

Nelhans's critique of Strömholm shows traces of the functional socialist position which originated with Undén.[93] Another critic of Strömholm, Fritz Kaijser, makes the same objection. Kaijser feels that the existing constitution (RF 1974, 8:2) is no obstacle to a system of employee investment funds. Kaijser's conclusion is that "[in] any case, this article of law strongly suggests that legislation on employee investment funds should be allowed."[94] Kaijser feels further that the parliament has taken a position against unequivocal constitutional protection for private property. He feels that the functional socialist approach—"according to the artichoke method"—has gradually cut away at ownership rights.

Strömholm's answer to Kaijser's and Nelhans's criticism is that the parliament *can* decide upon a fund system, but that this would happen against the opinions and advice of jurists. Strömholm also feels that a constitutional amendment *is necessary* and that it may not be difficult legally, but that it is surely difficult politically. A constitutional amendment is necessary, says Strömholm, because the constitution and its precursors recognize a protection of property. Strömholm feels that the construction of the constitution is such that it does not expressly establish "the basic norms" in a legal system (e.g., freedom of contract, private ownership) and that the article of law referred to by Kaijser only constitutes "one part of the ambitious attempt by the authors of the constitution to establish a boundary between the parliament and the normative authority of the government."[95] The ruling establishes, according to Strömholm, what the government *cannot* legislate.

Strömholm supports his argument that Meidner's proposal entails the transfer of property from one legal subject to another with the rules which protect property against confiscation. This "basic norm" has, according to Strömholm, "been partially expressed in the constitutional rule of expropriation."[96]

Strömholm concludes his article by stating that it "is perhaps possible" that there are certain principles which justify "the right of the workers to co-determination over their own labor contributions," but when it comes to the results of labor, says Strömholm, there is no support in Swedish law for influence based on labor. This is merely a labor union program and endeavor.

It is hard to reach any other conclusion than that Strömholm's argument is superior to that of his critics. Strömholm's analysis, as well as the earlier one of, for example, Undén, shows clearly that the right of ownership of the labor product is connected to the right of ownership of capital. A change in this would undoubtably be so extensive as to necessitate a constitutional amendment. If the principle of the rights of labor is judged to be sufficiently important to be implemented, then we cannot expect this to occur through mere minor modifications of existing rules for ownership and the administration of capital.

An entirely different question arises in connection with the expression "confiscation." The principle of the rights of labor means that labor is the basis for original acquisition. In accordance with this, passive capitalownership cannot be asserted as the primary basis for acquisition. Consequently, neither Meidner's proposal nor any other proposal based on the rights of labor (e.g., Wigforss's idea of social companies without owners) entails any confiscation. In order for something to be confiscated, it must first exist. According to the principle of the rights of labor, that which is produced is acquired *at the moment of creation,* i.e., at the moment it comes into existence through the contribution of labor. Thus, there is no question of the confiscation or expropriation of capital; to the extent that private capital is supplied there may be reason to compensate the person who supplies it, but the *right to ownership* of that which is produced derives from labor, not from the capital investment.

9.2 Functional Socialism: An Attempt at Asserting Civic Rights Against Private Ownership Rights

In this section we will elucidate the conflict between civic rights and private ownership rights. Our starting point will be the demands of functional socialism. According to its advocates, functional socialism is a method of gradually limiting private ownership rights by means of political power (civic rights). Because it controls the legislative institutions, political power may institute laws which are deemed necessary for the protection of the public civic interest, even if this involves cutting back the rights of the private owners of wealth.[97]

Two Social Democratic politicians, Östen Undén and Nils Karleby, are usually considered the founders of functional socialism in Sweden. We have dealt with Östen Undén's views of ownership rights in Chapter 2, and Nils Karleby's position is discussed in detail in Chapter 8. During the postwar period, the subject was dealt with by Gunnar Adler-Karlsson.

We shall first attempt to indicate the meaning of functional socialism in terms of demands and premises. The question is what chance functional socialism has to counteract certain consequences of private ownership. Functional socialism's goals are expressed by Adler-Karlsson as follows:

> First of all, production must be organized efficiently so that a rapid and balanced economic development takes place and full employment is maintained. . . . Second, the results of production must be distributed among society's citizens in a way which is seen as just and reasonable.[99]

Adler-Karlsson calls functional socialism both an ideology and a method. Functional socialism is an ideology because "one can say that we have retained the goals of socialism but chosen other *means* for their realization than the socialization of the means of production."[100]

Functional socialism is a method which entails seeking "the best solution which is practically possible under existing conditions."[101] According to Adler-Karlsson, the premises of the "practical method" which is functional socialism are the following:

- the conviction that power should be balanced;
- an aversion to violent means for the solution to social problems;
- a pragmatic attitude on the question of how private enterprise and state intervention should be balanced in economic life; and
- a realization of our basic values with the aid of functional socialism.

To these should be added the idea that ownership is divisible into a number of functions.

Let us examine Adler-Karlsson's stated points of departure. The first, that power should be balanced, is common in political theory and derives from Montesquieu. We have run into it also in the economist Assar Lindbeck. During the nineteenth century the notion occurs among several economists of the marginalist tradition.

Usually the thesis means that power is defined in terms of an institutional division of power between the courts, the political system, the economic system and the public administration. Historically, the notion is relatively new, and part of the protest of the bourgeois revolution was against the accumulation of all power by the lords in feudal society.

The idea is that power should be distributed in a balanced way between the various institutions. The difficulty with the theory and its practical application, however, is that the balance of power is constantly changing because various interests always strive for hegemony over other interests.

Adler-Karlsson takes as an example of the balance of power that in Sweden we have, on one hand, a concentrated private economy, but "on the other, for more than 30 years we have had a Social Democratic government and a very strong labor union movement, which together have been able to keep this wealthy upper hierarchy in balance."[103] This has been due to "the common interest of all members of society in a growing economy."[104] According to Adler-Karlsson, there exists a higher notion of harmony which is possible to preserve so long as the economy is growing.

> When the capitalist gets a larger profit, then he is more prepared to share it with his employees, and when the workers notice that their standard of living is constantly improving, then their willingness to peaceful cooperation in the existing society similarly increases.[105]

This idea that there exists a common interest is ultimately founded on the belief that production factors are equal and that there is no real conflict between labor and capital. Adler-Karlsson argues from the perspective of only two production factors, land and capital, even though he recognizes that conflicts exist between "the capitalist and the working classes."[106] But Adler-Karlsson claims that this conflict is subordinate to the public interest.

We are of the opinion that there is no evidence that the capitalist will for rational economic reasons be "more prepared to share" his profit if it increases. Political, rather than economic, reasons are what create this willingness. If the capitalist actually accepts wage increases, then this occurs primarily against the background of a relationship of mutual strength between the two parties. For example, if the wage-earner organization can gain the support of a government which is friendly to labor, then its strength increases. Without this support, the capitalist's strength increases.[107]

In summary, functional socialism draws its support from two questionable premises. They are questionable from both the theoretical and practical political perspectives.

There is an additional troublesome and incomplete premise in Adler-Karlsson's argument. It concerns the goal of functional socialism which, according to Adler-Karlsson, it has in common with socialism. Regardless of which socialism we are thinking of (state, council, guild, or some form of popular socialism—"the right of determination over production and its distribution should be put in the hands of all the people"), this goal involves a *change of mandator,* meaning that private ownership of the means of production ceases and is transferred to the state, the workers, the labor unions, or political bodies. According to Adler-Karlsson, functional socialism's goal is economic growth and just distribution. These goals are common to other forms of socialism, but the decisive goal—a democratic control over *production*—is not expressly present in functional socialism. The decisive difference between functional socialism and other forms of socialism is the third premise of functional socialism—"a pragmatic attitude on the question of how private enterprise and state intervention should be balanced in economic life"—which in principle means that private ownership of the means of production lacks significance. This premise also builds upon two basic assumptions which recur in Nils Karleby:

(1) Economic praxis is determined by an objective and scientific law which is valid regardless of the political system.[108] In the theoretical sense, there is no difference between a socialist and a capitalist economy. Adler-Karlsson completes his reasoning by presenting a convergence theory: the economies of the United States and the Soviet Union are developing in the same direction and toward the same final point. This is true both of the orientation and goals of the economies as well as of their decision-making processes.[109]

(2) Karleby feels that "from the perspective of the economic machinery, it is completely unimportant to *whom* the right of ownership and thus the income from the actual production factors belongs."[110] Adler-Karlsson presents the same line of thought.[111] From the legal point of view, he says, the owner in a capitalist country can "do whatever he wishes with his property within the limits of the law." In a socialist country the state can do whatever it wishes as owner, says Adler-Karlsson, while the individual can only do what the state allows. He continues:

> From the economic point of view, however, these definitions entail the same rights in a capitalist society as in a socialist one. For example, in a socialist society a factory manager may legally take the same actions and make the same decisions as the director of a company in a capitalist society.[112]

As the quotation shows, Adler-Karlsson uses what for this argument is an important and fateful ambiguity when he discusses ownership rights as a question of *executive* power. If two company directors, one in the United States and the other in the Soviet Union, seem to actually make the same production decisions, then this does not necessarily say anything about what rights the owners of the companies have or about the conditions which ultimately determine the decisions. The central question now is how Adler-Karlsson, like Karleby, can come to the conclusion that it is in practice uninteresting who owns the means of production.

According to Adler-Karlsson, functional socialism starts from Östen Undén's theories of ownership rights. He continues:

> Östen Undén's contribution was that he made it clear that the concept of ownership rights is not indivisible but on the contrary contains several different ownership functions which can be separated. Ownership, 0, includes, so to speak, not only ownership in general, but it also contains the functions a, b, c, etc., or expressed differently, $0 = a + b + c \ldots + n$. The consequence of this reasoning is that it becomes necessary to institute full socialization in order to attain the socialist goals. It may be advisable, and even economically advantageous, to socialize only certain of the functions of ownership, for example a and b, but not c.[113]

Adler-Karlsson explains in several contexts that ownership is equal to a number of functions, each of which signifies a relationship between the owner and that which is owned. These functions can now quite simply be distributed among various power subjects (state, organizations, individuals) and thus the sought-after balance of power can also be attained.[114] The question we now must ask is: Is ownership really equal to a number of clearly definable functions which can be "socialized"?

WHAT IS OWNERSHIP?

As we have already shown, the functional socialist position on ownership is built upon ideas which were presented by Undén, Hedenius, Lundstedt, and others (see Chapter 2). We shall now briefly examine certain of Undén's theses on ownership which are crucial to functional socialism.

Undén starts from the current politicoeconomic position that labor, land, and capital are production factors of equal value.[115] "Equal" means here that in the theoretical and formally legal sense it is of no importance whether the individual acquired the property through labor (wages) or through capital (interest) and, further, that all three production factors have the same value-creating significance. Undén's position draws support from arguments in contractual law. The worker, capitalowner, and land-owner appear formally as *equal parties* who enter into contracts with each other regarding compensation for their efforts. Ownership is constituted by ownership of the means of production (previously produced commodities). Labor is a value-creating production factor, remunerated through contractual wages; it cannot be the basis for ownership demands. This is the conclusion of Undén's presentation on this point.

The bases for ownership are, according to Undén, the three production factors land, capital, and labor, but with the reservation that the owner of capital or land is assured of a greater legal protection. In other words, labor is not equal to capital in the legal sense. The question upon which we shall dwell here is: Apart from the origin and basis of private ownership, are the legal rules which regulate the "function," i.e., the relation between the owner and that which is owned, equal? Are all owner relationships equal in the sense that one can sum them up in the concept ownership and also subtract one after another of the owner relationships (functions)?

In order to clarify Undén's position on this point we must add two further concepts to the discussion. Within right of ownership, Undén differentiates between right of possession/protection of possession and right of disposition/protection of disposition. Undén feels that ownership rights are the *strongest* property rights and that "there are many intermediate forms between the right of ownership and weaker rights."[116]

The right of ownership is the strongest of the property rights. It means authority to command a thing in different respects, to command it in its totality within the limits drawn up by every legal system and with respect to the limits which the owner has placed upon himself through legal agreements with other persons.[117]

As we were able to show in Chapter 2, the notions of ownership contain a core—the given relationship between the owner and the thing owned. This relationship is defined by protection of possession and freedom of disposition. Limitations and regulations exist, but it seems that several commentators agree that because of the freedom of disposition there are certain *fundamental* rights in ownership which may not be regulated. As Hedenius expresses it, these are the right to sell, transfer or sign a contract, "or without any contract to give away, will away, abandon or destroy the thing which is owned."[118]

Hedenius's definition of the freedom of disposition agrees with Becker's and Honoré's.[119] First, Becker and Honoré assume that the right of ownership of capital is the most fundamental right. Second, Becker feels that the core of the right of ownership is the right to "destroy, consume, and alienate."[120] Even Honoré seems to feel that there exist such fundamental principles of ownership rights which, above all regarding capital, cannot be modified in any degree. This is true, for example, of the right to use capital according to one's own discretion, the right to transfer it, the right to destroy it, the right not to use the capital at all, i.e., to let it be unproductive, the right to have physical control over it and the right to gain income from it.

We may summarize the meaning of private ownership in the following way: The right to private ownership of the means of production (capital) comprises the most fundamental element in the right of ownership. The same right is also the strongest property right and has the strongest protection. It may be limited, but not in such a way that the fundamental right is abandoned. The rights which follow from private ownership of the means of production are a precondition for a capitalist economy and thus objects of political and labor union interest. These are the rights to

- buy the labor of others,
- organize the labor of others,
- control the labor of others,
- make decisions concerning the goals of the labor of others, and
- use the surplus-value of the labor of others.

These rights may be modified by laws, contracts, and regulations on working hours, the working environment, wages, worker influence, etc. But the right to buy the labor of others by virtue of private ownership of the means of production may not be regulated by degree. That right either exists or does not exist. Nor may the right to refrain from buying the labor of others be regulated. If the owner of the means of production for some reason does not want to use these rights to the labor of others, then he can choose between the rights to

- — not use his capital as a means of production;
- — destroy the capital by, say, not providing for its profitability; or
- — alienate the capital.

The most fundamental right with far-reaching consequences for society is the right to let capital be unproductive or to destroy it.

This fundamental right is clearly established in Swedish law. The stock company legislation states the rights which fall exclusively to the share-holders' meeting (the owners). And certain of the rights given to the owners may not be delegated to any other body in the company.[121] This sovereignty given to the owners in the stock company legislation is so absolute that it could not be repealed without extensive social changes. It has been established that the stock company legislation is placed above all other laws which give employees the right to a certain influence.[122] We also feel, in agreement with Strömholm, that if one wanted to change the right of ownership to the means of production, then this would necessitate a constitutional amendment.[123] Such a change implies a shift in the principle of mandate from the present private owners to some other form of mandator.

THE IMPORT AND CONSEQUENCES OF THE RIGHT OF OWNERSHIP FOR FUNCTIONAL SOCIALISM

The goals of functional socialism are said to be identical to those of socialism. The primary goal of socialism, regardless of what form of socialism we are referring to, must be said to be a change of mandator. Such an interpretation is, however, denied by the functional socialists, who feel that growth and equitable distribution are the primary goals.

Functional socialism seems to assume that a change in mandator is not a precondition for the attainment of socialism's goals and that private ownership is not a precondition for growth. But then one could ask who shall have control over the means of production if they are neither socialized nor privately owned. It is our interpretation of Adler-Karlsson that the answer is the state. The state can regulate private ownership through legislation so that the state gains control over the means of production, thereby weakening the significance of private ownership to the extent that it becomes inoperative. One may functionally socialize ownership because it consists of a number of functions. Further, says Adler-Karlsson, it does not make any difference who owns the means of production because the executive makes the same economic decisions regardless of the form of ownership.

It is our opinion that these conclusions are based on a misunderstanding of the significance and effects of ownership rights. Ownership does not consist of a number of functions which can be separated from each other through legislation. In order to understand the core of ownership, we can find assistance in the delineation into freedom of disposition and protection of possession.[124] Freedom of disposition with respect to capital-ownership is the supreme legitimizing principle of private ownership. The rights of possession may be limited with the intent of protecting the public interest and third parties, while the right not to use, to destroy, or to alienate capital can only be altered by a constitutional amendment leading to a change of mandator.

Certain other rights important to production relations, such as the right to buy, organize, and control the labor of others, the right to make decisions concerning the goals of production, and the use of the surplus-value, may in some sense be open to modification, but on the whole they are the exclusive rights of the owner of capital.

Since the 1920s functional socialism has been held forth as a method for breaking the sovereignty and power of private ownership on the basis of civic rights. We can see that some rights have been limited and regulated. The person who owns the means of production and has employees is forced by law to pay taxes and make other payments to the state and the municipality. This has been attained in part as a consequence of a strong political and labor organization within the workers' movement. We can also see that private ownership and its sovereignty are undisturbed. The advantages achieved at the cost of capital are not to be taken for granted. The owners of the means of production may still choose not to use, to destroy, or to alienate their capital and thus to influence the preconditions for the maintenance of the relative advantages which have been achieved.

9.3 Summary

The various concepts of rights exist side by side. They vary in potency depending on the economic and political situation, but in some ways they also stand in logical conflict with each other. In this chapter we have dealt with two such conflicts. The conflict between private ownership of the means of production and collective capitalownership has been exemplified by the debate on employee investment funds, especially the discussion resulting from the proposal by Rudolf Meidner et al.

Given that some kind of collective ownership is instituted, the concept "collective" must be defined. The choice here is between the category "citizen" and the collective "wage earners." Functional socialism comprises a philosophy of gradual transfer of control over production to the public, i.e., to the citizens. A characteristic feature of functional socialism is that it avoids dealing with the question of the right to capital and the consequences of this right for the chances of controlling the use of the capital. The private right to capital means, among other things, that the initiative to where the capital will be invested (or not invested) is outside democratic control. The moving and closing of companies is mainly the product of private decisions. The state and the municipality are forced to a great extent to accept the conditions offered by private industry. A change in these conditions cannot be brought about by "functionally socialist" means. This demands a shift in the legal basis for the ownership of capital, i.e., it means a qualitative change in mandator relationships.

A third problem arises in the borderline area between civic rights and the rights of labor. The solution to this problem is central to all systems of collective capitalownership. Demands for influence from those groups who create value through their role in production must be weighed against demands for influence and equitable distribution from groups who lack any direct connection to production. This is the subject of our final chapter.

Chapter 10

THE RIGHTS OF LABOR AND ECONOMIC DEMOCRACY

Summary and Conclusions

Should the right of determination over companies be exercised on the basis of civic rights or on the basis of labor rights? In the preceding chapters we discussed the grounds for both of these principles of rights. It is now time to summarize our discussion and to deal with the problems of principle and organization involved in the application of the rights of labor. Our intent is to point out the potential of such a system as well as the problems associated with it.

10.1 Original Acquisition

A theory of ownership must be founded on a discussion of *original* acquisition (see Section 2.7). This is a matter of going beyond the strictly positive law analysis which has as its starting point property relations as they exist in society today. It is not sufficient to point out, as Strömholm does, that property has "been accumulated" in companies.[1] The important question in the discussion of private vs. collective ownership is *how* this accumulation has been brought about and on what legal premises the property accumulated in companies is founded.

Private property has "been accumulated" largely as a result of a system of composite production (individual capitalownership combined with purchased labor). It was during the historical development of this system that control over production and its preconditions increasingly passed from the direct producers to the private capitalowners.

CIVIC RIGHTS

Civic rights developed as a complement to private ownership of the means of production. Liberal writers were eager not only to extend suffrage, but also to limit it, so that the newly won influence of bourgeois and industrialist groups was not lost to demands for power from the working class.[2]

Thus, civic rights carry a heavy burden if and when they are introduced as the basic principle of economic democracy. Historically, civic rights are tied to liberal arguments for private property and economic freedom.

Politically, the fact that the labor movement confined itself to universal suffrage as its primary means of struggle has meant the acceptance of a sharp distinction between political and economic power, and the labor movement has contented itself with participation in the former. Such a thought was rather alien to the classical liberals: political power was for them indivisibly tied to economic power.

THE LABOR THEORY OF VALUE AND THE RIGHTS OF LABOR

The foundation of the labor theory of value is the notion that the value of a commodity is equal to the amount of work (Marx: "socially necessary labor-time") which is incorporated into it. The labor theory of value contains the notion of a real value, different from market-value or exchange-value. An additional cornerstone of the theory, which is important to the issue of original acquisition, is the genetic reasoning that capital originates through labor. The assumption of the labor theory of value that production relations and class relations are connected is yet another element which makes the labor theory of value an important instrument in the analysis of the economic and political development of society.

The labor theory of value refines and clarifies the dimension upon which such an analysis must for the most part build—the relation between capital and labor, the relation between the two interests which are opposite poles in the capitalist mode of production.

CONFLICTS BETWEEN THE NOTIONS OF RIGHTS

To date, the strongest challenge to the private ownership of the means of production has come from demands for employee investment funds (see Section 9.1). Especially in the report of the Meidner group, the conflict between private and collective ownership is clear: In the treatment to which the proposal has been subjected—and in which the demands of the labor organizations have been weighed against those of the Social Democratic party—important parts of it have been so attenuated that at this time (the end of 1979) it is unclear whether "employee investment funds" will really entail a change of mandator and a change in ownership relations in the economy.

An explanation for this development would seem to be the Swedish labor movement's traditionally strong commitment to civic rights arguments. One problem has been that, on the issue of fund formation, wage-earner interests and demands for labor rights do not entirely agree with the interests and demands of other civic groups. Wage earners have argued, however, that the conflict between wage-earner interests and civic interests has been exaggerated and that wage-earner organizations have both the will and the capability to represent public interests.[4]

The conflict between the public interest and the rights of labor may be the most important problem which must be solved by a system of economic democracy.

10.2 Political Democracy and Industrial Democracy

There is a parallel to the above-mentioned in the debate on co-determination in the public sector. It has been pointed out from various quarters that there is a danger that wage-earner demands could eclipse the influence of the public interest in decisions on, say, health care, education, and public communications. Especially the political scientists Nils Elvander, Agne Gustafsson, and—at an early stage—Jörgen Westerståhl and Mårten Persson have been active critics of wage-earner participation in decisions within the public sector.[5] There has also been a lively debate in the Social Democratic journal Tiden.[6]

Nils Elvander feels that the application of co-determination in the public sector carries with it risks of the endangerment of political democracy and may be the first step on the road to a corporate system. By corporatism, Elvander means "a system in which the decision-making organs at various levels in the state and communities are entirely or partially appointed by interested groups and not through elections with universal and equal suffrage."[7] It is not possible, according to Elvander, to apply within the public sector the general point of view of industrial democracy which is used for private companies. Westerståhl and Persson write: "Employee representation in state administrative bodies must be formed in such a way so as not to infringe upon general civic interests."[8]

In the public sector the problem has been legally solved in such a way that wage-earner demands for co-determination have been recognized in principle to the same extent as in the private sector, but in practice influence has been limited in various ways. The problem is given special attention in the preliminary work on the Law on Public Employment (LOA). Further, a special commission has been appointed to resolve possible conflicts between the public interest and wage-earner interests.[9] In negotiations in the municipal sector today there is often an explicit separation of "political" and "unionist" questions.

The discussion is in no way limited to the public sector and political democracy in the usual sense.

The same conflict between democratic interests and wage-earner interests may arise in charitable and nonprofit organizations as well as in companies owned by popular movements and so-called "opinion companies" (e.g., newspapers). Article 2 of the Law of Co-determination intends to regulate the relationship between mandator and employees:

> Employer activity of religious, scientific, artistic or similar nature, or which has cooperative, labor union, political, or other opinion-making intentions, is exempted from the area of applicability of the law as regards the goals and orientation of the activity.

The term "goals and orientation" indicates that the legislator has defined the comprehensive and long-term issues as the exclusive domain of the mandator in these kinds of organizations, while in *other* kinds of com-

panies employee interests are expressly allowed to influence even mandator issues.[10]

10.3 A Society Founded on the
Rights of Labor: Possibilities

In the preceding we have rejected the right of private ownership of the
means of production and argued for collective ownership (Chapters 5, 7,
and 8). As for the two main principles of collective ownership—civic rights
and the rights of labor—we are critical of civic rights. There is insufficient
reason for basing argumentation for collective ownership on a theory with
a strong egotistical character, a theory which emphasizes individual economic freedom and thus may seriously neglect demands for equality of
opportunity to influence economic conditions and the equitable distribution of the results of production. Both in principle and by definition, civic
rights are individual and noncollective.

UNLIMITED LOCAL WAGE-EARNER CONTROL?

"Civic rights" and "public interest" are not synonymous concepts.
Both contain the principle of universal and equal suffrage. Beyond this,
however, the concept "public interest" has an important connotation
concerning the distribution policy: Letting the public interest assert itself
means limiting tendencies toward local egoism and is also important for
comprehensive social functions, such as commerce, foreign, and defense
policies. A general representative assembly should, in other words, have
the right, if need be, to make decisions contradicting those of representative assemblies on lower levels (local, regional). The aim is to prevent
smaller groups, who may have greater resources, from shirking obligations
to the larger collective or from gaining advantages at the expense of this
collective. Examples of measures aimed at counteracting excessive self-
interest are progressive taxation, regional policies, and social, and educational policies.

In the debate on employee investment funds, fears have been raised
that a mandator role for wage earners would lead to "company egoism"
and would undermine the wage solidarity policy. The LO-SAP committee
on employee investment funds writes:

> That the funds are to be a step in the democratization of working life means
> that all wage-earner groups should be given influence over the funds while at
> the same time influence should be rooted as close to the members as possible,
> without, however, binding it entirely to the individual company.[11]

The example of Yugoslavia is a warning here: since the introduction of
the self-management system, regional inequality has grown greatly. Those

regions which were well developed at the start have succeeded in increasing their advantage over poorer regions even more.[12]

The risk that Sweden would follow the path of Yugoslavia after any introduction of wage-earner management of companies is probably modest. The reasons for this have been developed earlier. They are, in summary, that Sweden is far more homogeneous than Yugoslavia in cultural, political, and economic respects, and Sweden has an important tradition of sociopolitical and unionist solidarity.[13]

This, however, is not sufficient. A society founded on the rights of labor must be able to *guarantee* that local striving for advantages will be held within reasonable limits—among other things, for the simple reason that the conditions for continued employment are dependent upon what part of their profits successful companies can forgo in order to support less successful companies. How can company egoism be limited and still be reconciled with the principle of the rights of labor? How can the rights of be combined with equitable distribution?

As we have maintained, the solution must be sought within the framework of the labor theory of value. Equitable distribution should be seen in terms of production first and only thereafter in terms of consumption, for the simple reason that consumption follows production, which is consequently primary. Before anything can be distributed and consumed, it must first exist.

"Equitable distribution" is thus a matter of equitable distribution of the control over the means of production and over the preconditions of production. Those who are employed gain power over production by virtue of the fact that they create social property. Those who are not employed gain power over society's property because they, in accordance with the ethical premises of the labor theory of value, are adjudged the right to work and have a legitimate interest in seeing that this right is realized through social measures.

The "rights of labor" signify a recognition of labor as the human being's primary source of consciousness and development. The right to work must be unconditional: *Everyone shall have the right to meaningful employment and be able to demand in political assemblies that measures be taken so that this goal is attained. The "rights of labor" can therefore not be equated with a system in which only those who are employed have political influence.*

Workers in companies have a legitimate mandator role with respect to existing production, but they cannot be recognized as the only mandator regarding the determination of the distribution of production results or with respect to decisions concerning the continued development of production. The rate of development of employment and the distribution of employment opportunities are issues which especially concern the *un*employed; they must therefore be represented in the assemblies which make these decisions.

POLITICAL REPRESENTATION

The above-mentioned suggests a system of political representation, the primary goal of which is to guarantee the right to work, i.e., to create work with express consideration of those who lack employment and who are especially dependent on a solidary solution to issues of distribution. The primary means of attaining this goal is the combination of *the right to make decisions* concerning production and *the right to execute the decisions.* Political and economic power is founded on original acquisition of the type "production through one's own labor"; in the exercise of this power those people participate who now contribute to capital growth with their labor, who previously contributed, and who will continue to contribute in the future.

It would carry us too far to examine all the technical details of how a system of political representation governed by the principle of the rights of labor would be formed. Several alternatives are possible. *One* possible solution may, however, be suggested in rough outline. The link between the political and economic roles of workers should be made as strong as possible. This means that actively employed people should nominate and elect representatives through their work organizations.

The concept "work organization" includes companies producing both commodities and services and includes the organizations which provide public service, i.e., schools, hospitals, agencies, etc. Several companies and organizations may be grouped together, regionally and/or by branch.

Unemployed people may be represented on the basis of a geographic division which accords with the grouping of companies: this against the background of the desire to keep together, as far as is possible, political representation and the economic issues which are to be handled by the decision-making assemblies. The election of representatives to regional (state, municipal) assemblies can thus occur in two kinds of constituencies, representing employed and unemployed people. Representatives to the central decision-making assembly (the parliament) can be elected according to the same classification principle, either on the same election day or through a special parliamentary election. There may be reasons which call for a strengthening of the influence of the regional organs in the parliament: in that case a certain portion of the seats could be filled in indirect elections under the direction of the regional assemblies (broken line in Figure 10.1).

This sketch does not include any allocation of seats by quota among either employed or unemployed people; rather, both groups are represented in regional and central assemblies on the basis of proportional elections. In our opinion, the idea of interest representation—that is, that a certain number of seats in the decision-making assemblies be reserved for certain interest groups—should be rejected. "There is simply no way to give any generally rational basis for the determination of the number or proportion of representatives for various interests. This is a problem which

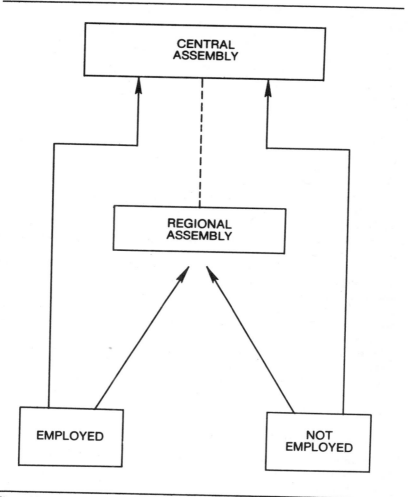

Figure 10.1

confronts anyone who tries to put together an organ with representatives of interests." [14]

FUND FORMATION

Capital is formed in companies, but—for reasons mentioned above—the capital may not be unilaterally controlled by them. The right of determination over capital formation must be distributed among three different levels: the companies, regions, and society. Disbursements to collective funds at each level can occur from a part of the company's profits—which presupposes that profit exists and that its amount can be determined somewhat clearly—and/or from a part of the total wage payment, as in the proposals for the formation of employee investment funds presented by the LO/SAP and the TCO.[15] Expressed schematically, the company's revenues can be said to consist of three parts: (1) the wages which go to the workers; (2) the funds set aside for new investments; (3) surplus. The latter can go to (a) improvement in the income of the workers, (b) increasing the company's solvency, and/or (c) external funds for the defrayment of collective needs, according to decisions made regionally and/or centrally. Each of these issues will be the object of political discussion: for obvious reasons, no final division between 1,2, and 3 and between 3a, 3b, and 3c can be established. Rather, the division will vary with the economic situation and the judgment of the political majority. For reasons of regional and distribution policy, it may be advisable, for example, during an economic upswing, to keep both wages and solvency at a relatively low level in order to increase societal or regional flexibility in the establishment of new firms, to expand public services, and to insure the goals of financial and stabilization policies.

This means that the power over the comprehensive economic decisions—including decisions on fund formation—lies with the central political assembly. The governing of the economy is carried out through the establishment of a framework for the activity of the labor organizations, not through direct administrative intervention in their detailed decisions or in the composition of their decision-making assemblies. Society forms the rules for the functioning of the economic system and watches over their fulfillment. Within the framework of these rules, the companies should be left free to the greatest possible extent and should be responsible for their own market assessments, product developments, and investment plans (cf., Hansson, pp. 206-207). For a discussion of plan and market, see below.

THE ORGANIZATION OF THE COMPANY

To an excessive degree, the debate on the potential of worker control has begun with the *inner* organization of the company; the goal has been to deal first with the control of the workers over their own labor and then perhaps to discuss the relations of the companies to each other and to society as a whole.[16] It is not uncommon for the latter problem to be solved through the general assumption of the existence of a socialist consciousness: If the wage earners just gain control over production in the companies, then it is thought that this will lead to a general increase in feelings of solidarity and in the willingness of those with greater resources to forgo some of what they have for the benefit of those who have less. Every form of state or central supervision can thus be deemed alien to a system of the rights of labor. In an interview on the Yugoslavian self-management system, the Yugoslavian sociologist Zaga Golubović gives the following answer to the question, "With what functions and what means of power should the state be equipped?"

All decisions in society should be based on democratic assent by all free producer associations. . . . If an association cannot accept what has been democratically agreed upon, then it should be able to go its own way, but it must, of course, be prepared to take all the consequences of the divorce. . . .

Question: Shouldn't the state have any means of power?

Answer: No. The task should only be to bring these wills together to a common view, a public interest, not to direct these units from above.

One problem which Zaga Golubović disregards is that a "divorce" can be more disastrous for society than for the producer association which breaks away. A separation is tempting to the rich companies: one may exploit one's strong position with no obligation to the whole. The same separation is a threat to the poorer companies who lose the possibility of benefiting from contributions from the wealthier part.of the producer family.

Thus, the question of how guarantees will be made to the weaker parties must be answered first. We tried above to suggest some basic features of a possible solution. How the control and production of the company will then be arranged internally is a comparatively simple question. For example, these problems may be solved through a structure of the kind proposed by Branko Horvat.[18]

The company is seen as composed of two subsystems, one representative and the other producing. The base of the representative system is the wage-earner collective, which is the mandator of the company. The mandators appoint from within their ranks representatives to various levels in the company, and they choose the executive board (worker council) which takes care of daily decisions. The task of the producing system is to carry out production as efficiently as possible. It is led by an employed executive leadership which is in close contact with the company's management. The employees function here as the base of the producing system, and they are incorporated into a production and labor management system which looks traditional. The organization of the company may be illustrated by the hourglass model in Figure 10.2. (To the company may also be added certain market analysis, administrative and ombudsman functions which for the sake of simplicity have been left out here.)

The hourglass organization is based on the observation that there are two fundamentally different spheres of activities or decision-making. The first is concerned with value judgments and, consequently, each individual counts as one. In the second, technical decisions are made as a function of technical competence and expertise. The first group of decisions are policy directives, the second are technical directives. The former were based on political authority as exercised by the members of the organization, the latter on professional authority specific to each member due to the division of labor.[19]

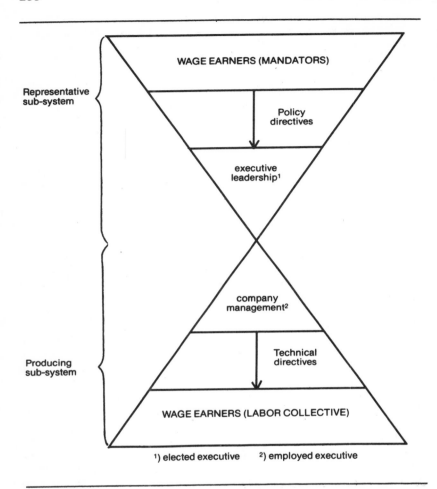

Figure 10.2

10.4 A Society Founded on the
Rights of Labor: Problems

The principle of the rights of labor seems to be the most reasonable path to follow if the goal is economic democracy. It offers possibilities for a reunification of political and economic power, power which derives from labor and which is placed in the hands of those who through their labor create the foundation for society and its continued development.

However, the principle of the rights of labor brings up a number of problems and raises a series of questions which demand answers. The questions may be divided into two groups: the first concerns internal relations in the companies, and the second concerns characteristics of the social system as a whole. As was the case earlier, the most important problems make themselves felt on the level above the individual work organizations.

QUESTIONS OF THE ORGANIZATION OF THE COMPANIES AND UNION ACTIVITY

(1) *Are wage earners competent to run the companies?* It is not uncommon in the discussion of wage-earner control and employee investment funds to run into the thesis that workers lack the competence to run the companies and that the institution of wage-earner control must be therefore a long-term issue.

> As for wage-earner ownership in companies, it is obvious that a long period of edification is necessary. Wage earners are today the clear underdogs in relation to capitalowners. A number of indispensible insights and experiences regarding the running of companies are still reserved for the groups which until now have had the right of determination, i.e., the present owners and the corporate leaderships appointed by them. This head start must be made up if wage-earner ownership influence is to be a reality. This can only happen if wage earners have the time to grow into a new role, to broaden their experiences, and to gradually increase their active involvement in issues concerning the future of the companies.[20]

> Advanced technical knowledge or facts from technical experts [are needed] in order to be able to really participate in the planning for a large company. Among those who represent the workers there are hardly any who possess such knowledge. [Labor unions do not possess] the technical, administrative or commercial experience which is necessary to run a large company.[21]

The meaning of the concept "competence" needs clarification. Administrative and technical competence is required to manage the daily activity of companies, and this competence should be suitably distributed throughout the various levels and positions which make up stages in the production of goods and services. This is true of competence within the producing subsystem. However, another distinction is also central—the distinction between mandator and executive. Our argumentation above concerns the take-over of the *mandatorship* of the producing organizations and not, at first, the executive responsibilities. It is a reasonable assumption that wage earners today are not competent to control all aspects of all the special functions included in managing a large company. One cannot make people into heating and ventilation engineers, computer systems specialists, corporate lawyers, or foreign language secretaries in the wink of an eye. It is even questionable if the long-term goal *should* be that everyone be able to do all jobs. Complicated and extensive production tasks often require complicated and extensive education and a rather extensive division of labor.

This is also true, for the most part, of administrative competence—the knowledge needed to plan and coordinate production. However, "competence" in this sense is more ambiguous and not as clearly connected to detailed knowledge and special education. The duties of corporate leadership are largely based on experience and an overall understanding of production: it is a matter of understanding how the various parts of the operation contribute to the creation of the final product, singly and in combination. Detailed technical knowledge about individual steps in the production process is is not a self-evident advantage in the completion of executive duties. More important is often a thorough knowledge of the company's external relations (to other companies and to the domestic and international markets) and of the conditions for conflict resolution and cooperation internally in the company. It is, of course, not impossible that a group of wage earners may find among themselves persons with sufficient experience and knowledge to provide the strategy and the micropolicy involved in the management of production.

However, the "rights of labor" are not dependent upon this. This principle concerns the transfer of the *mandator role,* i.e., the role which is exercised by the shareholders' meeting in private companies. The mandator has the right to appoint and dismiss the executive; and the issue of the rights of labor concerns first and foremost the mandator control over the executive. The question which must be raised thus concerns the competence of the wage-earner collective as compared to the *shareholders' meeting.*

There is no immediate reason to judge the competence of present stockholders to exercise power over the company to be greater than that of the wage earners. Stockownership is not based on competence but rather on interest. The stockholder is primarily interested in realizing a return on his invested capital, and he is interested in the company being managed in such a way as to maximize the possibility for this. The stockholder is a member of the shareholders' meeting by virtue of his capital investment, and he exercises his right of decision with the aim of increasing the amount of this investment. He may, if the company does poorly, terminate his involvement (though at an economic loss) and move his investment to a more profitable area. There is no special interest in seeing that a specific company continues to exist, and the sale, merger, or closing of a company is evaluated against the background of the consequences for the individual's capital investment. This requires neither especially detailed knowledge of the internal state of the company nor any larger perspective on the future existence of the company.

The wage-earner assessment can be expected to be different. Wage-earners are members in the mandator group by virtue of their labor investment: they exercise their right of decision in order to influence the short-term results (which have consequences for the wages they may exact) but also in order to insure that production and employment can be maintained in the future. Further, from the perspective of the private capitalowner, it makes no difference where his investment is placed geographically. The opposite is often true of the wage earner: His investment may not be arbitrarily moved, since this would cause relocation problems for him and his family. The geographic relocation of production can also have negative socioeconomic consequences which the wage earners would want to minimize because they are the ones who must ultimately pay. It seems therefore reasonable to expect that the interests of the workers as mandators will be both deeper (greater personal involvement) and broader (concerning more aspects of the company's activity) than those of the private capitalowners. The motivation for obtaining knowledge and competence concerning the current situation and the future potential of the company can be assumed to be greater in the wage-earner collective than among the representatives of private capital. The potential for the workers' active participation in the administration and running of the company thus seems to be largely connected to a take-over of the mandator role.

(2) *What happens with co-determination?* Those problems which are of special interest today regarding the application of the Law of Co-determination are related to the formal subordination of co-determination to stock company legislation (see Section 2.4) and to the question of which levels of decision the Law of Co-determination affects.

In principle the Law of Co-determination makes co-determination possible for wage earners at all levels in the company, even in areas concerning the company's goals and orientation (exceptions here are companies with scientific activity, activity based on charitable interests, mass media companies, etc., as regulated by Article 2 of the Law). But in practice private capitalowner interests take precedence over wage-earner interests in co-determination. A change in mandator would mean by definition that wage earners would also gain the right of determination of overall issues. Thus, under a system where labor has taken precedence over capital, there is no formal reason to press for the workers' co-determination demands via a special law.

Informally, however, things are different. Even if wage earners become mandators of the companies—and the conflict within the company between capitalowner and worker disappears—it cannot be assumed that this would eliminate conflicts in the *production organization.*

Strikes are theoretically ruled out in a system based on the rights of labor. In practice it is to be expected that differing views between the labor management and individual workers (or work groups) concerning the planning of work can lead to strikes and other labor conflicts. (A study in Yugoslavia shows that at least 2,000 strikes occurred between the years 1958 and 1968. Most were small and brief and pretty closely followed the pattern of wild-cat strikes in Sweden.)[22] Labor management exercises its role through a mandate from the *entire* wage-earner group; it is thus not reasonable for management simply to give in to demands from small groups on individual issues. A wage-earner-controlled company should therefore contain a special democratically appointed body for the resolution of this kind of conflict.

(3) *Does the trade union organization have any purpose?* What will be the position of the labor union movement in a system based on the rights of labor? There are two kinds of argument here. First of all, it is claimed that the existing adversary relationship in the labor market cannot be abandoned. It is an indispensible part of our economic system. A departure from this system would place wage earners "on both sides of the negotiating table," which is seen as a self-contradiction and which could have serious consequences. The newspaper *Dagens Nyheter* wrote about the Meidner proposal: "The LO as employers' association: certainly a risk to be aware of."[23] And in the SAF report "Corporate Profits, Capital Supply, Employee Investment Funds," Erland Waldenström et al. write:

> The double role of the labor unions as owners of the main part of the economy and at the same time as representatives of the employees' union interest must—like their position as a state within the state on the whole—seem questionable even from the perspective of the union movement itself, perhaps not least from the aspect that in the end it would nevertheless seem to be the state which would gain the upper hand. "Mixed socialism" can easily slip into a classical state socialism.[24]

The objection is based on the premise that the economy *must* be organized on the basis of private capital ownership. The Waldenström group has "*assumed that* the increased influence for the employees will be realized within the framework of the market economy system with a retained right for private institutions and persons to own companies."[25] In the preceding we presented reasons why this premise cannot be accepted. If labor is given precedence over capital, then the workers themselves will be able to determine the distribution of company revenues. However, there must still be some negotiations on wage increases. In accordance with the lines of reasoning we have developed, the right of determination over capital and its yield is exercised on different levels: local, regional, and central.[26]

As has been mentioned above, unlimited local wage-earner control cannot be accepted. The mandatorship for fund formation and capital administration is in the hands of comprehensive bodies; wage-earner demands must be balanced against the public demands which may be presented by these bodies. The size of the available margin for wage increases must be determined; the main difference from today is that wage earners will have more opportunity to get an overall view on the societal level of what the available wage increase margin actually is. Then it will be a matter of forming a contract between society and the companies in the most suitable way possible, contracts which allow for societal demands for solidarity as well as for wage-earner demands for reasonable economic incentives (see below). The contract may include clauses on wage level and wage development as well as on investment assistance and other resources coming from society to the company. The workers will, of course, be "on both sides of the negotiating table," but as representatives of different social levels: public interest will be opposed to subinterests. This conflict always exists, regardless of the economic system. It can thus not be used as an argument for wage earners not being the mandators of production.

Second, it is claimed that the labor union movement will generally not have anything to do in a social organization based on the rights of labor. "Meidner's proposal will be the death of the unions," wrote the business magazine *Veckans Affärer* in September 1975. There is good reason to believe that this fear is greatly exaggerated. The question has been dealt with by P. H. Hugenholz among others.[27]

The theory of the death of the labor unions in the worker-controlled economy rests on several incorrect assumptions, says Hugenholz: (1) the assumption that all workers are sufficiently competent to manage the company, (2) the assumption that all workers are equal and strive for the same thing, (3) the assumption that all sectors of the economy are equally strong and independent of each other, and (4) the assumption that the economy in which the labor union movement works is isolated from the surrounding environment.

Instead, says Hugenholz, the circumstances are the following: (1) An extensive need for education and training for the tasks of self-management exists. This requires large resources and must be organized centrally. The labor union movement has a necessary role here. (2) Values of equality and solidarity in wage policy must be guaranteed. The union movement is the natural organization for this. (3) The same is true of the position of branches of industry vis-à-vis each other. The union movement also has an important task with respect to the coordination of production, agreements between companies, etc. (4) Export policy and solidarity with workers in other countries are important questions, as is aid to developing countries. The union movement is also important here as a leader in debate, origin of ideas, and organization.

There is hardly reason to believe that the union movement's tasks will *lessen* in a wage-earner-controlled economy, and there is reason to assume that they will even increase in number and scope. Contributions from a strong labor union movement are of vital importance for the successful functioning of the system.

QUESTIONS ON PRODUCTION IN GENERAL AND ON THE POLITICAL SYSTEM

(1) *The market, incentives, and efficiency.* A system based on the rights of labor must be a compromise between local wage-earner control over companies and central democratic control over capital formation and capital supply. Expressed differently, the mandator role of the workers will be divided up among various levels, with increased direct influence for the workers the further down in the system one goes, and—in the opposite direction—with an increasingly broad right of determination for social institutions the more extensive the decisions become.

There is no reason to apply a detailed central plan to the production stage. On the contrary, the market principle should be used as far as possible. The market is a *means* to smoothly coordinate supply and demand, a means which in important ways has proved its efficiency over the planning systems of the socialist countries. As an *end,* however, the market principle is debatable. If the market is an end, then this means that the creation of inequality and the other negative effects of the system must be accepted. The subjective theory of value sets up the market, exchange, and consumption as primary goals. This must be rejected for the reasons we have presented, but this does not mean that the market *elements* in the economy also must be rejected. The market can and must be supervised and, when required, adjusted.

Critics of the employee investment fund notion readily depict a fund system under wage-earner control as synonymous with central control, bureaucracy, and strictly planned regulation of the economy. The Waldenström group, for example, reasons as follows:

> The question which we are justified in asking is what place consumers are allotted in the labor union-controlled economy which is the final goal of the Meidner system. In the Meidner proposal the emphasis is on seeing that the employees, rather than capital, attain a decisive influence over the company. *But ultimately, the economy does not exist for the employees—or for capital-owners—but rather for the consumers of goods and services.* Production and employment are means to satisfy consumer needs. Ultimately, it is still the ability of the economic system to fulfill this task which is the decisive criterion for its ability to function.[28]

The quotation contains two basic thoughts. Consumption should take precedence over production. Wage-earner influence over fund formation entails "labor union control" and the risk of state intervention ("[the solution would seem to be] that the state through various means of economic policy directs and intervenes both with respect to investment planning and capital supply"[29]).

The basic thoughts imply in turn that the outlined state of affairs would sharply deviate from what is true of today's Swedish economy. It is suggested that today's economy exists primarily for the consumers of goods and services. Further, it is tacitly implied that state intervention in the area of capital supply does not occur today, or in any case that it is far less than would be the case in a system of employee investment funds.

In reality, companies try in a number of different ways to direct consumption both with regard to amount and content. They do this with the aid of various means for influencing consumer preferences. The thesis of consumer sovereignty is largely a myth. The party with the main interest in this myth formation is industry, whose continued profitability and existence depend upon avoiding unexpected oscillations in the market. Modern industrial production is extraordinarily capital-demanding and requires a long planning time; it is therefore important to see to it that consumers are ready when a new product is launched. This has been investigated by, among others, John Kenneth Galbraith in *The New Industrial State*.[30]

It should be added that the Waldenström group's concern for consumers almost without exception relates to the consumption of *privately* produced goods and services. The report speaks in a much softer voice about the need for direct public production so that public needs may be better met. But when consumers are given the opportunity to choose whether they want to invest a potential wage increase in private consumption or in an expansion of public service, the choice almost always falls on the latter.[31]

As for state interventionism, it should be pointed out that in most industrialized countries today a close cooperation between state and industry is a rule rather than an exception. This was not changed by the fact that in 1976 a non-Social Democratic government came to power in Sweden. On the contrary, during the lifetime of this government there was an increase in the amount of economic support to companies, e.g., in the form of subsidies for education and hiring, temporary employment subsidies to large companies, branch subsidies to the steel and shipping industries, recruitment subsidies, branch subsidies to the forestry sector, regional development funds, and company-specific loans.[32] The main reason for the cooperation between industry and state is not to be found in the political color of the existing government, but rather in the fact that company closings and restructuring of industry have had increasingly extensive consequences for the economy and employment, due, for example, to the concentration of capital and labor in fewer and larger companies. Society *must* intervene in many cases; and it seems under these circumstances to be a reasonable demand that the workers themselves, via control over capital, gain the opportunity to take the initiative in active efforts in economic policy. It seems plausible that such initiatives can be taken both earlier and with greater effect if wage earners at the local level have a good overall view of the market situation and development of the companies, and if at the central level they can direct investment finances to branches and companies which need special measures. This is not a "labor union-controlled economy left to itself," as the Waldenström group expresses it, but rather an economic system with a mixture of market elements and potential for broad economic considerations and general direction under democratic control.[33] That wage earners are well organized for this is to be seen as a special advantage of the system.

On incentives. Systems for collective capital formation and wage-earner influence over industry are often rejected by pointing out that such systems run the risk of eliminating the incentive resulting from the expectation of private profit. The subjective theory of value—and its interpretations in liberal political theory—emphasizes *material* incentives as the primary impetuses for human action. The standard case is piece-work wages, where compensation is directly related to the labor achievement. Seen on a larger scale, the material motive recurs also as the main explanation for technical innovation and creativity.[34]

A fairly complete review of the incentive problem reveals considerably more kinds of impetus than the material one. Incentives can be connected to force, material factors, normative stimuli (to do things in order to fulfill formal or informal rules or moral commands), and impetuses inherent in the task itself.[35] Normative incentives can be divided up further into those connected with group pressure, identification, and moral and ideological conviction.

It would, of course, be senseless to deny that many of our actions are motivated by material impetuses. First of all, however, the connection between material incentives and action is far from unequivocal. A higher piece-work wage, for example, sometimes leads to a greater, sometimes to a lessened, and sometimes to an unchanged level of achievement.[36] Second, the material motive does not preclude the effort being made *along with other people*. In other words, there are collective material impetuses. Competition between groups may replace competition between individuals.[37] An economic system based on wage-earner-controlled companies—where the employees have an opportunity to influence the size of the wages—is an application of the material incentive.

And quite a bit of production is carried out in work organizations where there is almost no way of seeing the connection between achievement and wages. Work in education, health care, and public administration often contains rewards which are mainly of a social character: One works out of solidarity with the work group, the students, the patients, or for moral and ideological motives.

Further, people often work because the labor is rewarding in itself. "An example is the researcher, who has been caught up in an intellectual problem to such an extent that he cannot stop thinking about it," writes Mats Friberg.[38] However, says Friberg, today's industrial jobs give the worker little opportunity to develop his creative ability and express his individuality. The content of labor needs therefore to be expanded both horizontally and vertically.

> The work should include more subtasks. These should comprise a meaningful whole and demand some care, skill, and practical intelligence. The individual must have control over his part of the production process and participate in the planning and establishment of goals. He must be able to choose himself the method of carrying out the work, and he must be regularly informed of his achievements.[39]

It is usually denied by the classical school of organization theory (Taylorism) that inherent impetuses exist, or that they play any significant role. "It is assumed that the human being by nature is lazy and unindustrious, works as little as possible, dislikes responsibility—in short, that he is interested in nothing but his wage."[40]

As Friberg points out, it is a natural goal for the good society to strive for a system in which inherent impetuses govern labor to a great degree. It would seem that creativity and innovative ability are related to a significant extent to the individual's fascination with and interest in a problem which is in need of solution. The fact, then, that the invention or intellectual creation arouses interest in others (social motives) or pays well (material incentives) only emphasizes the complexity of the set of impetuses which govern labor.

In summary: A system based on the rights of labor does not exclude material incentives or the thought that works in innovative or efficient companies should have the opportunity for reasonable compensation for their extra contributions. It must, however, be a question of a balance between this compensation and the common need for a wage solidarity policy. There must be sufficient guarantees against company egoism; and the cumulative results of production must be used for, among other things, a gradual development of working life, so that inherent impetuses can increasingly come into play. In short, labor must become more human and more interesting. The methods for attaining this in direct assembly-line production are largely known (job expansion, job rotation, self-supervising groups, etc.). But to a great extent it must also be a question of reestablishing the connection between planning and executing labor, a connection which more and more tends to be broken in today's industrial production.[41] The conflict with the previously mentioned demand for a rational use of expert and specialized knowledge, which arises here, cannot be definitively resolved but rather must be dealt with from case to case, depending upon economic and organizational conditions.

Wage-earner self-rule means improved possibilities for ending alienation and increasing participation in the solution of common problems. Thus, efficiency, in the long term at least, should increase. Various manipulations aimed at increasing the workers' production (time studies, the MTM system, piece-work rates, etc.) will no longer be necessary since workers will no longer have any interest in restraining their efforts. Such an interest does, however, exist under private capitalist circumstances, as Ernst Wigforss pointed out in 1919:

> When the worker does not exert himself to the utmost, when on the whole he does not do more than is absolutely necessary for him to keep his job, then he is doing nothing more than applying the principle which according to the defenders of the present society forms the indispensible foundation for our entire economic life, i.e., the principle of the greatest possible profit.[42]

On the establishment of new firms and on inventions. A commonly presented argument against wage-earner-controlled systems is that they do not provide sufficient incentive for the establishment of new firms.[43] Why should one take any initiative if one must share the earnings of an invention with others?

As we have stated, the incentive question cannot be reduced to a mere economic affair; other motives for labor are common. But nevertheless, the objection must be answered. A society based on the rights of labor must not be a hindrance to innovations and new companies, and it can, of course, not be denied that economic incentive plays a considerable role here.

One possible solution to the problem is to leave room for the establishment of smaller companies but at the same time to set a limit on the number of employees a company may have under private ownership. Yugoslavia has a system where the limit is five employees. If the company becomes bigger, then it becomes public property and wage-earner managed; the initiator of the company can then be part of the company, employed, for example, as executive director. The system sets limits on extreme profits and private capital accumulation, while at the same time it seems to allow enough opportunity so as not to restrain initiative and innovation.

If the development of an invention requires a greater work force than mentioned here, then it would seem that the required capital investment from society would be so great that a widening of the mandator influence to people other than the initiator would be warranted.[44]

(2) *The party system and political participation.* There exist today a number of tendencies which suggest that the traditional political party structure may be on the verge of change. Changes of political sympathy even across coalition boundaries have become more common, and the variety of political groupings which cannot be sensibly incorporated into the traditional right-left scale has grown. For many of today's voters the differences between parties have become increasingly blurred, and the parties no longer appear, as they once did, to be clearly tied to different property-owning—or property-less—groups.

The readiness on the part of the traditional party system to articulate demands from various subgroups (sometimes collected under the label "discontentment groups") has not always been great. The Vietnam movement, environmentalists, opinions on the nuclear power issue, demands from various women's rights groups, and various small municipal party formations are examples of elements in the political structure which indicate that its legitimacy may be undergoing reevaluation.

At least two consequences of this are worth careful consideration and discussion.

The first consequence concerns the ideological stability of the system. The subgroups are often organized around relatively limited and temporary issues which sometimes lack obvious importance for overall social development. This is worth reflection since to a great extent politics concerns programs for overall social development. There is a risk that readiness for and interest in a discussion of long-term issues may diminish.

The second consequence has to do with the relationship of this politics of subgroups to work interests. Very few of the spontaneous movements of recent years have had any connection with wage-earner issues, wage-earner organizations, or with working life in general. To the extent that trends toward topic specialization continue in politics, it is conceivable that issues of working life will recede into the background. They are less dramatic than, say, decisions concerning nuclear power or local environmental issues. Further, the solution of labor problems cannot be dealt with as easily as specific issues, demanding instead extensive economic and political planning.

In both of these respects we feel that the principle of the rights of labor can offer ideas for an alternative development. Compared with the ideologies of the subpolitical movements, it offers a coherent politico-economic value system, rooted in a theory of original acquisition and oriented toward *conditions* for society's development. Further, it takes into express consideration the need for humanization and democratic control over the human being's most important area of activity.

Political participation. Trends toward centralization within the political system could cause a decrease in political participation. Municipal mergers during the 1960s and 1970s have drastically decreased the number of political offices. "Before the municipal reform of 1962 there were an estimated 150,000-200,000 municipal posts. When the Bureau of Statistics did a study in 1968, there were approximately 105,000 regular municipal posts. It is evidenced in the study executed by the municipal democracy investigation that the number of posts decreased to around 60,500 in 1971 and to around 42,000 in 1974."[45]

It is generally true that the larger organizations become, then the less participation there is, measured in the percentage of members who participate in an organization's meetings.[46] The work load on elected representatives has increased sharply during recent years, and this would seem to be one of the reasons behind the growing difficulty in recruiting political and union representatives as well as behind the, as it seems, increasingly common resignations from political posts.

A high rate of participation is a basic condition for a political system fulfilling demands for representativeness. If wage earners are given a mandator role in companies, then the potential for a broadened participation in important social issues increases, a participation which, as we discussed above in detail, concerns both decisions and their execution.[47]

(3) *Social Democracy and ownership.* Why did Social Democracy accept bourgeois economics with its subjective theory of value, its emphasis on consumption, and its equation of labor and capital? What were the circumstances which forced issues of power, ownership rights, and control

over the means of production into the background, and which kept them there until the 1970s?

Compared to other countries, Swedish industrialism developed relatively late. Due to the crisis on the international market until 1880, development in Sweden did not get under way until the 1890s. The preconditions for the workers forming a conscious political class. which industrialism is traditionally considered to bring about, did not develop with the 1890s. This means that at the turn of the century, the traditional one-family mill system dominated, with its patriarchal rule and carefully controlled, unorganized workers, all of whom were dependent upon the mill management for housing, employment, school, food, clothes, etc. In many mill towns, labor union and political organizations were not formed until the 1930s and 1940s. The changes in the social structure which are caused by industrialism, and which make up part of the preconditions necessary for the rise of a working class, did not exist in Sweden until the beginning of the twentieth century.

One may add to this that the difficult economic years around 1870-1880 led one million Swedes to emigrate. This, of course, diminished the conditions for an early organization and class consciousness.

In short, the labor movement lacked a mass base before the 1890s. It was mainly well-educated workers and craftmen who took the initiative in the formation of the Social Democratic party. These initiators drew mainly on social-liberal ideas. Labor organizations were often patterned on temperance and revivalist organizations. In a fictional account, P.-O. Enquist has shown how the traditional ideals of liberty counteracted the attempts at organization.[48]

Bunny Ragnerstam, also in a fictional account, has shown how the temperance and revivalist organizations and their representatives often took over the leadership of party organizations.[49] Sven Lundqvist has supported this with evidence from historical study within the framework of the research project "The Class Society's Functions: The Popular Movements."[50]

These organizational and intellectual bases contributed to making the "social question" the central problem for the worker organizations. Social misery was at the center of all attention, not questions of power and interest. From very early on, the activity took on a pragmatic and rather untheoretical orientation. The great socialist debate on the Continent generally missed the Swedish labor movement. International influences gained greater importance only through Hjalmar Branting and his participation in the Second International from 1890 on.

Swedish Social Democracy developed parallel to the labor union movement and the cooperative movement. This simultaneous development of various branches of the movement often made the struggle unclear: was it a change in production which was the primary goal, or was it political rights for all? As we tried to describe in Chapter 8, there was an inner conflict here. The labor union struggle for control over production was put off into the future. Cooperation with the liberals for universal suffrage became an important element in the party's political activity. The labor union struggle for control over capital was in practice put off into the future and not seriously revived again until the beginning of the 1970s.

Thus, between 1850 and 1900, the conditions for forming a workers' party and mobilizing wage earners on the ownership issue were limited. There was a series of resistance factors: competing movements (temperance, religious, liberal labor associations); the bourgeois counteroffensive in repressive forms and direct open resistance through legislation and the army; the mill town milieu which entailed the physical splitting up of workers in various mill towns and which traditionally bound workers tightly to the mill; the late—and slow—development of industrialism; and the recruitment of many of the party's leading members from among well-educated craftsmen and academics. All of this contributed to the development of the party strategy and tactics. These factors also explain in part the fact that the path chosen was one of struggle toward universal suffrage in cooperation with the liberals.

The chosen alternative, i.e., a reformistic development of the labor movement, has, however, had serious consequences in its lack of a firm theoretical position and development of a view of society. There have been no attempts (with certain exceptions, e.g., Karleby) to create an independent socio-philosophic base upon which to stand. Much has been reduced to pragmatism. One may also express it as Lindhagen did: The cooperation with the liberals led to the loss of feeling for and understanding of the origin of political action and the alternatives open to the labor movement. The "double consciousness" was lost and was replaced by the party's view of itself as mainly social liberal.

The party's lack of its own social theory and a clear understanding of society's goals caused problems in deciding upon the means necessary for society's development. Stated simply, this is exemplified in the distribution policy ambitions which have guided Social Democracy. The distribution policy has mainly been concerned with the *results* of production, not with the determining conditions. It is especially true that the right to capital—the most fundamental determinant of production—for all intents and purposes has been left out of the discussion.

Functional socialism has been presented as Social Democracy's main strategy in the struggle for economic democracy. Ownership rights would be attacked with the artichoke tactic: the power of private ownership would be stripped away leaf by leaf. But an artichoke consists not only of leaves. What is lacking is a strategy for what is to be done with the heart of the artichoke—the right to private ownership of the means of production. The handling of this heart was begun with the discussion of employee investment funds and economic democracy in the 1970s. The principle of the rights of labor is the principle for the reunification ot decision-making *and* executive power over production—a reunification which is a necessary part of economic democracy.

NOTES

Notes to
Chapter 1

1. Nozick, Robert, *Anarchy, State and Utopia*, 1974: 178.
2. Vedung, Evert, *Det rationella politiska samtalet*, 1977.
3. Myrdal, Gunnar, *Vetenskap och politik i nationalekonomin*, (1929) 1977.
4. Macpherson, C.B., *The Political Theory of Possessive Individualism*, (1962) 1977.

Notes to
Chapter 2

1. Furniss, Norman, "Property rights and democratic socialism," in *Political Studies*, 1978: 460.
2. Marx, Karl, *Capital: A Critical Analysis of Capitalist Production*, 1957: 160.
3. Marx, Karl, 1957: 160.
4. Marx, Karl, 1957: 160-161.
5. Marx, Karl, 1957: 162.
6. Marx, Karl, 1957: 823.
7. For a commentary on this, see, for example, *Vem äger Sverige?*, 1971: 31; and Chapter 9.
8. Honoré, A. M., "Ownership," in A.G. Guest (ed.) *Oxford Essays in Jurisprudence*, 1961.
9. Becker, L. C., *Property Rights*, 1977: 20.
10. Honoré, A. M., 1961: 132.
11. More on the concept "mandator" in Abrahamsson, *Bureaucracy or Participation: The Logic of Organization*, 1977: 26-30, 171-182.
12. For a more detailed discussion of the connection between the concepts "mandator" and "executive," and of some problems with the definition of "executive," see Abrahamsson, 1977, Chapter 10. For an exchange of opinion concerning the fruitfulness of these concepts, see the articles by Jan-Erik Lane and Bengt Abrahamsson in *Statsvetenskaplig tidskrift*, Nos. 2 and 3, 1978.
13. At this time we shall not go into the interesting discussion of the power of the shareholders' meeting vis-à-vis the executive board and executive directorship. There is much to indicate that the mandator role of the private capitalowners appears primarily when the company is in a financial crisis and the continued interest yield

on the capital is threatened. Normally it is the executive board and the executive directorship which exercise the visible influence over the organization. For a short summary of the discussion concerning power over the company, with well-known contributions by, among others, Berle and Means, James Burnham, and C. H. Hermansson, see *Vem äger Sverige?*, 1971: 11-42. Note also Lidén, 1966, and Engvall, 1967.

14. "Förhållandet mellan medbestämmandelagen och viss annan lagstiftning," *Arbetsmarknadsdepartementet*, 1977: 20.

15. Johansson, Sten, in *Arbetet*, October 6, 1975.

16. For an argument along these lines, see Bodström, Lennart, "TCO, partierna och den politiska pressen," in *Tiden*, No. 7, 1978: 381-391.

17. Hedenius, Ingemar, *Om rätt och moral*, 1941: 10.

18. Myrdal, Gunnar, *Vetenskap och politik i nationalekonomin*, 1972.

19. Hägerström, Axel, *Socialfilosofiska uppsatser*, 1966: 55, 57.

20. Strömholm, Stig, *Allmän rättslära*, 1976a: 19.

21. Lundstedt, V., 1928: 84.

22. Lundstedt, V., 1928: 84.

23. Strömholm, Stig, 1976a: 19.

24. Hedenius, Ingemar, 1941: 67-85.

25. Hedenius, Ingemar, 1941: 70.

26. Strömholm, Stig, 1976a: 51.

27. Lantz, Göran, *Eigentumsrecht—ein Recht oder ein Unrecht?*, 1977.

28. Strömholm, Stig, 1976a: 50.

29. Strömholm, Stig, 1976a: 50.

30. Eckhoff, T., "Litt om det juridiske rettighetsspråk," in *Festskrift for Alf Ross*, 1969: 65.

31. Eckhoff, T., 1969: 65; and Lantz, Göran, 1977: 27.

32. Hedenius, Ingemar, "Analysen av äganderättsbegreppet," in Belfrage and Stille (eds.) *Filosofi och rättsvetenskap*, 1975.

33. Hedenius, Ingemar, 1975: 42.

34. Hedenius, Ingemar, 1975: 43.

35. Hedenius, Ingemar, 1975: 54-55.

36. Hedenius, Ingemar, 1975: 55.

37. Hedenius, Ingemar, 1975: 50.

38. Hedenius, Ingemar, 1975: 54.

39. Hedenius, Ingemar, 1975: 53, 59.

40. Undén, Östen, *Svensk sakrätt, I. Lös Egendom*, (1927) 1976: 71-72.

41. Undén, Östen, 1976: 73.

42. Undén, Östen, 1976: 85.

43. Kahn-Freund, O., "Introduction," in Karl Renner, *The Institutions of Private Law and Their Social Functions*, (1949) 1976: 24; cf., Macpherson, C. B., on "simple market society," 1977: 51 ff.

44. Cf., Meek, R. L., *Studies in the Labor Theory of Value*, 1973: 26.

45. Kahn-Freund, O., 1976: 25.

46. Ambjörnsson, Ronny, *Idé och klass*, 1972: 33.

47. Cf., note 107 in Renner, Karl, *The Institutions of Private Law and Their Social Functions*, 1976: 103.

48. Kahn-Freund, O., 1977: 27.

49. Renner, Karl, 1976: 117.

50. Undén, Östen, 1976: 85.

51. Hydén, Håkan, *Rättens samhälleliga funktioner*, 1978: 213.
52. Malmström, Åke, *Civilrätt*, 1977: 123.
53. Hydén, Håkan, 1978: 213.
54. Hydén, Håkan, 1978: 213.
55. Undén, Östen, 1976: 86. Concerning the importance of the value relationship in foreign law, see also Honoré, A. M., 1961: 136.
56. Undén, Östen, 1976: 87.
57. Renner, Karl, 1976: 121.
58. Renner, Karl, 1976: 121-122.
59. Flodgren, Boel, *Fackföreningen och rätten*, 1978: 28.
60. Ståhl, Ingemar, "Ägande och makt i företagen—En debattinledning," in *Ekonomisk debatt*, No. 1, 1976: 62-75.
61. Rhenman, Eric, *Företagsdemokrati och företagsorganisation*, 1964: 28.
62. For commentary, see Therborn, Göran et al., *En ny vänster*, 1966; Karlsson, Lars-Erik, *Demokrati på arbetsplatsen*, 1969: 31ff.; Abrahamsson, B., *Bureaucracy or Participation*, 1977, Chapter 9.
63. Westholm, C. J., "Majoritetsprincipen och kontraktsrätten," in *Ekonomisk debatt*, No. 3, 1976: 239.
64. Westholm, C. J., *Ratio och universalitet. J. S. Mill och dagens demokratidebatt*, 1976: 280.
65. Westholm, C. J., in *Ekonomisk debatt*, No. 3, 1976: 242. Italics in original.
66. Cf., Meyerson, P.-M., *Löntagarfonder eller . . . ägande och demokrati i en marknadsekonomi*, 1978: 109-110.
67. Honoré, A. M., 1961: 147.
68. Becker, L. C., 1977: 120, note 11.

Notes to
Chapter 3

1. Vedung, Evert, *Det rationella politiska samtalet*, 1977.
2. Vedung, Evert, 1977: 170.
3. Vedung, Evert, 1977: 173.
4. Vedung, Evert, 1977: 173.
5. Vedung, Evert, 1977: 173.
6. Vedung, Evert, 1977: 174.
7. Vedung, Evert, 1977: 175.
8. Vedung, Evert, 1977: 175-176.
9. Vedung, Evert, 1977: 176.
10. Vedung, Evert, 1977: 176.
11. Vedung, Evert, 1977: 177-178.
12. Vedung, Evert, 1977: 178.
13. Myrdal, Gunnar, *Vetenskap och politik i nationalekonomin*, (1929) 1972.
14. Myrdal, Gunnar, (1929) 1972: 251-252.
15. Myrdal, Gunnar, *Objektivitetsproblemet i samhällsforskningen*, 1969.
16. Myrdal, Gunnar, 1972: 259.

17. Winch, Donald, "The emergence of economics as a science 1750-1870" (1971) in C. M. Cipolla (ed.) *The Fontana Economic History of Europe. The Industrial Revolution*, 1977: 509ff.

18. Winch, D., 1977: 509.

19. Cf., Qvist, Gunnar, in *Dagens Nyheter*, November 11, 1978.

20. Winch, D., 1977: 523.

Notes to
Chapter 4

1. Winch, D., "The emergence of economics as a science 1750-1870" (1971) in C. M. Cipolla (ed.) *The Fontana Economic History of Europe. The Industrial Revolution*, 1977: 510.

2. Hilton, Rodney, "Introduction," in R. Hilton (ed.) *The Transition from Feudalism to Capitalism*, 1978: 30, 14-15.

3. Dobb, Maurice, "From feudalism to capitalism," in R. Hilton (ed.) *The Transition from Feudalism to Capitalism*, 1978: 165.

4. Hobsbawm, Eric, "From feudalism to capitalism," in R. Hilton (ed.) *The Transition from Feudalism to Capitalism*, 1978: 161-162.

5. Hobsbawm, Eric, 1978: 163.

6. Merrington, John, "Town and country in the transition to capitalism," in R. Hilton (ed.) *The Transition from Feudalism to Capitalism*, 1978: 186.

7. Tilly, Charles (ed.) *The Formation of National States in Western Europe*, 1975: 399.

8. Lilley, Samuel, "Technological progress and the Industrial Revolution 1700-1914" (1970) in C. M. Cipolla (ed.) *The Fontana Economic History of Europe. The Industrial Revolution*, 1977: 187ff.

9. Lilley, Samuel, 1977: 188-189.

10. LeGoff, Jacques, "The town as an agent of civilisation 1200-1500" (1971) in C. M. Cipolla (ed.) *The Fontana Economic History of Europe. The Middle Ages*, 1976: 87.

11. Lilley, Samuel, 1977: 191.

12. Lilley, Samuel, 1977: 191.

13. Thrupp, Sylvia, "Medieval industry 1000-1500" (1971) in C. M. Cipolla (ed.) *The Fontana Economic History of Europe. The Middle Ages*, 1976: 265.

14. Thrupp, Sylvia, 1976: 249.

15. Macpherson, C. B., *The Political Theory of Possessive Individualism*, (1962) 1977: 287-291.

16. Sella, Domenico, "European industries 1500-1700" (1970) in C. M. Cipolla (ed.) *The Fontana Economic History of Europe. The Sixteenth and Seventeenth Centuries*, 1976: 400.

17. Thrupp, Sylvia, 1976: 252.

18. Sella, D., 1976: 397-400.

19. Sella, D., 1976: 400.

20. Meek, R. L., *Studies in the Labor Theory of Value*, 1973: 18.

21. Meek, R. L., 1973: 19.

22. Sweezy, Paul, "A Critique," in R. Hilton (ed.) *The Transition from Feudalism to Capitalism*, 1978: 49-50.

23. Dobb, Maurice, *Studies in the Development of Capitalism*, 1946: 42-43.

24. Sweezy, 1978: 36-37; cf., Hilton, 1978: 26.

25. Sweezy, 1978: 40.

26. Sweezy, 1978: 103.

27. Le Goff, J., 1976: 92.

28. Roehl, Richard, "Patterns and Structure of Demand 1000-1500" (1970) in C. M. Cipolla (ed.) *The Fontana Economic History of Europe. The Middle Ages*, 1976: 123.

29. See, for example, Cassel, Gustav, *The Nature and Necessity of Interest*, (1903) 1971: 3ff., 153-154.

30. Sella, D., 1976: 409; 411.

31. Sella, D., 1976: 412.

32. Tilly, C. (ed.), 1975: 418.

33. Sella, D., 1976: 362.

34. Mols, S. J. Roger, "Population in Europe 1500-1700" (1972) in C. M. Cipolla (ed.) *The Fontana Economic History of Europe. The Sixteenth and Seventeenth Centuries*, 1976: 38.

35. Sella, D., 1976: 384-388.

36. Macpherson, C. B., 1977: 51.

37. For a longer presentation than is possible here, see Ambjörnsson, R., *Idé och klass*, 1972: 167ff.

38. Macpherson, C. B., 1977: 52.

39. Macpherson, C. B., 1977: 51.

40. Macpherson, C. B., 1977: 48.

41. Macpherson, C. B., 1977: 54.

42. Macpherson, C. B., 1977: 55.

43. Macpherson, C. B., 1977: 55-56.

44. See Lantz, Göran, *Eigentumsrecht—ein Recht oder ein Unrecht?*, 1977, Chapter 5; and Roehl, R., 1976: 45-50.

45. Meek, R. L., 1973: 13.

46. Meek, R. L., 1973: 13.

47. Meek, R. L., 1973: 14.

48. Meek, R. L., 1973: 14.

49. Meek, R. L., 1973: 15.

50. Meek, R. L., 1973: 14ff.

51. Meek, R. L., 1973: 17.

52. Thrupp, S., 1976: 245.

53. Tilly, C. (ed.), 1975.

54. Lilley, S., 1977: 196.

55. Lilley, S., 1977: 195.

56. Lilley, S., 1977: 213.

57. Lilley, S., 1977: 211.

58. Lilley, S., 1977: 215.

59. Bergier, J. F., "The industrial bourgeoisie and the rise of the working class 1700-1914" (1971) in C. M. Cipolla (ed) *The Fontana Economic History of Europe. The Industrial Revolution*, 1977: 399.

60. Bergier, J. F., 1977: 400-401.

61. Meek, R. L., 1973: 18-19; Marx, K., *Capital: A Critical Analysis of Capitalist Production*, 1957, Chapter 14.
62. Meek, R. L., 1973: 18, note 1.
63. Meek, R. L., 1973: 18.
64. Meek, R. L., 1973: 20.
65. Meek, R. L., 1973: 20.
66. Meek, R. L., 1973: 23.
67. Meek, R. L., 1973: 25-26.
68. Meek, R. L., 1973: 26.
69. Meek, R. L., 1973: 27.
70. Meek, R. L., 1973: 27.
71. Meek, R. L., 1973: 31.
72. Burke, Edmund, *Reflections on the Revolution in France*, 1969: 270.
73. Smith, Adam, *Wealth of Nations*, (1776) 1977: 136.
74. Smith, A., 1977: 109-110.
75. Smith, A., 1977: 112.
76. Smith, A., 1977: 435.
77. Smith, A., 1977: 429-430.
78. Meek, R. L., 1973: 124.
79. Hansson, Sven Ove, *Marx och Engels i politiken*, 1976a: 41-42; cf., Gustafsson, Bo, "Klassicism, marxism och marginalism," in *Häften för kritiska studier*, Nos. 1-2, 1968: 15.
80. Bergier, J. F., 1977: 397-451; Marx, Karl, 1957, Chapter 15; Hellner, Brynolf, "Brukens arbetare" in Lindblom, A. (ed.) *Den svenska arbetarklassens historia*, 1943: 195-216; Andrén, Erik, "Städernas arbetare," in Lindblom, A. (ed.), 1943: 183-194; Heckscher, Eli F., *Svenskt arbete och liv*, (1957) 1976.
81. Bergier, J. F., 1977: 419, 433.
82. Bergier, J. F., 1977: 429.
83. Marx, K., 1957: 411.
84. Marx, K., 1957: 417.
85. Marx, K., 1957: 426.
86. Bergier, J. F., 1977: 431.
87. Marx, K., 1957: 395.
88. Andrén, Erik in Lindblom, A. (ed.), 1943: 87-88. For a credible and detailed fictional description of the living conditions of the workers, see Ragnerstam, 1975-1978.
89. Bergier, J. F., 1977: 443.
90. Thomson, David, *Europe since Napoleon*, (1966) 1970: 230.
91. Bergier, J. F., 1977: 436.
92. Macpherson, C. B., *Property*, 1978: 9.

Notes to
Chapter 5

1. On philosophic radicalism, see, for example, Halévy, Elie, *The Growth of Philosophic Radicalism*, 1955; and on empiricism, see, for example, Kolakowski, L., *Positivist Philosophy*, 1972: 91ff.
2. Myrdal, Gunnar, *Vetenskap och politik i nationalekonomin*, 1972: 54-55.

3. Tingsten, Herbert, *De konservativa idéerna*, (1939) 1966: 19-82.
4. Tingsten, H., 1966: 77.
5. Tingsten, H., 1966: 78.
6. Tingsten, H., 1966: 20; cf., McClosky, Herbert, "Conservatism and Personality," in *American Political Science Review*, 1958: 27-45.
7. Tingsten, H., 1966: 19
8. Tingsten, H., 1966: 19.
9. Tingsten, H., 1966: 20.
10. Tingsten, H., 1966: 24-25.
11. Tingsten, H., 1966: 26.
12. Tingsten, H., 1966: 19-20, 24-26.
13. Lantz, Göran, *Eigentumsrecht—ein Recht oder ein Unrecht?*, 1977: 99.
14. Lantz, G., 1977: 99-100.
15. Lantz, G., 1977: 102.
16. Lantz, G., 1977: 84.
17. Becker, L. C., *Property Rights*, 1977: 36-41 for a critique of the "one's-own-body" argument.
18. Macpherson, C. B., 1977: 221.
19. Macpherson, C. B., 1977: 201ff.
20. Macpherson, C. B., 1977: 201.
21. Macpherson, C. B., 1977: 211-212.
22. Macpherson, C. B., 1977: 212.
23. Macpherson, C. B., 1977: 204.
24. Macpherson, C. B., 1977: 215.
25. Macpherson, C. B., 1977: 214-215.
26. Macpherson, C. B., 1977: 194.
27. On Locke and the contract, see Macpherson, C. B., 1977: 218.
28. Macpherson, C. B., 1977: 258.
29. Lantz, G., 1977: 80.
30. Bentham, Jeremy, *An Introduction to the Principles of Morals and Legislation* see Everett, Charles, *Great Lives and Thought: Jeremy Bentham*, 1966: 111.
31. Locke, John, *An Essay Concerning Human Understanding*, 1894: 37.
32. Bentham, J., see Everett, C., 1966: 112.
33. Bentham, J., see Everett, C., 1966: 135ff.
34. Bentham, J., see Everett, C., 1966: 140.
35. For a modern discourse on the security principle, see Becker, L. C. 1977: 101-102.
36. Halévy, E., 1955: 46.
37. Everett, C., 1966: 65.
38. Halévy, E., 1955: 46.
39. Halévy, E., 1955: 53-54.
40. Halévy, E., 1955: 51.
41. Parekh, Bhikhu, *Bentham's Political Thought*, 1973: 260.
42. Parekh, B., 1973: 281.
43. Bentham, J., see Parekh, B., 1973: 282.
44. Mill, John Stuart, see Fletcher Ronald, *John Stuart Mill: A Logical Critique of Sociology*, 1971: 218.
45. Mill, J. S., see Fletcher, R., 1971: 218.
46. Mill, J. S., see Fletcher, R., 1971: 220.
47. Mill, J. S., see Fletcher, R., 1971: 220.
48. Mill, J. S., see Fletcher, R., 1971: 221.
49. Mill, J. S., see Fletcher, R., 1971: 221.

50. Mill, J. S., see Fletcher, R., 1971: 222.
51. Mill, J. S., see Fletcher, R., 1971: 223.
52. Mill, J. S., see Fletcher, R., 1971: 223.
53. Mill, J. S., see Fletcher, R., 1971: 223.
54. Mill, J. S., see Fletcher, R., 1971: 223.
55. Mill, J. S., see Fletcher, R., 1971: 224.
56. Mill, J. S., see Fletcher, R., 1971: 231. "Fair agreement" would seem
synonymous with various kinds of contract, such as employment contract.
57. Mill, J. S., see Fletcher, R., 1971: 232.
58. Mill, J. S., see Fletcher, R., 1971: 232.
59. Mill, J. S., see Fletcher, R., 1971: 223.

**Notes to
Chapter 6**

1. Hayek, F. W. von, *Vägen till träldom,* 1944; Tingsten, Herbert, *Demokratins problem* (1960) 1969, the chapter "Demokrati och socialism."
2. Tunberg, Sven and Ernst Söderlund, *Svensk historia för gymnasiet,* 1951: 312-313.
3. Tunberg, Sven and Ernst Söderlund, 1951: 322.
4. Tingsten, H., 1969: 9.
5. Tingsten, H., 1969: 9.
6. Tingsten, H., 1969: 17.
7. Tingsten, H., 1969: 26.
8. Tingsten, H., 1969: 25.
9. Tingsten, H., 1969: 66-67.
10. Tingsten, H., 1969: 35.
11. Tingsten, H., 1969: 35.
12. Tingsten, H., 1969: 65-66.
13. Tingsten, H., 1969: 159.
14. Tingsten, H., 1969: 65.
15. Tingsten, H., 1969: 152.
16. Tingsten, H., 1969: 110-136.
17. Höglund, Zeth, *Hjalmar Branting och hans livsgärning, Part II,* 1929: 240.
18. Höglund, Zeth, 1929: 247.
19. Gerdner, Gunnar, "Ministären Edén och författningsrevisionen," in Hadenius, Stig (ed.) *Kring demokratins genombrott i Sverige,* 1966: 108.
20. Gerdner, G., in Hadenius, Stig (ed.), 1966: 91.
21. Gerdner, G., in Hadenius, Stig (ed.), 1966: 100.
22. Gerdner, G., in Hadenius, Stig (ed.), 1966: 100.
23. Gerdner, G., in Hadenius, Stig (ed.), 1966: 97.
24. Gerdner, G., in Hadenius, Stig (ed.), 1966: 110.
25. Gerdner, G., in Hadenius, Stig (ed.), 1966: 104.
26. Gerdner, G., in Hadenius, Stig (ed.), 1966: 113-114.

27. Bachrach, Peter and Morton S. Baratz, "Decisions and nondecisions: an analytical framework," in *American Political Science Review*, 1963: 632-642.
28. Tingsten, H., 1969: 14.
29. Tingsten, H., 1969: 13.
30. Tingsten, H., 1969: 22.
31. Tingsten, H., 1969: 22.
32. Tingsten, H., 1969: 22.
33. Macpherson, C. B., *The Political Theory of Possessive Individualism*, 1977: 108.
34. Macpherson, C. B., 1977: 107.
35. Macpherson, C. B., 1977: 123-124.
36. Macpherson, C. B., 1977: 137-148.
37. Ambjörnsson, R., *Idé och klass*, 1972: 39.
38. Macpherson, C. B., 1977: 158.
39. Locke, J., see Macpherson, C. B., 1977: 223.
40. Locke, J., see Macpherson, C. B., 1977: 224.
41. Locke, J., see Macpherson, C. B., 1977: 224.
42. Locke, J., see Macpherson, C. B., 1977: 145 ff., 219, 231.
43. Macpherson, C. B., 1977: 233.
44. Macpherson, C. B., 1977: 252.
45. Macpherson, C. B., 1977: 196.
46. Macpherson, C. B., 1977: 236.
47. Macpherson, C. B., 1977: 258.
48. Tingsten, H., 1969: 49.
49. Tingsten, H., 1969: 50.
50. Bentham, Jeremy, see Parekh, B., *Bentham's Political Thought*, 1973: 195.
51. Bentham, J., see Parekh, B., 1973: 207-208.
52. Bentham, J., see Parekh, B., 1973: 282.
53. Bentham, J., see Parekh, B., 1973: 293.
54. Johansson, Sten, *Politiska resurser*, 1971; Pateman, Carole, *Participation and Democratic Theory*, (1970) 1975.
55. Tingsten, H., 1969: 52; cf., Johansson, Sten, 1971: 10-12.
56. Westholm, C. J., *Ratio och universitalitet, John Stuart Mill och dagens demokratidebatt*, 1976b: 109.
57. Westholm, C. J., 1976b: 108-109.
58. Mill, J. S., *Representative Government*, 1966: 278.
59. Mill, J. S., 1966: 279.
60. Mill, J. S., 1966: 280.
61. Westholm, C. J., 1976b: 109; Tingsten, H., 1969: 152.
62. Tingsten, H., 1969: 53.
63. Mill, J. S., 1966: 284.
64. Mill, J. S., see Fletcher, R., *John Stuart Mill: A Logical Critique of Sociology*, 1971: 407.
65. Tocqueville, Alexis de, *Jämlikheten vårt öde*, 1970: 96.
66. Tocqueville, Alexis de, 1970: 96.
67. Tocqueville, Alexis de, 1970: 96.
68. Tocqueville, Alexis de, 1970: 97.
69. Tocqueville, Alexis de, 1970: 97.

70. Tocqueville, Alexis de, 1970: 98.
71. Korpi, Walter, in *Dagens Nyheter*, April 5, 1979.
72. Korpi, Walter, in *Dagens Nyheter*, April 5, 1979.
73. Ross, Alf, *Varför demokrati?*, 1963: 128.
74. Tingsten, H., 1969: 54.
75. Thomson, D., *Europe since Napoleon*, (1966) 1970: 32.
76. Lefebvre, Georges, *1789, Den franska revolutionens bakgrund och orsaker*, 1963: 187.

Notes to Chapter 7

1. Marx, K., see Roll, Eric, *A History of Economic Thought*, (1938) 1978: 261.
2. Baumol, William J., "The transformation of values: what Marx 'really' meant (an interpretation)," in *Journal of Economic Literature*, 1974, 1: 51-61.
3. Baumol, W. J., 1974: 57-58. In *Journal of Economic Literature*, 1974, 1 the transformation problem is discussed by Baumol, Samuelson, and Morishima.
4. Smith, Adam, *Wealth of Nations*, 1977: 133. See also the introduction to *Wealth of Nations* by Andrew Skinner, 1977: 49.
5. Smith, A., 1977: 133.
6. Ricardo, D., *The Principles of Political Economy and Taxation*, 1976: 6-7.
7. Ricardo, D., see Meek, R. L., *Studies in the Labour Theory of Value*, 1973: 99.
8. Ricardo, D., 1976: 7; cf., Meek, R. L., 1973: 118.
9. Marx, K., *Theories of Surplus Value*, 1951: 203.
10. Meek, R. L., 1973: 123-124; cf., Gustafsson, Bo, "Klassicism, marxism och marginalism," in *Häften för Kritiska Studier*, 1968, 1-2: 7-9.
11. Gleisner, P.-A., S. Iger, M. Pettersson, and B. Svensson, *Värde och profit hos Marx och Sraffa*, 1974; another and somewhat longer presentation is given by Roll, 1978: 260-281.
12. Meek, R. L., 1973: 127.
13. Meek, R. L., 1973: 128.
14. Meek, R. L., 1973: 128.
15. Marx, K., *A Contribution to the Critique of Political Economy*, 1904: 70-71.
16. Marx, K., 1904: 25; cf., Meek, R. L., 1973: 167-168.
17. Marx, K., 1904: 71-72; cf., Meek, R. L., 1973: 177f.
18. Marx, K., 1904: 72-73; cf., Meek, R. L., 1973: 177-178.
19. Marx, K., *Capital: A Critical Analysis of Capitalist Production*, 1957: 6.
20. Marx, K., see Meek, R. L., 1973: 184.
21. Meek, R. L., 1973: 177.
22. Meek, R. L., 1973: 123-124.
23. Marx, K., *Capital*, Vol. III, 1960: 629-630.
24. Meek, R. L., 1973: 178.

25. Marx, K., 1957: 43-44.
26. Marx, K., see Meek, R. L., 1973: 142.
27. Blaug, M., *Economic Theory in Retrospect*, 1968: 299.
28. Roll, E., 1978: 424ff.
29. Roll, E., 1978: 318.
30. Roll, E., 1978: 318.
31. Roll, E., 1978: 319.
32. Roll, E., 1978: 320.
33. Roll, E., 1978: 321.
34. Roll, E., 1978: 163. See the reference there to Smith, A., *Wealth of Nations*.
35. Roll, E., 1978: 321.
36. Roll, E., 1978: 322; cf., Cassel, G., *The Nature and Necessity of Interest*, 1971: 25-27.
37. Roll, E., 1978: 345.
38. Roll, E., 1978: 347.
39. Myrdal, G., *Vetenskap och politik i nationalekonomin*, 1972: 123.
40. Cf., Roll, E., 1978: 349-350.
41. Marx, K., 1957: 156-157; cf., Marx's view on labor under capitalism in the "Economic and philosophic manuscripts of 1844," quoted in Bottomore, T. and M. Rubel, *Karl Marx: Selected Writings in Sociology and Social Philosophy*, 1964: 167.
42. Roll, E., 1978: 372.
43. Roll, E., 1978: 372.
44. Roll, E., 1978: 373.
45. Roll, E., 1978: 370-371.
46. Allport, 1959: 10-13.
47. Myrdal, G., 1972: 46ff.
48. Myrdal, G., 1972: 123.
49. Roll, E., 1978: 324; cf., Myrdal, G., 1972: 121-122.
50. Roll, E., 1978: 424-479.
51. Udéhn, L., 1978: 1.
52. Böhm-Bawerk, E. von, *Karl Marx and the Close of His System*, 1949: 65.
53. Böhm-Bawerk, E. von, 1949: 70-73.
54. Marx, K., 1957: 7.
55. Sweezy, P. M., Introduction in Sweezy, P. M. (ed.) *E. von Böhm-Bawerk, Karl Marx and the Close of His System, and R. Hilferding, Böhm-Bawerk's Criticism of Marx*, 1975: xii-xiii.
56. Cassel, G., 1971: 87.
57. Gustafsson, Bo, 1968: 12.
58. Gustafsson, Bo, 1968: 15.
59. Gustafsson, Bo, 1968: 7-9, 13-16.
60. Nozick, R., *Anarchy, State and Utopia*, 1974: 175-176.
61. Horvat, B., 1977: 39-40.
62. Roll, E., 1978: 382.
63. Nozick, R., 1974: 174-175; Becker, L. C., *Property Rights*, 1977: 40 cities and agrees with Nozick's argument.
64. Nozick, R., 1974: 302; cf., also page 182 and the "minimal state" model in Chapter 10.

Notes to
Chapter 8

1. See *Från Palm to Palme. Den svenska socialdemokratins program 1882-1960*, 1972: 14. On page 23 the international character of the movement is emphasized. Concerning this, see also Bäckström, K., *Arbetarrörelsen i Sverige*, 1971, I:100-101 and 196. Tingsten summarizes the various dependencies of Swedish Social Democracy as follows:

> The German influence on Swedish politics and the cultural debate was extraordinarily important. Marxism, as well as social conservatism, are results of this influence. The young men who were in the vanguard of Swedish socialism drew their ideas mainly from Germany, and their theoretical contributions were mainly paraphrases of the preaching of the German authorities. The ideological studies of the older leaders were contained for the most part within a very narrow framework. For example, the discussion in Sweden of anarchism and syndicalism shows that the primary writings in these movements were unknown to the Swedish leaders. As for the Swedish working class, its position on Marxism before the turn of the century needs no discussion: the great mass of the working class was not Social Democratic. By the time Social Democracy later became representative of the majority of Swedish workers, its Marxism had already been attenuated. Still, a number of important Marxian notions was accepted, and there is reason to state that for a couple of decades more the movement had a mainly Marxist coloring.

> These circumstances must be kept in mind when one raises the question of the reasons for Swedish Social Democracy's abandonment of Marxism and, more generally, its transition from radical social protest to the politics of welfare. Social Democracy's development cannot be entirely identified with that of the working class; early Social Democracy did not represent the working class.

> Concerning what has been posed as the main question, it should above all be emphasized that Social Democracy's history may be viewed from entirely different perspectives. The ideological changes in the Swedish party may be seen as one part of an international process. In every country where it has won a significant position of power, Social Democracy has undergone essentially the same development as in Sweden. This is evident in our recollections of international Social Democracy in the first part of this work, but it is more clearly evident in a study of Social Democratic parties in different countries: the International, where one could speak and resolve with a certain irresponsibility, was permeated with a greater measure or Marxism and radical terminology than the particular parties of which it was composed.

> The Swedish movement's peculiarity lies not in its theoretical development but rather in its extraordinary success—which certainly led to its theoretical development in some areas progressing somewhat further than in other areas, although the direction of the development was the same. Judging from a cursory examination, it would be possible, with respect to a number of countries, to draw quite complete parallels to the present work. It would be wrong, as often happens, to view moderns Swedish Social Democracy as the result of conditions peculiar only to Sweden. It should also be remembered in this context that the Swedish movement in later times has drawn its most important influences from other places than before. During the 1880s and

1890s the German influence was decisive; during more recent decades contact with the English debate has been most fruitful.

Further, the development of Social Democracy should be seen against the background of the Swedish environment in which it took place. The fact that the movement early took on a moderate and reformist character was caused by the strong traditions of freedom and rights in Swedish society [Tingsten, *Den svenska socialdemokratins idéutveckling*, 1967, II:369-370].

2. Branting maintained as late as 1902 that Swedish Social Democratic agitation was mainly based on "popularization brochures"; even if some of them (on Lassalle and Liebknecht, our note) were "gems," "the lack of fully adequate expressions of what theoretical socialism can achieve in our language has become increasingly noticeable" (Branting, Foreword and notes to "Socialismens utveckling" by Engels in *Tal och skrifter*, 1926: 267).

The largest labor library in the country, the library of the Social Democratic Union in Stockholm, contained mainly specialized literature. Concerning this, see Gustavsson, R. and L. Rydqvist in *Ord & Bild*, no. 5, 1978: 50-51:

"Social issues and socialism," the second largest division in the library, had the highest lending rate. The most commonly borrowed titles included the books by the founder of the German Social Democratic Party, August Bebel, *Women: Past, Present and Future* (1885) and *What We Want* (1886), plus the American economist Henry George's *Social Problems* (1884) and Ferdinand Lassalle's *The Labor Estate and Our Time* (1885).

3. Gunnarsson, Gunnar in Lindhagen, J. (ed.) *Bilden av Branting*, 1975: 206-245, quote 213.

4. Gustafsson, Bo, *Marxism och revisionism*, 1969: 30:

The Gotha Program was marked throughout by Lassalle's outlook. This explained that all other classes besides the working class formed "merely a reactionary mass," that the party strove "with all legal means for a free state" as well as for "the breakdown of the iron law of wages." The program also demanded, "in order to extend the solution to the social question, the establishment of socialist production cooperatives with state aid."

See also Bäckström, 1971, I: 103; Fran Palm till Palme, 1972: 15.

5. Marx writes in his letter:

Er [Lassalle] hatte einen förmlichen Kontrakt mit Bismarck eingegangen. . . . Ende September 1864 sollte er nach Hamburg und dort Bismarck zur Inkorporation von Schleswig-Holstein zwingen, dass heisst, solche im Namen der "Arbeiter" proklamieren etc. Wogegen Bismarck allgemeines Wahlrecht und einige sozialistische Scharlatenerien versprochen. Es ist schade dass Lassalle diese Komödie nicht ausspielen konnte! [Kautsky, Marx och Lassalle, in *Der Kampf*, 1923: 90].

6. Brandes, Georg, *Lassalle*, 1906, II: 95ff.

7. Kirkup, Thomas, "Lassalle," in *Encyclopaedia Britannica*, Vol. 13, 1951: 734; see also Finer, H., "Lassalle," in *The Encyclopaedia of the Labour Movement*, p. 183.

8. Brandes, Georg, 1906.

9. Droz, Jacques, *Histoire Générale du Socialisme,* 1972: 480, summarizes Lassalle's program as follows:

> Il s'agissait dans sa pensée, qui était résolument dirigée contre la pratique du liberalisme parlementaire, de former un parti ouvrier entièrement independant à la fois du gouvernement et de la bourgeoisie—de cette bourgeoisie qui se revoélait incapable dans le conflit constitutionel de défendre efficacement les droits de la démocratie—, et de conquérir de haute lute de suffrage universel et direct que continuait à refuser obstinement le Parlement prussien, attachée au système des trois classes, il s'agissait enfin, une fois la conquête politique de l'Etat assureé et établie "la dictature de l'intelligence" d'obtenir du pouvoir la création de cooperatives de production qui permettraient à la classe ouvrière de concurrencer victorieusement l'économie capitaliste et, par des voies pacifiques et légales d'assurer un ordre conforme à la justice."

10. Droz, J., 1972: 498.
11. Gustafsson, Bo, 1969: 28.
12. Gustafsson, Bo, 1969: 28.
13. Gustafsson, Bo, 1969: 28.
14. Gustafsson, Bo, 1969: 28.
15. Hansson, Sven Ove, *Marx och Engels i politiken,* 1976a: 192, 195.
16. Hansson, Sven Ove, 1976a: 192.
17. Engels, F., "Einleitung zum Neudruck von Marx' 'Klassenkämpfe in Frankreich 1848-1850'," in *MEW,* Vol. 13, 1978: 123.
18. Branting, Hjalmar, "Den revolutionära Generalstrejken," in *Tal och Skrifter,* VIII, 1929: 124-125.
19. Marx, K., *MEW,* Vol. 1, 1978: 231-232.
20. Hansson, Sven Ove, 1976a: 129-131.
21. Hansson, Sven Ove, 1976a: 131.
22. Marx, K., 1957: 788-789.
23. The best presentation in Swedish of Bernstein and the theoretical precursors of his revisionism appears in Gustafsson, Bo (1969). Two other important presentations of Bernstein are Angel, P., *Eduard Bernstein et l'évaluation du socialisme allemand* (1961) and Angel, P. and P. Gay, *The Dilemma of Democratic Socialism: Eduard Bernstein's Challenge to Marx* (1962) upon which Droz, Jacques (1972) mainly bases his presentation.
24. Bernstein, E., *Socialismens förutsättningar och socialdemokratins uppgifter,* 1907b:30.
25. Bernstein, 1907b: 13.
26. Bernstein, 1907b: 15.
27. Bernstein, 1907b: 16.
28. Bernstein, 1907b: 17, 29.
29. Bernstein, 1907b: 151.
30. Bernstein, 1907b: 276-277.
31. Bernstein, 1907b: 140.
32. Bernstein, 1907b: 145.
33. Bernstein, 1907b: 245, 276-277.
34. Bernstein, 1907b: 281.
35. Bernstein, 1907b: 280.
36. Bernstein, 1907b: 202.
37. Bernstein, 1907b: 203.

38. Bernstein, 1907b: 195.
39. Bernstein, 1907b: 194.
40. Bernstein, 1907b: 198.
41. Bernstein, 1907b: 196-197.
42. Bernstein, 1907b: 204-206.
43. Bernstein, 1907b: 10-11.
44. Bernstein, 1907b: 12.
45. Bernstein, 1907b: 45.
46. Roll, E. A., *History of Economic Thought*, 1978: 377-378.
47. Bernstein, 1907b: 74.
48. Bernstein, 1907b: 79.
49. Bernstein, 1907b: 103.
50. Bernstein, 1907b: 90.
51. Bernstein, 1907b: 97.
52. Bernstein, 1907b: 110.
53. Bernstein, 1907b: 137.
54. Bernstein, 1907b: 140.
55. Bernstein, 1907b: 159.
56. Kautsky, Karl, *Socialdemokrati och socialism*, 1908: 89-131, 132, 181ff.
57. Bernstein, 1907b: 71.
58. Gustafsson, Bo, 1969: 161.
59. Two historians as different as Herbert Tingsten and Knut Bäckström are close to describing the Swedish labor movement as Marxist. Most things indicate that this is not the case. From the middle of 1880 individual people such as Danielsson and Sterky may be described as *more* Marxist than the dominant faction led by Branting. The movement as a whole can hardly be described as Marxist. Branting's revisionism, the origins of which can be dated from the Gävle speech of 1886, is completely dominant during the 1890s, even though the SAP program of 1897 is a copy of the Marxist Kautsky's Erfurt program. Cf., Bäckström, K., 1971, I: 103ff.; and Tingsten, H., *Den svenska socialdemokratins idéutveckling*, 1967, I: 67, 137.
60. Tingsten, 1967, I: 52:62.
61. Gunnarsson, Gunnar (ed.) *Arbetarrörelsens genombrottsår i dokument*, 1965: 16.
62. Bäckström, 1971, I: 86.
63. Tingsten, 1967, I: 71.
64. Från Palm till Palme, 1972: 14.
65. See *Fabian Essays in Socialism*, 1962.
66. Tingsten, 1967, I: 67.
67. Tingsten, 1967, I: 137.
68. Tingsten, H., *Mitt liv* (1962) 1971, II: 289, see also 1971, III: 100 ff.
69. Meurling, Per, "Det revolutionära 80-talet," in Lindhagen, J. (ed.) *Bilden av Branting*, 1975: 56; and Palmgren, Y. in Lindhagen, J. (ed.), 1975: 71.
70. Meurling, 1975: 56.
71. Höglund's characterization appears as an introduction to Branting's Gävle speech in Branting, *Tal och skrifter*, I. *Socialistisk samhällssyn*, I., 1926: 87.
72. Branting, "Varför arbetarrörelsen måste bli socialistisk," in *Tal och skrifter*, I, 1926d: 87ff.
73. Branting, 1926d: 108.
74. Branting, 1926d: 95.
75. Branting, 1926d: 96.

76. Branting, 1926d: 96.
77. Branting, 1926d: 90.
78. Branting, 1926d: 107.
79. Branting, 1926d: 102.
80. Branting, 1926d: 104.
81. Kautsky also worked diligently on the staff of *Vörwarts*, and in 1887 he published his *Karl Marx' ökonomische Lehren.*
82. Branting, Hjalmar, Foreword and notes to "Socialismens utveckling" by Engels in *Tal och skrifter*, I, 1926a: 272.
83. Branting, H., 1926a: 274.
84. Branting, Hjalmar, "Nya riktningar inom socialdemokratin," in *Tal och skrifter*, I, 1926c: 258.
85. See Bernstein's *Socialismens forutsättningar och socialdemokratins uppgifter*, in which he in the spirit of neo-Kantianism incessantly emphasizes the significance of morals and will. See, for example, 1907b: 15-16, 196ff.
86. Branting, H., *"Varför arbetarrörelsen måste bli socialistisk,"* *Tal och skrifter*, I, 1926d: 115.
87. Branting, H., "De närmaste framtidsutsikter," in *Tal och skrifter*, III, 1927a: 33.
88. Branting, H., 1927a: 34.
89. Branting, H., 1927a: 34.
90. Bäckström, 1971: 180.
91. Gunnarsson, G., 1975: 206-245.
92. Mehr, Hjalmar, "Hjalmar Branting—människan, ledaren, statsmannen," in Lindhagen, J. (ed.), 1975: 414, 417.

Excursus on Branting and Bernstein: It would be wrong to call Branting a revisionist in the sense of being a direct descendant of Bernstein. Revisionism was a general phenomenon in Europe of the 1890s, and Bernstein was merely its chronicler. Branting developed what was in part his own, Swedish variant of revisionism, although with a clear dependence on Bernstein. Most people who have dealt with the history of Social Democracy have shown that in some cases Branting directly borrowed his opinions from Bernstein (see, for example, Tingsten, 1967, I: 151, 186; Bäckström, 1971, I: 276-277; and Lindhagen, J., *Socialdemokratins program*, 1972, I: 79). The best proof of a direct influence is, of course, Branting's own texts, in which one finds in several places that Branting makes direct references to Bernstein (see, for example, Branting, *Tal och skrifter*, I, 1926: 253, 255, 258, 276; and *Tal och skrifter*, II, 1926: 71ff. and 84ff.) In two cases Branting has more or less translated portions of Bernstein's "Förutsättningar" and taken his argumentation almost word for word. (This is true of Branting's discussion of the theory of value in *Tal och skrifter*, II, 1926: 71ff., which should be compared to Bernstein, 1907b: 66; and Branting's presentation of new trends in Social Democracy in *Tal och skrifter*, I, 1926: 255, which is to be compared with Bernstein, 1907b: 66.) Zeth Höglund, who published and edited Branting's *Tal och skrifter*, writes in the introduction to an essay (in Vol. I, 1926: 251):

> Branting, who on several points (the evaluation of the unionist movement, the materialist view of history, the catastrophe theory) had to some extent anticipated Bernstein's critique, naturally greeted its arrival with sympathy, even though he did not consider it to be entirely correct.

Of course, Branting and Bernstein, as representatives in the Second International, had numerous opportunities to meet, visit with each other, and exchange letters. In a letter to the leader of the Austrian Social Democratic party, Bernstein wrote that Branting in principle shared his views on revisionism. The year was 1896 (see Gustafsson, Bo, 1969: 162).

93. Hentilä, S. "Orsaker till reformismens genombrott i svensk social-demokrati," 1974: 7-8.

94. Branting, H., "Socialismen," in *Tal och skrifter*, II, 1927d: 13.

95. Branting, H., "Varför arbetarrörelsen måste bli socialistisk," in *Tal och skrifter*, I, 1926d: 96.

96. Branting, H., "Kritiken av socialismen på Arbetarinstitutet," in *Tal och skrifter*, I, 1926b: 206-207.

97. Branting, H., 1926b: 211.

98. Branting, H., "Socialismen i arbetarrörelsen," in *Tal och skrifter*, II, 1927e: 336.

99. Branting, H., 1927e: 336.

100. Branting, H., 1927e: 337.

101. Branting, H., 1927e: 338.

102. Branting, H., "Klasskamp och skiljedom," in *Tal och skrifter*, VII, 1928: 69.

103. Branting, H., "Rösträtt och arbetarrörelse," in *Tal och skrifter*, III, 1927c: 141.

104. Branting, H., 1927c: 156.

105. Branting, H., "Nyare riktningar inom socialdemokratin," 1926c: 255.

106. Branting, H., "Socialismen," 1927d: 81.

107. Branting, H., "Demokratins genombrott," in *Tal och skrifter* IV, 1927b: 310.

108. Tingsten, 1967, I: 254.

109. Tingsten, 1967, I: 254.

110. Tingsten, 1967, I: 213-214.

111. Tingsten, 1967, I: 215.

112. Tingsten, 1967, I: 220. Tingsten writes: "during a period of around two years, from the end of 1918 until after the second-chamber election in 1920, the socialization issue came to the fore as never before or later."

113. Tingsten, 1967, I: 220.

114. Ernst Wigforss (1881-1977), Ph.D., was one of the most prominent publicists of the Swedish Social Democratic party, and during two periods Minister of Finance. Much inspired by G.D.H. Cole and English guild socialism, he wrote extensively on ideas of socialism, economics and welfare politics. An excellent introduction to Wigforss' workings is given by Tilton (1979).

115. Tingsten, 1967, I: 223, 224. In our opinion, Tingsten is unable to do the debate justice. In the debate, especially in Ernst Wigforss's writings, there were relatively clear signs of a desire to differentiate between, on the one hand, economic democracy, and on the other, industrial democracy. Even Gustav Möller shows signs in his writing which indicate that he differentiates between economic and industrial democracy. In the 1918 essay, "Den sociala revolutionen," Möller says that socialization will begin through industrial democracy. See Möller, G., *Revolution och socialism*, Tiden, (1918) 1976: 80-100.

116. Undén, Ö., 1976: 58ff.; Karleby, N., 1976: 70-78. Tingsten, 1967, I: 225 cites an election brochure written by Gustav Möller for the second-chamber election in 1920. He maintains that when the necessary socialization (i.e., of natural resources

and such) has been concluded, then it will be "extremely easy to *abolish private exploitative capital by means of our tax legislation.* We could gradually collect it all by means of an inheritance tax or a tax on wealth." It is thus Möller's thesis that legal political power is a sufficient prerequisite for directing the right of disposition of private capital over surplus-value ("the exploitative capital"). See also Gunnarsson, G., 1965: 278-283.

1'17. Tingsten feels that: "On the whole, the new premises are distinguished by greater formal firmness than the old ones. From the point of view of content, they primarily entail a sharpening of the general Marxist perspective, a new interpretation of the development which is presumed to lead to socialism, and a stronger and more sophisticated assertion of the socialization demand" (1967, I: 233).

We feel that Tingsten in his interpretation of the program change exaggerates the Marxist element and overlooks the significant revision of Marxism contained in the relativistic approach to the concept of ownership rights. In our opinion, Tingsten's own reasoning on the import of the 1920 program revision shows that the important thing in the line of reasoning is the functionalistic differentiation between possession or lack of possession and between possession and disposition or degree of disposition (Tingsten, 1967, I: 239-240).

118. Tingsten, 1967, I: 288.
119. Tingsten, 1967, I: 260.
120. Quoted in Tingsten, 1967, I: 273.
121. Quoted in Tingsten, 1967, I: 275. See also 1967, I: 278, where Tingsten points out that Sandler in the same debate renounced Marx and other "theoreticians' systems."
122. Myrdal, G., *"Prisbildningsproblemet och föränderligheten,"* 1927.
123. SOU 1936: 7, *Socialiseringsproblemet. Allmänna synpunkter,* Stockholm, 1936, Tidens förlag. Later there appeared SOU 1937: 1 and SOU 1937: 2, both Stockholm 1937 and Tidens förlag.
124. Tingsten, 1967, I: 335.
125. Tingsten, H., *Den svenska socialdemokratins idéutveckling,* Part II, 1967: 361.
126. Tingsten, 1967, I: 301.
127. Tingsten, 1967, I: 312.
128. Quoted in Tingsten, 1967, I: 270.
129. Lindhagen, Jan, *Bolshevikstriden, Socialdemokratins program,* 1972, II: 216-226.
130. Lindhagen, 1972, II: 105.
131. Lindhagen, 1972, II: 190.
132: Lindhagen, 1972, II: 231.
133. Lindhagen, 1972, II: 223.
134. Lindhagen, 1972, II: 286.
135. See Bottomore, T. and P. Goode, *Austromarxism,* 1978: 209. The Austromarxists, primarily Max Adler, Otto Bauer, Rudolf Hilferding, and Karl Renner, have probably had a relatively large importance for Swedish Social Democracy. The reason may be that they presented a rather detailed and concrete alternative to other forms of Marxism existing during the first decades of the twentieth century. Tom Bottomore (Bottomore and Goode, 1978: 1-44) has written an excellent summarizing essay on the Austromarxists in which he says, among other things:

I think it can be argued that this was one of the most thorough, consistent, and intelligent attempts yet made to develop Marxism as an empirical social science, and that the neglect it has suffered is less the consequence of a considered intellectual judgement than the product of a collocation of unfavourable historical events [p. 7.].

See also Hilferding, Rudolf, *Finanskapitalen,* 1976.
The idea of organized capitalism has been described by Hardach, G. et al. (1978: 55) as follows:

(1) technical progress in general and in particular the utilization of chemistry, since the latter made production independent of natural raw materials;
(2) the organization of the economy into trusts and cartels;
(3) internationalization;
(4) the gradual replacement of free competition by the planned administration of society "in reality therefore organized capitalism means the replacement of the capitalist principle of free competition by the socialist principle of planned production!" [Hilferding, R., 1976, I: 65].

At the concrete politico-economic level the equivalent to the theoretical concept of organized capitalism was the idea of "economic democracy." This expressed a programme of democratic control of the economy through workers' participation. Just like "organized capitalism," "economic democracy" was seen as ultimately leading to the final goal of socialism.

136. Lindhagen, 1972, II: 290.
137. Three factions were party to the conflicts:

(1) A rightist faction which was expressely anti-Marxist. This was, for example, Herbert Tingsten, Torsten Gårdlund, Richard Lindström, and Karl Fredriksson.
(2) A "middle line" represented by Per-Albin Hansson, Richard Sandler, and Gustav Möller.
(3) A leftist faction including Artur Engberg, Per Emil Brusewitz, and Georg Branting—and perhaps even Ernst Wigforss, although to some extent he represented his "own line."

See Jonsson, U., "Social reformism kontra marxism," in *Från Palm till Palme,* 1972: 99; Lindhagen, J., 1972, II: 293-294; Lewin, L., Planhushallningsdebatten, 1967: 215ff.

138. Lindhagen, J., 1972, II: 295.
139. Öhman, B., *Svensk arbetsmarknadspolitik 1900-1947,* 1970: 138.
140. Öhman, 1970: 142-143.
141. Öhman, 1970: 144.
142. Öhman, 1970: 146.
143. Öhman, 1970: 149.
144. Öhman, 1970: 183, note 37.
145. Lewin, L., 1967: 68.
146. Unga, N., *Socialdemokratin och arbetslöshetsfrågan 1912-1934,* 1976: 17.
147. See, for example, Karleby, N., *Socialismen inför verkligheten,* (1926) 1970: 132, 156, 183, 213-216; and Erlander, T., *Tage Erlander 1901-1939,* 1972: 122-128.
148. Erlander, T., 1972: 25. Others were Östen Undén and Karl Fredriksson. Richard Lindström's importance was more as a catalyst. Östen Undén gave the liberal economic ideas a legal clothing. Together, these ideas constitute what has since come to be called functional socialism.

149. Erlander, T. and Björn von Sydow in Nils Karleby, *Socialismen inför verkligheten,* 1976: 305-312.

150. Lindhagen, 1972, II: 226-227.

151. Lindhagen, J., 1972, II: 227 adds in a footnote that Ernst Wigforss in his review of Karleby's book "points out between the lines" a probable "risk of a social-reformist interpretation."

152. Lindhagen, 1972, II: 229.

153. Erlander, T. and B. von Sydow, 1976: 321.

154. Erlander, T. and B. von Sydow, 1976: 324.

155. Erlander, T. and B. von Sydow, 1976: 328.

156. Erlander, T. and B. von Sydow, 1976: 285.

157. Erlander, T. and B. von Sydow, 1976: 341.

158. Karleby, N., 1976: v, 3.

159. Karleby, N., 1976: vii.

160. Karleby, N., 1976: 105, 114.

161. Karleby, N., 1976: 233.

162. Karleby, N., 1976: 132.

163. Karleby, N., 1976: 22.

164. Karleby, N., 1976: 106.

165. Karleby, N., 1976: 116-117.

166. Karleby, N., 1976: 54.

167. Karleby, N., 1976: 53.

168. Karleby, N., 1976: 61.

169. Karleby, N., 1976: 82.

170. Karleby, N., 1976: 101-102.

171. Karleby, N., 1976: 102-103.

172. Karleby, N., 1976: 62.

173. Karleby, N., 1976: 63.

174. Karleby, N., 1976: 162.

175. Karleby, N., 1976: 172.

176. Karleby, N., 1976: 205.

177. Karleby, N., 1976: 81; cf., the Austromarxists' ideas on organized capitalism. Karleby often refers to several of the Austromarxists; cf., also note 136.

178. Karleby, N., 1976: 137.

179. Karleby, N., 1976: 143.

180. Karleby, N., 1976: 87ff.

181. Karleby, N., 1976: 156.

182. Karleby, N., 1976: 171.

183. Karleby, N., 1976: 78, 101, 171.

184. Karleby, N., 1976: 172.

185. Karleby, N., 1976: 180.

186. Karleby, N., 1976: 172-173.

187. Karleby, N., 1976: 179.

188. Karleby, N., 1976: 182.

189. Karleby, N., 1976: 215.

190. Karleby, N., 1976: 180.

191. Karleby, N., 1976: 183.

192. Karleby, N., 1976: 183.

193. Karleby, N., 1976: 226.

194. Karleby, N., 1976: 209.
195. Erlander, T., 1972: 127.
196. Erlander writes: "whether Nils Karleby has understood Marx correctly is something I cannot judge today and could judge even less during the 1920s" (1972: 125).
197. Erlander, T., 1972: 126.
198. Erlander, T., 1972: 126.
199. Erlander, T., 1972: 126.
200. Erlander, T., 1972: 128-129.
201. Karleby, N., 1976: 275-281.
202. Karleby, N., 1976: 281.
203. Lindhagen, J., 1972, II: 283-284.
204. Lindhagen, 1972, II: 288.
205. Lindhagen, J. and Macke Nilsson, *Hotet mot arbetarrörelsen,* 1970: 165.
206. Lindhagen, J. and Macke Nilsson, 1970: 166.
207. Lindhagen, J., and Macke Nilsson, 1970: 167-168.

Notes to
Chapter 9

1. Meidner, R. et al., *Löntagarfonder,* 1975: 42-44.
2. See Elvander, N., *Företagsdemokrati och politisk demokrati,* 1976; Gustafsson, Agne, *Företagsdemokratin och den offentliga sektorn,* 1978; Gustafsson, Agne, "Facket, medborgarna och demokratin," in *Tiden,* Nr. 1, 1979: 25-35; Bodström, Lennart, "TCO, partierna och den politiska pressen," in *Tiden,* Nr. 7, 1978: 381-391; Gustafsson, Sverker, "Varför tillåts demokratiskt uppbyggda organisationer?" in *Tiden,* Nr. 7, 1978: 374-380; Westerståhl, J. och M. Persson, *Demokrati och intresserepresentation,* 1975.
3. Elvander, N., 1976; Gustafsson, Agne, 1978; and Westerståhl, J. and M. Persson, 1975.
4. Hansson, Sven Ove, "Att välja modell för den ekonomiska demokratin" in *Tiden,* Nr. 4, 1977: 212 presents the following models for a socialist economy:

(1) state socialism
(2) different forms of ownership
    (a) forms of ownership varying according to branch
    (b) competing forms of ownership
(3) Company executive boards including all parties
(4) Employee-managed companies, subordinate to planning bodies
    (a) state planning bodies
    (b) planning bodies composed of parties to the labor market
    (c) worker-controlled planning bodies
(5) autonomous employee-managed companies

5. The presentation concerning certain historical occurrences is based on Åsard, E., *LO och löntagarfondsfrågan,* 1978: 14-42, 145-148, 185-190; and on Meidner, R. et al., 1975: 9-28.

6. See Günnarsson, Gunnar, *De stora utopisterna*, II, 1973: 7, 23, 64-66, 181.
7. Mill, J. S., *Principles of Political Economy*, 1965: 768-769.
8. Thunberg, Anders (ed.), *Strejken*, 1970; Dahlström, E. et al., *LKAB och demokratin*, 1971.
9. Korpi, Walter, *Arbetarklassen i välfärdskapitalismen*, 1978.
10. Dahlström, Edmund et al., *Arbetet, facket och medbestämmandet*, 1977: 14ff.
11. Dahlström, E. et al., 1977: 14-17.
12. LO-SAP, *Löntagarfonder och kapitalbildning*, 1978: 7.
13. Opinions of the party executive board on motions to the party convention concerning economic democracy, 1978: 4-5, 11, SAP, Stockholm, 1978.
14. LO-SAP, 1978: 61.
15. LO-SAP, 1978: 61.
16. TCO, *Löntagarfonder ur TCO-perspektiv—en debattskrift*, 1978: 56.
17. TCO, 1978: 57.
18. TCO, 1978: 58.
19. Hedborg, Anna, "Makten är odelbar," in *Tiden*, Nr. 4-5, 1976: 222.
20. Åsard, E., 1978: 123.
21. Meidner, R. et al., 1975: 15-16.
22. Motion 305 from the Steelworkers' Union, in Meidner, R. et al., 1975.
23. Meidner, R. et al., 1975: 17.
24. Meidner, R. et al., 1975: 17-18.
25. Meidner, R. et al., 1975: 18ff.
26. Meidner, R. et al., 1975: 19.
27. Meidner, R. et al., 1975: 19.
28. Meidner, R. et al., 1975: 19.
29. Meidner, R. et al., 1975: 19.
30. Meidner, R. et al., 1975: 19.
31. Meidner, R. et al., 1975: 20.
32. Meidner, R. et al., 1975: 81.
33. Meidner, R. et al., 1975: 107.
34. See the following writings, *Solidariskt medbestämmande*, 1976: 10, where the argument for equitable distribution is presented as follows: "The right to influence the conditions for one's own life and labor has an intrinsic value. It need not be derived from anything except the human being's intrinsic value."

The power argument is presented as follows: "Labor is the base for all welfare. Capital is the result of everyone's cumulative labor contributions. It is, then, labor which should be the basis for the right of co-determination."

The arguments are also presented together as follows: "Society could be changed only through collective efforts. The demand for these changes grew from the intrinsic value of labor. Labor in itself, not capital, legitimizes the demand for influence and the right of determination. It is therefore natural that labor be the basis for the right of co-determination in working life. The reform of labor legislation is aimed at strengthening labor, the wage earners' power in the work-place" (1976: 37).

During the discussion of the report at the LO convention in 1976, the following statements were submitted (1976: 113-117): "Our position [is that] labor is the basis for all welfare. Our position [is that] democracy is indivisible." Further, concerning the power argument, the following was maintained: "It is unreasonable that the person who invests himself, his labor, should be subservient to the person who owns the capital. Human labor must be given precedence because it is always labor which creates capital."

And further, concerning equitable distribution: "It is not for the sake of power that we demand co-determination—but rather it is for the sake of the people. . . . Our aim is to provide the companies with an important resource, the knowledge and experience of the employees." In the last quote, the demand for justic is united with an argument for efficiency. The demands for equitable distribution and influence (power) recur also in the convention report *Kollektiv kapitalbildning* (1976: 16-17). Sven Ove Hansson uses both arguments in support of the demand for economic democracy, in *Tiden*, Nr. 6, 1976: 299-307; Nr. 1, 1977: 8-9; Nr. 4, 1977: 212.

35. In an article by Sten Johansson in *Tiden*, Nr. 7, 1975: 361, a form of moral argumentation is used with respect to economic democracy. He writes: "The labor movement must establish in its program the great undertaking on the basis of the force of its own conviction of the necessity of socialism." Bo Södersten, in *Tiden*, Nr. 4-5, 1976: 197, feels with respect to Meidner's proposal that "its primary motivation is the demand for justice"; and in an article with G. Johansson and A. Andersson (*Aftonbladet*, 1977, May 2) he writes:

> The employer monopoly on the determination of the future of the companies must be broken. The employees must have the decisive influence over the companies' investments which by all rights should fall to them, since they are the ones who have the greatest interest in insuring the existence of jobs in the long term. [And a little further down there is a justice argument:] Therefore, a new technique is needed for transferring to the employees more of the company's returns without damaging the competitive power of the company.

36. See *Tiden*, Nr. 3-4, 1978: 157-167. In an earlier article, "Makten är odelbar," in *Tiden*, Nr. 4-5, 1976: 217-225, Hedborg maintains the thesis that democracy in its full sense may not exclude working people from participation. Those who press the justice argument (i.e., who demand an equitable distribution of the results of labor) end up arguing for a state-socialist economic system, says Hedborg.

37. Hedborg, A., "Löntagarfonder—en förstärkning av demokratin," in *Tiden*, Nr. 3-4, 1978: 158.

38. Hedborg, A., 1978: 163.

39. Hedborg, A., 1978: 165.

40. Hedborg, A., 1978: 166.

41. Hansson, Sven Ove, "Kapitalets roll i socialismen," in *Tiden*, Nr. 7. 1977: 419-429.

42. Hansson, 1977c: 419.

43. Hansson, 1977c: 422.

44. Hansson, 1977c: 423.

45. Hansson, 1977c: 422.

46. Hansson, 1977c: 420-421.

47. Hansson, 1977c: 428-429.

48. LO-SAP, 1978: 24.

49. LO-SAP, 1978: 4.

50. LO-SAP, 1978: 27.

51. LO-SAP, 1978: 5.

52. LO-SAP, 1978: 17.

53. LO-SAP, 1978: 25.

54. Karleby, N., *Socialismen inför verkligheten,* 1976: 3, 105, 116.

55. Jan Lindhagen writes in the *LO-tidningen,* Nr. 30, 1978: 8-9: "We would have to really search through the party's history—otherwise so full of unclear discussions—in order to find anything as ambiguous as the debate on employee investment funds."
Lindhagen feels that Meidner's original proposal and the one adopted by the LO convention of 1976 are "social revolutionary," while the SAP is asserting a "social reformist" line which is: "the path of liberalism—making way for the 'welfare society' while preserving but modernizing capitalism (or, in the words of a clever slogan, advocating 'social reforms without socialism')."
Lindhagen's thesis is that these conflicting views make the debate ambiguous and that the labor movement must develop a debate on the "social revolutionary" alternative. Otherwise, the labor movement is pushed toward a social reformist "solution to the question of employee investment funds *as long as we lack knowledge concerning what we shall put in the place of the mixed economy*" (our italics).

56. See, among others, Lindbeck, Assar, *Fondfrågan,* 1979; the so-called Waldenström report, *Företagsvinster, kapitalförsöjning, lontagarfonder,* Sveriges Industriförbund and SAF (1976); and Meyerson, P.-M., *Löntagarfonder eller. . . .,* 1978.

57. Lindbeck, A., 1979: 10-11.

58. Lindbeck, A., 1979: 11.

59. Lindbeck, A., 1979: 102.

60. Lindbeck, A., 1979: 43.

61. Lindbeck, A., *Can Pluralism Survive?* 1977: 11; also published in *Ekonomisk debatt,* Nr. 5, 1976 and in *Fondfrågan,* 1979: 23-25.

62. Lindbeck, A., 1977: 12-13.

63. Lindbeck, A., 1977: 13-14.

64. Lindbeck, A., 1977: 14.

65. Lindbeck, A., 1977: 15.

66. Lindbeck, A., 1977: 16-17.

67. Lindbeck, A., 1977: 17.

68. Lindbeck, A., 1977: 22.

69. Lindbeck, A., 1977: 23.

70. Cf., note 61.

71. Lindbeck, A., 1977: 14.

72. Lindbeck, A., 1979: 15.

73. Lindbeck, A., 1979: 16.

74. Lindbeck, A., 1979: 100-106.

75. Lindbeck, A., 1979: 102.

76. Lindbeck, A., 1979: 33.

77. Lindbeck, A., 1979: 39.

78. Strömholm, Stig, "Förslaget om sk löntagarfonder i rättslig belysning," in *Svensk Juristtidning,* 1976: 452-468.

79. By "other legislation," Strömholm is referring to *"expropriation, taxation,* and intervention such as *requisition and disposition* (as well as so-called *emergency laws*)," 1976b: 453.

80. Strömholm, S., 1976b: 454.

81. Strömholm, S., 1976b: 454.

82. Strömholm, S., 1976b: 456.

83. Strömholm, S., 1976b: 460-461.
84. Strömholm, S., 1976b: 467.
85. Strömholm, S., 1976b: 461: 467.
86. Strömholm, S., 1976b: 468.
87. Strömholm, S., 1976b: 454.
88. Strömholm, S., 1976b: 455:468; cf., Hydén, Håkan, *Rättens samhälleliga funktioner,* 1978: 214-215.
89. Nelhans, J., "Den Meidnerska löntagarfonden i Stig Strömholms rättsliga belysning," in *Svensk Juristtidning,* 1976: 648.
90. Strömholm, S., 1976c: 658.
91. Nelhans, J., 1976: 649.
92. Nelhans, J., 1976: 649.
93. Undén, Ö., *Svensk sakrätt,* I, 1976.
94. Kaijser, Fritz, "Om de s.k. löntagarfondernas grundlagsenlighet – ett genmäle," in *Svensk Juristtidning,* 1976: 655.
95. Kaijser, F., 1976: 659.
96. Strömholm, S., "Replik," in *Svensk Juristtidning,* 1976: 660.
97. "The best solution which is practically possible under existing circumstances," writes Adler-Karlsson. He gives the following examples of functional socialism in practice:
(1) The growth of the public sector (1967: 25-27).
(2) The co-existence of labor and capital (1967: 27-32).
(3) Indirect methods through financial and monetary policy plus labor market policies. Concerning the latter, Adler-Karlsson says: "Labor market policy consists mainly of reeducating workers who have become unemployed along with society's assistance in relocating surplus labor from one area of unemployment to regions where there is a demand for labor" (1967: 33).
(4) Direct methods (legislation) aimed at
   (a) creating what is called "security from cradle to grave" – the example is social policy;
   (b) "limiting conceivable asocial behavior on the part of owners of land and capital." This, says Adler-Karlsson, is "more difficult to exemplify. But let us try." The examples he gives are
      (1) The State Price and Cartel Agency.
      (2) The Council on Industrial Freedom.
      (3) Land lease legislation.
      (4) Forestry legislation.

Adler-Karlsson's conclusion is: "In this way an extensive functional socializing of private ownership has been accomplished. The best catalogue of these measures is found in the Laws of the Kingdom of Sweden" (1967: 36).

98. Adler-Karlsson, Gunnar, *Funktionssocialism. Ett alternativ till kommunism och kapitalism,* 1967.
99. Adler-Karlsson, G., 1967: 23.
100. Adler-Karlsson, G., 1967: 19.
101. Adler-Karlsson, G., 1967: 19.
102. Adler-Karlsson, G., 1967: 11-12.
103. Adler-Karlsson, G., 1967: 14.
104. Adler-Karlsson, G., 1967: 18.

105. Adler-Karlsson, G., 1967: 18.
106. Adler-Karlsson, G., 1967: 40, 18.
107. Korpi, W. and M. Shalev, 1978: 28-30.
108. Karleby, N., 1976: 74, 180.
109. Adler-Karlsson, G., 1967: 65-74.
110. Karleby, N., 1976: 173.
111. Adler-Karlsson, G., 1967: 20.
112. Adler-Karlsson, G., 1967: 20.
113. Adler-Karlsson, G., 1967: 20-21.
114. Adler-Karlsson, G., 1967: 43.
115. Undén, Ö., 1976: 71-72.
116. Undén, Ö., 1976: 57. The description of Undén's concept of ownership
rights is founded on his book *Svensk sakrätt*, I. *Lös egendom*; and on his essay
"Några synpunkter på begreppsbildning inom juridiken," in *Festskrift tillägnad Axel
Hägerström*, 1928: 170-177.
117. Undén, Ö., 1976.
118. Hedenius, I., "Analysen av äganderättsbegreppet," 1975: 55.
119. Becker, L., *Property Rights*, 1977; and Honoré, A. M., *Owndership*, 1961.
120. Becker, 1977: 20.
121. Kedner, G. and C. M. Roos, *Aktiebolagslagen*, 1977: 194; and the report by
the Labor Department *Förhållandet mellan MBL och viss annan lagstiftning*, 1977:
20.
122. Arbetsmarknadsdepartementet, 1977.
123. Strömholm, S., 1976b: 461.
124. Hedenius, I., 1975: 54-55.

Notes to
Chapter 10

1. Strömholm, Stig, "Förslaget om s.k. löntagarfonder i rättslig belysning," in
Svensk Juristtidning, 1976: 454.
2. Cf., Clarke, Peter, *Liberals and Social Democrats*, 1978: 6: "Liberalism
accepted democracy only when it was tempered by implicitly elitist assumptions."
3. Alf Ross says in his classic work *Varför demokrati?* that democracy should
be seen as "a political method, a pan-ideology, not as a norm for the ordering of the
content of social relation" (1963: 128). As we have seen, the classical theoreticians
of democracy were most often quite conscious of the fact that "the ordering of the
content of social realtions" (i.e., property relations) was of extraordinary importance
for the form of democracy *they* wished to see realized.
4. Bodström, Lennart, "TCO, partierna och den politiska pressen," in *Tiden*,
Nr. 7. 1978: 381-391.
5. Elvander, Nils, "Foretagsdemokrati och politisk demokrati," in *Organisationerna i det moderna samhället*, 1976; Gustafsson, Agne, *Företagsdemokratin och
den offentliga sektorn*, 1978; Westerståhl, J. and M. Persson, *Demokrati och intresserepresentation*, 1975.

6. Gustafsson, Sverker, "Statskunskap, socialismen och demokratin," in *Tiden*, Nr. 3, 1979: 151-161.

7. Elvander, N., 1976: 71.

8. Westerståhl, J. and M. Persson, 1975: 42.

9. Proposition 1975/76: 105, Appendix 2, Subappendix 2:3.

10. Proposition 1975/76: 105, Appendix 1: 209-210.

11. LO-SAP, *Löntagarfonder och kapitalbildning*, 1978: 13.

12. Abrahamsson, Bengt, *Exemplet Jugoslavien och den svenska debatten om löntagarstyre*, 1976: 148ff.

13. Abrahamsson, B., 1976: 172-174.

14. Westerståhl, J. and M. Persson, 1975: 21.

15. LO-SAP, 1978: TCO, *Löntagarfonder ur TCO-perspektiv*, 1978.

16. Cf., Håkansson, Kaj, *Socialism som självstyre*, 1973: 72-75.

17. Interview with Zaga Golubović in *Frihetlig socialistisk tidskrift*, Nr. 2-3, 1975.

18. Horvat, Branko, *Between East and West while Opting for Socialism: Comparative Social Organizations*, 1977.

19. Horvat, B., 1977.

20. LO-SAP, 1978: 6.

21. Clegg, H., *Industrial Democracy and Nationalization*, 1951: 73.

22. Jovanov, N., *Radnicki strajkovi u SFRJ od 1958 do 1969*, 1974; Korpi, Walter, *Varför strejkar arbetarna?*, 1970.

23. *Dagens Nyheter*, June 3, 1975.

24. *Företagsvinster, kapitalförsöjning, löntagarfonder*, Sveriges Industriförbund and SAF, 1976: 128-129 (the so-called Waldenström report).

25. *Företagsvinster, kapitalförsöjning, löntagarfonder*, 1976: 15.

26. Cf., Lindbeck, Assar, "Skall SAFLO ta makten över kapitalet?" in *Fondfrågan*, 1979: 52-57.

27. Hugenholz, P. H., "The task of the trade unions in a system of workers' selfmanagement," in Brookmeyer, M. (ed.) *Yugoslav Workers' Selfmanagement*, 1970: 63-66.

28. *Företagsvinster, kapitalförsöjning, löntagarfonder*, 1976: 128.

29. *Företagsvinster, kapitalförsöjning, löntagarfonder*, 1976: 128.

30. Galbraith, John Kenneth, *The New Industrial State*, 1967.

31. Ahrne, Göran, *Den gyllene kedjan*, 1976; Zetterberg, Hans and Karin Busch, "Allmänhetens prioritering av offentlig och privat konsumtion," in Tarschys, Daniel et al., *Offentlig sektor i tillväxt*, 1975: 79-105.

32. Lundberg, Lars, *De statliga industrisubventionernas framväxt*, 1979.

33. *Företagsvinster, kapitalförsöjning, löntagarfonder*, 1976: 128.

34. Hedelius, Tom, "Tar vi vara på innovatörerna?" in *Dagens Nyheter*, April 14, 1979.

35. Friberg, Mats, "Incentiveproblem under socialismen," in *Sociologisk Forskning*, Nr. 4, 1975: 52-65; Friberg, Mats, "Är lönen det enda som sporrar oss att arbeta?" in *Sociologisk Forskning*, Nr. 1, 1976: 24-37.

36. Friberg, M., 1976: 27.

37. Friberg, M., 1976: 25.

38. Friberg, M., 1976: 36.

39. Friberg, M., 1976: 36-37.

40. Friberg, M., 1976: 36

41. Cf., Bråverman, H., *Arbete och monopolkapital*, 1977.
42. Quoted in Bergström, V., *Kapitalbildning och industriell demokrati*, 1973: 122.
43. Lindbeck, A., 1979: 15ff.
44. Cf., Bergström, V., 1973: 141.
45. SOU 1975: 41: 28.
46. Abrahamsson, Bengt, *Organisationsteori*, 1978: 190-192.
47. Questions of political participation are discussed in detail by, among others, Abrahamsson, 1978; Bachrach, P., *The Theory of Democratic Elitism*, 1969; Lewin, L., *Folket och eliterna*, 1970; Pateman, C., *Participation and Democratic Theory*, 1975.
48. Enqvist, P.-O., *Musikanternas uttåg*, 1978.
49. Ragnerstam, Bunny, *Innan dagen gryr*, 1974; *Uppbrottets timme*, 1975; *Vredens dag*, 1977; *Skall jorden bliva vår*, 1978.
50. Lundkvist, Sven, *Folkrörelserna i det svenska samhället 1850-1920*, 1977.

BIBLIOGRAPHY

Åsard, Erik (1978) LO och löntagarfondsfrågan. En studie i facklig politik och strategi [LO and the Employee Investment Fund Issue: A Study in Union Politics and Strategy]. Fackföreningsundersökning 5. Östervåla: Rabén & Sjögren.

——— (1979) "Employee participation in Sweden 1971-1978. The issue of economic democracy." Uppsala: Uppsala University, Statsvetenskaplig institutionen (mimeo).

Abrahamsson, Bengt (1970) "Homans on exchange: hedonism revived." American Journal of Sociology (November).

——— (1976) Exemplet Jugoslavien och den svenska debatten om löntagarstyre [The Example of Yugoslavia and the Swedish Debate on Employee-Management]. Stockholm: AWE/Gebers.

——— (1978a) Organisationsteori. Om byråkrati, administration och självstyre (2nd ed.). Stockholm: AWE/Gebers. [English edition: (1977) Bureaucracy or Participation: The Logic of Organization. Beverly Hills, CA: Sage.]

——— (1978b) "Genmäle till Jan-Erik Lane" [Reply to Jan-Erik Lane]. Statsvetenskaplig tidskrift 3.

Adler-Karlsson, Gunnar (1967) Funktionssocialism. Ett alternativ till kommunism och kapitalism [Functional Socialism: An Alternative to Communism and Capitalism]. Oskarshamn: Prisma Verdandi.

Ahlsén, Bengt et al. (1972) Från Palm till Palme. Den svenska socialdemokratins program 1882-1960. Kommentar och dokument utgivna av Föreningen Socialistisk Debatt [From Palm to Palme: The Program of Swedish Social Democracy 1882-1960. Commentary and Documents Published by the Union for Socialistic Debate]. Stockholm: Rabén & Sjögren.

Ahrne, Göran (1976) Den gyllene kedjan. Studier i arbete och konsumtion [The Golden Chain: Studies in Labor and Consumption]. Falköping: Prisma Verdandi.

Allport, Gordon W. (1954) "The historical background of modern social psychology," in Handbook of Social Psychology, Vol. I. Reading, MA: Addison-Wesley.

Ambjörnsson, Ronny (1972) Idé och klass. Texter kring den kommersiella revolutionens England i urval [Idea and Class: Selected Texts on the Commercial Revolution in England]. Stockholm: Bokförlaget Pan/Norstedt.

Andrén, Erik (1943) "Städernas arbetare" [Urban Workers], pp. 183-194 in Andreas Lindblom (ed.) Den svenska arbetarklassens historia. Arbetaren i helg och söcken. Kulturhistoriska studier, I. Hus och hem [The History of the Swedish Working Class: Workers on Weekdays and Holidays. Studies in Cultural History, I. Houses and Homes]. Stockholm: Tidens förlag.

Bachrach, Peter (1969) The Theory of Democratic Elitism. London: University of London Press.

——— and Morton S. Baratz (1963) "Decisions and nondecisions: an analytical framework." American Political Science Review: 632-642.

Bäckström, Knut (1971a) Arbetarrörelsen i Sverige, I. Den svenska arbetarrörelsens uppkomst och forening med socialismen [The Labor Movement in Sweden, Vol. I. The Emergence of the Swedish Labor Movement and Its Union with Socialism]. Stockholm: Rabén & Sjögren.

––– (1971b) Arbetarrörelsen i Sverige, II. Den politiska arbetarrörelsens sprangning och ett nytt revolutionärt arbetarpartis uppkomst [The Labor Movement in Sweden, Vol. II. The Split of the Political Labor Movement and the Emergence of a New Revolutionary Workers' Party]. Stockholm: Rabén & Sjögren.

Baumol, William J. (1974) "The transformation of values: what Marx 'really' meant (an interpretation)." Journal of Economic Literature 1: 51-61.

Becker, Lawrence, C. (1977) Property Rights: Philosophic Foundations. London: Routledge & Kegan Paul.

Belfrage, Bertil and Leif Stille [eds.] (1975) Filosofi och rättsvetenskap [Philosophy and Legal Science]. Lund: Bokförlaget Doxa.

Bentham, Jeremy (1962) The Works of Jeremy Bentham. Published under the Superintendence of His executor John Bowring, Vol. I. New York: Russell & Russell.

Bergier, J. F. ([1971] 1977) "The industrial bourgeoisie and the rise of the working class 1700-1914," pp. 397-451 in C. M. Cipolla (ed.) The Fontana Economic History of Europe: The Industrial Revolution. Glasgow: Fontana/Collins.

Bergström, Villy (1973) Kapitalbildning och industriell demokrati [Capital Formation and Industrial Democracy]. Stockholm: Tidens förlag.

Berle, Adolf A. and G. C. Means (1934) The Modern Corporation and Private Property. New York: Macmillan.

Bernstein, Eduard (1907a) Socialdemokrati och parlamentarism [Social Democracy and Parliamentarianism]. Malmö: Socialdemokratiska ungdomsförbundets förlag. [German edition: (1906) Parlamentarismus und Sozialdemokratie. Berlin: Pan-Verlag.]

––– (1907b) Socialismens förutsättningar och socialdemokratins uppgifter. Stockholm: Bjorck & Borjesson. [German edition: (1899) Die Vorausetzungen des Sozialismus und die Aufgaben der Sozialdemokratie. Stuttgart: Dietz Verlag; abridged English edition: (1961) Evolutionary Socialism. A Criticism and Affirmation. New York: Schocken.]

Birney, Robert C. and Teevan C. Richard [eds.] (1961) Reinforcement. New York: Van Nostrand.

Blaug, M. (1968) Economic Theory in Retrospect. London: Heinemann.

Bodström, Lennart (1978) "TCO, partierna och den politiska pressen" [The TCO, the Parties and the Political Press]. Tiden 7: 381-391.

Böhm-Bawerk, Eugen von (1975) "Karl Marx and the close of his system," in Paul M. Sweezy (ed.) Karl Marx and the Close of His System. London: Merlin.

Bottomore, Tom and Patrick Goode (1978) Austromarxism. Oxford: Clarendon.

Bottomore, Tom and Maximilian Rubel (1964) Karl Marx: Selected Writings in Sociology and Social Philosophy. New York: McGraw-Hill.

Brandes, Georg (1903) Lassalle, Vol. I. Stockholm: Marcus boktryckeri. [English edition: (1925) Ferdinand Lassalle. New York: B. G. Richards.]

Branting, Hjalmar (1926a) Foreword and notes to "Socialismens utveckling" [Socialism's development] by Engels (1902), pp. 266-282 in Tal och skrifter, I. Socialistisk samhällssyn, I [Speeches and Writings, Vol. I. Socialist Social View, Vol. I]. Stockholm: Tidens tryckeri.

––– (1926b) "Kritiken av socialismen pa Arbetarinstitute (1897)" [The critique of socialism at the Labor Institute (1897)], pp. 204-211 in Tal och skrifter, I.

Socialistisk samhällssyn, I [Speeches and Writings, Vol. I. Socialist Social View, Vol. I]. Stockholm: Tidens tryckeri.

――― (1926c) "Nyare riktningar inom socialdemokratin (1900)" [New directions within social democracy (1900)], pp. 251-265 in Tal och skrifter, I. Socialistisk samhällssyn, I [Speeches and Writings, Vol. I. Socialist Social View, Vol. I]. Stockholm: Tidens tryckeri.

――― (1926d) "Varför arbetarrörelsen måste bli socialistisk (det s.k. Gävletalet, 1886)" [Why the labor movement must become socialist (the so-called Gävle-speech of 1886)], pp. 87-119 in Tal och skrifter, I. Socialistisk samhällssyn, I [Speeches and Writings, Vol. I. Socialist Social View, Vol. I]. Stockholm: Tidens tryckeri.

――― (1927a) "De närmaste framtidsutsikter (1886)" [Prospects for the near future (1886)"], pp. 27-34 in Tal och skrifter, III. Kampen för demokrati, I [Speeches and Writings, Vol. III. The Struggle for Democracy, Vol. I]. Stockholm: Tidens tryckeri.

――― (1927b) "Demokratins genombrott (1918)" [The breakthrough of democracy (1918)], pp. 289-314 in Tal och skrifter, IV. Kampen för demokratin, II [Speeches and Writings, Vol. IV. The Struggle for Democracy, Vol. II]. Stockholm: Tidens tryckeri.

――― (1927c) "Rösträtt och arbetarrörelse (1896-1899)" [Suffrage and the labor movement (1896-1899)], pp. 128-157 in Tal och skrifter, III. Kampen för demokrati, I [Speeches and Writings, Vol. III. The Struggle for Democracy, Vol. I]. Stockholm: Tidens boktryckeri.

――― (1927d) "Socialismen ((1892) 1906)" [Socialism ((1892) 1906)], pp. 5-88 in Tal och skrifter, II. Socialistisk samhällssyn, II [Speeches and Writings, Vol. II.

――― (1927e) "Socialismen i arbetarrörelsen (1907)" [Socialism in the labor movement (1907)], pp. 325-345 in Tal och skrifter, II. Socialistisk samhällssyn, II [Speeches and Writings, Vol. II. Socialist Social View, Vol. II]. Stockholm: Tidens tryckeri.

――― (1928) "Klasskamp och skiljedom (1898)" [Class struggle and arbitration (1898)], pp. 67-71 in Tal och skrifter, VII. Ekonomisk och social arbetarpolitik [Speeches and Writings, Vol. VII. Economic and Social Labor Policy]. Stockholm: Tidens tryckeri.

――― (1929) "Den revolutionära generalstrejken (1906)" [The revolutionary general strike (1906)], pp. 118-136 in Tal och skrifter, VIII. Stridsfrågor inom arbetarrörelsen [Speeches and Writings, Vol. VIII. Issues of Conflict in the Labor Movement]. Stockholm: Tidens tryckeri.

Braverman, Harry (1977) Arbete och monopolkapital [Labor and Monopoly Capital]. Stockholm: Rabén & Sjögren.

Burke, Edmund (1969) Reflections on the Revolution in France. New York: Pelican.

Burnham, James (1941) The Managerial Revolution. New York: Day.

Cassel, Gustav ([1903] 1971) The Nature and Necessity of Interest. New York: Augustus M. Kelley.

Cipolla, Carlo M. [ed.] (1976) The Fontana Economic History of Europe: (1) The Middle Ages; (2) The Sixteenth and Seventeenth Centuries; (3) The Industrial Revolution; (4) The Emergence of Industrial Societies; (5) The Twentieth Century; (6) Contemporary Economics. Glasgow: Fontana/Collins.

Clarke, Peter (1978) Liberals and Social Democrats. Cambridge: Cambridge University Press.

Clegg, H. A. (1951) Industrial Democracy and Nationalization: A Study Prepared for the Fabian Society. Oxford: Oxford University Press.

Dahl, Robert A. (1970) After the Revolution? New Haven, CT: Yale University Press.

Dahlström, Edmund et al. (1971) LKAB och demokratin [LKAB and Democracy]. Stockholm: Wahlström & Widstrand.

——— (1977) "Arbetet, facket och medbestämmandet" [Labor, unions, and employee participation]. Gothenburg: Sociological Institute, Gothenburg University (mimeo).

Dobb, M. (1946) Studies in the Development of Capitalism. London: NLB.

——— (1978) "From feudalism to capitalism," in R. Hilton (ed.) The Transition from Feudalism to Capitalism. London: NLB.

Droz, Jacques [ed.] (1972a) Histoire générale du socialisme. Vol. I: Des origines à 1875. Paris: Presses Universitaires de France.

——— [ed.] (1972b) Histoire générale du socialisme. Vol. II: De 1875 à 1918. Paris: Presses Universitaires de France.

——— (1972c) "Les origines de la socialdémocratie allemande," in J. Droz (ed.) Histoire générale du socialisme, Vol I. Paris: Presses Universitaires de France.

Eckhoff, T. (1969) "Litt om de juridiske rettighetsspråk" [Something about the juridical language of rights], in Festskrift for Alf Ross. Copenhagen: Juristforbundets forlag.

Ekdahl, Lars-Olof and Hans Eric Hjelm (1978) "Reformismens framväxt inom svensk arbetarrörelse" [The emergence of reformism in the Swedish labor movement]. Häften för Kritiska Studier 2: 4-26.

Elvander, Nils (1976) "Företagsdemokrati och politisk demokrati" [Industrial democracy and political democracy], in Organisationerna i det moderna samhället [Organizations in the Modern Society]. A symposium in Skokloster, April 8-9. Uppsala: State Council on Social Research.

Engels, Friedrich (1895) Einleitung (Zum Karl Marx' "Klassenkämpfe in Frankreich 1848 bis 1850"), p. 509 in MEW, Vol. 22.

——— (1969) Familjens, privategendomens och statens ursprung (3rd ed.). Stockholm: Arbetarkulturens forläg. [English edition: (1942) The Origin of the Family, Private Property and the State. New York: International Publishers.]

Engwall, Lars (1967) "Styrelsekarakteristika i Norge och Sverige—en jamforelse" [Management characteristics in Norway and Sweden—a comparison]. Statsekonomisk Tidskrift 3-4.

Enqvist, P. O. (1978) Musikanternas uttåg [The Musicians' Exodus]. Stockholm: Norstedt.

Erlander, Tage (1972) Tage Erlander 1901-1939 (4th ed.). Stockholm: Tidens förlag.

——— and Björn von Sydow ([1926]1976) Postscript on pp. 283-346 of Nils Karleby, Socialismen inför verkligheten [Socialism in the Face of Reality]. Stockholm: Tidens förlag.

Everett, Charles W. (1966) Great lives and Thought: Jeremy Bentham. London: Weidenfeld & Nicolson.

Finer, H. (1975) "Lassalle," pp. 183 in H. B. Lees-Smith (ed.) The Encyclopaedia of the Labour Movement, Vol. II. London: Caxton.

Fletcher, Ronald (1971) John Stuart Mill: A Logical Critique of Sociology. London: Michael Joseph.

Flodgren, Boel (1978) Fackföreningen och rätten. En jämförande studie av föreningsrätten i Sverige och USA [Labor Unions and the Law: A Comparative Study of the Right of Association in Sweden and the U.S.]. Lund: Norstedts.

Företagsvinster, kapitalförsöjning, löntagarfonder [Company Profits, Capital Supply, Employee Investment Funds] (1976) Report from an industry work group (The so-called Waldenström Report). Stockholm: SAF's förlagssektion.

Fogelklou, Anders (1978) Den orättfärdiga rätten [The Unjust Right]. Stockholm: Norstedts.

Friberg, Mats (1975) "Incentiveproblem under socialismen" [The problems of incentive under socialism]. Sociologisk Forskning 4: 52-65.

——— (1976) "Är lönen det enda som sporrar oss att arbeta?" [Are wages the only thing that Spurs us on to work?]. Sociologisk Forskning 1: 24-37.

Furniss, Norman (1978) "Property rights and democratic socialism." Political Studies 26, 4: 450-461.

Galbraith, John Kenneth (1967) The New Industrial State. Boston: Houghton Mifflin.

Gamby, Erik (1978) Pär Götrek och 1800-talets svenska arbetarrörelse [Pär Götrek and the Swedish Labor Movement of the Nineteenth Century]. Stockholm: Tidens förlag.

Gerdner, Gunnar (1966) "Ministären Edén och författningsrevisionen" [The Edén Cabinet and the constitutional revision], in Stig Hadenius (ed.) Kring demokratins genombrott i Sverige [On the Emergence of Democracy in Sweden]. Stockholm: Wahlström & Widstrand.

Gleisner, P.-A., S. Iger, M. Pettersson, and B. Svensson (1974) "Värde och profit hos Marx och Sraffa" [Value and profit in Marx and Sraffa]. Stockholm: Stockholms universitet, Nationalekonomiska institutionen (mimeo).

Golubović, Zaga (1975) "Interview." Frihetlig socialistisk tidskrift 2-3.

Guest, A. G. [ed.] (1961) Oxford Essays in Jurisprudence: A Collaborative Work. London: Oxford University Press.

Gunnarsson, Gunnar [ed.] (1965) Arbetarrörelsens genombrottsår i dokument [The Labor Movement's Years of Emergence in Documents]. Stockholm: Prisma.

——— (1970a) Arbetarrörelsens krönika i ord och bild 1881-1938 [The Chronicle of the Labor Movement in Words and Pictures 1881-1938]. Stockholm: Tidens förlag.

——— (1970b) Arbetarrörelsens krönika i ord och bild 1939-1970 [The Chronicle of the Labor Movement in Words and Pictures 1939-1970]. Stockholm: Tidens förlag.

——— (1973) De stora utopisterna. (2) Från Babeuf till Quiding [The Great Utopians. (2) From Babeuf to Quiding]. Stockholm: Tidens förlag.

——— (1975) "Kautsky, Bernstein och Marx" [Kautsky, Bernstein, and Marx], pp. 206-245 in J. Lindhagen (ed.) Bilden av Branting [Portrait of Branting]. Stockholm: Tidens förlag.

Gustafsson, Agne (1978) Företagsdemokratin och den offentliga sektorn [Industrial Democracy and the Public Sector]. Lund: Studentlitteratur.

——— (1979) "Facket, medborgarna och demokrati" [Unions, citizens, and democracy]. Tiden 1: 25-35.

Gustafsson, Bo (1968) "Klassicism, marxism och marginalism" [Classicism, Marxism, and marginalism]. Häften för kritiska studier 1-2: 3-16.

——— (1969) Marxism och revisionism. Eduard Bersteins kritik av marxismen och dess idehistoriska forutsattningar [Marxism and revisionism: Eduard Bernstein's critique of Marxism and Its Theoretical Precursors]. Ekonomiska-historiska studier, Nr. 4. Uppsala: Svenska bokförlaget.

―――(1978) "A new look at Bernstein: some reflexions on reformism and history." Scandinavian Journal of History: 275-296.

Gustafsson, Sverker (1978) "Varför tillåts demokratiska uppbyggda organisationer?" [Why are democratically constructed organizations allowed?]. Tiden 7: 374-380.

―――(1979) "Statskunskapen, socialismen och demokratin" [Political science, socialism, and democracy]. Tiden 3: 151-161.

Gustavsson, Per and Lars Rydqvist (1978) "Arbetarbibliotek i Sverige" [Labor libraries in Sweden] Ord & Bild 5: 50-57.

Håkansson, Kaj (1973) Socialism som självstyre [Socialism as Selfmanagement]. Stockholm: Prisma.

Hägerström, Axel (1966) "Om moraliska föreställningars sanning (Installationsföreläsning 1911)" [On the truth of moral notions (Inaugural lecture, 1911)], in Socialfilosofiska uppsatser [Social-Philosophic Essays]. Stockholm: Orion/Bonniers.

Halevy, Elie (1955) The Growth of Philosophic Radicalism. Boston: Beacon.

Hansson, S. [ed.] (1969) Moderna ideologier [Modern Ideologies]. Stockholm: Wahlström & Widstrand.

Hansson, Sven Ove (1976a) Marx och Engels i politiken. Demokratins roll i deras politiska och vetenskapliga verksamhet [Marx and Engels in Politics: The Role of Democracy in Their Political and Scientific Activity]. Kristianstad: Tidens förlag.

Hansson, Sven Ove (1976b) "Socialismens långsiktiga målsättningar" [Socialism's long-term goals]. Tiden 6: 298-307.

―――(1977a) "Arton argument mot löntagarfonder" [Eighteen arguments against employee investment funds]. Tiden 1: 6-19.

―――(1977b) "Att välja modell för den ekonomiska demokratin" [Choosing a model for economic democracy]. Tiden 4: 206-219.

―――(1977c) "Kapitalets roll i socialismen" [The role of capital in socialism]. Tiden 7: 418-429.

Hardach, Gerd and Dieter Karras, in collaboration with Ben Fine (1978) A Short History of Socialist Economic Thought. London: Edward Arnold.

Hayek, F. W. von (1944) Vagen till traldom. Stockholm: Timbro. [English edition: (1944) The Road to Serfdom. Chicago: University of Chicago Press.]

Heckscher, Eli F. ([1957]1976) Svenskt arbete och liv. Från medeltiden till nutiden. Stockholm: Aldus/Bonniers. [English edition: (1954) An Economic History of Sweden. Cambridge, MA: Harvard University Press.]

Hedborg, Anna (1976) "Makten är odelbar" [Power is indivisible]. Tiden 4-5: 216-225.

―――(1978) "Löntagarfonder - en förstärkning av demokratin" [Employee investment funds—a strengthening of democracy]. Tiden 3-4: 158-167.

Hedelius, Tom (1979) "Tar vi vara på innovatörerna?" [Are we making good use of our innovators?]. Dagens Nyheter (April 14).

Hedenius, Ingemar (1941) Om rätt och moral [On Rights and Morals]. Stockholm: Tidens förlag.

―――(1975) "Analysen av äganderättsbegreppet" [An analysis of the concept of ownership rights], in B. Belfrage and L. Stille (eds.) Filosofi och rättsvetenskap [Philosophy and Legal Science]. Lund: Bokförlaget Doxa.

Hellner, Brynolf (1943) "Brukens arbetare" [Mill workers], pp. 195-216 in Andreas Lindblom (ed.) Den svenska arbetarklassens historia. Arbetare i helg och söcken. Kulturhistoriska studier I. Hus och hem [The History of the Swedish Working

Class. Workers on Weekdays and Holidays. Studies in Cultural History. I. Houses and Homes]. Stockholm: Tidens förlag.

Hentilä, Seppo (1974) "Orsaker till reformismens genombrott i svensk socialdemokrati" [Reasons for the emergence of reformism in Swedish social democracy]. Arkiv för studier i arbetarrörelsens historia 5: 3-20.

Hilferding, Rudolf (1976) Finanskapitalen. Socialdemokratiets opgaver i republikken. Pragermanifestet, Del I og II [Finance Capital: The Tasks of Social Democracy in the Republic. The Prager Manifesto, Parts I and II.] Copenhagen: Rhodos.

Hilton, Rodney [ed.] ([1976]1978) The Transition from Feudalism to Capitalism. London: NLB.

Hobsbawm, Eric (1976) "From feudalism to capitalism," in R. Hilton (ed.) The Transition from Feudalism to Capitalism. London: NLB.

Höglund, Zeth (1926a). "Förord till Brantings uppsats 'Varförarbetarrörelsen måeste bli socialistisk'" [Foreword to Branting's essay "Why the labor movement must become socialist"], p. 87 in Tal och skrifter I. Socialistisk samhällssyn I. Stockholm: Tidens tryckeri.

––– (1926b) "Förord till Brantings uppsats 'Nyare riktningar inom socialdemokratin'" [Foreword to Branting's essay "New directions within social democracy"], in Tal och skrifter I. Socialistisk samhällssyn I. Stockholm: Tidens tryckeri.

––– (1928) Hjalmar Branting och hans livsgärning, Del II. [Hjalmar Branting and His Life's Work, Part II]. Stockholm: Tidens tryckeri.

Honoré, A. M. (1961) "Ownership,'. in A. G. Guest (ed.) Oxford Essays in Jurisprudence: A Collaborative Work. London: Oxford University Press.

Horvat, Branko (1977) "Between East and West while opting for socialism: comparative social organizations." Presented at the anniversary symposium, Uppsala University (mimeo).

Hugenholz, P. H. (1970) "The Task of the trade unions in a system of workers' selfmanagement," in Marius S. Broekmeyer (ed.) Yugoslav Workers' Selfmanagement. Donlrecht: D. Reidel.

Hutchison, T. W. (1962) A Review of Economic Doctrines 1870-1929. Oxford: Clarendon Press.

Hydén, Håkan (1978) Rättens samhälleliga funktioner [The Social Functions of Law]. Lund: Studentlitteratur.

Johansson, Sten (1971) Politiska resurser. "Om den svenska befolkningens deltagande i de politiska beslutsprocesserna. Utkast till kap. 10 i betänkande om svenska folkets levnadsförhållanden" [Political Resources. "On the participation of the Swedish population in the political decision-making processes: draft of chapter 10 in the report on the living conditions of the Swedish people"]. Stockholm: Allmänna förlaget.

––– (1975) "Om övergången till socialismen" [On the transition to socialism] Tiden, 7: 349-361.

Jovanov, Neca (1974) Radnicki strajkovi u SFRJ od 1958 do 1969. Belgrade: SFJ.

Kahn-Freund, O. ([1949]1976) "Introduction," in Karl Renner, The Institutions of Private Law and Their Social Functions. London: Routledge & Kegan Paul.

Kaijser, Fritz (1976) "Om de s.k. löntagarfondernas grundlagsenlighet–ett genmäle" [On the constitutionality of the so-called employee investment funds–a reply]. Svensk Juristtidning 61: 650-656.

Karleby, Nils ([1926]1976) Socialismen inför verkligheten. Studier över socialdemokratisk åskådning och nutidspolitik [Socialism in the Face of Reality: Studies in the Social Democratic Outlook and Current Policy]. Stockholm: Tidens förlag.

Karlsson, Jan (1977) Om arbete—en studie av arbetets ställning i skilda sämhallen. En delrapport från studien "Arbetslivet i framtiden" [On labor—a study of labor's position in various societies: a report in the study "working life in the future"]. Stockholm: Sekretariatet för framtidsstudier.

Karlsson, Lars-Erik (1969) Demokrati på arbetsplatsen [Democracy in the workplace]. Stockholm: Prisma.

Kautsky, Karl ([1899]1908) Socialdemokrati och socialism. En kritik av Bernsteins arbete Socialismens förutsättningar och socialdemokratins uppgifter. Stockholm: Björck & Börjesson. [German edition: (1899) Bernstein und der sozialdemokratische Program. Eine Antikritik. Stuttgart: Dietz.]

——— (1923) "Marx und Lassalle" [Marx and Lassalle]. Der Kampf. Sozialdemokratische Monatschrift 3: 87ff.

Kedner, G. and C. M. Roos (1977) Aktiebolagslagen, Del I. [Stock company legislation, Part I]. Stockholm: Norstedts.

Kirkup, Thomas (1951) "Lassalle," in Encyclopaedia Britannica.

Kolakowski, Leszek (1972) Positivist Philosophy: From Hume to the Vienna Circle. New York: Penguin.

Korpi, Walter (1970) Varför strejkar arbetarna? [Why Do the Workers Strike?]. Stockholm: Tidens förlag.

——— (1978) Arbetarklassen i välfärdskapitalismen. Arbete, fackförening och politik i Sverige [The Working Class in Welfare Capitalism: Labor, the Labor Union, and Politics in Sweden]. Stockholm: Prisma/Institute for Social Research.

——— (1979) "USA kör historien baklänges" [the U.S. runs its history backwards]. Dagens Nyheter (April 5).

——— and Michael Shalev (1978) "Strikes, power, and politics in the Western nations, 1900-1976." Stockholm: Swedish Institute for Social Research; Madison, WI: Industrial Relations Research Institute, University of Wisconsin (mimeo).

Landsorganisationen (LO) (1976a) Kollektiv kapitalbildning genom löntagarfonder. Rapport till LO-kongressen 1976 [Collective Capital Formation Through Employee Investment Funds: Report to the LO Convention 1976]. Stockholm: Prisma.

——— (1976b) Solidariskt medbestämmande. Rapport till LO-kongressen 1976 [Solidarity and Co-determination: Report to the LO Convention 1976]. Lund: Prisma.

——— and Sveriges socialdemokratiska arbetareparti (SAP) (1978) Löntagarfonder och kapitalbildning. Förslag från LO-SAP's arbetsgrupp [Employee Investment Funds and Capital Formation. A Proposal from the LO-SAP Work Group]. Stockholm: Tiden-Barnängen.

Lane, Jan-Erik (1978) "Begreppslabyrinter i administrativ forskning: om begreppen byråkrati och decentralisering" [Conceptual labyrinths in administrative research: on the concepts bureaucracy and decentralization]. Statsvetenskaplig tidskrift 2: 110-125.

Lantz, Göran (1977) Eigentumsrecht—ein Recht oder ein Unrecht? Eine kritische Beurteilung der etischen Argumente für das Privateigentum bei Aristoteles, Thomas Aquino, Grothius, Locke, Hegel, Marx und in den modernen katholischen Sozialenzykliken [Property Rights—a Right or a Wrong? A Critical Evaluation of the Ethical Arguments for Private Property in Aristotle, Thomas Aquinas, Grothius, Locke, Hegel, Marx, and in the Modern Catholic Social Encyclicals]. Acta Universitatis Upsaliensis. Uppsala Studies in Social Ethics, Nr. 4. Uppsala: Almqvist & Wicksell.

Lees-Smith, H. B. [ed.] (n.d.) The encyclopaedia of the Labor Movement. London: Caxton.

Lefebvre, Georges (1963) 1789: Den Franska revolutionens bakgrund och orsaker. Lund: Aldus/Bonniers. [English edition: (1968) The Coming of the French Revolution, 1789. New York: Vintage.]

Le Goff, Jacques ([1971]1976) "The town as an agent of civilization 1200-1500," pp. 71-106 in C. M. Cipolla (ed.) The Fontana Economic History of Europe. The Middle Ages. Glasgow: Fontana/Collins.

Lewin, Leif (1967) Planhushållningsdebatten [The Planned Economy Debate]. Uppsala: Almqvist & Wicksell.

——— (1970) Folket och eliterna [The people and the elites]. Stockholm: Rabén & Sjögren.

Lidén, Lars (1966) Makten över företaget [The power over the Company]. Stockholm: SNS.

Liedman, Sven-Eric [ed.] (1965) Karl Marx. Människans frigörelse [Karl Marx: The Liberation of Man]. Stockholm: Aldus/Bonniers.

Lilley, Samuel ([1970]1977) "Technological progress and the Industrial Revolution 1700-1914," pp. 187-254 in C. M. Cipolla (ed.) The Fontana Economic History of Europe. The Industrial Revolution. Glasgow: Fontana/Collins.

Lindbeck, Assar (1977) "Can pluralism survive?" The eleventh annual William K. McInally memorial lecture, Graduate School of Business Administration, University of Michigan.

——— (1979) Fondfrågan [The Fund Issue] Stockholm: Bokförlaget ALBA.

Lindblom, Andreas [ed.] (1943) Den svenska arbetarklassens historia. Arbetaren i helg och söcken. Kulturhistoriska studier I. Hus och hem. [The History of the Swedish Working Class. Workers on Weekdays and Holidays. Studies in Cultural History. I. Houses and Homes]. Stockholm: Tidens förlag.

Lindhagen, Jan (1972a) Socialdemokratins program, Första delen. I rörelsens tid 1890-1930 [Social Democracy's Program, Part I. The Time of Movement, 1890-1930]. Stockholm: Tidens förtag.

——— (1972b) Socialdemokratins program, Andra delen. Bolshevikstriden [Social Democracy's Program, Part II. The Bolshevik Struggle]. Stockholm: Tidens for-läg.

——— [ed.] (1975) Bilden av Branting [The Portrait of Branting]. Stockholm: Tidens förlag.

——— and Macke Nilsson (1970) Hotet mot arbetarrörelsen [The Threat to the Lábor Movement]. Stockholm: Tidens förlag.

Locke, John (1894[1st ed. 1690]) An Essay Concerning Human Understanding. Oxford: A. C. Frazer.

Lundberg, Lars (1979) "De statliga industrisubventionernas framväxt" [The growth of state industrial subsidies]. Uppsala: Uppsala University, Institute of Sociology and Business (mimeo).

Lundkvist, Sven (1977) Folkrörelserna i det svenska samhället 1850-1920 [Popular Movements in Swedish Society 1850-1920]. Stockholm: Seber Förlags AB.

Lundstedt, Vilhelm (1928) "Har Duquits rättsteori något underlag i fakta?" [Is Duquit's theory of rights supported by facts?], pp. 84-110 in Festskrift tillägnad Axel Hägerström den 6. september 1928 av Filosofiska och Juridiska föreningarna i Uppsala. Uppsala: Almqvist & Wicksell.

Macpherson, C. B. ([1962]1977) The Political Theory of Possessive Individualism: Hobbes to Locke (7th ed.). Oxford: Oxford University Press.

––– [ed.] (1978) Property. Toronto: University of Toronto Press.

Malmström, Åke, with the assistance of Anders Agell and Tore Sigeman (1977) Civilrätt [Civil Law]. Lund: LiberLäromedel.

Marx, Karl (1904) A Contribution to the Critique of Political Economy (N. I. Stone, trans.). Chicago: Charles H. Kerr.

––– (1951) Theories of Surplus Value (G. A. Bonner and E. Burns, trans.). London: Lawrence & Wishart.

––– (1957) Capital: A Critical Analysis of Capitalist Production (S. Moore and E. Aveling, trans.). London: Allen & Unwin.

––– (1960) Capital, Vol. III. London: Lawrence & Wishart.

––– (1965) The German Ideology. London: Lawrence & Wishart.

McClosky, Herbert (1958) "Conservatism and personality." American Political Science Review: 27-45.

Meek, Ronald, L. (1973) Studies in the Labor Theory of Value (2nd ed.). London: Lawrence & Wishart.

Mehr, Hjalmar (1975) "Hjalmar Branting–människan, ledaren, statsmannen" [Hjalmar Branting–the man, the leader, the statesman], in Jan Lindhagen (ed.) Bilden av Branting [The portrait of Branting]. Stockholm: Tidens förlag.

Meidner, Rudolf, in collaboration with Anna Hedborg and Gunnar Fond (1975) Löntagarfonder. Stockholm: Tidens förlag. [English edition: (1978) Employee Investment Funds: An Approach to Collective Capital Formation. London: Allen & Unwin.]

Merrington, John (1978) "Town and country in the transition to capitalism," in R. Hilton (ed.) The Transition from Feudalism to Capitalism. London: NLB.

Meurling, Per (1975) "Hjalmar Branting och arbetarinternationalen" [Hjalmar Branting and the labor International], in Jan Lindhagen (ed.) Bilden av Branting [The portrait of Branting]. Stockholm: Tidens Förlag.

Meyerson, Per-Martin (1978) Löntagarfonder eller . . . ägande och demokrati i en marknadsekonomi [Employee Investment Funds or . . . Ownership and Democracy in a Market Economy]. Stockholm: Norstedts.

Michaels, Robert (1962) Political Parties: A Sociological Study of the Oligarchical Tendencies of Modern Democracy. New York: Free Press.

Mill, John, Stuart (1965) Principles of Political Economy with Some of Their Applications to Social Philosophy, Book IV, Chapter vii, §4. London: Routledge & Kegan Paul.

––– (1966) On Liberty. Representative Government. The Subjection of Women: Three Essays. London: Oxford University Press.

Möller, Gustav (1975) Revolution och socialism [Revolution and Socialism]. Stockholm: Tidens förlag.

Mols, S. J. Roger ([1972]1976) "Population in Europe 1500-1700," pp. 15-82 in C. M. Cipolla (ed.) The Fontana Economic History of Europe. The Sixteenth and Seventeenth Centuries. Glasgow: Fontana/Collins.

Morishima, Michio (1973) Marx' Economics. Cambridge: Cambridge University Press.

Montgomery, A. (1976) See E. F. Heckscher, Svenskt arbete och liv.

Myrdal, Gunnar (1927) Prisbildningsproblemet och foranderligheten [The Problem of Price Formation and Variability]. Stockholm: Almquist & Wicksell.

––– (1969) Objektivitetsproblemet i samhallsforskningen [The Objectivity Problem in Social Research]. Uddevalla: Raben & Sjogren.

Nelhans, Joachim (1976) "De Meidnerska löntagarfonderna i Stig Strömholms rättslig belysning" [Meidner's employee investment funds from Stig Strömholms legal perspective]. Svensk Juristtidning 61: 647-649.

Nozick, Robert (1974) Anarchy, State and Utopia. New York: Basic Books.

Öhman, Berndt (1970) Svensk arbetsmarknadspolitik 1900-1947 [Swedish Labor Market Policies 1900-1947]. Stockholm: Prisma.

Palm, August (1904) Ur en agitators liv [From the Life of an Agitator]. Stockholm: Knut Griberg.

Palmgren, Yngve (1975) "Trojkan" [The troika], in J. Lindhagen (ed.) Bilden av Branting [The portrait of Branting]. Stockholm: Tidens förlag.

Parekh, Bhikhu (1973) Bentham's Political Thought. New York: Harper & Row Barnes & Noble.

Pateman, Carole ([1970]1975) Participation and democratic Theory. Cambridge: Cambridge University Press.

Ragnerstam, Bunny (1974) Innan dagen gryr [Before Dawn]. Ostervala: Gidlunds.

——— (1975) Uppbrottets timme [Time to Rise]. Kristianstad: Gidlunds.

——— (1977) Vredens dag [The Day of Anger] : Avesta: Gidlunds.

——— (1978) Skall jorden bliva var [And the Earth Shall Be Ours]. Avesta: Gidlunds.

Renner, Karl ([1949]1976) The Institutions of Private Law and Their Social Functions. London: Routledge & Kegan Paul.

Rhenman, Eric (1964) Företagsdemokrati och företagsorganisation. Stockholm: Norstedts. [English edition: (1968) Industrial Democracy and Industrial Management. London: Assen, Van Gorcum.]

Ricardo, David ([1911]1976) The Principles of Political Economy and Taxation. London: Dent & Sons.

Roehl, Richard ([1970]1976) "Patterns and structure of demand 1000-1500," pp. 107-142 in C. M. Cipolla (ed.) The Fontana Economic History of Europe. The Middle Ages. Glasgow: Fontana/Collins.

Roll, Eric ([1938]1978) A History of Economic Thought (4th revised and expanded ed. London: Faber & Faber.

Ross, Alf (1953) Om ret og retfaerdighed. Copenhagen: Nyt nordisk forlag. Arnold Busck. [English edition: (1958) On Law and Justice. London: Stevens.]

——— (1963) Varför demokrati? Stockholm: Tidens förläg. [English edition: (1952) Why Democracy? . . . Cambridge, MA: Harvard University Press.]

Rossiter, Clinton ([1955]1962) Conservatism in America: The Thankless Persuasion (2nd ed.) New York: Vintage.

Samuelson, Paul (1974) "Insight and detour in the theory of exploitation: a reply to Baumol" Journal of Economic Literature 1: 62-70.

Sandler, Richard (1936) Socialiseringsproblemet. Allmänna synpunkter. Utkast till principbetänkande [The socialization problem. General viewpoints. Draft of report of principle]. Stockholm: SOU 1936: 7. Tidens förlag.

——— (1937a) Socialiseringsidéer och socialiseringspraxis i Sovjetunionen [Socialization: ideas and practice in the Soviet Union]. Stockholm: SOU 1937: 2. Tidens förlag.

——— (1937b) Socialiseringsproblemet, II. Hushållsräkningens problem och faktorer [The socialization problem, II. Economic calculation—problems and factors]. Stockholm: SOU 1937: 1. Tidens förlag.

Sella, Domenico ([1970]1976) "European Industries 1500-1700," in C. M. Cipolla (ed.) The Fontana Economic History of Europe. The Sixteenth and Seventeenth Centuries. Glasgow: Fontana/Collins.

Skinner, Andrew (1977) "Introduction," to Adam Smith, The Wealth of Nations. New York: Penguin.

Smith, Adam ([1776]1977). The Wealth of Nations, Books I-III. New York: Penguin.

Södersten, Bo (1976) "Den sanna pluralismen. Teser om löntagarstyre" [The true pluralism: theses on worker-management]. Tiden, 4-5: 197-209.

——— G. Johansson, and D. Andersson (1977) "Kapitalismens hot mot demokratin och löntagarna" [Capitalism's threat to democracy and wage earners]. Aftonbladet (May 2).

Ståhl, Ingemar (1976) "Ägande och makt i företagen—En debattinledning" [Ownership and power in companies—an introduction to debate]. Ekonomisk debatt 1: 62-75.

Strömholm, Stig (1976a) Allmän rättslära. En första introduktion (3rd ed.) [General Legal Theory: An Introduction]. Stockholm: Norstedts.

——— (1976b) "Förslaget om s.k. löntagarfonder i rättslig belysning" [The proposal on so-called employee investment funds from a legal perspective]. Svensk Juristtidning 61: 452-468.

——— (1976c) "Replik" [Rebuttal]. Svensk Juristtidning 61: 656-660.

Sweezy, Paul, M. (1975) "Introduction," in P. M. Sweezy (ed.) E. von Böhm-Bawerk, Karl Marx and the Close of His System, and R. Hilferding, Böhm-Bawerk's Criticism of Marx. London: Merlin.

——— (1978) "A critique," in R. Hilton (ed.) The Transition from Feudalism to Capitalism. London: NLB.

Tarschys, Daniel et al. (1975) Offentlig sektor i tillväxt [The Growing Public Sector]. Stockholm: SNS.

Therborn, Göran (1976) Science, Class and Society: On the Formation of Sociology and Historical Materialism. London: NLB.

——— et al. (1966) En ny vänster [A New Left]. Stockholm: Rabén & Sjögren.

Thomson, David ([1966]1970) Europe since Napoleon. New York: Penguin.

Thrupp, Sylvia ([1971]1976) "Medieval industry 1000-1500," in C. M. Cipolla (ed.) The Fontana Economic History of Europe. The Middle Ages. Glasgow: Fontana/Collins.

Thunberg, Anders (1970) Strejken [The Strike]. Stockholm: Rabén & Sjögren.

Tilly, Charles [ed.] (1975) The Formation of National States in Western Europe. Princeton, NJ: Princeton University Press.

Tilton, Timothy (1979) "A Swedish road to socialism: Ernst Wigforss and the ideological foundations of Swedish Social Democracy." American Political Science Review (June).

Tingsten, Herbert ([1939]1966) De konservativa idéerna [The conservative Ideas]. Stockholm: Aldus/Bonniers.

——— ([1941]1967) Den svenska socialdemokratins idéutveckling, Del I och II. Stockholm: Aldus/Bonniers. [English edition: (1973) The Swedish Social Democrats: Their Ideological Development. Totowa, NJ: Bedminster.

——— ([1960]1969) Demokratins problem [The Problems of Democracy]. Stockholm: Aldus/Bonniers.

——— (1971a) Mitt liv: Mellan trettio och femtio, Del II [My life. Between Thirty and Fifty, Part II]. Stockholm: Bokförlaget Pan/Norstedts.

——— (1971b) Mitt liv. Tidningen 1946-1952, Del III [My life: The Newspaper 1946-1952, Part III]. Stockholm: Bokförlaget Pan/Norstedts.

Tjänstemännens Centralorganisation (TCO) (1978) Löntagarfonder ur TCO-perspektiv–en debattskrift [Employee Investment Funds from the TCO Perspective: A Contribution to Debate]. Stockholm: TCO.

Tocqueville, Alexis de (1970) Jämlikheten vårt öde. Tankar om demokratins möjligheter och blindskär [Equality Is Our Fate: Thoughts on the Potentials and Pitfalls of Democracy]. Selected and translated by Anders Byttner. Stockholm: Rabén & Sjögren.

Tunberg, Sven and Ernst Söderlund (1951) Svensk historia för gymnasiet [Swedish History for High School]. Stockholm: Norstedts.

Udéhn, Lars (1968) "Methodological individualism–a critical appraisal." Uppsala: Sociological institutionen (mimeo).

Undén, Östen (1928) "Några synpunkter på begreppsbildning inom juridiken" [A few perspectives on concept formation in jurisprudence], in Festskrift tillägnad Axel Hägerström den 6. september 1928 av Filosofiska och Juridiska föreningarna i Uppsala.

––– ([1927]1976) Svensk sakrätt, I. Lös egendom. [Swedish property law, I. Personal Property]. Lund: Liber-Läromedel.

Unga, Nils (1976) Socialdemokratin och arbetslöshetsfrågan 1912-1934. Framväxten av den "nya" arbetslöshetspolitiken [Social Democracy and the Unemployment Issue 1912-1934: The Emergence of the "New" Unemployment Policy]. Arkiv Avhandlingsserie, Nr. 4. Kristianstad: Archive for Studies in the History of the Labor movement.

Vedung, Evert (1977) Det rationella politiska samtalet. Hur politiska budskap tolkas, ordnas och prövas [Rational Political Dialogue: How Political Messages Are Interpreted, Ordered, and Tested]. Stockholm: Aldus/Bonniers.

Westerståhl, Jörgen and Mårten Persson (1975) Demokrati och intresserepresentation. En principdiskussion [Democracy and Interest Representation: A Discussion of Principle]. Stockholm: Liber-Läromedel.

Westholm, Carl Johan (1976a) "Majoritetsprincipen och kontraktsrätten" [The majority principle and contract law]. Ekonomisk debatt 3: 239-243.

––– (1976b) Ratio och universialitet. John Stuart Mill och dagens demokratidebatt [Ratio and Universality: John Stuart Mill and Today's Democracy Debate]. Statsvetenskapliga föreningen i Uppsala, Nr. 72. Kungälv: Rabén & Sjögren.

Winch, Donald ([1971]1977) "The emergence of economics as a science 1750-1870," in C. M. Cipolla (ed.) The Fontana Economic History of Europe. The Industrial Revolution. Glasgow: Fontana/Collins.

Zetterberg, Hans and Karin Busch (1979) "Allmänhetens prioritering av offentlig och privat konsumtion" [The public's priorities with respect to private and public consumption], pp. 79-105 in D. Tarschys et al., Offentlig sektor i tillväxt [The Growing Public Sector]. Stockholm: SNS.

Public Documents

Arbetsmarknadsdepartementet [Department of Labor] (1977) Förhållandet mellan medbestämmandelagen och viss annan lagstiftning [The relation between the Law on Co-determination and certain other legislation]. Memorandum by a group of experts within the government. DsA 1977: 2.

Proposition 1975/76: 105. Bilaga 2. Finansdepartementet. Arbetsrättsreform: Lag om offentlig anställning [Finance Department. Labor law reform: The Law on Public Employment].

Proposition 1975/76: 105. Bilaga 1. Arbetsmarknadsdepartementet. Arbetsrättsreform: Lag om medbestämmande i arbetslivet [Department of Labor. Labor law reform: The Law on Codetermination].

Vem äger Sverige? Fakta om makt och ägande ur Koncentrationsutredningen [Who owns Sweden? Facts on Power and Ownership from the Concentration Investigation] (1971). Stockholm: Prisma.

Der Bundesminister fur Arbeit und Sozialordnung (1979) Mitbestimmung. Bonn, March.

SOU 1975: 41 (1975) Utredningen om den kommunala demokratin. Kommunaldemokrati. Huvudbetänkande [The investigation of municipal democracy. Municipal democracy. Main report]. Stockholm.

INDEX

Subject Index

absolutism, 51
abstinence, 131
abstract ("average") labor, 125
acquisition, 34-39
Austromarxists, 178

Bolshevik Struggle, 176-178
bourgeoisie and the bourgeois class, 66

capital, 13, 20, 22-23, 34, 66-67, 68,
    71-72, 81, 90, 93, 123
capitalism, 37, 54ff, 59-60, 66, 80
categorical value judgments, 46
citizen rights 13, 23, 27, 42, 97ff,
    108-115, 193, 229
    defined 20
    suffrage 162
civic funds, 209ff
Co-determination, Law of, 26-27,
    241-242
collective ownership, 140-142
collective ownership, arguments for,
    140-142
Commission on Socialization, 171,
    173-175, 180
Communism, 91ff
competence, employee, 239
composite production (or production
    through the labor of others), 20,
    36-37, 87, 90, 117
    defined 34
conservatism, 79ff
"constitutive authority," 97, 108ff
contract, right of contract, 37, 39-41
control over capital 22, 42-43, 95
custom; tradition, 83

democracy, 100ff, 108ff, 204ff, 212,
    231f
    Marx on, 153
democratic rights, 98
derived acquisition, 34
determinism, 100
dictatorship of the proletariat
    Marx on, 153

disposition, freedom of; protection of,
    32-34
distribution and distribution policy, 16,
    158, 166-167, 171, 177, 182, 188f

economic democracy, 13, 17, 43,
    172-173, 229-252
economic power, 15, 41, 97, 105ff, 115
efficiency and wage-earner control, 206,
    243ff
"embodied labor" vs. "commandable
    labor," 120
employee investment funds, 194ff
    the expropriation question, 217ff
    constitutionality, 217ff
    the LO/SAP proposal, 207ff
enlightened development model, 98
equality principle, 89, 110
establishment of new firms, 247
exchange value, 121, 124ff, 130
executive, 26, 216
    defined, 25
    executive power, 223
explanatory models, 50-51, 69
extinctive acquisition, 34, 37-39

feudalism, 54ff, 59
functional socialism, 17, 187, 219,
    220ff, 251
fund, 23
fund formation, 235

genetic arguments, 81, 145
"Goals and Orientation" (Art. 2 of Law
    of Co-determination), 231

historic compromise, 76

idealism, 51, 166
incentives, 18, 146, 172, 245ff
Industrial Democracy, Investigation of,
    171, 175-176
industrial revolution, 66
instrumental value judgments, 47-48
instruments of labor, 21
intermediary concept 31-32

ABOUT THE AUTHORS

BENGT ABRAHAMSSON is professor of sociology at the Swedish Center for Working Life (*Arbetslivscentrum*) and is also affiliated with Uppsala University. His present fields of interest are work organization and administration. Among his publications are *Military Professionalization and Political Power* (Sage Publications, 1972) and *Bureaucracy or Participation: The Logic of Organization* (Sage Publications, 1977). He is currently engaged in a research project on economic democracy, economic power, and ownership.

ANDERS BROSTRÖM has a Ph.D. in sociology from Uppsala University. Also working at the *Arbetslivscentrum*, he has published books on communication and the sociology of education. He is now doing research on economic democracy, trade union strategies for co-determination, and principles of private vs. collective ownership.